CIVIC COMMUNITY IN LATE MEDIEVAL LINCOLN

CIVIC COMMUNITY IN LATE MEDIEVAL LINCOLN

Urban Society and Economy in the Age of the Black Death, 1289–1409

Alan Kissane

THE BOYDELL PRESS

First published 2017
The Boydell Press, Woodbridge

ISBN 978 1 78327 163 4

The Boydell Press is an imprint of Boydell & Brewer Ltd
PO Box 9, Woodbridge, Suffolk IP12 3DF, UK
and of Boydell & Brewer Inc.
668 Mt Hope Avenue, Rochester, NY 14620–2731, USA
website: www.boydellandbrewer.com

A catalogue record for this book is available
from the British Library

Contents

Illustrations

Figures

Maps

All maps © English Heritage

Tables

Acknowledgements

My research for this book began under the watchful eyes of Rob Lutton and Richard Goddard, an experience which, to this day, remains one of the most enjoyable of my professional life. Not only did they offer unwavering support during the initial years of research but they have, since its completion, offered yet more words of advice and encouragement. I owe a huge debt of thanks to Gwilym Dodd, Sarah Rees Jones, Paul Dryburgh, Marianne Wilson and David Stocker for reading some or all of my work in its current and former guises and for providing timely and much needed criticism. My sincerest thanks also go to David M. Smith, who has lent his considerable expertise on ecclesiastical matters and Latin grammar, and Chris Johnson, who has provided me with several useful databases and allowed me to read his book on Lincoln's ancient houses prior to its publication. I must offer my heartfelt thanks to the staff at The National Archives at Kew and the Bodleian, Oxford; Nicholas Bennett, former Vice-Chancellor and Librarian of Lincoln Cathedral Library; and Mike Rogers at Lincoln Archive Office, for aiding me in my pursuit of various manuscripts, sources and answers. Friends both in England and abroad have also provided me with support and guidance, going out of their way to read and pass comment on drafts of this book, in particular Lucy Lynch, Matthew Phillips, Dan Ellin and Teresa Phipps, whilst a number of others have pushed me with words of encouragement from the sidelines; they know who they are. Finally, I cannot finish without thanking my beautiful and understanding wife, Harriet, who has dealt with my many late nights, research trips and moments of crisis when things weren't quite going my way. Still, it all pales into insignificance when I consider that she has borne me the three most wonderful gifts anyone could ever ask for, our beautiful children, Noah, Eli and Kitty. It is to all of them that this work is dedicated.

Publication of this volume was aided by a generous grant from Lincoln Record Society.

Abbreviations

AASRP	*Architectural and Archaeological Societies Reports and Papers*
BB	*Burwarmote Book*, Lincoln Cathedral Library, MS169
BH	*The Blickling Homilies*, Princeton University Library, Digital Collections, Scheide Library M71
CChR	*Calendar of Charter Rolls*
CCR	*Calendar of Close Rolls*
CFR	*Calendar of Fine Rolls*
Chantry Certificates	C. W. Foster and A. H. Thompson, 'The Chantry Certificates for Lincoln and Lincolnshire returned in 1548 under the Act of Parliament of 1 Edward VI', *AASRP*, 36, 2 (1922): 183–295
CIM	*Calendar of Inquisitions Miscellaneous*
CIPM	*Calendar of Inquisitions Post Mortem*
CLR	*Calendar of Liberate Rolls*
CPR	*Calendar of Patent Rolls*
CSML	D. Owen, *Church and Society in Medieval Lincolnshire* (Welwyn Garden City, 1971)
CUHB	D. M. Palliser (ed.), *Cambridge Urban History of Britain, vol. 1: 600–1540* (Cambridge, 2008)
ELW	A. Gibbons, *Early Lincoln Wills* (Lincoln, 1888)
English Guilds	T. Smith (ed.), *English Guilds* (Oxford, 1870)
Export Trade	E. M. Carus-Wilson and O. Coleman, *England's Export Trade, 1275–1547* (Oxford, 1963)
Historical MSS	W. D. Macray (ed.), *Historical MSS, 14th Report: The Manuscripts of Lincoln, Bury St Edmunds and Great Grimsby Corporations and of the Deans and Chapters of Worcester and Lichfield, etc.* (London, 1895)
LAO	Lincoln Archive Office
LCL	Lincoln Cathedral Library
Liber Cant.	*Liber de Ordinationibus Cantariarum*, Lincoln Cathedral Library, Dean and Chapter, A/1/8

LW	R. E. G. Cole (ed.), *Lincoln Wills, vol. 1: 1271–1526* (Lincoln, 1914)
Medieval Lincoln	J. W. F. Hill, *Medieval Lincoln* (Cambridge, 1948; reprint, Stamford, 1990)
Medieval Lincolnshire	G. Platts, *Land and People in Medieval Lincolnshire* (Lincoln, 1985)
Reg. Antiq.	*Registrum Antiquissimum*, Lincoln Record Society, 10 vols (1931–73): vols 1–3, C. W. Foster (ed.); vol. 4, C. W. Foster and K. Major (eds); vols 5–10, K. Major (ed.)
Rot. Hund.	*Rotuli Hundredorum*, vol. 1 (London, 1812)
Rot. Parl.	*Rotuli Parliamentorum*, vols 1–5 (London, 1783)
Royal Charters	W. Birch de Gray (ed.), *The Royal Charters of the City of Lincoln* (Cambridge, 1911)
LCL VCH	W. Page (ed.), *The Victoria History of the County of Lincolnshire*, vol. 2 (London, 1906)
WB	*White Book*, Lincoln Archive Office, L1/3/1

Note on the Text

All forenames and locations have been modernised. Surnames appear as in the original, with the exception of standardised place-names. Standard abbreviations and contractions have been silently expanded in citations from manuscript sources. All dates are based on the year beginning 1 January. All unpublished documents cited here are held at The National Archives (Public Record Office, London) unless otherwise stated. All maps are adapted from D. Stocker (ed.), *The City by the Pool* (Oxford, 2003); they remain the copyright of English Heritage and have been reproduced here with its kind permission.

Introduction

This is a study of Lincoln's civic community between the late thirteenth and early fifteenth centuries, a period which begins with the suspension of civil liberties in 1289 and ends with the city being granted urban county status in 1409. It explores how those living within the jurisdiction of the mayor and civic government dealt with and adapted to the challenges of the period, in particular plague, famine and war, and questions to what extent economic and social changes influenced urban patterns of living, local customs and social relations.

It is generally acknowledged that the turn of the fourteenth century marked a new phase in English society, signalling an end to two centuries of economic growth, a period which had otherwise seen a dramatic rise in population, expansion in the number and size of towns and markets and the emergence of a more sophisticated commercial economy.[1] However, as many of these trends began to reverse, English society saw the population begin to outstrip its resources as prices rose and foodstuffs became scarce. The significance of this shift in fortunes was that pockets of society, in particular agrarian communities, began to be pushed towards the edge of subsistence, a phenomenon known in historiography as the 'Malthusian crisis'.[2] While it is possible that, in isolation, these difficulties might have been managed, they were exacerbated by several other factors, including the increasing fiscal demands of the crown, much of which was used to pay for foreign wars, the commutation of labour services to monetary rents, a declining seigniorial system, a

1 D. M. Palliser (ed.), *Cambridge Urban History of Britain, vol. 1: 600–1540* (Cambridge, 2000); E. Miller and J. Hatcher, *Medieval England: Towns, Commerce and Crafts, 1086–1348* (Harlow, 1995).

2 For a discussion of this issue and some criticisms, see S. H. Rigby, 'Introduction', in R. Horrox and W. M. Ormrod (eds), *A Social History of England: 1200–1500* (Cambridge, 2006), 10–30; B. M. S. Campbell (ed.), *Before the Black Death: Studies in the 'Crisis' of the Early Fourteenth Century* (Manchester, 1991); J. Drendel (ed.), *Crisis in the Later Middle Ages: Beyond the Postan–Duby Paradigm* (Turnhout, 2015).

fall in the available money supply and widespread famine and animal disease.[3] The impact of this complex amalgam of problems was that wealth began to be redistributed throughout the kingdom, in particular towards London, East Anglia and the south-east, as different areas of the country proved more resilient than others.[4] Whilst it appears that Lincolnshire fared badly during this period – for example, in 1290 it ranked as the wealthiest county in England, whereas by the 1310s it had fallen to ninth place[5] – the impact on Lincoln has not yet been determined in any systematic way. This study seeks to redress this issue by situating Lincoln within a broader framework of late medieval urban history.

According to the most comprehensive analysis of late medieval demography yet undertaken for British towns, Lincoln housed a population of approximately 12,300 at the beginning of the fourteenth century,[6] a figure considerably higher than that of its nearest neighbours, Boston (6,200) and Stamford (4,500).[7] Standing on a par with other provincial capitals, including Bristol (14,400) and Norwich (12,000), Lincoln's population placed it within the second tier of English towns, some way behind York (22,700) and further still behind London (60,000). Even after subsequent bouts of plague from 1349 onwards, Lincoln's population stood somewhere in the region of 7,500 in 1377,[8] ranking it the sixth largest town in all England.[9] In a purely demographic sense, these figures set Lincoln apart from the majority of England's estimated 600 towns (c.1270–c.1540), most of which housed populations of somewhere between 300 and 2,000 inhabitants,[10] though naturally it remained dependent on smaller towns and communities to function as a provincial capital.[11]

3 R. Britnell, *The Commercialisation of English Society, 1000–1500* (Manchester, 1996), 155, 164–71, 179–85; W. M. Ormrod, 'The Crown and the English Economy, 1290–1348', in Campbell, *Before the Black Death*, 149–83; W. C. Jordan, *The Great Famine: Northern Europe in the Early Fourteenth Century* (Princeton, 1996); P. Slavin, 'The Great Bovine Pestilence and its Economic and Environmental Consequences in England and Wales, 1318–50', *Economic History Review*, 65, 4 (2012): 1239–66.

4 P. Nightingale, 'The Lay Subsidies and the Distribution of Wealth in Medieval England', *Economic History Review*, 57, 1 (2004): 1–32

5 Nightingale, 'The Lay Subsidies', 20–3.

6 B. M. S. Campbell, 'Benchmarking Medieval Economic Development: England, Wales, Scotland, and Ireland, c.1290', *Economic History Review*, 61, 4 (2008), 908, table 4.

7 This is higher than previous estimates for the city, usefully reviewed in A. Vince, 'The New Town: Lincoln in the High Medieval Era (c.900 to c.1350)', in D. Stocker (ed.), *The City by the Pool: Assessing the Archaeology of the City of Lincoln* (Oxford, 2003), 166–8 and fig. 9.6.

8 This figure is based on Lincoln's taxable population of 3,569 in 1377: C. C. Fenwick (ed.), *The Poll Taxes of 1377, 1379 and 1381: Part 2, Lincolnshire-Westmorland* (Oxford, 2001), 34; C. Dyer and T. Slater, 'The Midlands', in *CUHB*, 626–7.

9 A. Dyer, 'Appendix 5: Ranking of Towns by Taxpaying Population: the 1377 Poll Tax', in *CUHB*, 758.

10 C. Dyer, 'Small Towns 1270–1540', in *CUHB*, 505–40, at 511.

11 For more on this issue, see chapter two.

The Black Death in Towns

> In 1349 there was that great pestilence in Lincoln which spread over all parts of the world beginning on Palm Sunday in the year aforesaid until the Nativity of St John the Baptist [24 June] next following, when it ceased, God be praised who reigns for ever and ever, Amen[12]

Recorded in the margins of the *Blickling Homilies* shortly after 1349,[13] these words mark the passing of the Black Death in Lincoln, a disaster which swept away as much as half of the city's population in just a few short months,[14] including at least a dozen civic officials and the incumbent mayor, John de Fenton. Somewhat surprisingly, this passage remains the only direct reference to the Black Death in Lincoln's surviving records at this time,[15] though as the experience of other late medieval towns indicates,[16] this bore little semblance to plague's overall impact on the city.[17] At Winchester and Norwich, for example, by the late 1350s numerous houses and churches had begun to fall down through neglect, whilst in Norwich in 1369 the area of the marketplace was reduced in order to enlarge the churchyard of St Peter Mancroft.[18] At Exeter work on the west façade sculpture of the cathedral was delayed by approximately twenty-five years due to the loss of craftsmen from local workshops, a pattern mirrored at London, where brass manufacturing shifted away from small workshops to two main centres due to a collapse of

12 Translated from R. Willard (ed.), *The Blickling Homilies: the John H. Scheide Library, Titusville, Pennsylvania* (Copenhagen, 1960), fo. 128v. Palm Sunday took place on 5 April in 1349.

13 For more on the *Blickling Homilies*, see chapter four.

14 No exact figure can be placed on Lincoln's losses, though 103 wills were enrolled in 1349, against an annual average of approximately three (2.9) for fifty-three years between 1308 and 1376 (excluding the years 1309, 1311–13, 1319–20, 1325–26, 1332–33, 1372–74 for which there is no data). The breakdown is as follows: February (1); March (1); May (9); June (45); July (32); August (3); September (6); November (6). *BB*, fos 183–209v. Note, however, that these dates are not adjusted according to administrative delays with the date of probate being unknown. For more on this problem, see O. J. Benedictow, *The Black Death, 1346–1353: The Complete History* (Woodbridge, 2008), 126–31, 138–40. For clerical losses in the city, which have been estimated at 60 per cent, see A. H. Thompson, 'The Registers of John Gynewell', *Archaeological Journal*, 68 (1911), 312.

15 Note, however, that plague was blamed for the death of Juliane de Threkyngham in 1369: JUST 2/67, rot. 46.

16 Estimates on losses vary: for a third upwards, see J. Hatcher, 'England in the Aftermath of the Black Death', *Past and Present*, 144 (1994), 3; for 30–40 per cent, J. Bolton, '"The World Upside Down": Plague as an Agent of Economic and Social Change', in M. W. Ormrod and P. G. Lindley (eds), *The Black Death in England* (Stamford, 1996), 26, 28–9; for 40–50 per cent, R. Britnell, 'The Black Death in English Towns', *Urban History*, 21, 2 (1994), 195–204; and for 45–50 per cent, Benedictow, *Black Death*, 377–9.

17 Take, for example, W. H. Bliss and J. A. Twemlow (eds), *Calendar of Papal Registers Relating to Great Britain and Ireland*, vol. 3, 1342–1362 (1897), 289, for papal recognition of the difficulties facing the city and diocese.

18 D. Keene, *Survey of Medieval Winchester*, vol. 1 (Oxford, 1985), 116; B. Green and R. M. R. Young, *Norwich: The Growth of a City* (Norwich, 1963), 17; B. Brödt, 'East Anglia', in *CUHB*, 656.

infrastructure.[19] At Great Yarmouth, too, an extension begun on the west end of the church of St Nicholas had to be discontinued on account of the plague, whilst in Oxford student halls stood empty for several years.[20]

Despite these setbacks, the response of towns throughout the second half of the fourteenth century was not one of inertia: many benefitted from, and in some cases actually encouraged, migration from rural areas.[21] At York, for example, admissions to the freedom of the city quadrupled in 1350 when compared to the average of the five previous years,[22] whilst in 1364 the rental arrears from the vicars' estates returned to their pre-plague level.[23] At Colchester the influx of hundreds of highly skilled Flemish textile workers served to kick-start the town's own industry, which grew well into the fifteenth century, offering a timely reminder that not all migrants were necessarily English or local.[24] Elsewhere other towns began to experience steady economic growth reflecting inward migration, including Coventry, which saw a rise in the number of debts enrolled in the local court after 1355, a development attributed to increased business confidence brought about by a burgeoning textile industry.[25] Gloucester likewise experienced growth through its role as a distributive centre, particularly in exports of grain and manufactured iron goods,[26] while both Norwich and Exeter, two towns cited previously for their troubles, rose to great prominence by the late fifteenth century through successful commercial ventures based respectively on the worsted industry and overseas trade.[27]

Taken collectively these urban experiences present a complex picture, one without defined pace or rhythm, with towns re-emerging from the devastation on their own terms. Given the lack of any single pattern to recovery, it is clear that the Black Death presents significant interpretive problems for historians, in particular in terms of its demographic, social and economic impact,[28] though this has not stopped several scholars from describing it as 'the most significant turning point in

19 P. Lindley, 'The Black Death and English Art', in Ormrod and Lindley, *The Black Death*, 142; B. Sloane, *The Black Death in London* (Stroud, 2011), 158–9.

20 Britnell, 'Black Death', 201; Sloane, *The Black Death*, 155.

21 This point is explored more fully in chapter one.

22 B. Dobson, 'Admissions to the Freedom of the City of York in the Later Middle Ages', *Economic History Review*, 26, 1 (1973), 17–18.

23 S. Rees Jones, *York, The Making of a City, 1068–1350* (Oxford, 2013), 293–4.

24 B. Lambert and M. Pajic, 'Drapery in Exile: Edward III, Colchester and the Flemings, 1351–1367', *History*, 99, 338 (2014): 733–53; R. Britnell, *Growth and Decline in Colchester, 1300–1525* (Cambridge, 1986), 72–85.

25 R. Goddard, *Lordship and Medieval Urbanisation: Coventry, 1043–1355* (Woodbridge, 2004), 256–89; *idem*, 'Commercial Contraction and Urban Decline in Fifteenth-century Coventry', *Dugdale Society Occasional Papers*, 46 (2006), 16–24.

26 R. Holt, 'Gloucester in the century after the Black Death', in R. Holt and G. Rosser (eds), *The Medieval Town, 1200–1540: A Reader in English Urban History* (Harlow, 1990), 141–59.

27 M. Kowaleski, *Local Markets and Regional Trade in Medieval Exeter* (Cambridge, 2002); P. Dunn, 'Trade', in C. Rawcliffe and R. Wilson (eds), *Medieval Norwich* (London, 2004), 213–34.

28 J. Hatcher, *Plague, Population and the English Economy 1348–1530* (London, 1977); A. R. Bridbury, 'The Black Death', *Economic History Review*, New Series, 26, 4 (1973): 577–592; M. Kowaleski, 'The Demography of Maritime Communities in Late Medieval England', in M. Bailey and S. Rigby (eds), *Town and Countryside in the Age of the Black Death* (Turnhout,

late medieval British urban history'.[29] The genesis of this statement lies in the extent to which towns are judged to have declined in size, wealth and importance as a result of the Black Death and subsequent plagues, an issue known in historiography as the 'urban decline' debate.[30] Unsurprisingly, the methods by which urban fortunes can be measured remain a matter of some dispute,[31] though for Stephen Rigby 'for better or worse, it is population size which remains our main indicator of changes in urban fortunes'.[32] While this is hardly surprising given the unprecedented demographic upheaval wrought by successive plagues, as Jim Bolton argues, seeing urban decline as a synecdoche for the fifteenth-century economic malaise does little to advance our broader understanding of the fortunes of the English economy during this period or indeed their social consequences.[33] Perhaps a more effective means of exploring the fortunes of towns would be to place human agency at the forefront of analysis, in particular concepts of volition. It goes without saying that the choices of peasants, consumers, traders and manufacturers remained central to the fortunes of towns, many of them seeking out better wages and standards of living, with more still investing various amounts of time and energy into making local markets a success. To what extent these choices reflected the economic fortunes of towns is less well understood, however, in particular during periods of perceived crisis. Nevertheless, this approach is gaining currency in scholarship, including in the work of James Davis, for example, who analyses the impact of plague on the day-to-day commercial practices of the small market town of Clare (Suffolk) during the late fourteenth century. Specifically he identifies how royal and urban regulation remained less effective at suppressing prices than market forces as consumers became fussier about the quality of food they were able to buy, a concern resulting from the growth of local competition and choice, not top down legislation.[34]

A second contiguous approach would be to provide a more systematic analysis of towns in both the pre- and post-plague years than hitherto. Whilst it is true that the Black Death provides an expedient chronological stopping point for historical analysis, due primarily to the sheer magnitude of the population loss it brought about,[35] it arguably serves to demote the 'Malthusian Crisis' of the early fourteenth century or the outbreak of the Hundred Years War to something of secondary importance.

2012), 87–118. For contemporary understanding of the Black Death and subsequent bouts of plague, see R. Horrox (ed.), *The Black Death* (Manchester, 1994).

29 For example, B. Dobson, 'General Survey, 1300–1540' in *CUHB*, 276; Britnell, 'Black Death', 198.

30 The best introduction to this debate remains A. Dyer, *Decline and Growth in English Towns, 1400–1600* (Cambridge, 1991).

31 See chapter three for a detailed discussion of these issues.

32 S. H. Rigby, *Medieval Grimsby: Growth and Decline* (Hull, 1993), 146. See also *idem*, 'Urban Decline in the Later Middle Ages: the Reliability of the Non-statistical Evidence', *Urban History Yearbook*, 11 (1984): 45–60.

33 Bolton, '"The World Upside Down"', 63–70; Britnell, *Commercialisation of English Society*, 170–1, 184, 195–6.

34 J. Davies, 'Selling Food and Drink in the Aftermath of the Black Death', in Bailey and Rigby, *Town and Countryside*, 351–406.

35 B. F. Harvey, 'Introduction: the 'Crisis' of the Early Fourteenth Century', in Campbell, *Before the Black Death*, 3.

Such events remain extremely important, impacting upon the long-term fortunes of towns and the types of choices available to inhabitants in the aftermath of plague. Take, for example, the work of John Munro, who argues that the rise in the standard of living frequently cited by historians as a consequence of the Black Death actually only occurred after the mid-1370s.[36] This, he argues, was due to the fact that before 1349 wages had actually risen as a result of famine, peaking in 1334/35 before slumping again in the 1340s. Therefore the rise in wages so readily identified in the years immediately after 1349 actually only resulted in a return to the level of the 1330s. It was only after the mid-1370s when wages finally came to outpace inflation that there was a real rise in wages and standards of living. Similar conclusions have been drawn by Robert Braid, who analyses the commercial regulations of London's markets in the first half of the fourteenth century in order to explain the form and contents of the Ordinance of Labourers (1349).[37] In particular, he notes that the capital provided a 'natural inspiration for central regulation', with the ordinances being written most likely by the men who drafted London's regulations or at least by those familiar with them, thereby demonstrating a remarkable regulatory continuity at a time of demographic upheaval on the one hand and the ongoing influence of the capital on royal policy on the other.[38] Similarly Anthony Musson emphasises how the customary practices of local courts informed attitudes towards the enforcement of labour legislation after 1349, with the plague itself instituting little or no change.[39] In fact, it was not until the 1370s, following a shift in economic fortunes cited by Munro, that legislation for trespass and breaches of contract (writ of assumpsit) emerged in a regularised format specifically designed to deal with the ongoing problems of labour legislation. As these studies show, modern perceptions of the impact of plague on medieval society are heavily influenced by the chronological period being investigated. As such, it is important to be wary of this fact in order to avoid over-emphasising the effects of the Black Death, or worse still exaggerating its influence altogether.

Nowhere is this exaggeration clearer than in the claims that the Black Death ushered in a 'new kind of sensibility and religiosity' which prompted the rapid

36 J. Munro, 'Before and after the Black Death: Money, Prices, and Wages in Fourteenth-century England', *New Approaches to the History of Late Medieval and Early Modern Europe*, 104 (2009), 335–64. For standards of living: C. Dyer, *Standards of Living in the Later Middle Ages: Social Change in England, c.1200–1520* (Cambridge, 1998). For tensions over attracting servants and rural workers into towns after 1349, see C. Given-Wilson, 'Service, Serfdom and English Labour Legislation, 1350–1500', in A. Curry and E. Matthew (eds), *Concepts and Patterns of Service in the Later Middle Ages* (Woodbridge, 2000), 21–37.

37 R. Braid, 'Behind the Ordinance of Labourers: Economic Regulation and Market Control in London before the Black Death', *Journal of Legal History*, 34, 1 (2013): 3–30. For earlier work drawing attention to this development see, for example, S. Rees Jones, 'Household, Work and the Problem of Mobile Labour: the Regulation of Labour in Medieval English Towns', in J. Bothwell, P. J. P. Goldberg and W. M. Ormrod (eds), *The Problem of Labour in Fourteenth-century England* (York, 2000), 133–53.

38 Braid, 'Behind the Ordinance of Labourers', 29

39 A. Musson, 'New Labour Laws, New Remedies? Legal Reaction to the Black Death "Crisis"', in N. Saul (ed.), *Fourteenth Century England I* (Woodbridge, 2000), 73–88.

growth of socio-religious institutions and practices, such as guilds and chantries.[40] Whilst it has been suggested that in London the majority of fraternal growth took place after 1349, due to a heightened awareness and sensibility over the issues of death and dying, at York and Bristol foundations of perpetual chantries began to decline after 1350, pointing towards an altogether different pattern.[41] Whilst the reasons behind these idiosyncrasies remain complex, it is clear that geography, local custom, personal choice and wealth remained more significant factors in the development of pious devotions than they have hitherto been given credit for.[42] This study thus seeks to question the extent to which the Black Death influenced the customs and practices of urban life by challenging the assumption that it was a central turning point in the fortunes of English towns.

Medieval Lincoln: Modern Scholarship

In spite of the early efforts of John Ross to promote the civic history of Lincoln,[43] ever since the publication of Sir Francis Hill's seminal work, *Medieval Lincoln*, in 1948,[44] comparatively little work has been undertaken on this aspect of the city's history for the Middle Ages. This is not to say that no work has been undertaken on Lincoln, far from it, only that the majority of existing work has focused on other aspects of urban life. Foremost amongst these topics is Lincoln's ecclesiastical history, which has seen various studies on the cathedral and its clergy by Dorothy Owen, Kathleen Major, Alison McHardy and, most recently, Marianne Wilson;[45] on the role and function of Lincoln's medieval bishops by Rosalind Hill, Nicholas Bennett, Philippa Hoskin

40 For example, J. Le Goff, *The Birth of Europe* (Oxford, 2005), 159–62, at 161; P. Ziegler, *The Black Death* (London, 1998), 276–86; H. F. Westlake, *The Parish Gilds of Mediaeval England* (London, 1919), 26–35.

41 C. M. Barron, 'The Parish Fraternities of Medieval London', in C. M. Barron and C. Harper-Bill (eds), *The Church in Pre-Reformation Society* (Woodbridge, 1985), 13–37; C. Harper-Bill, 'The English Church and English Religion after the Black Death', in Ormrod and Lindley, *The Black Death*, 112.

42 G. Rosser, 'Guilds in Urban Politics in Late Medieval England', in I. A. Gadd and P. Wallis (eds), *Guilds and Association in Europe, 900–1900* (London, 2006), 32; Hatcher, *Plague, Population*, 34, 49–50. See chapters five and six for more on these issues.

43 J. Ross, *Civitas Lincolnia* (Lincoln, 1870).

44 J. W. F. Hill, *Medieval Lincoln* (Cambridge, 1948; reprint, Stamford, 1990).

45 For example, D. Owen (ed.), *A History of Lincoln Minster* (Cambridge, 1994); *idem*, *Church and Society in Medieval Lincolnshire* (Lincoln, 1971); K. Major, *Minster Yard* (Edinburgh, 1974); *idem*, 'The Finances of the Dean and Chapter of Lincoln from the Twelfth to Fourteenth Century', *Journal of Ecclesiastical History*, 5 (1954): 149–67; A. K. McHardy, 'The Lincolnshire Clergy in the Later Fourteenth Century', in W. M. Ormrod (ed.), *England in the Fourteenth Century: Proceedings of the Harlaxton Symposium* (Woodbridge, 1986), 145–151; *idem* (ed.), *Clerical Poll-Taxes of the Diocese of Lincoln, 1377–1381* (Lincoln Record Society, 1992); M. Wilson, 'Community, Kinship and Piety: Lincoln Cathedral Close, c.1450–1500' (Unpublished Ph.D Thesis, University of Nottingham 2014).

and others;[46] and on the mendicant friars by Michael Robson.[47] Earlier scholarship, too, also saw Edmund Venables write widely on Lincoln's church history and monuments,[48] whilst R. E. G. Cole offered detailed studies on the priory of St Katherine and the canonisation attempts of bishops Grosseteste and Dalderby, amongst other topics.[49] Whilst it is likely that this focus on ecclesiastical matters remains driven primarily by the broad scope of surviving archival material,[50] it has nevertheless prioritised the church at the expense of the majority of the city's inhabitants.

Beyond ecclesiastical matters, scholars have also been keen to elucidate other topics, including Stanley Kahrl and James Stokes, who have explored entertainment and drama from the late fourteenth century onwards,[51] Philip Lindley, who edited a volume of essays on the early history of Lincoln Castle,[52] and R. A. Pelham, Sumner Ferris and Anthony Verduyn, each of whom considered Lincoln's role within a broader political and judicial framework.[53] Extensive work has also been undertaken on Lincoln's medieval domestic properties in the *Survey of Ancient Houses* series,[54] which supplements the outstanding collection of publications by Lincoln Record

46 For example, R. M. T. Hill, *Oliver Sutton, Bishop of Lincoln, 1280–1299* (Lincoln, 1950); *idem* (ed.), *The Rolls and Register of Bishop Oliver Sutton, 1280–1299*, 8 vols (Lincoln Record Society, 1942–86); N. Bennett (ed.), *The Registers of Bishop Henry Burghersh, 1320–1342*, 3 vols (Lincoln Record Society, 1999–2011); P. Hoskin (ed.), *Robert Grosseteste as Bishop of Lincoln: The Episcopal Rolls, 1235–1253* (Lincoln Record Society, 2015).

47 M. Robson, 'The Greyfriars of Lincoln c.1230–1330: The Establishment of the Friary and the Friars Ministry and Life in the City and its Environs', in M. Robson and J. Rohrkasten (eds), *Franciscan Organisation in the Mendicant Context: Formal and Informal Structures of the Friars' Lives and Ministry in the Middle Ages* (Berlin, 2010), 113–37.

48 For example, E. Venables, 'A List and Brief Description of the Churches of Lincoln Previous to the Period of the Reformation', *AASRP*, 19, 2 (1887): 326–54; *idem*, 'The Shrine and Head of St Hugh of Lincoln', *AASRP*, 50, 1 (1893): 131–51.

49 For example, R. E. G. Cole, 'The Priory of St Katherine without Lincoln, of the Order of St Gilbert of Sempringham', *AASRP*, 27 (1903–04): 264–336; *idem*, 'Proceedings Relative to the Canonisation of Robert Grosseteste, Bishop of Lincoln', *AASRP*, 33 (1915): 1–34; *idem*, 'Proceedings Relative to the Canonisation of John de Dalderby', *AASRP*, 33 (1915): 143–76.

50 See, for example, R. M. Thomson, *Catalogue of the Manuscripts of Lincoln Cathedral Chapter Library* (Woodbridge, 1989).

51 S. J. Kahrl (ed.), *Records of Plays and Players in Lincolnshire, 1300–1585* (Oxford, 1974); J. Stokes, 'Staging Wonders: Ritual and Space in the Drama and Ceremony of Lincoln Cathedral and its Environs', in F. Andrews (ed.), *Ritual and Space in the Middle Ages: Proceedings of the 2009 Harlaxton Symposium* (Donington, 2011), 197–212; *idem* (ed.), *Records of Early English Drama: Lincolnshire*, 2 vols (London, 2009).

52 P. Lindley (ed.), *The Early History of Lincoln Castle* (Lincoln, Society of Lincolnshire History and Archaeology, 2004).

53 R. A. Pelham, 'The Provisioning of the Lincoln Parliament of 1301', *University of Birmingham Historical Journal*, 3 (1951–52): 16–32; S. Ferris, 'Chaucer at Lincoln (1387): The "Prioress's Tale" as a Political Poem', *Chaucer Review*, 15, 4 (1981): 295–321; A. Verduyn, 'The Revocation of Urban Peace Commissions in 1381: the Lincoln Petition', in S. Mews (ed.), *Religion and National Identity* (Oxford, 1982), 108–11.

54 S. Jones, K. Major, and J. Varley, *The Survey of Ancient Houses in Lincoln*, 3 vols (Lincoln, 1984–90); S. Jones, K. Major, J. Varley and C. Johnson, *The Survey of Ancient Houses in Lincoln: IV: Houses in the Bail: Steep Hill, Castle Hill, and Bailgate* (Lincoln, 1996). See also C. Johnson and S. Jones, *Steep, Strait and High: Ancient Houses of Central Lincoln* (Woodbridge, 2016).

Society on the charters of the Dean and Chapter, published in ten volumes under the title *Registrum Antiquissimum*.[55] Lincoln's role within the county is also discussed at some length by both Graham Platts and Paul Bischoff in two wide-ranging studies,[56] much of which has been integrated into the recent archaeological work of Alan Vince and others,[57] while work by Peter Sawyer has considered Lincoln's place within a pre-civic Anglo-Saxon setting.[58]

Despite the breadth of much of this material, it has only been more recently with the work of Louise Wilkinson on women during the thirteenth century,[59] Anne Sutton and Livia Visser-Fuchs on the piety of Lincoln's late fifteenth-century mayor John Eylestone,[60] and David Stocker and Stephen Rigby on the wealthy fourteenth- and fifteenth-century mercantile Sutton family[61] that matters touching upon the civic life of the city have truly begun to come to the fore. The relative absence of work on this area of the city's history is undoubtedly down to the relative paucity of surviving civic records, and it is to be regretted that no surviving court rolls, accounts, council minutes or lists of freemen survive before the early sixteenth century.[62] Undoubtedly this has made it difficult for historians to reconstruct Lincoln's civic history in any meaningful way for the Middle Ages, though as Francis Hill proved this is not impossible.

According to Hill, Lincoln emerged in the years after the Conquest as the dominant town in the Midlands and one of the most important urban centres in the realm after London. The growth of Lincoln, he argues, came about as a result of the city's strong cloth manufacturing output, its close links with royal and ecclesiastical government, its large and oftentimes wealthy Jewish population, and its precocious development as an independent civic authority.[63] By the fourteenth century, however, Hill argues that Lincoln had begun to lose its importance on the national stage, with the period after 1350 being characterised by physical decay, financial hardship and poverty,[64] a view which has largely persisted in secondary literature

55 *Registrum Antiquissimum*, Lincoln Record Society, 10 vols (1931–1973): vols 1–3, C. W. Foster (ed.); vol. 4, C. W. Foster and K. Major (eds); vols 5–10, K. Major (ed.). Volumes 8–10 deal specifically with Lincoln.

56 G. Platts, *Land and People in Medieval Lincolnshire* (Lincoln, 1985); J. P. Bischoff, 'Economic Change in Thirteenth Century Lincoln: Decline of an Urban Cloth Industry' (Unpublished Ph.D Thesis, Yale University, 1975), 277–91.

57 See Stocker, *City by the Pool.*

58 P. Sawyer, *Anglo-Saxon Lincolnshire* (Lincoln, 1998).

59 L. J. Wilkinson, *Women in Thirteenth-Century Lincolnshire* (Woodbridge, 2007), 13–26, 92–115.

60 A. F. Sutton and L. Visser-Fuchs, 'The Sun in Splendour and the Rose Reborn: A Yorkist Mayor of Lincoln and his Book of Hours', *Nottingham Medieval Studies*, 57 (2013), 195–245.

61 D. Stocker, '"A Very Goodly House Longging to Sutton …": A Reconstruction of 'John of Gaunt's Palace', Lincoln', *Lincolnshire History and Archaeology*, 34 (1999): 5–15; S. H. Rigby, '"John of Gaunt's Palace" and the Sutton Family of Lincoln', *Lincolnshire History and Archaeology*, 35 (2000): 35–9.

62 For example, LAO L/1/1/1, L/1/1/2. Lincoln's surviving civic records are touched upon at various points throughout this book.

63 *Medieval Lincoln*, chapters 3, 5, 8–11. For a discussion of Hill's analysis of civic government, see chapter four.

64 *Medieval Lincoln*, 251–6, 270–3, 286–8.

ever since.[65] Whilst there is undoubtedly an element of truth to this account, especially given the fortunes of many towns in the post-plague years, that Lincoln has been described by one historian as the 'yardstick' of urban decline highlights how the city has been treated in this regard.[66] This study thus seeks to re-evaluate this arguably selective interpretation of the evidence by placing it within a wider urban context. As will become clear, Lincoln was by no means powerless in the face of the plague, famine and war and, in the words of D. M. Palliser, 'we need not accept the orthodox opinions on individual towns simply because they have often been repeated'.[67]

A further aim of this study is to move the discussion of Lincoln's civic practices and customs beyond the largely narrative assessment of Hill, which focuses primarily on chancery records for the period between the thirteenth and fifteenth centuries, an approach sometimes lacking nuance or analysis.[68] In particular, there is little discussion of Lincoln's trade links (local and international) or manufacturing output, despite his claims that these were a driving force for the city's early success. There is also little discussion of Lincoln's lay-founded religious institutions, in particular guilds and chantries, although there is a large corpus of surviving material for both. Such institutions are a marker of urban status and wealth as recent studies have shown and they remain central concerns if a fuller understanding of Lincoln's economic well-being during the later Middle Ages is to be gleaned.[69] Finally, this study seeks to address Lincoln's status as county town, a subject to which Hill gave only passing attention,[70] and to question why this was important in framing the city's fortunes.

Terminology and Methodology

Hitherto the terms 'civic community' and 'city' have been used interchangeably throughout this introduction with little distinction, being described simply as those living within the jurisdiction of the mayor and civic government. Whilst this remains in the strictest sense true, thereby setting it apart from the separate jurisdictions of

65 For example, Bischoff, 'Economic Change', 277–91; A. Vince, 'Lincoln in the Early Modern Era (c.1350–c.1750), in Stocker, *City by the Pool*, 159, 168, 303–4; S. H. Rigby, '"Sore Decay" and "Fair Dwellings": Boston and Urban Decline in the Later Middle Ages', *Midland History*, 18 (1995): 52, 55; C. Phythian-Adams, *Desolation of a City: Coventry and the Urban Crisis of the Later Middle Ages* (Cambridge, 1979), 15; R. Dobson, 'Urban Decline in Late Medieval England', in Holt and Rosser, *The Medieval Town*, 265–86; S. Reynolds, *An Introduction to the History of English Medieval Towns* (Oxford, 1977), 155–7. For views challenging the extent of this decline, see A. R. Bridbury, 'English Provincial Towns in the Later Middle Ages', *Economic History Review*, 34, 1 (1981), 8–10; and D. M. Palliser, 'Urban Decay Revisited', in J. A. F. Thompson (ed.), *Towns and Townspeople in the Fifteenth Century* (Gloucester, 1998), 8.

66 Rigby, 'Urban Decline in the Later Middle Ages', 55, n. 118.

67 Palliser, 'Urban Decay Revisited', 15.

68 *Medieval Lincoln*, chapters 10, 12–13.

69 For example, J. Laughton, E. Jones and C. Dyer, 'The Urban Hierarchy in the Later Middle Ages: a Study of the East Midlands', *Urban History*, 28, 3 (2001): 331–57.

70 See, for example, *Medieval Lincoln*, 306–14.

the Bail and the Close, each of which maintained their own laws and rights (table 1 and map 1), it nevertheless disregards how divisions such as these were seldom clear cut. As this study demonstrates at various points, those living within one jurisdiction could and did express their allegiance to another, suggesting that communities were neither straightforward nor easily defined.

Table 1 Jurisdictions and rights in the city of Lincoln (c.1380)

The 'Bail', held by the Constable of the Castle on behalf of the earls of Lincoln and later the crown

- Held rights of jurisdiction over the Bail, its adjacent ditches and Battleplace within the suburb of Westcastle.
- Court Baron (formerly de la Haye) held each Tuesday at Bardolfhalle in St Clement near the postern gate for all pleas relating to those within the bounds of the Bail.
- Revenues drawn from:
    - assay of measures (bushels, gallons, pottels, quarts, ells and other measures of corn, wine and ale);
    - assay of weights (pounds, stones and other weights of all things sold by weight) and forfeitures;
    - amercements and other punishments for breach of the assize of bread and ale;
    - profits from vacant plots and ditches in the bail, including the plot called Batailplace, and rents for herbage and ditches;
    - stallage from vacant plots in times of fairs and markets;
    - windowtol (licence to retail small quantities of food and drink in the marketplace);
    - rents from tenants in the bail of the castle, and from foreign tenants in Kesteven and Lindsey for the guard of the castle.

The 'Close', held by the Dean and Chapter of the cathedral

- Held rights of jurisdiction over the cathedral precinct known locally as the Close.
- Galilee Court held weekly and daily for non-residents, to hear all pleas, including those relating to the crown.
- Revenues drawn from:
    - stalls and selds in the Close, and tolls from markets and fairs (days and dates not specified);
    - chattels of felons and fugitives;
    - amercement of brewers;
    - fines for trespass;
    - terrage (levy on harvested goods) and piccage (setting up a stall);
    - rents from tenants of the Close;
- Inhabitants of the Close exempt from summons, aletol (fixed payment to brew ale) and backestrigeld (viz. baxtergeld) (fixed payment to bake bread) levied in the civic franchise.

The 'City', held by the Mayor, Bailiffs and Commonalty

- Held rights of jurisdiction over the lower intramural area, all suburbs and the common fields.

- Burwarmote Court held weekly on Mondays and Thursdays, dealing with pleas of 'the same city', 'lands and tenements', debts of the city and market offences.
- Revenues drawn from:
  - assize of bread and ale and measures and weights;
  - infangthief and outfangtheif (the right to hang thieves);
  - chattels of felons, wayfs and strays;
  - scot and lot (individuals eligible for office who were liable to contribute to taxes);
  - tolls on all vendibles;
  - the 'office of the market', including fines for drunkenness, nuisance and carrying arms;
  - aletol, windowtol, backestrigeld.
- Citizens of Lincoln quit of all tolls and lastage (export duty on cargo aboard ships) throughout England.
- Three markets to be held each week (Mondays/Wednesdays/Fridays); a fair once per year in Newport from the feast of St Botolph to the Day of the Apostles (17 June–29 June).
- In 1409 a second fifteen-day fair was granted beginning on the feast of the burial of St Hugh (17 November); four justices of the peace were to be elected; mayor named as escheator.

Sources: For the castle: *CPR, 1389–92*, 220, 270–1; *CCR, 1330–33*, 255; *CIPM*, vol. 5, 153; DL 29/1/1, m. 9d; for the Close: *LCL VCH*, 82; *CCR, 1381–85*, 62; *CIM, 1377–88*, 200–3; *Reg. Antiq.* vol. 3, no. 963; for the City: *Royal Charters*, 1–8, 16, 48–50, 55, 59, 61, 63, 66–7; *CPR, 1266–72*, 270; *1377–81*, 461–2; *1389–92*, 260–1; *CCR, 1374–77*, 261; F. W. Brooks, 'Calendar of the Rolls of the Lincoln Court of Burghmanmote', LAO FL/Transcripts/U/28, 2, 15. For Lincoln's civic tolls, see 50–64.

Note that difficulties persist in pinning down the exact date of many of these developments, with many being known only from later evidence. For some insight into interpreting these problems, see *Royal Charters*, vi–xxxiii. For the changing ownership of the castle, see *Medieval Lincoln*, 82–106.

Concerns over the adoption of 'community' as a category of analysis have been rightly raised by both medieval and early modern historians, with many identifying early historiographical interpretations of community as problematic, it frequently being seen as a natural and immutable entity without distinction.[71] The origins of this belief stem primarily from the theory put forward by the nineteenth-century German sociologist Ferdinand Tönnies who remarked upon what he saw as a shift from community (*gemeinschaft*) to society (*gesellschaft*) in pre-modern Europe, a development which has subsequently been used to idealise and mythologise the past. In particular, Tönnies' ideas saw the emergence of a paradigm which attributed the 'decline of community' to 'various religious, political, and social transformations, including the Reformation, the French Revolution, and industrialisation'.[72] Such methods have been openly questioned in some quarters, with Miri Rubin arguing that 'if community can describe at once the realm, the village, the town, the

71 For example, S. Reynolds, *Kingdoms and Communities in Western Europe, 900–1300* (Oxford, 2nd edn, 1997), xi–lxvi; M. Rubin, 'Identities', in Horrox and Ormrod, *Social History*, 402–12.

72 S. S. Thomas, *Creating Communities in Restoration England* (Leiden, 2013), 2–6, at 3.

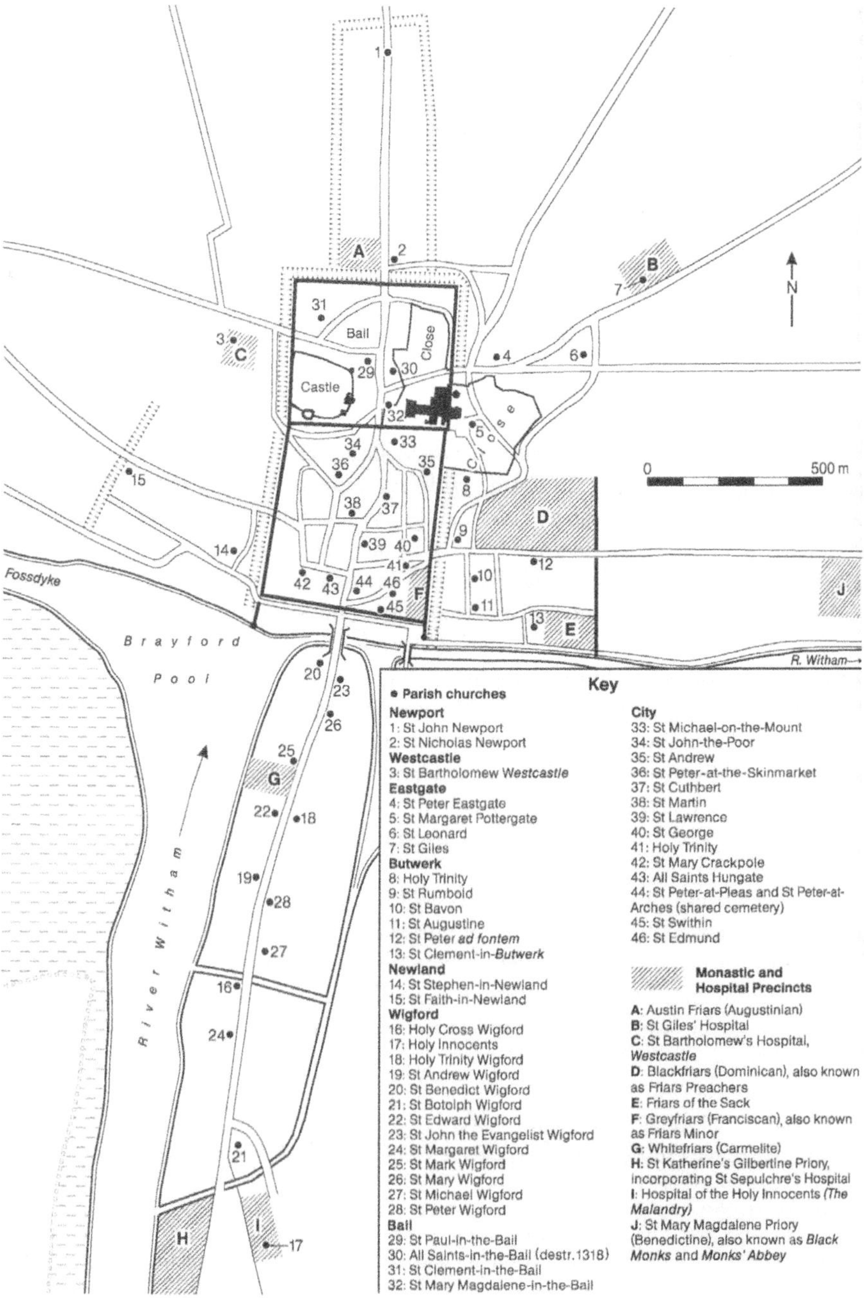

Map 1 Medieval Lincoln (c.1330)

neighbourhood, the fraternity, the parish, even the household, then surely it is not much of a category at all'.[73] More radically, this led Christine Carpenter to call for the term to be thrown out altogether; she suggests that 'community' has been used as 'shorthand for a whole series of complex and important issues', thereby proving more of a hindrance than anything else.[74] Whilst Carpenter's calls are perhaps a step too far in the other direction, such criticisms are not without merit and have ensured, if nothing else, that historians have become more mindful of applying concepts of 'community' without clearly defined boundaries and definitions.[75]

Fortunately the recent work of John Arnold has sought to shed new light on this problem by offering a flexible yet conceptual framework through which to understand and explore this concept. In particular, he contends that community is best understood as a 'process and activity, rather than as something innately ordered or static', emphasising how exclusion and inclusion remain central components in understanding how communities functioned.[76] An illustration of this comes from his discussion of funeral processions, where he identifies how there was a 'strict adherence to status for the deceased', with many frequently displaying 'their social level through clothing on the bier'. When this is set beside the various gifts and doles frequently distributed to the poor, it is clear that such acts of charity were nevertheless benevolent reminders of social status.[77] Identifying community as completely harmonious thus remains unrealistic, there being no 'single mechanism, no button marked "community" that, when pushed, causes all to fall dutifully into place'.[78] To put it another way, community as Arnold understands it was a product of its own divisions, not a passive holistic entity, with those living in towns and villages well aware of their role and their need to contribute to that society in order for it to function (be it through manufacture, service, knowledge or a multitude of other skills). In fact it was this functional element or understanding of social relations that kept communities from being riven by irreconcilable differences and torn apart by internecine strife.

Considered in this way it is useful to see Lincoln's 'civic community' or the 'city' as not only those who lived within the jurisdiction of the mayor and civic government but those who owed them allegiance and lived according to their rules, even if they lived outside of that jurisdiction in the Bail or the Close, two legally distinct entities.[79] In other words, by agreeing to live by the laws of civic government, which

73 M. Rubin, 'Small Groups: Identity and Solidarity in the Late Middle Ages', in J. Kermode (ed.), *Enterprise and Individuals in Fifteenth Century England* (Stroud, 1991), 134.

74 C. Carpenter, 'Gentry and Community in Medieval England', *Journal of British Studies*, 33, 4 (1994): 340–80.

75 See, for example, D. G. Shaw, *The Creation of a Community: The City of Wells in the Middle Ages* (Oxford, 1993); G. Rosser, 'Conflict and Political Community in the Medieval Town: Disputes between Clergy and Laity in Hereford', in T. R. Slater and G. Rosser (eds), *The Church in the Medieval Town* (Aldershot, 1998), 20–42.

76 J. H. Arnold, *Belief and Unbelief in Medieval Europe* (London, 2010), 106.

77 Arnold, *Belief and Unbelief*, 139.

78 Arnold, *Belief and Unbelief*, 142.

79 Note that the terms 'civic community' and 'city' will be used interchangeably throughout this book.

included engaging in events organised under its auspice, such as guild festivities, elections and market practices, individuals actively chose to become part of that 'civic community'.[80] Such a definition does not seek to deny the existence of smaller communities (such as parish or guild), which include those who may have felt disenfranchised in some way by the laws of civic government (the poor or non-citizens) or those who might have participated in more than one 'community' (merchants, for instance), but seeks to emphasise how the authority of civic government was the driving force behind how these disparate groups and individuals lived their day-to-day lives. Of course, it must be remembered that not everyone bought into this idea, or wished to live under the aegis of civic government. The inhabitants of the Cathedral Close, for example, saw themselves as independent of the 'city', and in the fifteenth century both lay and clerical residents frequently directed their pious devotions towards the cathedral, with many seldom looking beyond its walls, a practice which differed from the situation in Salisbury, for example, where local inhabitants were 'primarily concerned with embellishing their own parish churches'.[81] Where and how these divisions emerged, then, remains central to understanding how Lincoln's civic community formed and functioned, with self-image in particular being a prominent component of Lincoln's civic identity.

In order to establish the practices and customs of Lincoln's 'civic community', this book is divided into two main parts. The first, which spans chapters one to three, offers an economic and fiscal analysis of the city between 1289 and 1409, focusing in particular on the unique features of Lincoln's occupational structure and industry, its trading patterns and wealth, and the finances of civic government. Each chapter draws upon a large corpus of central government sources, principally because few civic records relating to these themes survive for Lincoln from this period. This is not insignificant as it predicates a narrative based upon town–crown relations and provides opportunities to explore new aspects of Lincoln's history and development hitherto analysed.

The second part of this book, spanning chapters four to six, considers various socio-religious, cultural and political developments, focusing in particular on the growth of civic government, the emergence of guilds and chantries and their links to popular beliefs and practices. Once again, records used throughout these chapters derive predominantly from central government sources, though they are supplemented by extant ecclesiastical and civic records, including bishops' registers, charters, deeds and wills, and the accounts of the Dean and Chapter, for example. The tenor of these records, in particular their links to land and property ownership, remains equally central to the narrative put forward in these chapters by providing an opportunity to explore the spatial dimension of these developments.

Collectively this two-tiered approach seeks not only to add nuance to the current understanding of civic institutions, how they emerged and evolved, but to explore how they influenced and shaped local customs and practices during a period of unprecedented demographic and political upheaval. The focus upon town–crown

80 Rubin, 'Identities', 403–4.
81 Wilson, 'Community, Kinship and Piety', 296–7.

relations likewise aims to elucidate how the ongoing dialogue with royal government, both as suppliers of goods and services and as financiers of crown policy, remained not only central to the daily concerns of local inhabitants, from the wealthy elite to ordinary townsmen and women, but was, as this book argues, the driving force behind the economic fortunes of the city during the later Middle Ages.

I

Urban Foundations: Occupational Structure

If population alone is used as an indicator of urban status, it is clear that Lincoln was one of the most important English towns during the later Middle Ages.[1] Yet what is it that marked out county towns, such as Lincoln, from other lesser towns and how was this reflected by local occupational structure? While existing work on this issue has shown that towns of different sizes and status often had common characteristics, such as guild foundations, hospitals, monasteries or a weekly market, for example,[2] larger towns nevertheless maintained 'more specialist activities and a deeper social structure than their smaller neighbours',[3] which came to be reflected by their greater diversity of trades.[4] More populous towns likewise maintained larger spheres of influence which, according to 'central place' theory, attracted consumers and traders from further afield than smaller towns and saw them become the focus for a region's trade, goods and services.[5] Together with these smaller centres, county towns formed an interlocking and interdependent regional hierarchy. Such a theory might reasonably be used to describe the position of Lincoln during the later Middle Ages, which not only housed the see of the bishop of Lincoln at the cathedral and the shire court and county gaol of the sheriff at the castle,[6] but also a large civic government ruled by a strong and wealthy mercantile elite.[7] To these important institutions must also be added Lincoln's numerous specialist markets,[8] its capacity to hold public entertainments and events, including tournaments, jousting and public preaching, peace treaties and even parliament itself, and its focus as a centre of pilgrimage and finance.[9]

1 Dyer and Slater, 'The Midlands', in *CUHB*, 621, 623. For Lincoln's population, 2.

2 C. Dyer, 'Medieval Small Towns and the Late Medieval Crisis', in Drendel, *Crisis in the Later Middle Ages*, 38.

3 Laughton, Jones and Dyer, 'Urban hierarchy', 331–57, at 331; Miller and Hatcher, *Medieval England*, 327–30.

4 Miller and Hatcher, *Medieval England*, 324–29.

5 Summarised in C. Dyer, 'Market Towns and the Countryside in Late Medieval England', *Canadian Journal of History*, 31 (1996), 19–20; though see H. Carter, *The Study of Urban Geography* (London, 4th ed., 1995), 25–98, for further details.

6 *Medieval Lincoln*, 64–99.

7 See chapters two and four.

8 See map 2 below.

9 For example, for entertainments and preaching: *Rot. Hund.*, 398; Stokes, *Early English Drama*, vol. 2, 651; S. E. M. Thomson, (ed.), *Chronicon Galfridi le Baker de Swynebroke* (London, 1889), 97; LAO Reg/3, fos 105v, 280v, 342v; *Reg. Antiq.* vol. 2, nos 406–423; for treaties: *CCR, 1327–30*, 185–6, 207–8, 219, 225; for parliament, see Pelham, 'Parliament of 1301' and appendix

An equally essential function of many large (and small) towns was their local manufacturing or trading specialism, which provided employment for dozens if not hundreds of local workers.[10] Chief amongst these specialisms was the cloth trade which came to dominate the economies of Colchester, Coventry, Norwich and Salisbury during the fourteenth century, for example.[11] For Salisbury in particular, John Hare has estimated that by 1377 at least a quarter of the entire male adult population worked within the trade (approximately 400).[12] Elsewhere large numbers of workers have been identified for the iron industry at York and Gloucester during the fourteenth century,[13] whilst at Newcastle there was a large and prosperous coal-mining community.[14] Manufacturing was not the only industry which demanded a large workforce, however, with Westminster, Oxford and Cambridge all retaining substantial retail economies based on the consumption of food and drink.[15] Ports such as Exeter and Southampton also required large transport infrastructures which served their hinterland.[16] Beyond the obvious benefit of providing local inhabitants with employment, these various industries and services provided merchants and traders with opportunities to distribute goods far and wide as part of a broader commercial network and to increase the wealth of local communities.[17]

Nonetheless, despite the economic interdependence of towns and industry, there remains a tacit assumption for the later Middle Ages that as manufacturing output declined, so did the fortunes of towns,[18] something argued for both Coventry and York during the fifteenth century, for example.[19] Whilst in many ways this remains axiomatic, it arguably demonstrates a largely deterministic view, with towns being

3; for markets, see Vince, 'The High Medieval Era', 206, 260–4, figs 9.46, 9.83; for pilgrimage, B. Nilson, *Cathedral Shrines of Medieval England* (Woodbridge, 2001), 113–17, 222; for Pentecostal and Rogation processions to Lincoln Cathedral, *CSML*, 106–9, 136; for finance, see chapter three.

10 For small town specialisms, see, for example, C. Dyer, 'Small Towns 1270–1540', 525.

11 Britnell, *Colchester*, 72–85, 181–92; R. Goddard, 'Commercial Contraction and Urban Decline in Fifteenth-century Coventry', *Dugdale Society Occasional Papers*, 46 (2006); Dunn, 'Trade', 215–21; J. Hare, 'Salisbury: The Economy of a Fifteenth-Century Provincial Capital', *Southern History*, 31 (2009): 1–26.

12 Hare, 'Salisbury', 6.

13 R. Holt, 'Gloucester', in Holt and Rosser, *The Medieval Town*, 147–8; H. Swanson, *Medieval Artisans* (Oxford, 1989), 69–72, 151, 170.

14 J. F. Wade, 'The Overseas Trade of Newcastle upon Tyne in the Late Middle Ages', *Northern History*, 30, 1 (1994): 31–48.

15 G. Rosser, *Medieval Westminster, 1200–1540* (Oxford, 1989), 119–43, 161–5; Miller and Hatcher, *Medieval England*, 328.

16 M. Hicks (ed.), *English Inland Trade, 1430–1540: Southampton and its Region* (Oxford, 2015), 36–8, 43–51; Kowaleski, *Medieval Exeter*, 273–4.

17 See, for example, J. Masschaele, *Peasants, Merchants, and Markets: Inland Trade in Medieval England, 1150–1350* (New York, 1997).

18 J. Kermode, 'The Greater Towns, 1300–1540', in *CUHB*, 453–4.

19 Goddard, 'Commercial Contraction', 8–37; Phythian-Adams, *Desolation of a City*, 220; J. N. Bartlett, 'The Expansion and Decline of York in the Later Middle Ages', *Economic History Review*, Second Series, 12 (1959–60), 29–33. For a reappraisal of York's fortunes, see P. Nightingale, 'The Rise and Decline of Medieval York: A Reassessment', *Past and Present*, 206, 1 (2010): 3–42.

seen as helpless in the face of economic change; yet as Heather Swanson identifies, the 'growing importance of county towns as administrative centres could to some extent mitigate … the migration of industry to new venues'.[20] To put it another way, how did towns react to changes in their urban manufacturing base and what attempts were made to mitigate its loss? Unfortunately very little work has been undertaken on this issue for late medieval towns, it being largely reserved for the early modern period, though as these studies have shown, towns were far from paralysed by shifting economic fortunes.[21]

It is the aim of this opening chapter to survey Lincoln's occupational structure over a period of approximately 120 years (1289–1409) and to challenge the idea that the reduction in manufacturing output was accompanied by economic decline. Conversely, it argues that the emergence of a non-specialised urban economy actually led to the growth of a strong localised administrative and service industry capable of supporting the needs of both the town and the region which, in turn, allowed Lincoln to maintain its status as one of the king's leading towns during a period of growing economic instability.

The Evidence

While existing studies of urban trades and industry have employed a variety of qualitative and quantitative methods to explore the economic foundations of late medieval towns, there remains no one single way to approach to the subject, with conclusions being shaped by the survival of evidence and the chronological period under consideration.[22] Certainly, historians seldom concentrate on single sources such as subsidies or poll tax records due to their obvious bias towards wealthy inhabitants,[23] with a much broader approach to the subject being preferred.[24] For the following survey, evidence is drawn from a wide range of central government (coroners' rolls, king's bench, justices of the peace) and civic records (accounts, charters, wills), all of which are listed in appendix 1. Collectively these reveal occupational data for 1,667 unique

20 H. Swanson, *Medieval British Towns* (Basingstoke, 1999), 63. For the economic importance of assize courts to towns, for example, see A. Musson, 'Centre and Locality: Perceptions of the Assize Justices in Late Medieval England', in R. Kaeuper (ed.), *Medieval Law and its Practices, vol. 14: Law, Governance, and Justice: New Views on Medieval Constitutionalism* (Leiden, 2013), 217–19.

21 P. Glennie and I. Whyte, 'Towns in an Agrarian Economy', in P. Clark (ed.), *Cambridge Urban History of Britain, 1540–1840*, vol. 2 (2000), 183–90.

22 See, for example, the differing approaches adopted by Goddard, *Lordship*, 188–9, 225–33, and Kowaleski, *Medieval Exeter*, 120–6, 350–2.

23 Though these are not without merit, see M. Curtis, 'The London Lay Subsidy of 1332', in G. Unwin (ed.), *Finance and Trade under Edward III* (Manchester, 1918), 35–60; and P. J. P. Goldberg, 'Urban Identity and the Poll Taxes of 1377, 1379 and 1381', *Economic History Review*, 43, 2 (1990): 194–216.

24 D. Keene, 'Continuity and Development in Urban Trades: Problems of Concepts and the Evidence', in P. J. Corfield and D. Keene (eds), *Work in Towns, 850–1850* (Leicester, 1990), 1–16; H. Swanson, 'Artisans in the Urban Economy: the Documentary Evidence from York', in Corfield and Keene, *Work in Towns*, 42–56.

individuals (table 2), all of whom have been placed into one of ten categories based upon shared economic interests, their use of raw materials and/or the general functions of their trade. These categories differ in some respects from those employed by Derek Keene for Winchester and Marianne Kowaleski for Exeter, for example, who based their studies on the relative wealth of property holders and heads of households respectively; such an approach is not practical here given the fact that the vast majority of individuals identified for this survey (93 per cent) are recorded only once.[25] This should not detract from the findings presented here, however, though it serves to highlight how in the absence of more detailed local records, reconstructing occupational hierarchies remains a task fraught with difficulty.

In order to identify individual occupations this survey draws primarily upon the evidence of occupational surnames and trade descriptions.[26] In particular, where the particles 'le' or 'la' (meaning 'the') precede an occupational title, they are regarded here as an acceptable means of identification until c.1360, at which point they begin to fall out of use, most likely due to the introduction of statutory measures demanding that occupational details recorded in court records be recorded.[27] Examples of this can be seen in the accounts of Robert le Venur dating from 1292/93,[28] which list Robert le Spicer, Peter le Pestur and Matilda la Skinner as paying fines to sell ale,[29] or the civic register known as the *Burwarmote Book*, which lists Henry le Carter, Thomas le Tannir and Alexander le Botteler in a variety of pleas in 1308.[30] In terms of eponymous surnames, these are considered only before 1330, as after this date many had become hereditary, no longer accurately reflecting an individual's occupational status. Take, for example, John Shipman, poulter, noted in 1337 or William Taverner, skinner, identified in 1342.[31] Whilst this strict cut off point means that some individuals are omitted from the overall data, for example John Mareschall or John Belman, both of whom were named in the 1350s,[32] there is not sufficient evidence to confirm their occupations one way or another.

In spite of this method of identification, the vast majority of data collected for this survey derive from explicit occupational references: for example, in 1321 Roger de Toft, carpenter, was noted as approving the will of William de Gretton of Lincoln;[33] in a charter dated 1333 Richard de Metheringham, *scriveyn*, was named

25 Keene, *Medieval Winchester*, 251; Kowaleski, *Medieval Exeter*, 124–5. See also Swanson, who focuses on the 1524 subsidy to ascertain levels of wealth in Tudor York: *Medieval Artisans*, 150–71.

26 For more on this approach, see D. A. Postles, *The North through its Names: A Phenomenology of Medieval and Early-Modern Northern England* (Oxford, 2007), 165–8.

27 See 140.

28 'Venur' being short for 'venator' or wine merchant: E 372/135, rot. 17d.

29 E 101/505/24, mm. 7–8.

30 *BB*, fo. 75. On this register, 128.

31 Welbeck Cartulary: Harleian MS, British Museum 3640, fo. 55 (held at LAO on microfilm: MF/2/117); *BB*, fo. 139.

32 *BB*, fos 214v, 218.

33 *BB*, fo. 87.

Table 2 Lincoln's occupational profile (1289–1409)

	Breakdown				
Category (no. of occupations)	**1289–1319 (%)**	**1320–49 (%)**	**1350–79 (%)**	**1380–1409 (%)**	**Total (%)**
i: Agriculture (16)	13 (2.9%)	14 (2.7%)	7 (1.7%)	14 (4.5%)	48 (2.9%)
ii: Artisans (14)	24 (5.4%)	24 (4.8%)	16 (3.9%)	20 (6.6%)	84 (5.0%)
iii: Building (13)	24 (5.4%)	32 (6.3%)	16 (3.9%)	35 (11.3%)	107 (6.4%)
iv: Clothing: Leather and Fur (12)	26 (5.8%)	56 (11.1%)	61 (15.0%)	36 (11.7%)	179 (10.8%)
v: Clothing: Textiles (24)	47 (10.5%)	43 (8.5%)	72 (17.7%)	55 (18.0%)	217 (13.0%)
vi: Distribution (6)	107 (23.9%)	78 (15.4%)	69 (17.0%)	23 (7.4%)	277 (16.6%)
vii: Metal (19)	43 (9.6%)	22 (4.4%)	14 (3.5%)	17 (5.6%)	96 (5.8%)
viii: Professionals/Administrative (7)	37 (8.3%)	112 (22.2%)	51 (12.7%)	24 (7.4%)	224 (13.4%)
ix: Service (37)	51 (11.4%)	64 (12.7%)	46 (11.3%)	52 (16.8%)	213 (12.8%)
x: Victualling (22)	75 (16.8%)	60 (11.9%)	54 (13.3%)	33 (10.7%)	222 (13.3%)
	n=447 (100%)	n=505 (100%)	n=406 (100%)	n=309 (100%)	n=1,667 (100%)

Key: see overleaf

Key to Table 2

(i) basketmaker (*skepper*; *peddar*), birdcatcher, dyker, farmer, forester, fowler, herder/herdswoman (*swynnard*), huntsmen (*corsour*), seeder, shearer, sheep-breeder, shepherd, tasker (*theker'/thressere*), tiller, turfleder, workman (*laborarius/werkman*)

(ii) archer, botteler, bower, bowlmaker, boxmaker, cartwright, carver, cooper, fletcher, horner, oiler/oilmaker, parchment dealer/maker, potter, soper

(iii) brickmaker (*kilner*), carpenter, glasswright, glazier (*glasyer*; *verreour*), joiner, mason (*cementarius*), painter (*pictor*), plasterer, pointer, quarrier (*quarreour/quarriour/quarryour*), thatcher, tiler (roofer: *spoliand'*), wright

(iv) bootmaker (*laster*), cordwainer (*patyner*; *souter*; shoemaker), currier, glovemaker, pelter, pouchmaker, saddler, sheather, skinner (also *parmenter*), tanner (*tannator; barker*), tawyer (leatherdresser; *allutarius*)

(v) bocher (mender of clothes), cardmaker, chaloner, draper (also *pannarius*; later *mercer*), dyer (dubber/*litster/greser*), embroider (*tredgold, broudestre*), flyer, fuller/walker, girdler, hair-cloth maker, hatcher, hatter, lacemaker, quilter (maker of soft armour), sherman, seamster, sewer (*sutore*), tailor (inc. *cissore*), upholder (second-hand clothes seller), weaver (*textor/webster*), woad-seller (*wadestre*), woolman, wool-packer, wool-winder (*vulwyndere*)

(vi) chandler (*chaundeler, candelmaker*), chapman, grocer, merchant (*mercator, merchaund, mercenarius*), wine merchant, wool merchant

(vii) armourer, bell-founder, coppersmith, cutler (*coteller/cultellarius*), farrier (*ferreour*), furbour, goldsmith (*aurifaber*), ironmonger, latoner (working with brass), lead-beater, locksmith, lorimer, marshal, pewterer, plumber, sealer, shear grinder, smith, spurrier (*sporiere*)

(viii) attorney, bookbinder, clerk, illuminator (*luminour/libraire*), notary, physician/surgeon (*medicus*), scribe (*scriptor/scriveyn*)

(ix) apprentice, barber, boatman/sailor/shipman, carter (*ledar*), cellarer, clarion player, cryer, falconer, fiddler (*fitheler*), groom (*garcio*; ostler; stableman), handmaid (*ancilla*), hangman, harpist, horse-keeper (*conreyur*), jongleur, lavender/laundress (*lotrix*), lecher (*leche'*), lute player, messenger, minstrel, nurse/midwife, organ player, packer, piper, porter, rent gatherer, scullion, servant, shield bearer (*scutiferus*), shipwright, soldier (*karnus/kerner*), squire, stacker, summoner (*sarmoner*), taverner/hosteler (also *herberger*), toller, warder (watchman; also *wyat*)

(x) apothecary/spicer, baker (*pestour*), brewer, butcher, cheesemaker, cook, fisherman/fishmonger (*fissher/pissenarius/piscator/pershoner/wayder*), flanner (pastry maker), fruiterer, fleshewer, food seller (seller of small non-standard quantities of food), huckster, miller (*molendarius/miln'/monier*), mustarder, panner (seller of small goods), poulter, salter, saucer, tapster, tester, victualler, vintner

as the son and heir of Ralph Carter de Neuport (the latter is not counted);[34] in 1360 Simon othe Castell de Lincoln, shepherd, was indicted for the theft of twelve sheep belonging to Robert de Scarle of Lincoln;[35] in 1368 Amice, former wife of John Lening, butcher, was adjudged to have died of natural causes by twelve jurors, including William Mercer, skinner, William de Snartford, cook, John de Basingham, tailor, and Thomas de Patryngton, tapster;[36] and in 1395 of twenty Lincoln men indicted for 'diverse felonies' in the county nineteen had their occupations listed (eight fishermen, six masons, two pointers, two tilers, and one wright).[37]

Of all the individuals listed, each is counted only once, being classified in one of four periods according to the earliest date they are recorded. For example, in 1339 John de Billesby is identified as a draper, hence he is recorded in the category 'Clothing: Textiles' for the period 1320–49.[38] Where different occupations are noted for individuals of the same name, each is listed separately. For example, in a witness list drawn from an inquisition *ad quod damnum* certificate from 1392 there are two men named William de Derby,[39] one of whom is described as a cordwainer, the other a fisher. The occupation of skinner is also ascribed to a man of the same name in the records of the justices of the peace dating from 1395.[40] Whilst it is possible that the cordwainer and the skinner or the fisher and the skinner were in fact the same man, the absence of corroborating evidence means it is impossible to be sure; hence there may be some duplication in a small number of cases. Such evidence naturally points to the issue of multiple forms of employment, a common feature of many towns.[41] As Heather Swanson demonstrates, a trade ascription rarely gives 'an adequate impression of the status or activity of the artisan to whom it applied', with many undertaking a multitude of roles.[42] This was undoubtedly true of Lincoln, though there is frustratingly little evidence: a limitation imposed by the lack of surviving civic records, which makes tracing individual histories particularly problematic, with the exception of only a handful of civic officials.[43]

The results of this survey show that Lincoln's occupational structure was similar in profile to many other large towns during the later Middle Ages, with over two fifths (43.5 per cent) of all occupations relating to food, drink, clothing and the building trades.[44] In many ways this is unsurprising as these were basic necessities for local townsmen and women. However, there is evidence for a much broader base of activities in the city beyond these four broad categories, with at least 170 different

34 LAO Dij 79/3/103.
35 JUST 3/32/2, m. 237.
36 JUST 2/67, rot. 47.
37 KB 29/41, m. 24.
38 LAO Dij 74/3/16.
39 C 143/412/23.
40 JUST 1/533, m. 5.
41 See, for example, Kowaleski, *Medieval Exeter*, 123, 344–5.
42 Swanson, 'Artisans in the Urban Economy', 48; J. Hatcher and M. Bailey, *Modelling the Middle Ages* (Oxford, 2001), 153.
43 See table 16 and appendix 2.
44 Kermode, 'The Greater Towns', 449; Miller and Hatcher, *Medieval England*, 324–8.

occupations being identified.[45] Collectively, the vast majority of these trades were non-agricultural (97.1 per cent), otherwise a feature of urbanisation in this period,[46] suggesting that there were plenty of opportunities for work in a variety of crafts and industries. Diversity was therefore a characteristic feature of large towns, with centres such as Coventry noting as many as 153 different trades in the thirteenth century, Norwich 130 in the early fourteenth century and York 125 at the turn of the fifteenth century, for example.[47] Of course, it is to be remembered that these numbers, while useful, are not absolute, revealing more about the survival of sources and their interpretation by historians than contemporary urban practices.[48] Despite this, there are several important indicators suggesting that Lincoln's occupational structure differed in several respects from other large towns and it is on these aspects that the remainder of this chapter focuses.

Clothing

While in some respects the pattern of cloth manufacturing at Lincoln mirrored that of many other large towns during the later Middle Ages – decline after the 1250s following two centuries of growth and then recovery during the 1330s and 1340s – in others it differed significantly.[49] The most obvious divergence was Lincoln's failure to keep pace with other leading cloth towns following its revival, which eventually saw cloth replace wool as the primary English export during the fifteenth century, in spite of its earlier position of strength. Certainly, during the twelfth and thirteenth centuries when the city's renowned luxury scarlet was exported widely throughout Europe and purchased by aristocrats and royalty, Lincoln stood at the epicentre of English urban cloth making and fashion.[50] By the close of the fourteenth, however, despite renewed efforts, cloth manufactured in the city fuelled only the domestic

45 Several specialist occupations, such as *patyner*, *souter* and shoemaker, have been subsumed under the heading cordwainer, for example.

46 Holt and Rosser, *The Medieval Town*, 4.

47 Goddard, *Lordship*, 160; E. Rutledge, 'Economic Life', in Rawcliffe and Wilson, *Medieval Norwich*, 158; 'The Later Middle Ages: Admissions to Freedom', in P. M. Tillot (ed.), *Victoria County History of the County of York* (London, 1961), 114–16.

48 C. Dyer, 'Luxury Goods in Medieval England', in B. Dodds and C. Liddy (eds), *Commercial Activity, Markets and Entrepreneurs in the Middle Ages* (Woodbridge, 2011), 232–5, esp. table 12.2. See also Goddard, *Lordship*, 164–8.

49 E. M. Carus-Wilson, 'The English Cloth Industry in the Late Twelfth and Early Thirteenth Centuries', *Economic History Review*, 14, 1 (1944): 32–50; E. Miller, 'The Fortunes of the English Textile Industry during the Thirteenth Century', *Economic History Review*, 18, 1 (1965): 64–82; J. Munro, 'The "Industrial Crisis" of the English Textile Towns, c.1290–c.1330', in M. Prestwich, M. R. Britnell and R. Frame (eds), *Thirteenth Century England VII: Proceedings of the Durham Conference, 1997* (Woodbridge, 1999), 105–15; A. R. Bridbury, *Medieval English Clothmaking: An Economic Survey* (London, 1982), 116; *Export Trade*, *passim*; E. Power, *The Wool Trade in English Medieval History* (Oxford, 1941), chapter 6; M. Bonney, 'The English Medieval Wool and Cloth Trade', *Local Historian*, 22, 1 (1992): 18–40.

50 Gifts of Lincoln scarlet were made to the Queen of Norway, for example. Carus-Wilson, 'English Cloth Industry', 32–3, 37; Miller, 'English Textile Industry', 65–9, 76–7, 79–80.

market,[51] a reversal of fortune which prompted A. R. Bridbury to ask 'What did they all do in Lincoln, if they no longer made much cloth, to keep so many people employed?'[52] What caused Lincoln's cloth industry to fail and how did the city react?

The initial resurgence of cloth manufacturing in the city took place sometime during the mid-1340s, slightly later than in many other towns which saw renewed growth in the 1330s.[53] Evidence of its development can be seen in both the sharp rise in the number of weavers identified in the city from three (1289–1349) to twenty-nine (1350–1409)[54] and the greater sums of money being invested in the manufacture and marketing of local cloth. Examples of this come from 1336 when Daniel de Grayingham of Lincoln, draper, lent John son of the former mayor Gilbert de Atterby (*viz.* Atherby), £60, possibly for the purchase of cloths or materials bought directly from him,[55] and 1349, when Hugh de Brunne of Lincoln, draper, borrowed £40 from John de Bury of Newark, a fellow draper, perhaps for similar reasons.[56] As surviving export accounts from this period show,[57] it is likely that the majority of this money was spent on the production of relatively inexpensive cloths dyed with madder or brasil opposed to grain (*panni curti sine grano*),[58] cloth otherwise central to England's resurgence,[59] marking a shift away from the production of expensive scarlets.[60]

Although evidence remains slight, it is perhaps no coincidence that of the weavers identified after 1350, names included John de Boston, John de Dancaster, John de Hul, Richard de Ponnfreyt (Yorkshire) and John de Fledburh (Nottinghamshire),[61] emphasising how Lincoln attracted skilled migrants from throughout the Midlands and the North.[62] By at least 1376 there were also a small number of aliens working within the trade,[63] with Herman de Coloyne and John Vaulynde of Brabant being two of thirteen local men listed as responsible for the payment of the annual weavers' farm (£6).[64] This, as recent studies have shown, was in keeping with the broader

51 Hatcher, *Plague, Population*, 33–4, 50; Britnell, *Commercialisation of English Society*, 170; Bridbury, *Clothmaking*, 63.

52 Bridbury, *Clothmaking*, 82.

53 E. M. Carus-Wilson, *Medieval Merchant Venturers* (London, 2nd edn, 1967), 241–3.

54 This was a far cry from the 1330s when it was claimed that there were no weavers in the city: *CPR, 1348–50*, 120–1.

55 C 241/109/219.

56 C 241/129/80. His lands were subsequently sold to pay his debts: *BB*, fo. 193v.

57 See 67.

58 'Grain' was the crushed body of insects found on a species of oak grown in the Mediterranean typically used in the manufacture of scarlet cloth: *Export Trade*, 14–15.

59 Munro, 'Industrial Crisis', 104–5, 116–17, 140. For the process of manufacture, see P. Walton, 'Textiles', in J. Blair and N. Ramsey (eds), *English Medieval Industries* (London 1991), 319–46.

60 Though it did not cease altogether, see, for example, E 356/7, mm. 10–10d; S. G. Uhler, 'English Customs Ports, 1275–1343' (Unpublished Ph.D Thesis, University of St Andrews, 1977), 93–4, 97–8, 100.

61 JUST 2/67, rots 48–50; *BB*, fo. 243.

62 For more on migration, see 61–2.

63 For example, JUST 3/159, m. 5a; JUST 3/142, rot. 51d.

64 Vaulynde lived in the city until 1388 when he was killed by Gerard Vaugrave, a fellow Brabanter: JUST 2/87, rot. 2; E 372/221, rot. 14d.

trend for alien weavers to settle in England during this period, suggesting that the economic drives of Edward III to attract foreign labour were largely successful.[65]

The resurgence of the textile industry in Lincoln was also accompanied, and perhaps even driven, by the re-foundation of the Weavers guild in 1346, following the successful acquisition of a new royal charter which forbade all weavers living within twelve leagues (*leucas*) of the city from practising the trade unless they joined the guild, an act no doubt designed to attract foreign labour and minimise competition.[66] However, only two years later a petition submitted by the guild claimed that several citizens were employing weavers who were not members of the guild, whilst others were refusing to contribute to the guild's annual farm, suggesting that the organisation was not altogether successful in its aims.[67] In 1365 the civic government proclaimed that no weaver, dyer or fuller was to make or dye cloth for his own use or he would face forfeiture, demonstrating renewed concerns over manufacturing output.[68] Nonetheless, as the problems of the Weavers guild demonstrate, this was seldom easy or straightforward.

Despite the growth of Lincoln's textile industry, it is clear from subsequent evidence that the revival of the industry was only temporary, there being a noticeable downturn in both exports and the number of workers associated with the trade after 1380 (table 3).[69] The declining numbers should be seen as a direct result of the financial decisions of local merchants who, as the main source of credit, chose to invest their monies into the more profitable wool trade, a decision undoubtedly successful in the short term but ultimately deleterious for local industry.[70] A second issue was that, despite the mid-fourteenth-century boom, Lincoln increasingly became a centre of consumption and marketing, not manufacture. For example, despite the relative absence of weavers during the first half of the fourteenth century, at no stage did Lincoln's marketing of cloth ever collapse, as has been suggested in some quarters.[71] In fact between 1320 and 1349 an impressive twelve drapers and mercers can be identified as living and working in the city.[72] The implication of this seems to be that they were buying up cloth manufactured in local areas before reselling it elsewhere.[73] As the occupational data also makes plain, this pattern continued well

65 J. Good, 'The Alien Clothworkers of London, 1337–1381', in L. E. Mitchell, K. L French and D. L. Biggs (eds), *The Ties that Bind* (Farnham, 2011), 7–19, esp. 10–11; Lambert and Pajic, 'Drapery in Exile', 733–53; A. Kissane and J. Mackman, 'Aliens and Local Justice in Late Medieval Lincolnshire', in W. M. Ormrod, N. McDonald, C. Taylor (eds), *Resident Aliens in Later Medieval England* (Turnhout, 2017).

66 The guild was dedicated to the Exaltation of the Cross: C 47/41/160; *CPR, 1348–50*, 120. This legislation was confirmed in 1414 and 1424: *CPR, 1413–16*, 238; *CPR, 1422–29*, 184. For a similar ordinance for Fullers: C 47/41/153. See chapter five for more on Lincoln's guilds.

67 *CPR, 1348–50*, 120; Miller, 'English Textile Industry', 79.

68 This ordinance echoes the *Provisions for the Government of the City* (c. 1300): *BH*, fo. 113v; *Medieval Lincoln*, 404.

69 For exports, see chapter two.

70 See 87–92.

71 Bischoff, 'Economic Change', 277–91.

72 A guild of Mercers was established sometime before 1349, the exact date is unknown: see 000.

73 *Medieval Lincolnshire*, 128, 182, 200–2, 224, 226. Note in the earlier period (1289–1319) cloth

Table 3 Clothing: textile occupations (ten or more)

	1289–1319 (n=47)	**1320–49** (n=43)	**1350–79** (n=72)	**1380–1409** (n=55)	**Total** (n=217)
Tailor	19	15	21	26	81
Draper/mercer	4	12	10	10	36
Weaver	1	2	21	8	32
Dyer	1	3	6	4	14
Fuller/walker	1	1	6	4	12

Note: All numbers in parenthesis in this and subsequent tables in this chapter relate to the overall number of individuals listed in this category during each period.

into the early fifteenth century as the number of weavers, dyers and fullers shrank, highlighting how this was a longer term trend.

The overwhelming number of tailors, too, points to the fact that Lincoln continued to make garments throughout periods of limited cloth manufacture (1289–1319, 1380–1409), presumably from imported cloth, thereby allowing it to maintain its dominant position within the regional textile industry. Certainly, Boston saw vast quantities of ungrained cloth imported in the opening decades of the fourteenth century, much of which would have found its way into the city.[74] The dominance of the tailors is also underscored by the fact that they were only one of three known guilds to build a guildhall in the city, with a 'Taillour's Hall' being established by 1483 at the very latest,[75] whilst by the final decades of the fourteenth century (1380–1409) they accounted for almost half of all textile workers. Such practices have much in common with early modern towns and, as Paul Glennie and Ian Whyte remark, during the seventeenth century urban centres often 'provided and consumed a range of professional and cultural services, which were most conspicuous where manufacturing growth was limited', more so in towns where there was a high proportion of the 'middling sorts' or individuals with designs on public or civic advancement.[76] Whilst many of the cultural aspects of this later development were not present at Lincoln at this time for obvious reasons – least of all changes to domestic living, new patterns of consumption and the greater emphasis on education and learning – the growth of clergy and lawyers as 'key "brokers" in social networks' of the region was nevertheless apparent, marking important similarities between the two periods.[77]

was also sold by merchants, such as Stephen de Stanham (mayor 1301–06, 1312–13): E. W. Moore, *The Fairs of Medieval England: An Introductory Study* (Wetteren, 1985), 65–7.

74 Uhler, 'English Customs Ports', 91, 95. See table 10 for tolls on textiles.

75 The other guilds were the Clerks and Cordwainers: see 172 n. 106. For the early and innovative devotional practices of the Tailor's guild, see 184.

76 Glennie and Whyte, 'Towns in an agrarian economy', 183–90.

77 See main text below.

Despite the dramatic rise of Lincoln's textile industry in the 1340s, by 1400 it fuelled only the domestic market. This is reflected in both the surviving aulnage accounts (1397/98, 1398, 1399/1400), which provide details of the volume and types of cloth being produced in the city,[78] and the Pipe Rolls, which record the total monies from the aulnage accounts returned to the Exchequer by local officials (table 4).[79]

Several observations can be made regarding this evidence. Firstly, when compared to other leading cloth towns, such as Coventry, which manufactured 1,443 whole cloths, 3,285 dozens (half-cloths), 81 Welsh cloths and 3,105¾ cloths of the assize in 1397/98 alone, or Salisbury, which manufactured 7,044 cloths in 1395/96 alone,[80] the output of Lincoln's cloth industry was modest to say the least.[81] Second, the output of cloth in the city was undoubtedly indicative of small units of production in domestic workshops, like at Colchester and Winchester,[82] with 254 unique individuals being listed as paying subsidy in the three surviving accounts,[83] a quarter of whom (50) were women.[84] The vast majority of these individuals produced only single cloths of various colours,[85] with higher units of production being restricted to only a handful of men,[86] some of which was bought up by local merchants and exported through Boston.[87]

A third observation is that by roughly 1410 the returns for Lincoln no longer accurately represented the level of manufacture in the city. Certainly, while there are recorded aulnage revenues of £2 16s 8d for the city between 1409 and 1414, £6 3s 4d for 1414–19 and £6 6s 8d after this date (Lincoln and Kesteven), it is highly unlikely that the exact same number of cloths were sealed each year.[88] The most likely explanation is that the city's aulnage was let out to farm, a practice not without precedent. For example, as early as 1370 Lincoln and Rutland's aulnage was leased for three years to Thomas de Thornhagh of Lincoln (mayor 1390/91) for £22, a value which, at that time, was higher than all other counties listed in the king's indenture (Yorkshire, Northumberland, Cumberland, Westmoreland, Kent, Surrey and Sussex).[89] When

78 P. Merrick, 'Taxing Medieval Cloth', *Local Historian*, 32, 4 (2002), 222–3.

79 For example, E 372/242, rot. 11d (Robert Ledes); E 372/246, rot. 24d (Robert Bury).

80 Bridbury, *Clothmaking*, 67, table 2.

81 Goddard, *Lordship*, 231, table 9.

82 Britnell, *Colchester*, 77–8, table 5.1; Keene, *Medieval Winchester*, vol. 1, 310, table 19.

83 Out of a total of 282 individuals.

84 For large workshops in the southern intramural area during the thirteenth century, see 149.

85 Colours listed at Lincoln included blue, blood, white, sand, green, marble and russet. For imports of dye, see table 10.

86 Richard de Thorp and John Houghton both produced the most with thirteen cloths, followed by John Norman with twelve, Robert Markham with eleven and the German weaver Arnest de Ruden with ten: E 101/340/2, m. 1; E 101/339/29, mm. 1–2; *CPR, 1396–9*, 463; *CCR, 1399–1402*, 286.

87 For example, S. Rigby (ed.), *The Overseas Trade of Boston in the Reign of Richard II* (Lincoln Record Society, 2004), 45 (John Shippeman), 47 (Seman Laxfeld), 106 (John Sutton), 112 (William Peeke); Britnell, *Colchester*, 77–8.

88 For a critique of these accounts, E. M. Carus-Wilson, 'The Aulnage Accounts: A Criticism', *Economic History Review*, 2, 1 (1929): 114–23; Bridbury, *Clothmaking*, 47–61, 64–5.

89 *CCR, 1369–74*, 172; *1374–77*, 368.

Table 4 Taxes on cloth: the aulnage and Pipe Roll accounts (1396–1420)

Year	Subsidy collected	No. of clothiers	No./type of cloth
1396/97	£1 19 9¾d	–	–
1397/98#	£4 22d	99	174 whole cloths
			8½ dozens^
			15 cloths (size 1/6th)
			5½ cloths (size 1/8th)
			17 long cloths
1398/99	£5½d	–	–
1399/1400†	£1 19 9¾d	70	110 short cloths
			7 dozens
			12 long cloths
1400/01~	£4 10s 3¾d	113	200 whole cloths
			20 dozens
			14 long cloths
1401/02	£4 10s 3¾d	–	–
1402/03	no data	–	–
1403/04	£2 3d	–	–
1404–08	no data	–	–
1408/09	£1 8s 4d	–	–
1409–14	£2 16s 8d	–	–
1414–19	£6 3s 4d*	–	–
1419/20+	£6 6s 8d*	–	–

Source: E 372
Key: * = Lincoln City and parts of Kesteven; ^ = a dozen was a half-cloth; # = E 101/339/29; † = E 101/339/30 (note the total values are not the same, it being noted as 45s in the detailed accounts); ~ = see E 101/340/2.

this is compared to 1451, however, when Lincoln and Kesteven raised revenues of only £1 7s 8d, the least of all those listed,[90] this evidence alone demonstrates the dramatic decline of cloth manufacture in the city and surrounding area in the intervening period.[91]

90 Merrick, 'Taxing Medieval Cloth', 225–7.

91 For renewed efforts by the civic authorities to kick-start the cloth industry in 1516/17: LAO L/1/1/1, fos 57v, 71, 81v.

In spite of the difficulties facing local cloth manufacturing in the final decades of the fourteenth century, it is clear that other aspects of Lincoln's clothing industry remained buoyant throughout the period. These included leather and fur goods which not only provided for the needs of the local community and surrounding areas but underlined Lincoln's status as a centre for local networks of trade (table 5). Take the leather industry which, like other aspects of the city's economy, began to experience renewed growth during the late 1330s following the national recession.[92] For example, in 1337 Thomas Frere of Lincoln, tanner, lent a fellow Lincoln tanner, John de Hibaldstow, £20 for the term of two years, perhaps in order to give him time to manufacture goods and to make a profit before repaying the debt;[93] in 1343 Roger Remay, tawyer, felt secure enough to lend £12 to Robert son of Hugh de Normanton of Nottinghamshire, though his trust was misplaced as the debt went unpaid;[94] and in 1342 John de Whyten of Lincoln, barker, was noted as being owed £8 by William de Bardfield of Atterby, possibly for leather goods or raw materials.[95] Three complaints brought against local craftsmen in 1372 also indicate the ongoing importance of the trade to the city's hinterland.[96] These relate to John Ribald and Nicholas de Wotton', cordwainers, who were accused of selling shoes in the city and 'elsewhere in different villages' (*et alibi in diversis villis*) for excessive profits, to the value of half a mark;[97] John de Coringham and John Prentys, two local tanners, who were accused along with a third man, Richard Barkere of Stainfield, tanner, of purchasing various ox-hides at East Rasen (forty untanned hides each) before selling them for excessive profits;[98] and William de Thornhagh (mayor 1362/63), who was accused by his business partner, William de Bramlee of Lincoln, bower, of stealing twenty-two carts of oak (*quercium*) called *bark* at Eagle (*Eykel*), a village some nine

Table 5 Clothing: leather and fur occupations (five or more)

	1289–1319 (n=26)	**1320–49** (n=56)	**1350–79** (n=61)	**1380–1409** (n=36)	**Total** (n=179)
Cordwainer	5	13	25	13	56
Skinner	4	12	17	5	38
Saddler	–	11	11	6	28
Tanner	3	11	2	9	25
Glovemaker	8	3	1	1	13
Tawyer	1	4	3	–	8

92 For more on this, see 86.
93 C 241/110/196. For his occupation, *BB*, fo. 202.
94 C 241/118/113. For his occupation, *BB*, fo. 206.
95 C 241/115/356.
96 For Lincoln's hinterland, see 61–3 and map 3.
97 R. Sillem (ed.), *Some Sessions of the Peace in Lincolnshire, 1360–1375* (Lincoln Record Society, 1937), 71–2 (no. 305).
98 Sillem, *Sessions of the Peace, 1360–75*, 58 (no. 243).

miles from the city, for which he was awarded 12 marks in damages.[99] The last case in particular shows the volume and scale of tanning taking place at Lincoln, much of which was seen on the banks of the Witham in Wigford.[100] This evidence echoes that of the thirteenth century when goods from Lincoln were frequently sold in the towns of Newark, Horncastle, Kirton, Market Rasen and Caistor, all of which lay within twenty-five miles of the city.[101]

A similar picture emerges for the fur trade, which arguably grew in importance as international fairs such as Boston and Stamford, where the majority of furs were traditionally bought and sold, began to decline after 1300.[102] Although the vast majority of skins scraped, manipulated and dressed for sale by Lincoln's skinners would have been sheep or lamb skins,[103] which reflected the city's growing dependency upon the wool trade after 1300,[104] more exclusive furs were available on the open market, with Lincoln's tolls recording skins of squirrel, ermine (miniver) and fox, for example.[105] In 1390, too, a 'man of Lincoln' was recorded as sending a bundle of otterskins worth 70s to Scotland,[106] whilst there was a rabbit warren located outside the castle by 1296,[107] an important development following the relatively recent introduction of the species into England at the beginning of the century.[108]

It is likely that many of these skilled workers lived and worked in Skinner's Row (*in rengia pellipariorum*), or Skinnergate as it was also known, which was located in the parish of St Martin (map 2),[109] it being first recorded in 1336 at a time when the number of skinners trebled from four (1289–1319) to twelve (1320–49).[110] Unlike at Winchester, however, which saw a decline in royal and aristocratic markets during the second half of the fourteenth century, the number of skinners identified at Lincoln rose steadily, suggesting that there remained a buoyant market for luxury

99 KB 27/459, rots 40, 59d. Bark was an important ingredient in the tanning process, making hides more resistant to water and flexible for manufacture. For more on this process, see J. Cherry, 'Leather', in Blair and Ramsey, *Medieval Industries*, 301–2.

100 Vince, 'High Medieval Era', 294. For fourteenth-century tanners living in Wigford, see Richard de Skarle, tanner (E 179/135/12, rot. 1d); John Frere, William de Filingham, John son of Richard of Lincoln, barker (*BB*, fos 121, 214, 248).

101 *Rot. Hund.*, 317. For a more detailed analysis of the role of towns in the manufacture of leather, see M. Kowaleski, 'Town and and Country in Late Medieval England: The Hide and Leather Trade', in Corfield and Keene, *Work in Towns*, 56–73.

102 Miller and Hatcher, *Medieval England*, 174–6; Moore, *Fairs of Medieval England*, 60–1, 63.

103 Cherry, 'Leather', 295–302; E. M. Veale, *The English Fur Trade in the Later Middle Ages* (Oxford, 1966), 58.

104 See chapter two for more on this.

105 Veale, *Fur Trade*, 69, 133–4, 137–8. See table 10.

106 G. G. Simpson and J. D. Galbraith (eds), *Calendar of Documents Relating to Scotland*, vol. 5 (Edinburgh, 1881), 275, no. 864.

107 DL 29/1/1, m. 9.

108 Veale, *Fur Trade*, 58.

109 For example, *BB*, fo. 170v; E 179/135/12, rot. 3; H. C. Maxwell Lyte (ed.), *A Descriptive Catalogue of Ancient Deeds in the Public Record Office*, vol. 4 (London, 1902), 76.

110 K. Cameron, *The Place-names of Lincolnshire, Part One: The Place-names of the County of the City of Lincoln* (Cambridge, 1985), 100.

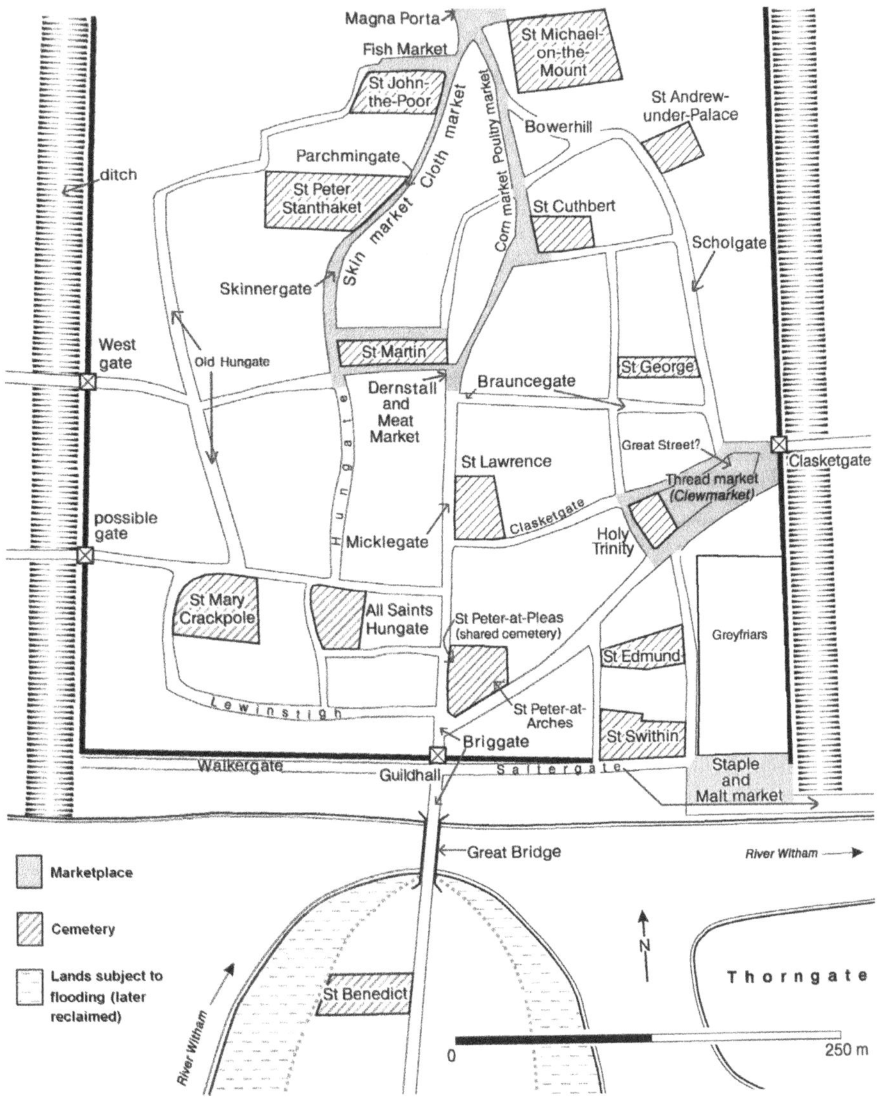

Map 2 The lower intramural area

goods in the city.[111] Certainly, several inhabitants were known to be in possession of expensive fur products, including hooded coats and gowns, many of which would have been purchased locally.[112]

[111] There is no indication that Lincoln's skinners simply marketed furs as at Winchester: Keene, *Medieval Winchester*, vol. 1, 286.

[112] *BB*, fos 121, 227v; *LW*, 5–7; LAO A/3/3, fo. 134. For the fifteenth century, see Wilson, 'Community, Kinship and Piety', 116, 118, 202–3.

In spite of the revival of Lincoln's textile industry in the decade before the onset of the plague, by 1400 it had once again contracted, this time permanently, as finance and opportunity drained away. No longer did it employ hundreds of workers in an industrial capacity as it had in the twelfth and thirteenth centuries. Lincoln's workers were now concentrating upon fulfilling the needs of the domestic market, highlighting the city's failure to keep pace with the leading cloth towns of Coventry, Colchester and Salisbury. Even so, not all sectors of the clothing industry shrank, with the production of furs and leather goods remaining buoyant until at least the opening decades of the fifteenth century, which came to be reflected by different areas of the city becoming associated with new and emerging crafts. Another key development during the fourteenth century was the increasing importance of the tailors. The growth of this trade emphasises how Lincoln rapidly became a finishing centre for cloth, much of which was manufactured outside the city, and a centre of consumption, characteristics shared with several early modern towns. Whilst in the broadest sense this marks a shift from the city's earlier dependency on manufacturing in the period before 1250, it also highlights how by 1400 textile production and marketing on an international scale no longer remained central to Lincoln's economic wellbeing, for better or worse.

Service

Like all medieval towns, Lincoln remained dependent upon a strong service industry – which included servants, musicians and entertainers, carters and labourers, barbers, taverners and hostelers, and an array of miscellaneous occupations – to support its various trades and industries. Taken collectively they comprised over an eighth of the city's entire workforce (12.8 per cent) throughout the period, a figure that rose to approximately a sixth between 1380 and 1409 (16.8 per cent). What is interesting about this evidence is how it dwarfs the findings for other towns of comparable size and wealth, including Norwich between 1275 and 1348 (where services stood at 3.3 per cent), York between 1307 and 1349 (5.1 per cent) and Coventry for the entire thirteenth century (9.09 per cent).[113] In fact, the proportion of service trades identified for Lincoln between 1289 and 1409 was only matched by York and Norwich during the second half of the fifteenth century (14 and 11 per cent respectively),[114] with York in particular seeing an increase in the number of innkeepers and taverners admitted to the freedom after 1450, a shift Jennifer Kermode links to the growing importance of the county court.[115] Whilst it is true that the disparity of the figures raises

113 Norwich data recalculated from Rutledge, 'Economic Life', 168–72, table 2 (categories 'miscellaneous services' and 'transport'); York data recalculated from Miller and Hatcher, *Medieval England*, 326 (categories 'transport' and 'miscellaneous'); Coventry evidence taken from Goddard, *Lordship*, 161, table 6.

114 R. Britnell, 'The Economy of British Towns 1300–1540', in *CUHB*, 326.

115 Kermode, 'Greater Towns', 452. There was also a rise in the number of attorneys and scriveners, reflecting the business of the court.

important questions over the methodology employed in achieving these results,[116] in particular their representativeness of poorer inhabitants who were most likely to have undertaken many of these roles, it is nevertheless noteworthy that it was during a period of declining manufacturing output that Lincoln's service trades began to increase, a situation analogous to that of Coventry during the sixteenth century.[117] It thus appears on a statistical level that as opportunities for manufacturing declined, individuals sought out other opportunities wherever possible.

A second important change, and one not incompatible with this hypothesis, is that in the decades after the Black Death a chronic labour shortage and, from the 1370s onwards, falling grain prices meant that service trades became more attractive to individuals seeking out work in towns, almost certainly due to the availability of higher wages.[118] This provides context for the decision of John Theker' in December 1393 to leave the service of Gilbert Blake of Harmston to work for John Sleyght, a butcher of Lincoln, or the choice of Roger Schepherde in November that same year to leave the service of Robert de Navenby, skinner, to work for William Clerk and Jacob de Barneby of Lincoln, pointer.[119] Additional, albeit circumstantial, evidence also hints towards the possibility of some migrants being willing to accept less skilled but better paid jobs in Lincoln. For example, in 1387 Matilda, daughter of Richard Neville, agreed to serve John Cotum of Snarford for a year as a spinner at Snarford but left his service before the end of the year to work as a servant for John Shipman of Lincoln, skinner.[120] Whether or not Matilda's opportunities were limited by the shrinking textile industry is unknown, though this remains a possibility. Unfortunately, the extent to which local men and women were affected by these changes lies largely beyond the scope of surviving records, though it is likely something similar was going on. It is certainly notable that there was a threefold rise in the number of unskilled agricultural occupations recorded after 1380, including threshers, foresters, basketmakers and turflayers, once again suggesting that work was being accepted wherever possible (appendix 1).[121]

Of all the occupations recorded within the service trades, the largest sub-group were those identified directly as 'servants' (*serviens, famula*) (table 6). Taken together they comprised 35 per cent of all those recorded (74 of 213) and 4.5 per cent of all

116 For example Goldberg has analysed the poll tax records of 1377 for a number of English towns, including Hull, York, Colchester, Carlisle and Rochester, estimating that between 20 and 30 per cent of the urban population were engaged in some form of domestic service (*not* service trades as discussed here). Such an approach, whilst extremely illuminating, nevertheless presents difficulties of comparison, as few other studies adopt it. P. J. P. Goldberg, *Women, Work, and Life Cycle in a Medieval Economy: Women in York and Yorkshire, c.1300–1520* (Oxford, 1992), 158–202.

117 Phythian-Adams, *Desolation of a City*, 204–220, esp. tables 18–19.

118 Goldberg, *Women, Work, and Life Cycle*, 74–6, 358.

119 E. Kimball, *Some Sessions of the Peace in Lincolnshire, 1381–96*, vol. 1 (Lincoln Record Society, 1953), 12 (nos 44, 46). For other cases, see 11 (nos 40–2), 30–1 (118); Sillem, *Sessions of the Peace, 1360–75*, 52 (no. 223). For the Statute of Labourers, see *Statutes of the Realm*, vol. 1, 311.

120 E. Kimball, *Some Sessions of the Peace in Lincolnshire, 1381–96*, vol. 2 (Lincoln Record Society, 1962), 49–50 (no. 138).

121 For complaints in 1375 by the city against the constable of the castle over the driving up of local agricultural wages, see *CCR, 1374–77*, 261–2.

Table 6 Service occupations (five or more)

	1289–1319 (n=51)	**1320–49** (n=64)	**1350–79** (n=46)	**1380–1409** (n=52)	**Total** (n=213)
Servant	4	18	21	31	74
Barber	8	7	4	10	29
Boatman/shipman/sailor	2	9	9	2	22
Taverner/hosteler	6	5	2	2	15
Musician/entertainer*	5	2	2	1	10
Carter	4	1	2	2	9
Summoner	5	2	–	–	7
Porter	–	2	2	1	5

* = includes clarion player, fiddler, harpist (2), jongleur, lute player, minstrel (2), organ player, piper

occupations surveyed here (out of 1,667), though it is likely that this figure grossly underestimates their overall proportion in the city.[122] For example, the evidence here does not include the dozens of servants hired by the sheriff and constable of the castle (messengers, watchmen, gatekeepers and gaolers), the mayor or bailiffs (clerks, chamberlains)[123] or the clergy, very few of whom can be identified by name.[124] The Poll Tax of 1377 likewise lists 157 lay inhabitants living in the Close,[125] many of whom would have found employment as servants of the Dean and Chapter, as they did in the fifteenth century.[126] Nevertheless, of those identified the vast majority were men (67 or 90 per cent), many of whom performed a variety of duties in their role as a servant.[127] They included John de Balderston, who, in the will of the William de Snelleston (mayor 1382/83) dated 1394, was described as 'my faithful servant and attorney (*attornatum*)',[128] and Walter, noted as the servant and shepherd of Avice de Crosseby in 1327.[129] Others also found employment with members of the gentry

122 See appendix 1.

123 Exceptions include William Thorp, *nuper gaolarius castri Lincolni*, noted in 1366 and William Lumnour, *gaolator*, listed in 1386, for example: KB 29/22, m. 25; JUST 3/173, m. 9d.

124 See 129–30.

125 Fenwick, *Poll Taxes*, 34.

126 Wilson, 'Community, Kinship and Piety', 30, 96–7, 191–3, 204, 213. For a comparative case study for York, see S. Rees Jones, 'God and Mammon: The Role of the City Estate of the Vicars Choral in the Religious Life of York Minster', in R. Hall and D. Stocker (eds), *Vicars Choral at English Cathedrals: Cantate Domino, History, Architecture and Archaeology* (Oxford, 2005), 192–9.

127 On the various connotations of the term 'servant', see P. J. P. Goldberg, 'What Was a Servant?', in A. Curry and E. Matthew (eds), *Concepts and Patterns of Service in the Later Middle Ages* (Woodbridge, 2000), 1–7.

128 *ELW*, 74.

129 *ELW*, 5–7.

and the clergy, including Robert Barbour, servant of William de Hawley, knight and sheriff (1363–68),[130] and William Cok, servant of the Prior of St Katherine *extra Lincoln*'; others still with wealthy merchants, including John son of Walter, servant of William de Dalderby, merchant (mayor 1383/84).[131] There were also those such as Robert, servant of Robert de Norton of Lincoln, carter, or John de Whyte, servant of Richard de Newcastle upon Tyne, baker, who served masters of more modest means.[132] Besides those identified directly as servants, the evidence from this survey records a scullion (kitchen-hand), several groomsmen, a horse-keeper, a squire, emphasising how males were seldom restricted to domestic roles, a conclusion at odds with that for women, the majority of whom were employed within a domestic setting, at least according to the testamentary evidence. They included Catherine, maidservant of Emma Nightingale, described as 'recently deceased' in the latter's will of 1349, possibly due to plague;[133] and Avote de Normanton, identified as maid-servant in the will of Gilbert Badde in 1330.[134] Nonetheless, as Louise Wilkinson has demonstrated for the late thirteenth century, women in Lincoln, much like those in many other large towns, frequently worked within a variety of industries and trades, including cloth, iron, carpentry and building, all of which supplemented more traditional female roles such as laundry, brewing and midwifery.[135]

Other occupations identified within the service industry included musicians and entertainers, some of whom doubtless joined the Minstrels and Entertainers guild, founded in honour of St Mary sometime before 1389.[136] There were also those, such as Thomas de Melton and Peter Pyper of York, who were able to find permanent positions as minstrels of the city in 1378 and who performed important roles in civic pageantry.[137] There were equally large numbers of individuals recorded in the transport industry, including boatmen, carters, porters, sailors and shipmen, highlighting the distributive element of Lincoln's economy, which is explored more fully in chapter two. In addition, those involved in a mixture of miscellaneous service professions included two lavenders (launderers), a falconer, a messenger, for example. The city was also home to a large number of barbers, for whom a guild dedicated to St John the Evangelist was founded in 1369,[138] suggesting that grooming remained an important part of life for many city inhabitants.[139] In 1440, for example, new ordinances regulating the trade were overseen by the civic government, including how no more than a farthing was to be charged for shaving the poor or a halfpenny for a priest;

130 *List of Sheriffs for England and Wales* (List and Index Society, New York, 1963), 79.
131 JUST 2/80, rot. 2; JUST 2/87, rot. 1; KB 29/41, m. 24.
132 JUST 2/67, rot. 48d; JUST 3/140, m. 30.
133 *BB*, fo. 207v.
134 *BB*, fo. 119.
135 Wilkinson, *Thirteenth-Century Lincolnshire*, 96–105; Goldberg, *Women, Work, and Life Cycle*, 82–137.
136 C 47/41/156. For further details on this guild, see 181.
137 *BH*, fo. 109v; *WB*, fo. 4v. For the mayoral procession, see 130.
138 C 47/41/151.
139 It is unknown whether Lincoln's barbers engaged in medical work as in the capital: J. Dobson and R. Milnes Walker, *Barbers and Barber Surgeons of London* (Oxford, 1979).

barbers visiting the houses of civic officials or conventual houses were to do so by agreement only; whilst all Sunday shaving was forbidden.[140]

One aspect of the service trade for which there is surprisingly little evidence is apprentices,[141] though as surviving guild ordinances demonstrate, they were undoubtedly common.[142] Certainly, by the opening decades of the sixteenth century an average of nine apprentices were enrolled as freemen each year over a thirty-year period (1512–42),[143] all of whom were required to serve for seven years in their masters' houses, before enjoying the benefits of citizenship.[144] According to ordinances recorded in 1422, all apprentices were required to pay 20d in their first year and 4d to the clerk for enrolment. At the conclusion of their apprenticeship they were also required to appear before the Burwarmote Court where they swore to having completed the term of their apprenticeship before performing an oath of obedience to the mayor and agreeing to abide by rules of their trade.[145]

The final occupations to consider within the service trade are taverners and hostelers, two interchangeable terms in the city for innkeepers. Providing temporary accommodation and provisions for visiting traders and pilgrims,[146] taverns and inns remained an important feature of all medieval towns.[147] While taverns are known to have been established at various places in the city, including in the parish of Holy Trinity near the Friars Minor,[148] in St Mary in Wigford,[149] in the Bail,[150] beneath the Stonebow,[151] and even in the Close, much to the consternation of the bishop and the Dean and Chapter,[152] on the whole they go unrecorded in much of the surviving evidence.[153]

Given their centrality to the local economy, it is perhaps unsurprising to note that some innkeepers were known to have taken advantage of their position. In the 1350s, for instance, both William de Betley and John de Torkesey were charged by crown officials for selling food and drink at excessive prices, whilst in 1365 fines were levied

140 *WB*, fos 10v–11.

141 For two runaway apprentices, R. R. Sharpe (ed.), *Calendar of Letters from the Mayor and Corporation of the City of London, c.1350–1370* (London, 1885), 74, 138.

142 For example, the Barbers, Fullers and Masons: C 47/41/151, 153–4.

143 J. W. F. Hill, *Tudor and Stuart Lincoln* (Stamford, 1956; reprint 1991), 23. For the policies of the Tudor civic government to apprentices, see G. A. J. Hodgett, *Tudor Lincolnshire* (Welwyn Garden City, 1975), 128–30.

144 For a draper's apprentice denied citizenship by his master: A. H. Thomas (ed.), *Plea and Memoranda Rolls, 1413–17* (London, 1943), 63.

145 *WB*, fo. 4v.

146 For numbers of pilgrims, see 166–7.

147 J. Hare, 'Inns, innkeepers and the society of later medieval England, 1350–1600', *Journal of Medieval History*, 39, 4, (2013): 477–497; Keene, *Medieval Winchester*, vol. 1, 274–8; Rees Jones, *York*, 257–60.

148 *BB*, fo. 127.

149 *BB*, fo. 130v.

150 JUST 1/527, m. 7d. For the twelfth-century Angel Inn located in the bail, see Vince, 'High Medieval Era', 210–12, figs. 9.52 and 9.54.

151 By 1523: LAO L/1/1/1, fo. 161.

152 *LCL VCH*, 87; D. Owen in *Ibid.* (ed.), *A History of Lincoln Minster* (Cambridge, 1994), 153.

153 For a former tavern turned into a shop in 1336: *BB*, fo. 130v.

by the civic government on hostelers abusing their right to sell bread and ale.[154] Such evidence goes some way towards explaining how men of the trade managed to establish substantial property portfolios, including Thomas de Kirketon of Lincoln who left four messuages upon his death in 1362,[155] or John de Torkesey who bequeathed a windmill and two shops to his two sons.[156] Frustratingly, however, very little is known of the commercial exploits of many innkeepers, though some were undoubtedly involved in the wine trade.[157] An illustration of this can be seen in the case of the aforementioned John de Torkesey who, along with his sons William (also a taverner)[158] and John, was granted a licence by the crown to import wine from Gascony through Boston up to the value of £100 in 1364.[159]

Lincoln housed a large and varied service industry, all of which was bound to support arterial networks of trade and communication, entertainment and domesticity, a picture consistent throughout the period analysed here. Nevertheless by the end of the fourteenth century the proportion of service trades began to grow as a result of both migration from the countryside and Lincoln's declining cloth manufacturing, an industry typically associated with a large and sophisticated workforce. Hence as opportunities for textile work receded, those living in and seeking out work in Lincoln found themselves in a position where it became necessary to look for work in any number of roles, both being a reflection and defining characteristic of the post-plague urban economic landscape.

Professionals and Administrative Work

Another conspicuous industry in the city was professional and administrative work (table 7), which included those engaged in the writing and recording of legal documents and those for whom reading or an understanding of the written word was a requirement (13.4 per cent).[160] While it is to be regretted that few details of these individuals can be glimpsed beyond their name and occupation, and less still transactions involving their goods and services, it is nevertheless clear that these men often dealt with the wealthy. Take, for example, John 'Libraire' of Lincoln, who was known to have sold a Roman de Renart' and a Psalter in 1359,[161] or John Liminour, who sold two books, including a missal, to John Plaint, godfather of Thomas in

154 JUST 1/527, mm. 5d, 7d; *BH*, fo. 26v.

155 *BB*, fo. 254v.

156 *BB*, fo. 102. This is the same John de Torkesey who served as bailiff in 1346/47 and undertook a pilgrimage to Rome in 1350. See appendix 2 and 194–5 and n. 262.

157 Kowaleski, *Medieval Exeter*, 143–7; Rosser, *Medieval Westminster*, 122–132.

158 JUST 1/523, m. 13. For his death in 1367: JUST 2/67, rot. 50d; E 13/90, m. 20d.

159 *CPR, 1364–67*, 17.

160 On problems associated with medieval concepts of literacy: M. T. Clanchy, *From Memory to Written Record: England 1066–1307* (London, 1979), 226–54.

161 M. A. Michael, 'English Illuminators, c.1190–1450: A Survey from Documentary Sources', in P. Beal and J. Griffiths (eds), *English Manuscript Studies, 1100–1700*, vol. 4 (London, 1993), 74–5.

Table 7 Professional and administrative occupations (all)

	1289–1319 (n=37)	**1320–49** (n=112)	**1350–79** (n=51)	**1380–1409** (n=24)	**Total** (n=221)
Clerk	28	69*	19	13	129
Attorney	1	34	27	8	70
Scribe	3	3	–	1	7
Illuminator	2	2	1	2	7
Notary	–	2	3	–	5
Physician/surgeon	2	1	1	–	4
Bookbinder	1	1	–	–	2

Key: * = the peak identified here is explained by the high number of wills enrolled in 1349, a third of which named clerks as executors or witnesses.

1394.[162] It is possible that these men, like Henry Baudenay, a wealthy illuminator who died in 1296, lived in Lumnour Lane, a place long associated with the trade, which straddled the parishes of St Rumbold and St Bavon in the suburb of Butwerk.[163] Further links to wealthy patrons can be identified for Robert de Metheringham, a local scribe (*scriptor*) who was named in 1319 among the provers of the will of Stephen de Stanham, a wealthy merchant and six-time mayor of Lincoln (1301–06, 1312/13),[164] and John le Graunt de Lincoln, *notar'*, who was named in a case involving Robert de Wakefeld and Henry Cheyney of London, both of whom were accused of falsifying documents to the value of £60.[165]

Despite the presence of these highly skilled occupations, Lincoln's professional and administrative trades were nevertheless dominated by two main groups: attorneys and clerks, both of which stand as testament to Lincoln's status as the focal point of judicial and clerical practices in the county and the diocese.[166] Take to begin with clerks, all of whom are distinguished here from chaplains,[167] with the term *clerici* being used in Lincoln as an occupational marker, akin to baker or fuller, much like in Norwich during the thirteenth century.[168] Typically it was the duty of a clerk to draft or copy accounts, prepare plaints, and record and witness wills and charters;[169] much of this work was enrolled into the records of various local courts.[170] Despite the secular function of many of the city's clerks, however, there

162 *CIPM, 1391–9*, no. 576.

163 *LW*, 4–5. For William Lumnour, son of Osbert Lumnour, who bequeathed several properties in this lane in the early 1340s: LAO Dij 74/1/24–5, 28, 30–1.

164 *BB*, fo. 82.

165 JUST 1/528, m. 16.

166 Swanson, *British Towns*, 62–3.

167 For the role of chaplains, see chapter six.

168 E. Rutledge, 'Lawyers and Administrators: the Clerks of Late-Thirteenth Century Norwich', in C. Harper-Bill (ed.), *Medieval East Anglia* (Woodbridge, 2005), 93.

169 *BB*, fos 104, 146v, 223. For an example of costs, see LAO Bj 2/7, fo. 82.

170 G. H. Martin, 'The English Borough in the Thirteenth Century', in Holt and Rosser, *The*

were also those who took minor orders and served in parish churches which, in practical terms, meant that they were able to perform auxiliary roles alongside local priests, including as an acolyte, reader, helper in exorcism, or even as a carrier of holy water.[171] Among these men were John de Lincoln, clerk of St Benedict's church, and Thomas Newport, late clerk of St Mary Magdalene in the Bail.[172] This distinction is reflected clearly by the ordinances of Clerks' guild, founded in honour of St Mary, St Nicholas and All Saints in St John in Wigford sometime before 1279, which make frequent reference to parish and lay clerks.[173] Further indication of the size and importance of this group can be gauged by the fact that, along with the Tailors and the Great Guild, they were one of only three guilds to establish a guildhall by 1424 at the latest, despite a number of ongoing fiscal problems.[174]

Equally influential were Lincoln's attorneys (*attornatus*) who, like clerks, found numerous opportunities for work in one or more of the city's six main courts.[175] These were the Court of de la Haye located 'before the gate of Lincoln castle' in Bardolfhalle in St Clement,[176] which heard pleas and matters pertaining to the market and jurisdiction of the Bail;[177] the county court, located in the Great Hall of the castle, which served the needs of the sheriff and the justices of the peace;[178] the Galilee Court housed in the cathedral, which heard pleas from residents of the Close and those living in properties belonging to the Dean and Chapter outside of Lincoln;[179] the ecclesiastical court of the Dean and Chapter, which held sessions at the Chapter House on matters relating to probate, marriage, sexual impropriety, defamation and other moral crimes;[180] and the Burwarmote and Statute Merchant courts held at the guildhall, which heard matters relating to the civic franchise and recorded and ratified contracts for credit on behalf of the crown.[181]

One such attorney was John de Thorp who defended the rights of a great number of clients, including the Dean and Chapter and the Abbot of Thornton, as well as several lay men and women.[182] Whilst it appears that Thorp's speciality was the rental

Medieval Town, 47–8; K. L. Bevan, 'Clerks and Scriveners: Legal Literacy and Access to Justice in Late Medieval England' (Unpublished Ph.D Thesis, University of Exeter, 2013), 101–5. For Lincoln's courts, see main text below.

171 M. Rubin, 'Sacramental Life', in M. Rubin and Walter Simons (eds), *Cambridge History of Christianity*, vol. 4 (Cambridge, 2009), 226.

172 *BB*, fos 106v (1328), 209v (1350). For other clerks with minor orders, see Bennett, *Registers of Bishop Henry Burghersh*, vol. 3, nos 2895, 3207.

173 The guild was founded 'before the Statute of Mortmain': C 47/40/148; *CPR, 1401–5*, 96.

174 *BH*, fo. 105v. See 192.

175 For the independent free court of the manor of Hungate known as Beaumont Fee, see J. W. F. Hill, 'The Manor of Hungate, or Beaumont Fee, in Lincoln', *AASRP*, 38 (1926–27): 175–208.

176 *CCR, 1318–23*, 596.

177 See table 1.

178 R. C. Palmer, *The County Courts of Medieval England, 1150–1350* (Princeton, 1982), 22, n. 99, 43.

179 *LCL VCH*, 82.

180 This was nevertheless a peripatetic court with no fixed location. L. R. Poos (ed.), *Lower Ecclesiastical Jurisdiction in Late-Medieval England: The Courts of the Dean and Chapter of Lincoln, 1336–1349, and the Deanery of Wisbech, 1458–1484* (Oxford, 2001).

181 See 000.

182 For example, *BB*, fos 112v, 117, 119, 122, 123v.

market,[183] he was also known to deal with pleas of lands and cases of essoin.[184] In 1335 he was also subject to a claim of unpaid rent himself, for which he defended himself (and won),[185] whilst in 1349 he proved the will of Simon de Grantham,[186] husband to the daughter of the former mayor, Stephen de Stanham,[187] demonstrating his standing locally. Simon Levelaunce was likewise another attorney who performed legal services for local inhabitants over a period of four decades, including Gilbert de Ledered, former sheriff (1338–41) in 1353,[188] William de Blyton (mayor 1327/28) in 1354,[189] and in 1365, in three separate pleas, John de Wilburn, Geoffrey Scrope and Adam de Lymbergh, cathedral clerks.[190] On two occasions, in 1358 and 1369, he also acted as an executor of the wills of Edmund de Burton and John de Lincoln, spicer,[191] while in 1359 he proved the will of John son of John son of Thomas of Lincoln, and defended the rights of Thomas son of William de Paris of Ouneby against Walter de Kelby (mayor 1350/51) in a plea brought by the sheriff in 1369.[192] Levelaunce himself brought a plea of land against John de Blythe along with his wife, Gillian, in 1366 though, unlike John de Thorp, he did not defend himself.[193] In 1351 he acted as a pledge for William de Hacthorn' (coroner 1322–47), who was accused of wandering at night,[194] whilst in 1367 he was named as one of Lincoln's coroners, a post he held for a decade.[195] Finally, in both 1376 and 1385 he was chosen to represent the civic authorities in disputes over lands and tenements in the city, thus bringing to a close a lengthy and distinguished career.[196]

What is clear from the Lincoln evidence is that some attorneys and clerks grew to great prominence during a period when the written culture of civic government reached new levels of sophistication and complexity.[197] As Michael Clanchy argues, the growth of the clerical profession was accelerated by events such as the passing of the Statute of Merchants in 1285, which required that all towns maintain a clerk 'to enrol recognisances of debt in duplicate and write out bills of obligation authenticated by a royal seal'.[198] Attorneys likewise emerged as a result of the increasing number of individuals seeking redress through the courts, the vast majority of whom were, in the words of Kitrina Bevan, 'unable to navigate the linguistically

183 *BB*, fos 113, 116v, 117, 127.
184 *BB*, fos 136v, 138, 143–143v.
185 *BB*, fos 130, 131.
186 *BB*, fo. 195v.
187 *BB*, fos 82–82v.
188 *BB*, fos 224, 226v. See also 218 for more on Ledered.
189 *BB*, fo. 226v.
190 *BB*, fo. 259v.
191 *BB*, fos 234v, 235v, 267v.
192 *BB*, fos 237v, 267v, 269v. For other cases involving Levelaunce, see *BB*, fos 101v–102, 222, 230, 257v–258, 261v, 268v.
193 *BB*, fo. 263; LAO Dij 80/3/58.
194 JUST 1/523, m. 12.
195 Appendix 2.
196 JUST 1/1486, m. 20; JUST 1/1488, mm 50, 51d.
197 Martin, 'The English Borough in the Thirteenth Century', 29–48; Bevan, 'Clerks and Scriveners', 81–90.
198 Clanchy, *Memory to Written Record*, 53.

and procedurally technical realm of English law'.[199] Collectively these developments brought with them varying degrees of status. Certainly, it is significant to note that of all the wills enrolled in 1349, over two thirds (73 of 103) referenced a clerk, whilst by the middle of the fourteenth century attorneys began to replace Lincoln's bailiffs as those tasked with returning the annual fee farm payment to the Exchequer on behalf of the civic government.[200] The knock-on effect of the latter was that by the 1380s attorney became a more frequent choice of profession for civic officials than previously.[201] While on the one hand this supports Derek Keene's theory that the legal profession prior to the fifteenth century has hitherto been underestimated in English towns,[202] it also supports the contention of Rosemary Horrox that attorneys were fundamental in the emergence of the urban gentry during the fifteenth century, with many being considered gentleman 'by virtue of their occupation'.[203] Literature and learning thus remained central to the concerns of towns and civic governments in particular, increasingly so by the fifteenth century.[204]

One of the more surprising aspects of this evidence, like that for the service trade, is how the proportion of administrative and professional occupations identified at Lincoln stands at a level usually only seen in other provincial capitals during the second half of the fifteenth century, including York, Canterbury and Chester.[205] In fact the only comparable centre for Lincoln was Westminster where the royal courts played a central role in the local economy.[206] Whilst it is possible that this is simply a reflection of the surviving evidence, it is nevertheless a possibility that the situation was also influenced by the decision of civic government to actively promote these occupations, thereby providing a forum through which they might emerge. This reflects the decision of the civic government to follow London's example when establishing its own Sheriff's Courts in 1409,[207] an act that brought great prestige and business to the city.[208] Certainly, as the occupational data shows, this may also have been driven in part by the relative decline in the proportion of professional and

199 Bevan, 'Clerks and Scriveners', 183; A. Musson, *Medieval Law in Context* (Manchester, 2001), 164; Rutledge, 'Lawyers and Administrators', 98.

200 See chapter 3.

201 For dates, see appendix 2.

202 Keene, *Medieval Winchester*, vol. 1, 252–3, 323, 352–3 (table 26), 437.

203 R. Horrox, 'The Urban Gentry in the Fifteenth Century', in J. A. F. Thomson (ed.), *Towns and Townspeople in the Fifteenth Century* (Gloucester, 1988), 30–1.

204 For links between 'gentlemen' attorneys and the gentry in the city, see *Medieval Lincoln*, 279–80; J. Mackman, 'The Lincolnshire Gentry and the Wars of the Roses' (Unpublished Ph.D Thesis, University of York, 1999), 20 (n. 55), 181.

205 See York, 'Services: other', for example, in Britnell, 'The Economy', in *CUHB*, 326. However, compare the treatment of professional groups in Norwich by Miller and Hatcher, *Medieval England*, 324–30, to that of Rutledge, 'Lawyers and Administrators', 83–98, with the latter placing much more emphasis on this group.

206 Rosser, *Medieval Westminster*, 201–6.

207 P. Tucker, *Law Courts and Lawyers in the City of London, 1300–1550* (Cambridge, 2007), 363.

208 For example, in 1413 the number of jurors alone brought before the sheriffs court on Thursday after the feast of St Margaret (20 July) was 120. JUST 3/33/8. See also A. Rogers, 'The Lincolnshire County Court in the Fifteenth Century', *Lincolnshire History and Archaeology*, 1 (1966): 64–78.

administrative occupations noted in the city between 1380 and 1409, most likely as a result of the changing fortunes of the Statute Merchant Registry.[209] Even so, alongside York and London, Lincoln was the only other urban county to hold a regular court of pleas presided over by civic sheriffs between monthly county courts, the legacy of which was memorialised in the city's custumal, 'copyled in drawn [and] owte of french *in* to inglish be Thomas Grantham' (mayor 1465/66) and recorded in the *White Book* in 1483,[210] a document Mary Bateson argues bears great similarity to the custumal recorded in London's own *Liber Albus*.[211]

The Arms and Parchment Industries

Implicit in the obligations of royally chartered towns was the need to satisfy the demands of the crown, which broadly speaking fell into two categories. The first was the responsibility for maintaining the rights of the market, dispensing the king's justice and keeping the peace, matters which, whilst not directly benefitting the crown, ensured that communities functioned according to the king's laws.[212] The second was fiscal or practical assistance in times of need, most frequently in the form of taxes or loans,[213] but which on occasion could involve the direct provisioning of grain and livestock, known by the fourteenth century as purveyance.[214] In times of war, towns were also expected to equip and provide troops and/or to construct ships and other sea-going vessels, a burden that typically fell to only the largest towns and ports.[215] Two ancillary measures that remained central to the needs of the crown, but which have received comparatively little attention from historians, were the manufacture of arms and the production of parchment,[216] two industries essential to the economic wellbeing of Lincoln.[217]

The first real indication of Lincoln's wide-scale involvement in the provisioning

209 See 78–90.

210 LAO L/1/3/1, mm. 46v–59.

211 M. Bateson (ed.), *Borough Customs*, vol. 1 (London, 1904–06), xxxvii.

212 Such obligations were noted in detail in surviving charters: *Royal Charters*, 1–33. See also A. Ballard and J. Tait (eds), *British Borough Charters, 1216–1307* (Cambridge, 1923), liv–lxxxviii.

213 Ormrod, 'The Crown and the English Economy', 149–83; C. Liddy, *War, Politics and Finance in Late Medieval English Towns: Bristol, York and the Crown, 1350–1400* (Woodbridge, 2005), 20–43; L. Attreed, *The King's Towns: Identity and Survival in Late Medieval English Boroughs* (Oxford, 2001), 181–212; G. L. Harriss, 'Aids, Loans, Benevolences', *Historical Journal*, 6, 1 (1963): 1–19.

214 J. R. Maddicott, 'The English Peasantry and the Demands of the Crown, 1294–1341', in T. H. Aston (ed.), *Landlords, Peasants and Politics in Medieval England* (Cambridge, 1987), 285–359.

215 Liddy, *War, Politics and Finance*, 43–57; Attreed, *The King's Towns*, 181–212; M. Kowaleski, 'Warfare, Shipping, and Crown Patronage: The Impact of the Hundred Years War on the Port Towns of Medieval England', in L. Armstrong and I. Elbl (eds), *Money, Markets and Trade in Late Medieval Europe* (Leiden, 2007), 233–54.

216 Though see Swanson, *Medieval Artisans*, 101–3, for bowers; and M. Mercer, 'King's Armourers and the Growth of the Armourer's Craft in Early Fourteenth-Century London', in J. S. Hamilton (ed.), *Fourteenth Century England VIII* (Woodbridge, 2014), 1–20.

217 See, for example, Goldberg who identifies 'armaments' as a category but does not discuss it: Goldberg, *Women, Work, and Life Cycle*, 44–8.

of arms for the crown dates from the time of the Anglo-French wars, when the responsibility for supplying armies with weapons was taken up directly by the royal government for the first time.[218] While previously infantrymen had to depend on arms purchased within their own regions, by the reign of Edward III it was not uncommon for sheriffs to be sent writs ordering a certain quantity of arms to be dispatched to the Tower of London.[219] An illustration of this comes from 1344 when 200 bows and 1,500 bow strings were bought at Lincoln,[220] along with a further 500 bows in 1349,[221] much of which provided work for local fletchers, bowers and archers (table 8).

Table 8 Select artisan occupations

	1289–1319 (n=24)	**1320–49** (n=24)	**1350–79** (n=16)	**1380–1409** (n=20)	**Total** (n=84)
Bower	3	12	10	10	35
Parchment dealer/makers	5	5	1	2	13
Fletcher	–	4	2	–	6
Archer	2	–	–	–	2

Alongside York,[222] Lincoln dominated the provincial manufacture of bows and associated components (bowstrings, arrows), a fact underscored by the quantities listed as being received from Lincolnshire at the Tower in 1355–56, which amounted to 454 painted bows, 2,356 white bows and 1,382 sheaves of arrows, and in 1382 when it dispatched 764 bows and 500 sheaves of arrows, figures higher than all other counties.[223] In 1341 and 1359 Lincolnshire also returned more bows for the war effort than every other county except London and Middlesex, the majority of which were sourced directly from Lincoln itself,[224] and as Herbert Hewitt remarks, Lincolnshire was well known for making arms in the Middle Ages.[225] During the 1350s, for example, John de Brakelond, who was put in charge of the production of

218 Note, however, that in 1303–04 the city contributed 36 crossbows, 286 bows, 1,200 quarrels and 1,200 arrows which were dispatched via Boston to Berwick, along with various grains and other foodstuffs for the war with Scotland, suggesting that there was a growing trade in the city by this time: E 101/569/19.

219 Swanson, *Medieval Artisans*, 101.

220 E 364/123, rot. 6/17.

221 *CPR, 1348–50*, 346.

222 Swanson, *Medieval Artisans*, 99.

223 E 101/400/22. M. J. Hewitt, *The Organization of War under Edward III, 1338–62* (Manchester, 1966), 64, table 5.

224 Hewitt, *Organization of War*, 64, table 6.

225 For the early fourteenth century, E 101/568/19; for the early fifteenth: *CCR, 1419–22*, 166. For imports of yew, used in the manufacture of bows, see Uhler, 'English Customs Ports', 91, 96; Rigby, *Overseas Trade*, 91–4, 96, 98. See also Swanson, *Medieval Artisans*, 102.

bows on behalf of the crown, was sent to Lincolnshire to acquire staff specialised in their manufacture.[226]

Such practices continued throughout the fifteenth century. In 1436, alongside York and Coventry, Lincoln's sheriffs,[227] Gilbert Fleccher and John Lyndon, were ordered to provide 100,000 goose wing feathers for arrows and to find 'sufficient workers and put them to work on the said arrows';[228] and in 1475 a general commission was issued to all counties demanding 'bowestaves', 'shefe arrowes' and arrowheads to be dispatched for the war with France.[229]

It is likely that much of this new manufacturing took place on the hill in the parish of St Michael, known by the middle of the fourteenth century as Bower Hill (*bowherhill*).[230] Certainly several individuals working within the trade are known to have resided there, including William Ermyn, bower, who lived in St Cuthbert; Robert Hare, bower, who bought an empty plot in St Michael, possibly with a view to building a workshop; and Thomas Colvill, bower, who owned a shop in St Michael.[231] However, it is the Maykyn family who best exemplify the tradition of manufacture in the city, with three successive generations being identified as bowers. Certainly, by 1391 the family had become sufficiently wealthy to alienate a messuage in St Benedict to the Dean and Chapter for the use of the community of vicars, who were instructed to pray for the soul of the founder, William, son of Maurice Maykyn, his mother and father and all the faithful dead.[232] The importance of the trade likewise continued well into the sixteenth century when the civic records reveal large numbers of apprentice bowyers being enrolled as freemen.[233]

Lincoln's involvement in the war effort was not confined to manufacture.[234] In 1314 the civic government supplied forty archers to fight at Berwick at a cost of £14;[235] in 1324 it equipped eighty men with actons, habergeons with plate-mail helmets and iron gauntlets;[236] during the reign of Edward III (no date) it provisioned eighty-four archers to fight in Gascony,[237] and in 1335 a further sixty mounted archers under the command of John Aldman, in the case of the last this was more

226 Hewitt, *Organization of War*, 69.

227 Note the term 'sheriff' replaced 'bailiff' following the grant of shire status in 1409. For further details, see 132.

228 *CPR, 1429–36*, 600.

229 *CPR, 1467–77*, 462.

230 *BB*, fo. 201v.

231 BB, fos 129v, 204; *CFR, 1377–83*, 174.

232 KB 29/3, m. 12d; *BB*, fo. 248; *CPR, 1391–96*, 30; C 143/406/19.

233 For example, LAO L/1/1/1, mm. 45v, 63v, 146, 190v, 202–202v, 272v. My thanks to Chris Johnson for drawing my attention to these records.

234 For some thirteenth-century munitions, see M. Prestwich, *Armies and Warfare in the Middle Ages: the English Experience* (New Haven, 1996), 299.

235 E 372/160, rot. 17d.

236 *CPR, 1324–27*, 79. Though see SC 1/36/41 for possible remission on the number of men equipped.

237 C 47/2/48/21. See also *CCR, 1330–33*, 487. For earlier provisions for the Anglo-Scottish War in 1298, excluding arms, see W. S. Thomson (ed.), *A Lincolnshire Assize Roll for 1298* (Lincoln Record Society, 1944), lx–lxvi.

than all the towns individually listed.[238] Furthermore, in 1324 the sheriffs of Lincoln, Nottingham, Warwick, York and London were ordered to build and supply heavy weaponry, all of which was to be sent directly to the Tower. Lincoln's contribution was six springalds (catapults) and 1,000 quarrels, all of which were dispatched from the castle,[239] a project that would have drawn upon local craftsmen, day labourers and carters. Finally, in three separate years (1374, 1377 and 1400) Lincoln, along with several other leading towns, was ordered to build a balinger (barge) for the defence of the realm.[240] The cost of the sea-going vessel in 1377 was £100, the money for which was raised by two leading merchants (Robert de Sutton and John Norman) who were repaid from the city's lay subsidy (£100).[241]

In peacetime Lincoln contributed to the needs of the crown through its manufacture of parchment. Locally this remained an important industry and one that can be identified as being on a similar scale to that of London and York during the fourteenth century.[242] Although there are no surviving ordinances for parchment makers at Lincoln before the second half of the sixteenth century,[243] it is likely that they were similar in content and form to those at York (undated, fourteenth century). There it was a requirement for all parchment makers to be well versed and expert in their craft, with searchers being appointed to root out false work. In 1422 additional rules also required parchment to be worked in the craftsmen's home or shop, whilst those rebelling against searchers were fined 40d; apprenticeships were set at seven years and work on Sundays and holy days was forbidden.[244]

However Lincoln's parchment industry was structured, it is obvious that it maintained a long-standing association with the area of the city known as *Parchemingate*, first identified in the early thirteenth century, a road that lay adjacent to the skinmarket in the northern intramural area (map 2).[245] Of the thirteen manufacturers and distributers of parchment identified in this survey, all but one was male. The sole woman, Cecilia Grubbe, most likely the widow of John Grobbe, a former parchment dealer,[246] was one of the leading dealers in the city during the opening decades of the fourteenth century, and she employed a number of specialists, given the

238 C. A. Candy, 'The Scottish Wars of Edward III, 1327–1338' (Unpublished Ph.D Thesis, University of Durham, 2004), 168, 281.

239 *CCR, 1323–27*, 246–8.

240 Liddy, *War, Politics and Finance*, 55; *CPR, 1370–77*, 233; *1377–81*, 628; *CCR, 1377–81*, 32–3, 44–5, 182; *1399–1402*, 238–9; Sillem, *Sessions of the Peace, 1360–75*, 43.

241 *CPR, 1377–81*, 628. For lay subsidies, see 118–19.

242 C. P. Christianson, 'Evidence for the Study of London's Late Medieval Manuscript-Book Trade', in J. Griffiths and D. Pearsall (eds), *Book Production and Publishing in Britain, 1375–1475* (Cambridge, 1989), 88; S. Gee, '"At the Sygne of the Cardynalles Hat": The Book Trade and the Market for Books in Yorkshire, c.1450–1550' (Unpublished D.Phil Thesis, University of York, 1999), 17.

243 These were recorded along with ordinances for Glovers, Girdlers, Skinners, Pinners, Pointers, Scriveners and Parchmentmakers in 1563: *Historical MSS*, 57.

244 Gee, 'The Book Trade', 77–80.

245 *Medieval Lincoln*, 154.

246 John Grobbe sold sixty-five dozen parchments, valued at £3 13s 7d, to the crown for use during the parliament of 1301. E 101/367/10.

lengthy and complex process involved in the product's manufacture.[247] Following the order of Walter de Norwich, royal treasurer, in 1315, Cecilia supplied thirty of the 140 dozen parchments transported by horse to Westminster, valued at £1 18s 2d,[248] along with thirty-five of the 225 dozen parchments in c.1315 at a cost of £2 4s 7d.[249] This compared favourably to the quantities of parchment manufactured by Henry, Robert and John de Oxonford, possibly relatives, who sold between them 225 dozen parchments over the same two periods for a total £12 19s 11d.[250] As subsequent records demonstrate, parchment manufactured at Lincoln remained important for royal business, and further orders and purchases were made in 1337, 1339, 1355, 1357, 1358/59, 1370, 1373, 1401, 1403 and 1407, reflecting a growing relationship between the city and the crown from the reign of Edward II onwards.[251]

Naturally Lincoln did not only supply parchment for the crown, with the church (the Dean and Chapter, monasteries, friaries and parish churches) and other secular institutions and individuals (guilds, civic government, shire administration in the castle, legal professionals) all acting as important customers.[252] For example, in 1304 the Dean and Chapter spent 11s 4d on parchment used for compiling a register of charters, whilst in December 1341 the sheriff of Lincoln spent 34s on twenty-five dozen parchments for county business.[253] Once again, however, evidence of trade within the city itself is limited.

The evidence presented here points not only to the sophisticated nature of the city's trade and manufacture, but its practical assistance to the crown in times of crisis and peace, all of which stands as testament to Lincoln's capacity to maintain a diverse and interdependent occupational structure. Equally it demonstrates how from the reign of Edward II onwards Lincoln's developing industries began increasingly to influence the topography of the city at a time when manufacturing in the city emerged out of the recession of the 1330s.

Conclusion

Lincoln was in many ways typical of English towns in the later Middle Ages. It was dominated on the face of it by the cloth, building and victualling trades, all of which provided for the basic needs of the townspeople and surrounding region. And yet, there were several features of the local economy that set Lincoln apart from not only

247 For this process and the likely numbers involved, see R. Clemens and T. Graham, *Introduction to Manuscript Studies* (Ithaca, 2007), 10–12. Note that there were two types of parchment typically made at Lincoln, good (*boni*) and medium (*mediocris*), both of which would have served different functions (i.e. draft and fair documents): E 101/332/11.

248 E 101/332/11.

249 E 101/699/23c.

250 E 101/332/11; E 101/699/23c.

251 *CCR, 1339–41*, 28; *CPR, 1334–48*, 384 (note that the collector, William de Cantebrigge, was a Lincoln man: *BB*, fo. 11); *1354–58*, 235, 612; *1399–1401*, 430, 438; *1401–05*, 313; *1405–08*, 312; E 101/334/7; E 101/334/9; E 101/334/14c.

252 LAO Bj 2/4, fo. 138v; C 62/121, m. 2.

253 Major, 'Finances of the Dean and Chapter', 164.

smaller towns but other provincial capitals too.[254] The most obvious divergence was Lincoln's role as an administrative and service centre,[255] two categories of occupation responsible for a quarter of the city's entire workforce. Whilst on the one hand this provided opportunities for a burgeoning class of professionals to emerge, on the other it ensured that the thousands of visitors entering the city on an annual basis were adequately provided for, legally and practically. The growing focus on professional and administrative roles in particular was driven as much by the development and needs of civic government as by the demands of the church and crown. The resolve of the civic government to establish its own sheriff's courts following the granting of shire status should be seen as a move to re-establish a trade suffering from the withdrawal of business from the Statute Merchant court, and the revenues associated with this expansion would have been welcomed during a period when the annual value of tolls began to decrease.[256]

The decline of textile manufacturing also marked Lincoln out from other towns, both large and small, with many experiencing substantial growth during the last quarter of the fourteenth century.[257] Given the trend for migrants to seek out work in towns following subsequent bouts of plague, newcomers were left with little choice but to accept less skilled jobs as servants or agricultural workers,[258] echoing to some extent the experience of some early modern towns. Whilst it is not yet clear whether this pattern continued until the end of the Middle Ages, it nevertheless explains Lincoln's ability to increase its share of the local taxable population in relation to the region as a whole during a period when the county was becoming poorer.[259] It also explains why Lincoln experienced a relatively drawn out economic decline. Certainly, over the long term, service and administrative work proved to be an ill-suited substitute for industry, however much it mitigated the initial problems of declining manufacturing output, whilst the city's wool trade was never quite as labour intensive.[260]

Although Lincoln maintained a largely non-specialised economy, it was not without manufacturing altogether and throughout the later Middle Ages it established itself as one of the leading centres of production for arms and parchment in the country. Much of this production was based upon the exploitation of local materials and imported goods, reflecting the ongoing demands of the crown. Not only

254 Laughton, Jones and Dyer, 'Urban Hierarchy', 344–6.

255 At Exeter, for example, professionals and administrators were the smallest occupational category: Kowaleski, *Medieval Exeter*, 171.

256 Britnell, *Commercialisation of English Society*, 157–8.

257 Goldberg, *Women, Work, and Life Cycle*, 76–7.

258 The latter was underscored by the establishment of a guild of husbandmen (*agellorum*) by at least 1453, see LAO, A/2/35, fo. 12v. For a Plough guild established sometime before 1470, see LAO, A/2/35, f. 129v. My thanks to Marianne Wilson for these references.

259 S. H. Rigby, 'Urban Population in Late Medieval England: the Evidence of the Lay Subsidies', *Economic History Review*, 63, 2 (2010), 405–11, esp. 409–10; A. Dyer, 'The Political Economy of Urban Decline in the Renaissance', in T. Slater (ed.), *Towns in Decline, AD100–1600* (Aldershot, 2000), 282–3; *idem*, 'Midlands', in Clark, *Cambridge Urban History*, 109–10. See also chapters three and four.

260 Compare Lincoln's population and tax contributions in 1524–25: A. Dyer, 'Appendix 6' and 'Appendix 7' in *CUHB*, 761, 765.

did the city provide for the needs of royal government in times of war and peace but it was evidently rewarded for doing so. This is seen by the fact that Lincoln was one of only seven provincial capitals named as an 'assay town' in a statute of 1423 (alongside York, Newcastle, Norwich, Bristol, Salisbury and Coventry),[261] which licensed Lincoln's goldsmiths to mark their own goods alongside the mark of the king (a leopard's head) despite only maintaining a relatively modest metal industry, and that Lincoln was awarded its own sheriff's courts following the grant of urban county status. The city was also successful in gaining the right to keep revenues from the sale of wool exported tax free in order to help with the payment of its civic finances during a period of increasing economic difficulty.[262] Lincoln's economic base therefore reflected not only its status as one of the king's leading towns, with both being bound in a state of mutual dependence, but also its willingness and readiness to adapt during a period of incessant warfare and plague.

261 M. Campbell, 'Gold, Silver and Precious Stones', in Blair and Ramsey, *Medieval Industries*, 141, 145–6.

262 See 115–21.

2

Lincoln as Entrepôt: Tolls, Trade and Credit

Located atop a steep limestone ridge amid the otherwise flat lands of the fens, the city of Lincoln was throughout much of the Middle Ages accessible by boat via the river Witham, which exited at the Wash to the south-east, and the Fossdyke, a Roman canal connecting Lincoln directly to the North Sea via the rivers Trent and Humber.[1] Two major roads also connected the city to the wider world, alongside a network of minor roads providing easy access to the surrounding hinterland (map 3). These were Ermine Street, which bisected the city along a north–south axis and ran directly southwards to London, and Fosse Way, which, according to Henry of Huntingdon writing in the twelfth century, passed directly 'through Lincoln' and provided access to south-west of England.[2] Such routes of communication and trade remained vital to the economic wellbeing of the city and surrounding areas, as it was in Lincoln that an array of goods and raw materials could be bought and sold.

This chapter explores Lincoln's trade and credit networks and aims to answer the following questions: how central was Lincoln to regional and international patterns of trade? How did legislative changes in the sale and distribution of wool impact upon the city's economy and the business decisions of merchants during years of growth and recession? How extensive were networks of credit in the city and region? And to what extent did bouts of plague and famine influence these patterns?

Tolls and Trade

The right to sell goods and raw materials in Lincoln's marketplaces was granted to two types of individual: those liable to pay tolls and those legally exempt. The former group included denizen non-citizens, including petty traders and craftsmen, and those from surrounding towns and villages; the latter, citizens who, as franchised members of the community, were free from all tolls in the city and elsewhere,[3]

1 M. W. Barley, 'Lincolnshire Rivers in the Middle Ages', *Lincolnshire Architectural and Archaeological Society Reports and Papers*, 1 (1936): 1–21.

2 A. Cooper, 'The King's Four Highways: legal fiction meets fictional law', *Journal of Medieval History*, 26, 4 (2000): 351–70, at 356; F. M. Stenton, 'The Road System of Medieval England', *Economic History Review*, 7, 1 (1936): 1–21.

3 Note the right to collect tolls was never explicitly stated in any surviving charters. The right for Lincoln's citizens to be quit of tolls throughout England was first recorded in 1194: *Royal Charters*, 3–5.

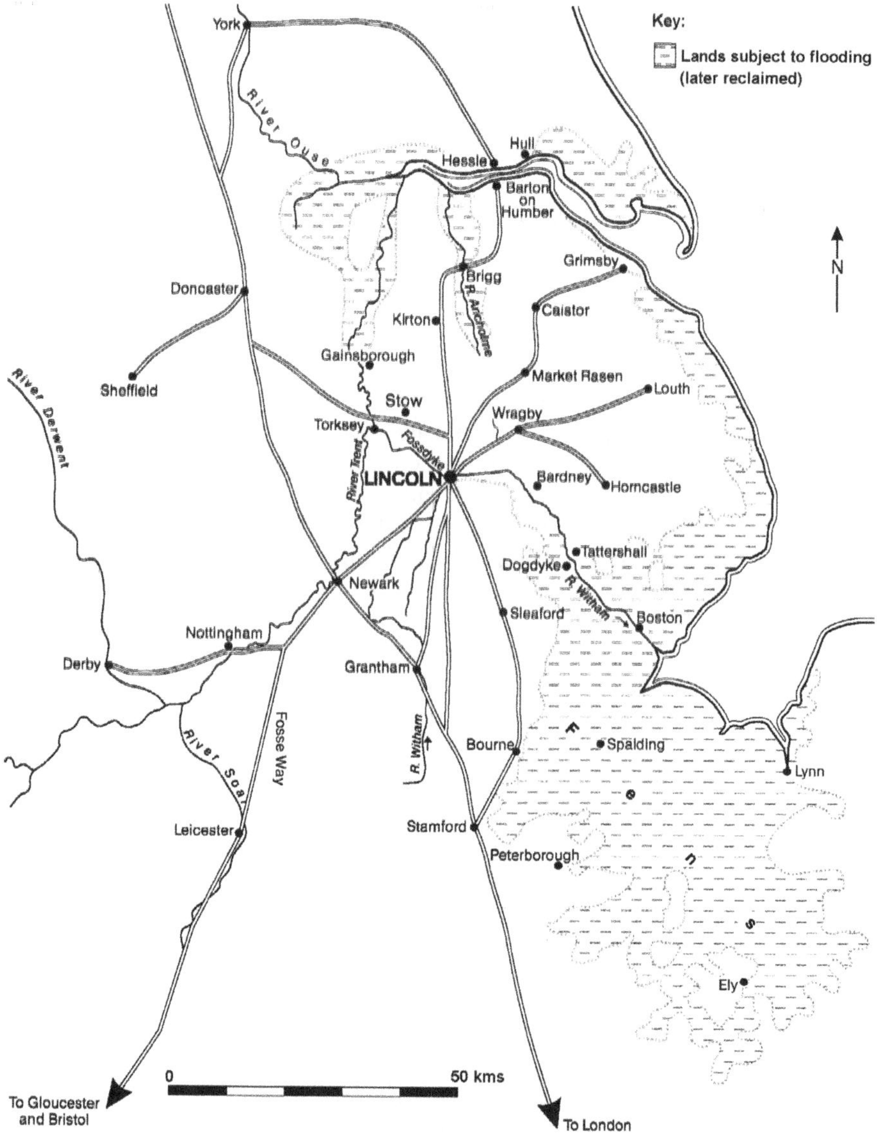

Map 3 Lincolnshire in the later Middle Ages

were granted rights of pasture in the common fields of the city and were eligible to serve in civic office,[4] along with merchants and traders from other towns who held priority of seisin (i.e. a charter pre-dating that of the town they wished to trade in).[5] For those liable to toll, goods were assessed at various collection points both within and without the city's walls, with tolls being recorded and preserved for accounting purposes.[6]

Lincoln's surviving civic toll accounts cover a ten-year period at the end of the thirteenth century (1290–99) during a period when the city's liberties had been suspended by the crown.[7] They contain, *inter alia*, six separate indices relating to incoming trade (table 9). For the two accounting years of 1292/93 and 1297/98 these are supplemented by more detailed records drawn up on behalf of the serving royal *custodes*, Robert le Venur and William Cause, both of which list in exacting detail the names and sums of those contributing to revenues in these years.

The first conclusion to draw from the evidence is that tolls for Lincoln were exceptionally high. Certainly when compared to other towns at the end of the thirteenth century, such as Northampton, Gloucester and Winchester, for example, which saw tolls of £44, £50 and £55 in peak years respectively,[8] Lincoln's average of £78 for the eight full years for which data is available, and an impressive £103 8s 9½d in 1292/93, mark the city out as one of leading commercial centres in England at this time. In fact, only Newcastle and London can be identified as recording higher revenues than Lincoln during this period: both attracted between £109 and £120 respectively through murage grants (a toll to raise revenues for wall repairs).[9] Secondly, tolls were collected all year round, including on Christmas Day in 1292 and Easter in 1293.[10] Unsurprisingly, they were highest during the warmer summer months when roads were generally in better shape, a peak coinciding with both the annual fair and the shearing and pilgrimage seasons.[11] Significant revenues were also raised in January and February, perhaps as a result of the sale of surplus stocks set aside for winter.

As this evidence indicates, tolls were collected on a fairly wide basis, including on storage in the cellar of *Clasketgate* (the civic prison), market stalls, fish (salmon), honey, salt and bread and winnow (grain separated from the chaff), alongside corn (*bladum*) and wool (*lana*),[12] two major commodities which were listed separately and are discussed in greater detail below. To these must also be added the large

4 R. Britnell, 'Town Life', in Horrox and Ormrod, *Social History of England*, 156.

5 J. Masschaele, 'Tolls and Trade in Medieval England', in Armstrong and Elbl, *Money, Markets and Trade*, 165, 168–70; Hicks, *English Inland Trade*, 7.

6 For toll collectors, see 132–3; for Lincoln's markets, 60.

7 For details of the suspension, see chapter four.

8 Masschaele, 'Tolls and Trade', 154; Keene, *Medieval Winchester*, vol. 1, 96.

9 Note, however, that toll grants (murage, pavage, pontage, for example) were typically higher than annual tolls: Masschaele, 'Tolls and Trade', 155; E. Harvey, 'Pavage Grants and Urban Street Paving in Medieval England, 1249–1462', *Journal of Transport History*, 31, 2 (2010), 154–5. It is likely that Newcastle's high value of tolls related to the ongoing war with Scotland. For details, see M. Prestwich, *Edward I* (Berkeley, 1988), 373, 556.

10 E 101/505/24, mm. 3–4.

11 See main text below and 166–7.

12 Corn was a generic term for barley, corn, oats, rye and wheat. See, for example, Sillem, *Sessions of the Peace, 1360–75*, 96 (no. 434).

Table 9 Excerpts from civic receipts (1290–99)

Years	**Weekly tolls†**	**Staithes***	***Minutis Theolonia* #**	**Fines for customary tolls^**	**Customs on brewing during Newport fair**	**Perquisites of court during Newport fair**	**Total**	**Total civic receipts**
1290/90	£41 2s 8½d	…	114s 1d	…	7s 4d	…	£47 4s ½d	£91 16½d
1290/91	£61 15s 1½d	4s 6d	£16 15s 2½d	79s 10d	…	68s 3d	£86 2s 2d	£165 3s 2d
1291/92	…	…	…	…	…	…	…	£181 11s 1d
1292/93	£76 1s 11½d	5s	£18 9s 3d	£6 13s 9d	7s	30s 10d	£103 8s 9½d	£179 11s 4½d
1293/94	£42 2s 10d	5s	£13 18s 3d	£6 19s 5d	7s	31s 5d	£65 3s 11d	£180
1294/95	£51 2s 3d	5s	£14 9s	£10 4s 9d	6s 4d	35s 9d	£78 3s 1d	£142 6s 5d
1295/96	£47 9s 6d	5s	£10 18s	£6 14s 2d	7s 4d	23s 9d	£66 7s 9d	£139 4s 9d
1296/97	£53 2½d	5s	£10 12s	£8 18s 5d	8s	23s 1d	£74 6s 8½d	£150 12s 2½d
1297/98	£53 11s 3½d	5s	£12 12s 9d	£6 6s 6d	6s 8d	22s 5d	£74 14s 7d	£159 13s 11½d
1298/99	£53 6s 10d	5s	£13 1d	£10 17s 10d	7s	38s	£79 14s 9d	£169 7s 3d

Key: † = includes corn (*bladum*) and wool (*lana*); * = *statheles*, or fines for mooring and delivering turf, faggots and other fuel (*turbis fagotis et aliis*); # = honey (*mensura mellis*), salmon and fish (*salmone et pischar'* [*viz.*]), salt (*salis*), baskets and winnow (*corbes et vanni*), stallage in the city (in High Market and Bread Market), and storage in the cellar of *Clasketgate*. They also relate to *landtolpeny* (an annual fine of 1d on each burgage plot held directly from the king), which formed a very small portion of the monies noted here, perhaps no more than £3 in any given year (for more on *landtol*, see 98); ^ = includes tolls for pigs, fish, bread and goods brought by boat, as well as stallage (i.e. rents for temporary market stalls presumably outside of the High and Bread Market).

NB: All dates run from Michaelmas (29 September) to Michaelmas, except for the first entry, which runs from May to September, the former being the month when the city was transferred from Robert de Chaddeworth, sheriff, to Robert le Venur, *custos* (E 372/136, rot. 27d). No accounts are recorded for 1299/1300, there being only an arrears of £131 18s 10½d relating to 25–26 Edward I (1296–98).

Sources: E 372/135, rot. 16d; E 372/137, rot. 7; E 372/138, rot. 20; E 372/139, rot. 28d; E 372/140, rot. 3d; E 372/141, rot. 23d; E 372/142, rot. 11; E 372/143, rot. 17d; E 372/144, rot. 10d; E 372/145, rot. 16d. For the accounts of Robert le Venur and William Cause corresponding to 1292/93 and 1297/98: E 101/505/24, 28.

number of unspecified goods and raw materials which, when subtracting tolls for grain and wool, left somewhere between 40 and 50 per cent of all annual revenues.[13]

Fortunately a surviving pavage grant from 1301 highlights the types of goods being brought into the city, with fifty-two different goods and raw materials listed (table 10).[14] Such evidence accords well with the surviving data for other towns including Ipswich, which listed fifty different items in a pavage grant in 1272, including ale, wood, cloth, hides, wool, stones, almonds, copper and lead;[15] and Coventry, which recorded sixty items in three separate murage and pavage grants in 1285, 1305 and 1329, including eleven different types of skin (e.g. cat, hare, fox), various dyes and materials (e.g. copperas, alum, woad, linen, samite), victuals (e.g. bacon, butter, deer, ham), metals (e.g. iron, cauldrons, nails), wood (e.g. boards, faggots) and other miscellaneous items (such as lime, grease).[16] Such evidence underscores the high level of sophistication characteristic of inland trade during this period.[17]

A second feature of these tolls is that they provide insight into local trading specialisms. For instance, sea-coal was frequently listed in northern towns, including at Newcastle, Whitby and Scarborough emphasising its importance to the area, whilst at Durham there was a toll on glass, perhaps reflecting close links with the cathedral there.[18] Similar specialisms can also be seen at Boston, where expensive items such as brasil (red dye), silk, incense, sugar, figs, rice, saffron, nutmeg, cinnamon and cloves were listed in a contemporaneous pavage grant (1285), reflecting its importance as an international port and fair.[19] At Lincoln bark, woad, linen, felt, wool and fleece emphasise the centrality of leather and textile manufacturing to local trade, whilst the inclusion of skins and furs, such as miniver, fox and squirrel, alongside various spices and foodstuffs, point to a more pervasive luxury market than in years previous.[20] Certainly, before the end of the thirteenth century such goods were usually only available at large fairs like Boston, St Ives or Winchester,[21] many of which were attended by Lincoln's merchants.[22] This shift marked both the end of the rapid expansion of new markets which characterised the previous two centuries as towns

13 See main text below.

14 C 66/121, m. 25. For the grant, see also *CPR, 1292–1301*, 576. Compare, for example, to the following: *Royal Charters*, 62–7.

15 Masschaele, 'Tolls and Trade', 146–8; T. Twiss (ed.), *The Black Book of the Admiralty*, vol. 2 (London, 1873), 187–91.

16 Goddard, *Lordship*, 299–300.

17 Hicks, *English Inland Trade*, *passim*; Masschaele, *Peasants, Merchants, and Markets*, *passim*.

18 C. M. Fraser, 'The Pattern of Trade in the North-East of England, 1265–1350', *Northern History*, 40 (1969), 46.

19 C 66/104, m. 20. For the grant, see *CPR, 1281–92*, 165. S. Rigby, 'Medieval Boston: Economy, Society and Administration', in S. Badham and P. Cockerham (eds), *'The beste and fairest of al Lincolnshire'. The Church of St Botolph, Boston, Lincolnshire and its Medieval Monuments*, British Archaeological Reports, 554 (2012), 6–28; H. Summerson, 'Calamity and Commerce: the Burning of Boston Fair in 1288', in C. M. Barron and A. F. Sutton (eds), *The Medieval Merchant: Proceedings of the 2012 Harlaxton Symposium* (Donington, 2014), 146–65.

20 Compare to the murage grant of 1253, which listed only forty items: C 66/64, m. 7; *CPR, 1247–58*, 203.

21 Miller and Hatcher, *Medieval England*, 164; Dyer, 'Luxury Goods', 217–38.

22 Moore, *Fairs of Medieval England*, 63–9, 195–6, 212.

Table 10 Tolls listed in a Lincoln pavage grant (1301)

Item	Toll	Item	Toll
Quarter of corn or malt	¼d	Measure of thistles	¼d
Last of herring	2d	Hundredweight of threshing	2d
Measure of herring	¼d	Cartload of lead	2d
Cartload of sea fish	4d	Bundle of bound cloths valued at 25s or more	1d
Horseload of sea fish	1d	Bundle of unbound cloths	¼d
Sack of wool	2d	Tun of white fish	2d
Wey of wool	½d	Tun of fish oil and *ter*	1d
Each horse, mare, oxen and cow	½d	Bacon [no weight given]	¼d
Fresh, leather or salted horse, mare, oxen or cow hides	¼d	Hundredweight of alum	2d
Last of ox hides	12d	Chalder of salt	1d
Ten pigs	1d	Measure of worked miniver	6d
Cartload of barley or timber per week	½d	Bundle of forty squirrel skins	½d
Hundredweight of faggots	¼d	Hundredweight of linen cloth of *canenaz*	1d
Cartload of bark per week	1d	Fresh bread	½d
Quarter of woad	2d	Hundredweight of skins from sheep with fleeces	2d
Wey of thyme, butter or cheese	¼d	Bundle of forty fox skins	1d
Hundredweight of pepper	2d	Hundredweight of rabbit and hare skins	½d
Hundredweight of almonds	1d	Twenty salmon	1d
Hundredweight of cumin	½d	Hundredweight of salted cod	1d
Basket of figs	½d	Hundredweight of felt	1d
Basket of raisins	1d	Sheaf of lattice	¼d
Horseload of herring	¼d	Millstones	½d
Horseload of onions	¼d	Horseload of honey	1d
Tun of wine	2d	Tun of honey	3d
Tun of potash	1d		
Chalder of sea-coal	½d		
Hundredweight of wax	2d		

Source: C 66/121, m. 25

became firmly established within regional urban hierarchies based upon the availability of various goods and services, and equally the decline of fairs as internationally important trading events.[23]

One of the more significant aspects of the city's annual tolls is how there was a discrepancy in the volume and value of corn and wool being brought into the city each year, a fact highlighted by the accounts of Venur and Cause (figures 1–2).[24] In particular, in 1292/93 there was an exceptionally high volume of wool brought into the city (a minimum of 6,264 sacks) as a result of the temporary ban put in place by the crown on exports in the previous year (1291/92).[25] According to Lloyd, the ban emerged as a result of competing claims between English and Flemish merchants over the theft of their respective goods.[26] It is thus possible that the peak identified in this year reflected wool initially earmarked for export but subsequently brought to market.[27] Whilst no direct comparisons for tolls on wool can be made with other years due to the absence of more detailed records, it is significant that in 1292/93 the tolls of wool contributed £52 1s 2d to the overall total of £76 1s 11½d for weekly tolls (roughly 70 per cent). Given that the figures for both 1292/93 and 1297/98 demonstrate a similar trading pattern, it would not be unrealistic to suggest that Lincoln received tolls on anywhere between 2,640 and 3,600 sacks of wool annually at the end of the thirteenth century, the equivalent of between 40 and 50 per cent of all tolls received (£22–£30).[28] Such figures must be seen as a minimum, however, as Lincoln's citizens and those holding priority of seisin did not pay tolls on their goods,[29] an important point given that these were the prime movers in the wool market. Moreover, as civic rules dictated, all wool being sold by Lincoln merchants was to be weighed in the city prior to export, whatever the destination,[30] a measure in place by at least the final quarter of the thirteenth century.[31] Even following the re-establishment of the Staple in 1353,[32] merchants from throughout

23 Miller and Hatcher, *Medieval England*, 409–11; C. Dyer, 'Trade, urban hinterlands and market integration, 1300–1600: a summing up', in J. A. Galloway (ed.), *Trade, Urban Hinterlands and Market Integration, c.1300–1600* (London, 2000), 104–5.

24 E 101/505/24, mm. 1–7; E 101/505/28, mm. 1–6.

25 This figure is based on a toll of 2d per sack of wool as per the pavage grant of 1301. However, given the uneven total for this accounting year, it is likely that tolls on wool varied depending on the quantity brought to market: Masschaele, 'Tolls and Trade', 163–4; Hicks, *English Inland Trade*, 7. Note that in 1310 the value of toll on each sack of wool entering the city doubled to 4d: *BH*, fo. 6.

26 T. H. Lloyd, *The English Wool Trade in the Middle Ages* (Cambridge, 1977), 74–6.

27 It is interesting to note that no similar peak can be identified for 1297 following the king's order that all wool be shipped into towns for the wartime prise, suggesting that many local traders ignored it: Lloyd, *Wool Trade*, 87–94. For the prise, see Thomson, *Lincolnshire Assize Roll*, xxxi, liii, lxx, lxxiv, 114, 182.

28 These figures are based upon the eight years for which there are full toll receipts (table 9), which average approximately £29 less than the peak year of 1292/93, thus ranging from £17 to £39. This, of course, presumes relative parity for all other incoming tolls.

29 Masschaele, 'Tolls and Trade', 172.

30 *CCR 1349–54*, 75.

31 *Export Trade*, 9; S. H. Rigby, 'Boston and Grimsby in the Middle Ages' (Unpublished Ph.D thesis, University of London, 1982), 165.

32 For background to this development, see Liddy, *War, Politics and Finance*, 110–19, and 69.

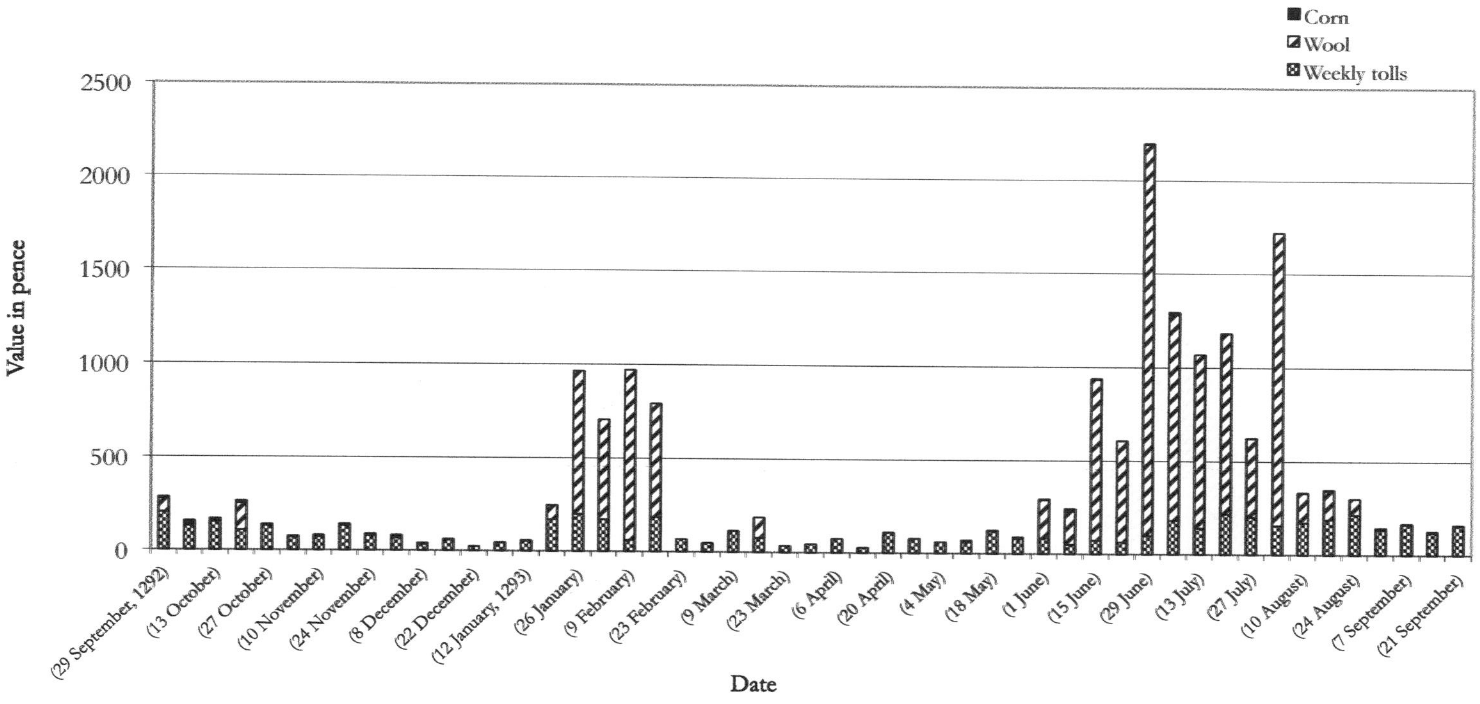

Figure 1 General tolls collected at Lincoln in 1292/93 (*Source:* E 101/505/24, mm. 1–7)

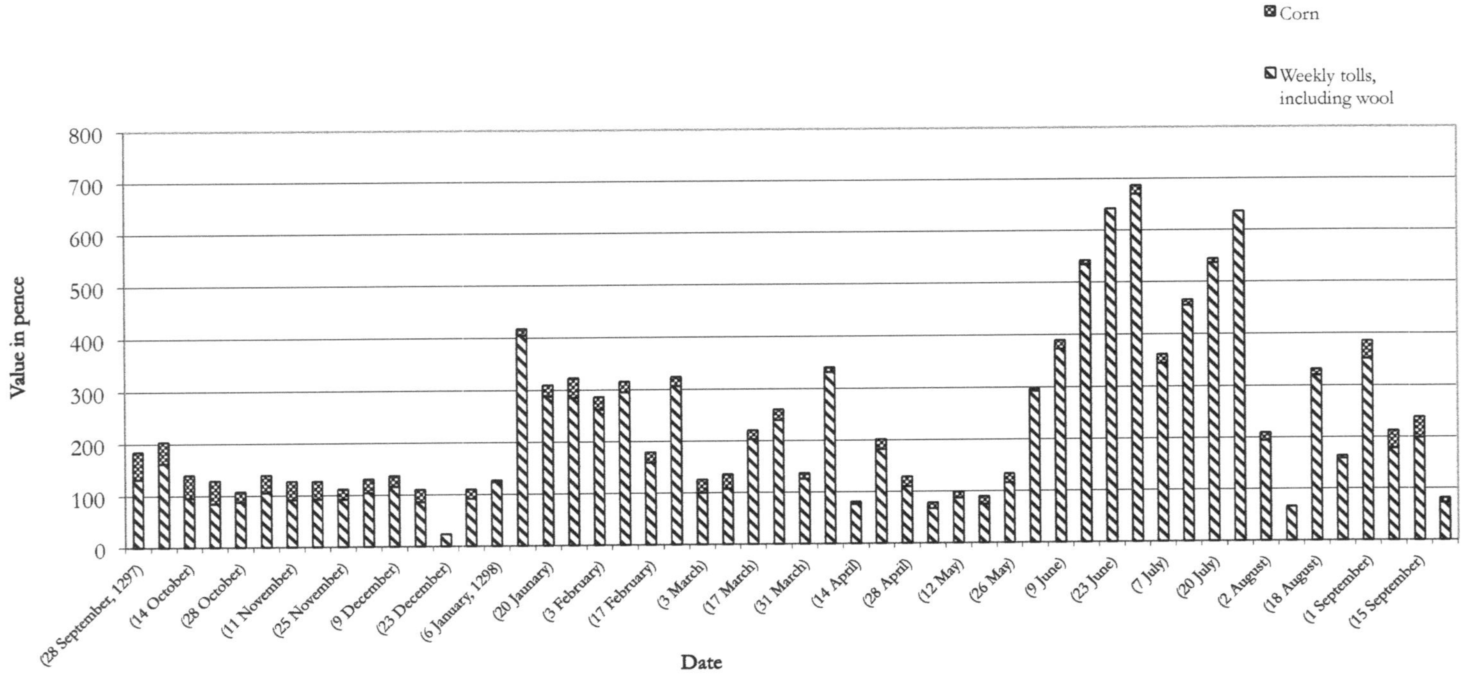

Figure 2 General tolls collected at Lincoln in 1297/98 (*Source:* W 101/505/28, mm. 1–6)

the county, including those from Boston, were compelled to bring their wool to Lincoln before exporting it.[33] Such legislation in no way diminished the central role played by Boston in the export of Lincolnshire's wool, as it undoubtedly remained one of the leading ports in England;[34] it merely highlights the fact that far more wool was brought to Lincoln prior to its departure than previously thought,[35] a fact no doubt linked to the greater availability of credit in the city.[36] Of course, not all wool brought into the city was destined for export, there being a demand from local cloth manufacturers.[37] Considered in this way, it is clear that by at least the 1290s wool was the leading commodity being bought and sold in the city.[38]

The impact of crown policies can also be seen on imports of corn. In 1292/93, for example, tolls totalled £1 0s 2½d, whereas in 1297/98 they stood at £4 3s 11d. Based upon a toll of ¼d per quarter, this equates to 970 and 4,028 quarters respectively. This fourfold growth can be explained by the royal prise of November 1296, which ordered that 3,000 quarters of corn be collected from the county to aid in the war with Scotland.[39] Even then, this left over 1,000 quarters for distribution amongst the city's inhabitants and the surrounding areas. As later evidence highlights, purveyed grains were frequently delivered from estates all over the county to Lincoln by river, such as in 1311, when thirty-eight quarters of grain and forty-one quarters of malt were transported to the city via the Witham from the abbeys of Barlings and Tupholme and from Bullington priory.[40] It is likely that in peacetime this practice continued, as there was a higher demand for grains in large towns, where they were liable to fetch higher prices.[41]

Such evidence demonstrates the importance of water transport to the city's economy, seen by the frequency with which grains were redirected upon their arrival. For example, in 1347/48, 180 quarters of wheat and 160 quarters of malt bought at Lincoln were shipped to Barton upon Humber and Boston via the rivers Witham and Humber (via the Fossdyke), along with a further 200 quarters of malt via Boston to Calais;[42] cargoes of wheat, malt and barley were similarly shipped from Lincoln to London in 1370 demonstrating a similar pattern in post-plague years.[43] Despite ongoing complaints over the city's rivers being blocked during much of

33 *CPR, 1354–58*, 433. For attempts to enforce this law: *CCR, 1349–54*, 75. For Boston merchants bringing cloth to the city, see for example: E 356/7, m. 6.

34 *Export Trade*, 36–74, 124–37; M. Kowaleski, 'Port Towns: England and Wales 1300–1540' in *CUHB*, 476–87.

35 Bischoff, 'Economic Change', 202, 268, n. 122, 273–4, n. 139.

36 See 78–90.

37 See main text below and 24–9.

38 For an account of the fortunes of Lincoln's wool trade in the twelfth and thirteenth centuries, see Bischoff, 'Economic Change', 193–214.

39 Thomson, *Lincolnshire Assize Roll*, lxxvi. This includes 1,500 quarters of corn, 500 quarters of barley and 1,000 quarters of oats.

40 E 101/568/31.

41 Dyer, 'Medieval Small Towns', 43.

42 E 101/621/11.

43 *CPR, 1367–70*, 363. For London, see J. A. Galloway, 'One market or many? London and the grain trade of England', in *idem*, *Market Integration*, 23–42.

the fourteenth century,[44] following the successful scouring of the Fossdyke in 1395, it was claimed that boats came 'to the city with divers victuals in greater numbers than they used to do'.[45] Lincoln thus played a central role in the region's grain trade, a fact underscored by the accounts of Robert de Nottingham, who, in 1324–25, was ordered to purvey wheat for the king, with Lincoln being the only place he visited twice.[46]

Excluding the intermittent tolls of corn and wool, the accounts of Venur (1292/93) indicate that the busiest day of the week was Friday, which brought in £5 18s 3¾d throughout the course of the year. This was followed by Wednesday (£3 4d) and, somewhat surprisingly, Sunday (£2 16s 11d). According to the accounts of Cause (1297/98), however, between November and January, and April and May, two periods when little, if any, wool was brought into the city,[47] the most popular trading days were Friday (£3 9s ½d), Wednesday (£2 12s 11d) and Thursday (£2 1s 1½d). Broadly speaking, this evidence reflects the city's chartered market days which were held on Mondays, Wednesdays and Fridays.[48] The popularity of Sundays and Thursdays can probably be attributed to the early arrival of traders setting up for market days. This certainly offers some explanation for the low level of tolls collected on Mondays in both years, ranking last in 1297/98 and second to last in 1292/93.

Another important aspect of the toll evidence is how by the end of the thirteenth century the city's annual fair, held in the suburb of Newport between St Botolph's Day and the feast of SS Peter and Paul (17–29 June),[49] had become a relatively successful event, raising £8 17s 6d in 1292/93 and £6 18s 7d in 1297/98,[50] which amounted to between 11 and 13 per cent of civic revenues in only a two-week period. Whilst it is true that the fair never approached the size or scale of the so-called 'great fairs' of St Ives, St Giles or Boston, for example,[51] it was undoubtedly important regionally, as the volume of tolls demonstrates. The success of the fair was certainly helped by the lack of any real competition within its immediate hinterland of roughly ten miles,[52] a situation similar to that of York.[53] Even so, it is regrettable that later accounts do not survive, as it is not possible to chart the long-term fortunes of the fair, especially in years during bouts of famine or plague. Even so, the fact that the city's annual fair was supplemented by a second fifteen-day fair in 1409, beginning on the feast of St Hugh (17 November),[54] suggests that, in spite of severe demographic upheaval

44 For example, *CPR, 1334–48*, 148, 203; *1381–85*, 500; KB 29/28, m. 33; SC 8/210/10453; SC 8/99/4939.

45 *CCR, 1392–96*, 413–14.

46 Other locations included York, Doncaster, Grantham, Stamford, Huntingdon and London: Stenton, 'The Road System', 13–14.

47 See main text below.

48 *Royal Charters*, 54; *Medieval Lincolnshire*, 136–8, fig. 47.

49 *Royal Charters*, 54, 57.

50 E 101/505/24, m. 1; E 372/138, rot. 20; E 101/505/28, m. 1; E 372/143, rot. 17d.

51 Moore, *Fairs of Medieval England*, *passim*.

52 *Medieval Lincolnshire*, 143–4, fig. 48.

53 Rees Jones, *York*, 250–2.

54 *Royal Charters*, 83.

and dubious complaints over the state of the city's economy,[55] Lincoln's existing fair must have continued with some success. Certainly, both were still in operation well into the sixteenth century, albeit for shorter durations, drawing traders from as far away as London.[56] These findings stand in accord with recent scholarship, which argues that provincial fairs continued to be successful throughout much of England and Europe during the later Middle Ages, meeting local demands by continuing to support commercial activities and changes in 'market networks'.[57]

Another indication of the importance of tolls derives from the fact that they yielded a significant proportion of the monies required to pay the town's fee farm, an annual payment made to the crown in lieu of certain rights and privileges, which typically raised between a third and over half of all civic revenues.[58] The volume of Lincoln's tolls provides important context for the fact that Lincoln's fee farm remained the third highest in all England throughout much of the Middle Ages, suggesting that there was a strong correlation between the two, both regionally and nationally. As discussed in the following chapter, the fee farm remained on ongoing concern for the civic government, reflecting its status as one of the king's leading towns.

The income from tolls also points to the fact that provincial towns such as Lincoln maintained large hinterlands through which many of their resources were drawn. Direct evidence of this can be seen from the locative surnames of those listed as paying customary tolls and shipping charges in the records of the Venur and Cause (map 4),[59] the majority of whom were drawn from towns and villages lying between eighteen and twenty-five miles away. Such evidence supplements the findings of James Masschaele, who revealed a similar geographical distribution for disputes over tolls between Lincoln's merchants and surrounding towns during the 1270s and 1290s,[60] as well as the evidence of migrants who, in the early fourteenth century, came predominantly from within a catchment area of approximately twenty miles.[61] Again, this pattern reflected the experiences of other provincial towns,[62] though, like these, Lincoln also saw its bonds of trade stretch well beyond this.[63] For example, in 1345 Richard de Bery of the cathedral priory of Durham travelled to Lincoln to purchased white garments (*albi vestimenti*), valued at £8, whilst in 1316 John le

55 See 116.

56 *Historical MSS*, 29, 32, 48, 49, 67.

57 J. S. Lee, 'The Role of Fairs in Late Medieval England', in Bailey and Rigby, *Town and Countryside*, 407–37, at 430; S. R. Epstein, 'Regional Fairs, Institutional Innovation, and Economic Growth in Late Medieval Europe', *Economic History Review*, 47, 3 (1994): 459–82. See also Britnell, *Commercialisation of English Society*, 155–64.

58 Masschaele, 'Tolls and Trade', 155.

59 E 101/505/24, m. 21; E 101/505/28, m. 17.

60 Masschaele, 'Tolls and Trade', 139–41 and map 6.1. See also SC 8/339/15961.

61 *Medieval Lincolnshire*, 198–200; D. Postles, 'Migration and Mobility in a Less Mature Economy: English Internal Migration, c.1200–1350', *Social History*, 25, 3 (2000), 298.

62 P. McClure, 'Patterns of Migration in the Late Middle Ages: The Evidence of English Place-Name Surnames', *Economic History Review*, New Series, 32, 2 (1979), 178–80; Rees Jones, *York*, 248–54; Goddard, *Lordship*, 266–70.

63 Masschaele, *Peasants, Merchants, and Markets*, 114–15, table 5.1.

Forbur senior of Nottingham brought swords and other things (*gladiis et aliis rebus*) by horse to Lincoln.[64]

Unsurprisingly, the size and shape of a town's hinterland were influenced by competition from other markets and the quality of communication links.[65] This was certainly true of Exeter, which had a far greater reach to the east than it did to the west due to the proximity of Dartmouth.[66] For Lincoln, a similar picture emerges, with very few traders coming from areas in and around the towns of Boston and Stamford, two important trading centres in their own right.[67] In fact, the greatest density came from within a radius of fifteen miles, from Lindsey and Kesteven, reflecting local patterns of credit.[68]

Despite the importance of water-borne transport for the delivery of grain, it is clear that many of the goods brought into the city came by road. An example of this can be seen in the case of Thomas Baxter of York who, in 1363, reportedly drove twelve oxen and five horses to the meat market in Dernstall (map 2) from beyond the fields of Caistor (*Castre*) via Welton near Dunholme before passing through Nettleham, a road located in the fields of Riseholme (*exinde extransverso camporum de Rysum*), and arriving at market, a distance of some thirty-five miles.[69] A similar route would doubtless have been taken by Ralph Notebroun who travelled from Messingham to Lincoln with an ox in 1297 and who was later accused of theft.[70] Such evidence supports the findings of R. A. Pelham who identified how much of the livestock (pigs, sheep, oxen) procured for the parliament of 1301 was driven to Lincoln during January on hardened frosty roads from places up to thirty-five miles away, the majority from Lindsey.[71] In 1341, too, it is clear that many of the goods purveyed and collected for the crown were brought to the city overland, including peas from Cherry Willingham and livestock (oxen, cows and horses) from Tathwell near Louth.[72]

Lincoln thus remained an important centre for inland trade within the county during the later Middle Ages, reflecting its status as a provincial town. This is seen both in the growing number of luxury goods available in the city by the beginning of the fourteenth century and equally in the sheer volume of goods and tolls brought into the city on annual basis. Although commercial links can be identified over long distances, merchants and traders were drawn to the city primarily from within a catchment area of approximately twenty-five miles. Of particular importance to the city's trade was Boston, which acted as the city's outport, especially for grain and

64 J. T. Fowler (ed.), *Extracts from the Account Rolls of the Abbey of Durham*, vol. 2 (Durham, 1899), 380; Nottingham City Archive, CA 1256, no. 718.

65 Britnell, *Colchester*, 44; Dyer, 'Small Towns, 1270–1540', 517–26.

66 Kowaleski, *Medieval Exeter*, 275–6.

67 A. Rogers, *Noble Merchant: William Browne (c.1410–1489) and Stamford in the fifteenth century* (Bury St Edmunds, 2012). For Boston, see n. 19 above.

68 See 89–90.

69 E 13/87, m. 9.

70 Thomson, *Lincolnshire Assize Roll*, 14–15, no. 62.

71 Pelham, 'Parliament of 1301', 26–9.

72 B. W. McLane (ed.), *The 1341 Royal Inquest in Lincolnshire* (Woodbridge, 1988), nos. 387, 494, 1106.

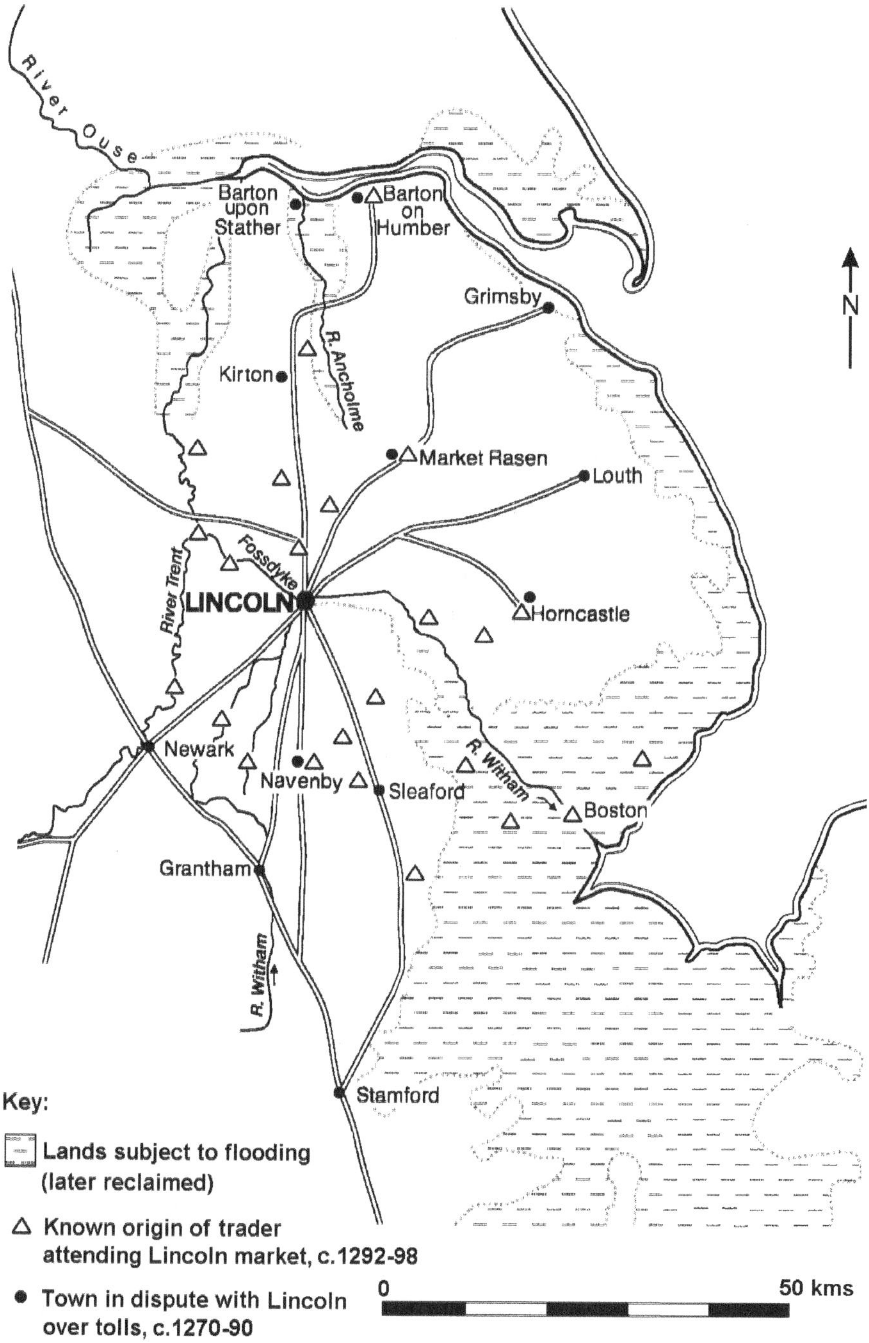

Map 4 Origins of traders travelling to Lincoln and locations of toll disputes

wool, though Lincoln retained commercial relationships with a number of religious houses and smaller towns, many of which would have acted as collection centres for the city's merchants.

International Trade

Despite the relative paucity of written records relating to the international trade of Lincoln's merchants, it is clear that they bought a wide variety of goods and raw materials from merchants overseas, much of which was sold in the city's markets or redistributed throughout the region. This was typical of many other towns to a greater or lesser degree, including those which, like Lincoln, were situated inland, such as Coventry, York, and Salisbury, all of which maintained an active and wealthy class of merchants.[73] Whilst it remains true that by the fourteenth century it was not commonplace for merchants to undertake journeys abroad themselves,[74] there were nevertheless a handful of local merchants, such as John de Blyton (mayor 1333/34) and William Peeke (bailiff 1398/99), who remained willing to do so.[75] The following section explores the variety of goods imported and exported by these men and considers their importance for the local economy.

According to a petition submitted to the crown in 1327,[76] Elias de Stubton (bailiff 1321/22) claimed that his ship called *La Bonane* of Boston, laden 'with divers goods' including salt (£100), ten tuns of wine (£40), two lasts of hides (£60), Irish cloth (£20), Spanish iron (£13 15s), two weighs (*peciis*) of wax (£6), seventeen beds and seventeen coffers containing 'robes, jewels, and silver by tale' (£66 5s), armour (£8), and victuals, including 'corn, meat, fish, and flour' (£6), had been confiscated by the citizens of Le Havre in France 'without reasonable cause'. After investigating his claim, the crown upheld his complaint and, following a period of silence from the French king on the matter, ordered the sheriff of Southampton to seize the goods of Norman merchants trading along the south coast until £460 had been repaid to Stubton for his loss, including damages.[77] Beyond the obvious details for the types of goods being traded by men such as Stubton, evidence such as this reveals how, luck permitting, merchants were able to reap great financial rewards by trading overseas.[78] Certainly, those wealthy enough to own their own ships were

73 Goddard, *Lordship*, 140, 214, 226, 270; Hare, 'Salisbury', 8–18; Rees Jones, *York*, 254–7.

74 R. Britnell, 'Sedentary Long-distance Trade and the English Merchant Class in Thirteenth-Century England', in P. R. Coss and S. D. Lloyd (eds), *Thirteenth Century England V* (Woodbridge, 1995), 131–5.

75 *CCR, 1318–23*, 433; Rigby, *Overseas Trade*, 65, 73.

76 SC 8/235/11715.

77 *CCR, 1327–30*, 175. For part satisfaction: *CCR, 1327–30*, 440.

78 For the risks of overseas trade, see J. Kermode, 'Merchants, Overseas Trade, and Urban Decline: York, Beverley, and Hull c. 1380–1500', *Northern History*, 23, 1 (1987), 52, 66; Goddard, *Lordship*, 270. For other losses by Lincoln merchants: H. Hall (ed.), *Select Cases Concerning the Law Merchant*, vol. 2 (London, 1930), 73–6; *CCR, 1307–13*, 378–9, 452, 541; *1318–23*, 412, 486, 608; *1374–77*, 424–4; *1405–9*, 43–4.

liable to benefit more than those who depended on the transportation of others.[79] These included William Peeke (bailiff 1398/99), who, in 1386, imported twelve lasts of herring valued at £32 20d and, in 1393, almost £500 worth of fish, oil and clipping (lamb skins used for hide) for foreign merchants.[80] In 1390 the ship of Robert Ledes (mayor 1387/88) imported twenty-nine tuns of wine into Boston, eleven of which belonged to John Sutton (mayor 1386/87),[81] whilst in 1383 Richard de Dalby purportedly owned several ships (*vessellamenta*) carrying woollen cloth and wool.[82] During the earlier period, too, several merchants can be identified as ship-owners, including Stephen de Stanham (mayor 1301–06, 1312/13), whose ship, the *Katerine de Sancto Botolpho*, carried beans and peas to Flanders for the king in 1297,[83] and William de Lincoln, whose ship was noted as importing ashes (*cineres*) (worth £29 6s) belonging to Gregory de la Porte in 1303, an important component for making lye, the alkalised water used in cloth manufacture.[84]

In spite of a number of merchants owning their own ships, there is nevertheless strong evidence for the existence of close ties between the city's merchants and foreign shipmasters, indicating that many of Lincoln's merchants hired cargo space.[85] Among such individuals were William Cause (*custos* and mayor 1297–1301) who, in 1303, imported bedding and blankets (worth £9 11s) aboard a German ship;[86] Simon Laxfeld (mayor, 1389/90) who imported smigmate (soap) and madder (red dye) (£41 9d), canvas and osmund (Swedish iron) (£105), a pack of canvas containing 1,440 ells of cloth (£12), two shipments of wax (£25 2s each), and 224lbs of onion seeds (28s) aboard Flemish and Brabant ships between 1384 and 1393;[87] Robert Sutton (mayor, 1379/80) who, in 1384, imported canvas, fustian (coarse cloth made of cotton and flax), madder and other goods (£137 10s 8 ½d); William Dalderby (mayor, 1383/84) who, in 1390, brought two tuns and a pipe of woad (a blue dye) from Amiens (£20); and John Driffeld (mayor 1391/92), John Heden (mayor 1395/96), Robert Harworth (mayor 1393/94), Robert Messingham (mayor 1388/89), John Norman (mayor 1385/86), Peter Saltby (mayor 1405/06) and Richard Wirsop (bailiff 1400/01), all of whom imported large quantities of canvas, presumably for the packing of wool, amongst other goods in 1390, all aboard foreign ships.[88] Such evidence is hardly surprising, given that ports such as Boston often saw the same ships month after month, year after year,[89] and it is likely that this provided opportunities for local merchants to buy up goods and raw materials directly from foreign traders at the

79 Britnell, 'Sedentary Long-distance Trade', 131–2.
80 Rigby, *Overseas Trade*, 63, 75, 200.
81 Rigby, *Overseas Trade*, 105.
82 E 13/101, m. 9.
83 Thomson, *Lincolnshire Assize Roll*, lxiv.
84 N. S. B. Gras, *The Early English Customs System* (Cambridge, 1918), 286.
85 Britnell, 'Sedentary Long-distance Trade', 132–3.
86 Gras, *Early English Customs*, 283.
87 Rigby, *Overseas Trade*, 40, 95, 167, 180, 201.
88 Including madder (£20), cloth (40s), wine (£15), woad (£32), smigmate (12s 2½d) and bolting cloth (20s): Rigby, *Overseas Trade*, 39, 40, 90, 95, 96, 104, 203.
89 Uhler, 'English Customs Ports', 156.

port, perhaps even aboard the ships themselves,[90] before transporting them overland or by river to the city.

One of the most important commodities brought into Lincoln was undoubtedly wine,[91] much of which originated from Gascony.[92] Exactly how much wine entered the city in a given year is impossible to say, however, as no complete figures survive. Nonetheless, evidence for other better documented provincial towns gives some indication of the likely volume. For example, in 1447/48 over 925 pipes of wine (462 tuns) were brought from Southampton to Salisbury.[93] It stands to reason that Lincoln would have received wine on a similar scale during the later fourteenth century, perhaps more so during the pre-plague period, as the two towns had roughly equal populations.[94] Certainly, in 1412/13 ten tuns of wine were being sold at the wholesale price of £6 13s 4d a tun at a time when the average price ranged between £4 and £7 per tun,[95] whilst at retail wine was sold for 10d per gallon in 1406 and 8d a gallon in 1413 when the average price was 8d.[96] Whilst it is true that the cost of wine was influenced by the costs of transport,[97] with water transport being significantly cheaper than overland,[98] it is also possible that these higher prices reflect a local taste for more expensive or exotic wines. In 1392, for example, Thomas Preston was recorded as selling one pipe of *Osey* wine (sweet wine from Portugal) and one pipe of red wine (*rubei*) worth 100s,[99] highlighting how Gascony was not the only available market for local merchants.[100]

Wine was also purchased by individuals or institutions lying outside of the civic jurisdiction, although evidence of this is limited. For example, it is known that the sheriff bought sixty tuns of wine in 1264 and a further forty in 1267/68 in preparation for the king's visit.[101] In 1301 he was also ordered to pay £60 for wine bought directly from Gascon merchants for the parliament at Lincoln,[102] and several years later four tuns of wine were brought from Torksey by road to the city for his own consumption.[103] While at present very little is known about the consumption patterns of the Dean and Chapter, in 1305 a 'due allowance' was nevertheless made

90 Kowaleski, *Medieval Exeter*, 271.
91 A toll of 2d per tun of wine was listed in the murage grant of 1253: C 66/64, m. 7.
92 For example, E 372/75, rot. 18; E 372/77, rot. 2; E 372/120, rot. 1; E. M. Carus-Wilson, 'The Medieval Trade of the Ports of the Wash', *Medieval Archaeology* (1962–63), 189–90.
93 Hare, 'Salisbury', 12–13 (table 42).
94 Based on the taxable population of 1377: Dyer, 'Ranking of Towns', in *CUHB*, 758.
95 E 13/127, m. 10.
96 E 13/124, m. 3; E 13/127, m. 6d; M. K. James, *Studies in the Medieval Wine Trade* (Oxford, 1971), 51–2.
97 James, *Wine Trade*, 147–9; Rigby, *Overseas Trade*, 37–40, 201–3.
98 C. Dyer, 'The Consumer and the Market in the Later Middle Ages', *Economic History Review*, 42, 3 (1989), 309–10. For wine transported overland: *CLR, 1267–72*, 43; *CIM, 1307–49*, 228, no. 916.
99 E 13/110, m. 11d.
100 W. Childs, 'A Paradise Hit is to Behold: Opportunities for Profit in Spain and Portugal in the Later Middle Ages', in Barron and Sutton, *Medieval Merchant*, 12–13.
101 *CLR, 1260–67*, 140; *1267–72*, 43.
102 E 101/367/10.
103 Pelham, 'Parliament of 1301', 28, n. 39.

for wine on the Monday after Holy Cross Day, in addition to 8d for wine for the precentor and the bishop's clerks at the cost of 5d each in 1396/97.[104] Earlier too, in 1301, the bishop of Lincoln had wine transported along the Witham from Boston to his palace in the city.[105]

Lincoln's merchants exported only two types of commodities: cloth and wool. For the former, evidence derives primarily from four surviving accounts dating from 1353 following the introduction of new staple regulations, though there are also some fragmentary accounts dating from the reign of Richard II.[106] These accounts show that between December 1353 and January 1355, 604 short cloths of various colours were exported abroad by denizens, followed by 699 between Easter 1355 and April 1356, 854½ between Easter 1356 and August 1357,[107] and 826½ between August 1357 and September 1358,[108] all of which stood in addition to a small number of cloths of various sizes and colours exported by aliens during the same period.[109] It has been estimated that Lincolnshire and Yorkshire were producing as much as 13 per cent of the country's entire output during this period.[110] Whilst it is certain that not all of these exports were manufactured in the city, with some coming from surrounding towns and rural areas,[111] that Lincolnshire's cloth farm stood highest of all recorded counties in 1370 suggests that the city's clothiers must have been manufacturing significant amounts of cloth at this time. This conclusion is supported by the high level of investment that took place in the city during the 1350s and 1360s before tailing off sharply in the 1370s.[112] When this is set alongside the aulnage evidence cited previously,[113] it thus seems clear that by the opening decades of the fifteenth century Lincoln's cloth industry had contracted severely,[114] perhaps to a quarter of what it had been only fifty years before. Hence Lincoln did not experience a period of sustained cloth manufacture like many other towns,[115] a fact undoubtedly influenced by the economic decisions of the city's leading merchants who invested primarily in wool, the city's leading export.

104 Major, 'Finances of the Dean and Chapter', 155, 163.

105 Carus-Wilson, 'Ports of the Wash', 190.

106 For example, Rigby, *Overseas Trade*, 11–13, 23 (Hugh Garwell), 47 (Seman Laxfeld), 109 (John Driffeld), 112 (William Peek).

107 E 356/30/8854, no. 372; E 356/30/8864d, no. 389; E 356/30/8864, no. 517.

108 E 356/30/8864d, no. 356.

109 For example, E 356/30/8854, no. 372.

110 H. L. Gray, 'The Production and Exportation of English Woollens in the Fourteenth Century', *English Historical Review*, 39, 153 (1924), 22.

111 Fenwick, *Poll Taxes*, 57; *Medieval Lincolnshire*, 182, 200, 202.

112 See main text below.

113 See 28–9 and table 4.

114 Direct comparisons between aulnage and exports are problematic. See Lambert and Pajic, 'Drapery in Exile', 750.

115 Hatcher, *Plague, Population*, 33–4, 50; Britnell, *Commercialisation of English Society*, 170; Bridbury, *Clothmaking*, 63.

The Wool Trade: Exports

The fortunes of the English wool trade in the later Middle Ages are well known.[116] As the leading English commodity during the later Middle Ages, its exports reached a peak of 45,000 sacks during the middle of the fourteenth century before beginning a slow decline in the 1360s, reaching a nadir of less than 5,000 sacks per annum during the 1430s before staging a minor recovery. Thereafter exports hovered at around 10,000 sacks per annum before tailing off again during the 1520s.[117]

Given its overall importance to the English economy, it is unsurprising that wool played an important role in the trade of many provincial towns, including Norwich, Salisbury, Winchester and York,[118] as well as in a number of smaller towns.[119] Whilst a large proportion of this wool was used in the manufacture of cloth, the vast majority was exported to the continent through major ports, including, in the case of the aforenamed towns, Bishop's Lynn, Southampton and Hull respectively. Unfortunately the level and volume of trade for these particular towns cannot be gauged with any degree of accuracy due to the absence of comprehensive inland taxation records unlike those for port towns, which retain a largely unbroken set of customs accounts from their inception in 1275 until the close of the Middle Ages in 1547.[120] Whilst it has been acknowledged that wool and other goods shipped from English ports did not necessarily reflect the overall level of trade conducted in them,[121] these accounts have, to some extent, privileged them over inland towns.[122] The importance of the wool trade within an urban context is thus deserving of more detailed analysis, especially for Lincolnshire, which, despite its rich tradition of sheep farming, is notably absent from existing historiography.[123]

The strength of the wool industry in Lincoln, and indeed all Lincolnshire, lay in the fact that it produced some of the highest quality wools in all England throughout the Middle Ages, particularly in the region of Lindsey.[124] This ensured that Lincolnshire wool was highly prized by merchants from all over Europe, in particular the Italians, who purchased it from numerous religious houses, including Thornton

116 Lloyd, *Wool Trade*.

117 *Export Trade*, 122–3; Lloyd, *Wool Trade*, 260–4, 314–17. See also J. Hatcher, 'The Great Slump of the Mid-fifteenth Century', in R. Britnell and J. Hatcher (eds), *Progress and Problems in Medieval England* (Cambridge, 1996), 237–72.

118 Dunn, 'Trade', 218–20; Hare, 'Salisbury', 14; Keene, *Medieval Winchester*, vol. 1, 292–5; J. Kermode, *Medieval Merchants: York, Beverley and Hull in the Later Middle Ages* (Cambridge, 1998), 160–5, 167–8. For a broader discussion of the importance of urban cloth manufacturing, see Carus-Wilson, 'English Cloth Industry', 32–50.

119 Dyer, 'Small Towns, 1270–1540', in *CUHB*, 515.

120 *Export Trade*, 1.

121 Kowaleski, *Medieval Exeter*, 231–2.

122 Hicks, *English Inland Trade*, 1; Nightingale, 'The Lay Subsidies', 18–25, 28–30.

123 A. R. Bell, C. Brooks and P. R. Dryburgh, *The English Wool Market, c.1230–1327* (Cambridge, 2007), 149.

124 See, for example, T. H. Lloyd, 'The Movement of Wool Prices in Medieval England', *Economic History Review Supplement*, 6 (Cambridge, 1973), 52–61. For the early history of the wool trade in Lincolnshire, see R. Faith, 'The Structure of the Market for Wool in Early Medieval Lincolnshire', *Economic History Review*, 65, 2 (2012): 674–700.

Abbey, Nun Cotham nunnery, the priory of Newsham, Templar House at Temple Bruer and the Priory of St Katherine at Lincoln;[125] and Lincolnshire's monasteries, much like those of Yorkshire, maintained a strong tradition of trading in wool,[126] the bulk of which was exported through Boston at the time of the annual fair.[127] There was also a significant trade in wool by manorial lords, including Henry de Lacy, earl of Lincoln, who had at over 5,000 sheep alone on his Lincolnshire estates in 1305.[128]

At Lincoln wool played an increasingly important role in local trade following the establishment of a wool market in or near Thorngate in the parish of St Swithun by at least 1270,[129] which lay in the south-west corner of the city adjacent to the river Witham and provided easy access for boats and carts loading and unloading wool (map 2).[130] In 1326 the area became a designated staple following the crown's decision to name Lincoln as one of fourteen towns in England, Wales and Ireland through which all 'wools, hides, skins, timber and tin' were to be exported.[131] The intermittent nature of the crown's staple policy relocated it from time to time to the continent, according to the exigencies of national politics; it was abolished in 1334 but then reintroduced in 1353 as 'part of the king's diplomatic weaponry during the Hundred Years War'.[132] By 1354 the re-established staple reportedly ran from 'the gate of Newelond on both sides of the water running through the middle of the city as far as Thornebrig',[133] thus spanning the entire lower city's access to the water. In 1369, however, the staple was relocated to Boston,[134] a decision greeted with great consternation by the inhabitants of Lincoln. Several years later, in 1376, the civic authorities petitioned the crown, claiming that the decision was to the 'great damage of the said commons and … to the disadvantage of our lord the king, as will be elucidated if necessary'.[135] Yet the crown remained unmoved and the staple remained at Boston. The reason behind this decision was seemingly one of practicality, with port towns being deemed more suitable for handling bulky exports than inland towns at a time when exports were beginning to recede.[136] York, for example, also lost its staple to Hull around this time.[137] Despite this setback, Lincoln's civic authorities did not sit idly by and were successful in securing the election of a number of the city's leading merchants to the post of mayor of the Boston staple well into the fifteenth century.[138]

125 Bell, Brooks and Dryburgh, *English Wool Market*, 61; J. P. Bischoff, 'Pegolotti: an Honest Merchant?', *Journal of European Economic History*, 6 (1977): 103–8.

126 Bell, Brooks and Dryburgh, *English Wool Market*, 59–63, 148–9; *CSML*, 65–9.

127 Summerson, 'Calamity and Commerce', 152–3.

128 P. Bischoff, '"I Cannot Do't without Counters": Fleece Weights and Sheep Breeds in Late Thirteenth-Century and Early Fourteenth-Century England', *Agricultural History*, 57, 2 (1983): 148.

129 For this period, see *Medieval Lincoln*, 320–5; Bischoff, 'Economic Change', 193–214.

130 *Rot. Hund.*, 311, 323; Bischoff, 'Economic Change', 200.

131 *Royal Charters*, 28–33, at 28.

132 Lloyd, *Wool Trade*, 99–121, at 121.

133 *CPR, 1354–58*, 8.

134 *CFR, 1377–83*, 107.

135 *Rot. Parl.*, vol. 2, 332–3.

136 *Export Trade*, 122, 126.

137 Liddy, *War, Politics and Finance*, 115–16.

138 *Medieval Lincoln*, 250–1.

According to Hill, the loss of the staple at Lincoln was one of the major reasons for the decline of the city's economy during the second half of the fourteenth century.[139] However, this cannot be so given that as early as 1363 all staples lost their 'economic function as the point at which all English wool exports had to be bought and sold', following the relocation to Calais.[140] Although after this date it remained a requirement that all wool still be registered and weighed at staple towns before being exported, meaning that they retained their importance as judicial franchises, it is likely that Lincoln's complaint stemmed primarily from the fact that it had lost valuable revenues on tronage (the duty on weighing wool), all of which contributed to the city's fee farm payment.[141] Whilst this did not adversely affect the sales or indeed the economic viability of wool traded in the city itself, primarily due to internal regulations,[142] it undoubtedly came as something of a blow to civic coffers: fewer incoming merchants and traders equalled fewer transactions on tronage, and less money spent on food, drink and hospitality. Nonetheless, it is significant that Lincoln retained its status as the leading debt registry in the county, recording seventy-five cases of defaulted debt between 1369 and 1399 in comparison to only twenty-three at Boston over the same period,[143] with many Bostonians even seeking out credit in Lincoln.[144] This points to the fact that whilst it may have been deemed more practicable by the crown for goods to be shipped directly from Boston, gaining access to credit through the Statute Merchant system (later the Statute Staple) was easier at Lincoln, although this was a position that did not go unchallenged.[145]

Lincoln's overall involvement in the wool trade can also be seen by the rise in the number of merchants identified as exporters from the late thirteenth century onwards. For example, in 1271–74 only three out of 327 merchants granted licences to export wool by the crown came from Lincoln, considerably fewer than those from London (96), Winchester (40), Southampton (19), Newcastle (15), Andover (15), Shrewsbury (12), Bristol (9) and York (7).[146] Lloyd sees the absence of merchants from Lincoln and other Midlands towns (Coventry, Leicester and Stamford) during this period as a result of the strength of Flemish trade, with locals acting primarily as middle men.[147] By the 1290s, however, the situation had changed dramatically, with Lincoln's merchants (including its Jewish population on the eve of its expulsion)[148]

139 *Medieval Lincoln*, 250. For a contrasting view of Lincoln's decline, Bischoff, 'Economic Change', 273–4.

140 Liddy, *War, Politics and Finance*, 115.

141 SC 8/321/E470. Note that tronage at Boston was charged at ½d per sack (for example, E 356/14, m. 12d). Hence when in the 1360s exports reached 9,162 sacks, tronage might possibly have been worth approximately £19–£20 per annum. For the fee farm, see chapter three.

142 See main text below.

143 My thanks to Richard Goddard for supplying comparative data for Boston.

144 For example, C 241/142/19; C 241/150/168; C 241/164/101; C 241/174/21.

145 For these developments, see main text below.

146 Lloyd, *Wool Trade*, 51, table 2. Despite this, several other merchants were shipping wool in these years: *CCR, 1268–72*, 593–5; *CPR, 1272–81*, 14, 67–8.

147 Lloyd, *Wool Trade*, 53.

148 The Jews dealt with approximately sixty-five sacks of wool per annum between 1288 and 1290: R. R. Mundill, *England's Jewish Solution: Experiment and Expulsion, 1262–1290* (Cambridge, 1998), 195–7.

exporting wool in far greater numbers than ever before, some of which was sold on advance contracts to Italian merchants.[149] In 1297 alone, for instance, sixteen Lincoln men exported wool.[150]

Even so, it was in the early years of the fourteenth century that Lincoln's merchants, like those of London, Boston, York and Hull, finally emerged as exporters in their own right, following the sharp reduction of Italian credit by 1305.[151] With the competition removed, English mercantile fortunes soared.[152] In the period between July 1310 and July 1312, for example, an unprecedented forty-one merchants from Lincoln exported wool through Boston, over double the number of its nearest Lincolnshire rival (Spalding with seventeen).[153] Of this group, seven men alone dispatched 1,044 sacks, with an impressive 2,062 sacks being exported in all,[154] a figure almost double that of all Spalding merchants combined (1,109 sacks). When it is considered that this was a period when approximately 10,000 sacks of wool were being shipped annually through Boston, it stands to reason that Lincoln's merchants controlled approximately 20 per cent of the county's wool trade.[155]

Trade continued well into the fourteenth century, with wool being exported directly to Flanders, the Low Countries, Italy and Germany.[156] Even following the intermittent home staple policy (1326–34), wool continued to be brought into the city on an unprecedented scale. For example, between January and September 1333, £403 18s 4½d was raised in customs on 2,423 sacks of wool exported by aliens from Lincoln,[157] with a further 7,357 sacks of wool, valued at £3,679 2s 4¾d, being exported by local and alien merchants between May 1333 and February 1334.[158] During the late 1330s and early 1340s, too, thirty-eight different merchants, including one woman, Isabella Blake, were listed as shipping wool to the continent via the ports of Boston and Hull.[159] Little is known of the exact volume of wool being shipped during this period by Lincoln's merchants, though it is possible to estimate the likely

149 These were John ad Fontem (bailiff, 1292/93), Robert le Venur (*custos*, 1290–97) and Adam Kokerel (bailiff, 1290/91): Bischoff, 'Economic Change', 252. For advanced contracts, see Bell, Brooks and Dryburgh, *English Wool Market, passim.*

150 John de Lincoln, Hugh de Lincoln, Hugh de Steynton of Lincoln, Alan de Skilington of Lincoln, Geoffrey de Thornhagh of Lincoln, John de Burton of Lincoln, John de Bliton of Lincoln, Hugh de Thorn of Lincoln, Stephen de Stanham, Richard de Beaufou of Lincoln, Hugh son of Adam of Lincoln, Geoffrey Chournay of Lincoln, Ralf Russell of Lincoln, Roger Faukes of Lincoln, William Russell, John ad Fontem: *CPR, 1292–1301*, 310–11, 299, 335; E 122/5/5A; E 122/5/5.

151 P. Nightingale, 'Alien Finance and the Development of the English Economy, 1285–1311', *Economic History Review*, 66, 2 (2013): 477–96, esp. 492, 494; G. A. Williams, *Medieval London, from Commune to Capital* (London, 1963), 113–14; Kermode, *Medieval Merchants*, 163.

152 Lloyd, *Wool Trade*, 99–143.

153 E 122/6/7.

154 Lloyd, *Wool Trade*, 131.

155 *Export Trade*, 41. Note the 1310–12 figure of 11,200 sacks includes denizens and aliens. It is likely that the number of denizens was a little less than half.

156 For example, *CCR, 1337–39*, 345; *CCR, 1341–43*, 332, 431; *CIM, 1307–49*, 398–401, no. 1628; *Rot. Parl.*, vol. 1, 330.

157 E 356/4, m. 15; E 356/10, m. 15.

158 E 356/5, m. 2.

159 *CCR, 1337–39*, 424–5, 427–30; *1339–41*, 46, 50, 52, 78, 307, 319, 361–2; *1341–43*, 48, 332.

totals based upon the value of loans made to the crown. In 1338, for example, wool valued at roughly £2,365 was shipped by twenty Lincoln merchants from Boston,[160] which equated to approximately 1,780 sacks.[161] When it is considered that this was a year when 4,973 sacks were dispatched from the port,[162] the share of Lincoln's merchants in the regional wool trade had almost doubled to 35 per cent, a significant rise on the early fourteenth century.[163] These years also marked a watershed for the wool trade, as changes in royal legislation saw to it that fewer merchants were able to export wools.[164] This was due both to the increase in export duty in 1337 to 33 per cent, a figure almost seven times greater than the 5 per cent on cloth,[165] and to the disastrous attempts at a wool monopoly by Edward III.[166] The effect of these measures was to price less affluent merchants out of the market,[167] a problem which, over the longer term, saw domestic sales of wool rise and the production of cloth increase, thereby hastening the downturn of wool exports after 1380.[168]

In the years immediately after the Black Death, direct evidence of Lincoln's involvement in the wool trade becomes scarce, though trade undoubtedly continued apace,[169] as it was during this decade that English exports reached their peak.[170] Despite the consolidation of London as England's major wool port,[171] Boston's share of national exports remained healthy, ranging between 3,500 and 6,500 sacks per annum, many of which were brought initially to Lincoln prior to export following the reintroduction of the staple in 1353. This placed the city's infrastructure under pressure following the heavy loss of population and in 1354 it was claimed that the roads 'running through the middle of the city as far as Thornebrig' had 'become so worn away and muddy ... by the frequent passage of carts and horses bringing merchandise and victuals to the staple ... that the transit of men and carriages is greatly impeded'.[172] Similar complaints were again voiced

160 *CCR, 1337–39*, 424–25, 427–30.

161 This conjectural figure is based on the fact that in 1349 an allowance (*viz.* loan) of £85 was the equivalent to roughly 64 sacks of wool (*CCR, 1349–54*, 6–7). Therefore the total cost of wool (rounded up to the nearest pound) is divided here by 85 and multiplied by 64 to get a very rough guide to the volume being exported.

162 This wool was exported in May 1338. The port accounts run from Michaelmas to Michaelmas. *Export Trade*, 35, 45.

163 To this figure must be added the £376 worth of wool (approximately 280 sacks) shipped by Robert de Dalderby and John de Snartford through Hull, as well as an unspecified amount shipped illegally: *CCR, 1337–39*, 427, 430; *CFR, 1337–47*, 154–5.

164 Kermode, *Medieval Merchants*, 171; Lloyd, *Wool Trade*, 170–2, 313.

165 Prices rose from 6s 8d per sack to 40s or more thereafter: *Export Trade*, 194–6; Lloyd, *Wool Trade*, 314.

166 E. B. Fryde, 'Edward III's Wool Monopoly: A Fourteenth-Century Royal Trading Adventure', *History*, New Series, 37 (1952): 8–24.

167 Lloyd, *Wool Trade*, 175, 182; Kermode, *Medieval Merchants*, 163.

168 *Export Trade*, 124.

169 At least 310 sacks were shipped in 1349: *CCR, 1349–54*, 6–7. See also *CCR, 1349–54*, 343–4.

170 *Export Trade*, 47–8, 122.

171 Williams, *Medieval London*, 110–16, 149–51.

172 *CPR, 1354–58*, 8.

in 1365,[173] suggesting that goods continued to flow in and out of the city.[174] Nevertheless, the civic government sought to address these problems, commissioning Peter Belassise (mayor 1358–60) and Roger de Tateshale (mayor 1360/61) to oversee repairs to the city's roads and bridges at this time.[175] In this they may be regarded as successful as by the 1420s much of the city was paved.[176]

In the decade after the first visitation of plague several cases were brought before the King's Bench complaining of fraud. For example, in 1353–54 John Martyn of Boston, Thomas Disny, William Kellesay, John Goldbeter of York and Roger Strykel were all accused of carrying wool out of the staple at Lincoln (206 sacks in total) under the false names of aliens.[177] In 1356 Richard Prentis of Newark, servant of Baudewin Fosse of Bruges, was accused of buying 100 sacks of wool at Lincoln and taking them without paying tax, including thirty sacks of wool from Henry Dyster of Leicester and thirty sacks from John Buckingham, bishop of Lincoln.[178] Similar problems also came to light in 1375 when Thomasyn Glaunchard, Lombard, complained that he, along with Nicholas Jon and other merchants of the society of Albertini of Florence, had bought 100 sacks of wool at £10 per sack from Thomas Pygot of Lincoln and other merchants, who, with the collusion and fraud of John Jolyff of Lincoln at Boston, had claimed that they had paid only 46s 8d per sack on duty as opposed to 50s, thereby defrauding the king.[179] Such evidence, though quantitatively lacking, points to the fact that Lincoln's involvement in the wool trade continued on an international scale.

By 1377/78 fourteen individuals can be identified as exporting wool,[180] though they dispatched an unprecedented 2,235 sacks from Boston, a figure remarkably similar to the 1330s, despite the overall downturn in the volume of wool exports.[181] Lincoln's leading exporter at this time was John de Sutton (mayor 1386/87), who was responsible for over 618 sacks, followed by John Norman with 327 sacks. Both lagged some way behind Boston's own Frederick Tilney, however, who shipped 723 sacks over the same period and who stood as the dominant wool exporter in the

[173] *CPR, 1364–67*, 89.

[174] For example, *CFR, 1356–68*, 120.

[175] *BH*, fo. 15.

[176] *WB*, fo. 5.

[177] KB 29/25, m. 23; JUST 1/526, m. 3.

[178] KB 29/25, m. 23d.

[179] KB 29/28, m. 31d. See also *CCR, 1374–77*, 440, 472–4.

[180] William Bylay, William Dalderby, Hugh Garwell, Robert Ledes, Robert Messingham, John Norman, William Snelston, John Sutton, Robert Sutton and Roger Tyrington, all of whom served as mayor. The four remaining men, John Carberton, John Chesterfeld, Thomas Clerk and Henry Overby, an alien living in Lincoln, never held civic office. Note that exact totals of wool are not always given. Rigby, *Overseas Trade*, 6–15, 18–21, 23. See appendix 2 for dates of office. Note, however, that nine other men were listed as trading with Florentine merchants in 1376 (John Bate, Nicholas Cameryngham, Gilbert de Kyme and Thomas Pigot, all of whom acted as bailiff; John Hudilston, Roger de Taterishale and John Toke, who acted as mayor; and Richard Chestirfeld and Thomas Serby, about whom nothing is known). *CCR, 1374–77*, 472–4; SC 8/64/3154; SC 8/343/16165.

[181] *Export Trade*, 44–6, 50–1, 126.

region.[182] Nonetheless, in a year when 6,226 sacks of wool were exported from the port,[183] Lincoln's involvement stood at roughly 36 per cent of the county's trade, thereby consolidating its earlier dominant position. Several years later, in 1380/81, Lincoln's merchants were responsible for 1,218 of the 3,506 sacks (35 per cent) shipped directly from Boston, highlighting that this was not a one-off.[184] By this stage, the vast majority of wool was transported to the continent by ships hailing from various Lincolnshire coastal towns, including Boston, Grimsby, Lynn, Saltfleethaven, Skegness and Wainfleet, a marked change from the early fourteenth century when Lincoln's merchants relied on foreign ships and one which placed Lincoln's merchants at the heart of the region's chief trade.[185]

The ongoing success of Lincoln's leading merchants in the wool trade can be seen finally in 1395/96 when there was a marginal increase in the number of identified exporters to twenty-one, all of whom were pardoned for 'contempts, trespasses, frauds, deceits and unjust and excessive weighings and purchases of wools contrary to statute'.[186] Fifteen of these individuals went on to serve as bailiff or mayor.[187] Three of these merchants, John de Chesterfeld, John Barkeworth (bailiff, 1394/95) and Robert de Sutton (mayor, 1379/80), also exported substantial quantities of wool from Hull during this period, dispatching 146 sacks, 65 sarplars and seven fardels of wool, along with 143 wool-fells,[188] again emphasising the strength of this select group.

On the eve of the fifteenth century, it is clear that, despite the diminishing volume of wool being exported from England, Lincoln's merchants were responsible for somewhere in the region of 1,100 sacks each year,[189] a figure just shy of York's exports.[190] Although in one sense this was a downturn from the peak years of the 1350s, it nevertheless represented Lincoln's continuing hold on the regional market. Moreover, despite the increased competition from merchants selling wool from the Cotswolds,[191] they were nevertheless fortunate enough to live in a county which produced some of the highest quality wools, an important consideration given that buyers were becoming more selective in their purchases.[192] With profits reckoned to be roughly 20 per cent per sack at the end of the fifteenth century,[193] Lincoln's merchants thus continued to make a healthy return on their investments and to

182 Rigby, *Overseas Trade*, 6–23, 223–5.

183 *Export Trade*, 51.

184 Rigby, 'Boston and Grimsby', 223.

185 This practice continued throughout the remainder of the Middle Ages: G. V. Scammell, 'English Merchant Shipping at the End of the Middle Ages: Some East Coast Evidence', *Economic History Review*, Second Series, 13, 3 (1961), 335, 341.

186 *CPR, 1391–96*, 626–9.

187 Many of whom were listed in 1377/78.

188 This was between June 1390 and June 1391: E 122/59/16, mm. 6–8. Note one entry is illegible.

189 This figure is based upon 35 per cent of 3,086 sacks, the average volume of exports from Boston between 1395 and 1405: *Export Trade*, 54–6.

190 Kermode, *Medieval Merchants*, 269, table 8.4. See also *CFR, 1377–81*, 40–1, 59.

191 Lloyd, *Wool Trade*, 309–10.

192 Lloyd, *Wool Trade*, 311–12.

193 A. Hanham, 'Profits on English Wool Exports, 1472–1544', *Bulletin of the Institute for Historical Research*, 55 (1982), 146–7.

provide much work for the local community, a matter to which this chapter now turns.

The Wool Trade: the Local Economy

To fully understand the significance of the wool trade in Lincoln it is necessary to consider the *Constituciones Civitatis Lincolnie*, a set of twelve ordinances written in Anglo-Norman French dating from c.1270–90 which outline the quality and sale of wool in the city.[194] They include rules prescribing how no merchant was to show or sell wool until it had been assessed by civic officials; that diseased or inferior wool was not to be mixed with good wool; that all wool sold to foreigners was to be weighed according to the king's trone; and that no wool was to be sold outside two ordained trading periods, the first of which began at the feast of Holy Innocents (28 December) and continued for approximately six to eight weeks, the second following the feast of St Augustine (26 May), continuing for twelve to fourteen weeks. On both feast days a meeting was ordained, at which point the constitutions were proclaimed and *purveyaunce* fixed, which in this context meant establishing all prices, tolls and contract particulars for the forthcoming trading period.[195] Wool merchants who did not attend these meetings were fined half a mark.

It should come as no surprise to note that the dates of the two ordained trading periods correspond exactly with the two peaks identified in the surviving tolls of Robert le Venur and William Cause (figures 1–2), periods when the bulk of the city's wool was collected. Nonetheless, it is clear from both the tolls and export accounts of the 1310s and 1370s that Lincoln merchants shipped wool from Boston all year round.[196] This differed from the earlier practice of the 1280s and 1290s when the vast majority of wool shipped from Boston was exported during the time of the annual fair (17 June until approximately early September by the end of the thirteenth century),[197] a development reflecting the general rise of English merchants in the trade and the decline of fairs for wool transactions previously noted.[198]

The constitutions also ordained that when a foreign merchant 'buys wool and takes the key of the house where the wool lies, as is the custom of the merchants … that wool is his as his own proper chattel without contradiction whether of the vendor or of the purchaser'.[199] An illustration of this practice can be seen through the surviving accounts of wealthy Hull merchant William de la Pole, who, as part of

194 *Royal Charters*, 34–7; Bischoff, 'Economic Change', 270. For similar ordinances for Leicester: Lloyd, *Wool Trade*, 302–4. It is possible that these constitutions were introduced to offset the losses of revenue listed in the Hundred Rolls relating to wool. However, without a fixed date of authorship for the constitutions this remains a matter of conjecture. See *Rot. Hund.* 309, 313.

195 More commonly meaning the right of the crown to buy goods at a fixed price: Maddicott, 'The English Peasantry and the Demands of the Crown', 285–359.

196 E 122/6/7; Rigby, *Overseas Trade*, 6–14, 17–23.

197 Summerson, 'Calamity and Commerce', 148, 152–3.

198 Bell, Brooks and Dryburgh, *English Wool*, 150–1; see 54–5.

199 *Royal Charters*, 35. For wool collected at Lincoln by foreign merchants, see A. Bell, C. Brooks

the proposed wool monopoly of Edward III in 1337, ordered two of his merchants, Robert de Dalderby of Lincoln and John de Canewyke of Lincoln,[200] to collect 205 sacks of wool from various parts of Lindsey and ship them to Hull. According to the accounts, all purchased wool was to be carried by cart to Lincoln (at 6d per sack) and wrapped in canvas (2s 6d per sack), as was custom.[201] There each sack was to be unloaded and stored in rented houses while the wools were dressed (*reparandis*) by a certain agreement (*ex certa convencione*) at the cost of 60s.[202] Following this they were then to be packed into sacks (6d each) and carried by cart (1d per sack) to Barton on Humber (2s 6d per sack) before travelling by boat to Hull (3d per sack) where they were to be stored for seventy weeks (½d per sack) before finally being shipped to Dordrecht (4s per sack). In addition to packing and transportation costs, de la Pole also set aside 12d per sack during the Lincoln leg of the journey for fodder, drink and hire of horses, and other necessaries (*et aliis necessariis*), as well as wages for those hired to pack the wool.[203] A second, less detailed example tells a similar story. Dating from 1339 it outlines how Roger de Wolsthorp and Henry de Tiddeswell, collectors of the king's wool, were ordered to receive 1,600½ ells of canvas from the sheriff (at a cost of £41 5s) for the packing of wool in Lincoln, £12 for rent for 'divers houses' storing the wool, and £2 for packing and other expenses.[204]

These accounts are significant as they reveal several important aspects of the wool trade within an urban context. Firstly, they show that men such as William de la Pole or the king's collectors did not pay tolls, meaning that there was a higher volume of wool coming into the city than the tolls suggest.[205] This was equally true of the city's merchants, who, as citizens, were similarly exempt. Secondly, the accounts underscore the importance of the wool trade to the city's service economy, both in terms of the steady stream of work afforded to individuals such as Walter Russell, packer, John de Halton, packer, John de Staunford, *wolpakker*, and John Maykyn, *vulwyndere*,[206] all of whom were engaged in the important process of packing and checking the wool,[207] and in terms of the business it provided for the numerous carters and porters employed in the transportation of wool, the latter of whom were paid 3d a day for their work in 1298.[208] The wool trade was equally significant in terms of the rents it provided through storage, including, for example, at *Allwolhouse*, which was located above the gate in St Mary Crackpole, where wool known

and P. Dryburgh (eds and trans), *Advance Contracts for the Sale of Wool, c.1200–c.1327* (List and Index Society, vol. 315) (Chippenham, 2006), nos 138, 162, 206, 207, 211, 213, 216.

200 *CIM, 1307–49*, 398–401, no. 1628.

201 *CCR, 1341–43*, 195.

202 For this process, see Bell, Brooks and Dryburgh, *English Wool*, 50–1.

203 E. B. Fryde (ed.), *The Wool Accounts of William de la Pole* (York, 1964), 16–17.

204 *CCR, 1339–41*, 152.

205 For earlier wool receipts (£433 17s) from the de la Pole family in Lincoln (1334/35): E 43/459/i.

206 *BB*, fo. 112; JUST 3/142, m. 47; JUST 2/85, rot. 2; KB 29/9, m. 34.

207 Kermode, *Medieval Merchants*, 199. For details of similar practices and associated problems, see M. Bateson, *Records of the Borough of Leicester* (London, 1899), 185–6, 189–90, 202–5, 229, 238–39, 262–3, 291–2.

208 Thomson, *Lincolnshire Assize Roll*, lxiv.

locally as *crakepullynge* was sorted (presumably also the origin of the parish name);[209] the Woolhouse (*Wlhous*) located in the parish of All Saints in Hungate owned by Simon son of Robert de Welton;[210] or the 'long chamber' called the Woolstead (*le Woolest*) located in St Bavon near the wool market which belonged to Hugh son of Simon de Edelyngton (mayor 1332/33).[211] It is likely, too, that a tower located in the parish of St Bavon near the staple port was purchased by the wealthy wool merchant John Norman (mayor 1385/86) with a view to storage.[212]

Aside from purpose-built warehouses, it was also common for many of the city's inhabitants to store wool in their own homes, including several Jews living in Brauncegate during the 1280s such as Jacob of Brauncegate, Elias Gubbay and Solomon of London;[213] Lawrence de Thorn of Lincoln, who was accused by Albreda, widow of Simon son of Gocelin, of receiving wool in his house in St Rumbold and selling it and keeping all profits for himself in 1331;[214] John Tolyngham and his wife, Alice, who kept 1½ sacks of wool and ½ sack of fleece in their house in Newport in 1341;[215] and John Herman, walker, and Nicholas de Stowe, walker, who kept 8 stones of black wool between them in their respective houses in St Swithun in 1395.[216]

The final constitution proclaimed that wool brought into the city from various parts of Lincolnshire, including Lindsey, Kesteven and 'of the Clay' (Holland?), was not to be mixed with wool from other regions. Whilst it is clear that this was used as a preventative measure against fraud, it also points to the fact that Lincoln's merchants purchased wools from a variety of sources. Evidence of this is plentiful and during the late thirteenth century, for example, small amounts of wool were purchased by Lincoln's Jews from South Kesteven, from the villages of Baston and Greatford, as well as from Nottingham, Tollerton, Holbeck, Kirton, Egmanton and East Markham to the west of Lincoln beyond the Trent. Primarily, however, it was brought from Barton, Riseholme, Ingleby, Stow St Mary, Upton, Fillingham and Hemswell to the north of the city; Hackthorn, Faldingworth, Newton by Toft in West Lindsey; and from Middle Rasen in the vale of Lindsey,[217] collectively reflecting the importance (and value) of wool from Lindsey.[218]

Given the overall centrality of the wool trade in the city, it is unsurprising to note that several of Lincoln's inhabitants reared their own sheep and/or stored wool outside the city, including William de Kylpyn, who kept twenty-four sheep at Thurlby in 1323, and William de Belesby of Lincoln, who kept wool and other goods in his house at Flixborough in 1375, traditionally a strategic staging post

209 *BB*, fo. 82 (1319); *Royal Charters*, 35.

210 *BB*, fo. 203 (1349).

211 *BB*, fo. 245 (1350).

212 *CPR, 1381–85*, 302–3. For warehouses located near the site of Blackfriars in Butwerk in the late thirteenth century, see *Rot. Hund.*, 311, 323; *LCL VCH*, 225.

213 R. R. Mundill, 'The Jews in England, 1272–1290' (Unpublished Ph.D Thesis, University of St Andrews, 1988), 294–5.

214 *BB*, fo. 125v.

215 McLane, *1341 Inquest*, no. 718.

216 JUST 1/532, m. 5.

217 Mundill, 'Jews in England', 350–2.

218 Lloyd, *Wool Prices*, 52–61.

for the transportation of wool along the river Trent.[219] Wealthier inhabitants who maintained links to the wool trade were also active in buying up meadowlands and pastures in surrounding areas, possibly with a view to rearing sheep, including John, son of John de Blyton (mayor 1333/34), who bought 148 acres of land and 12 acres of meadow in Canwick by Lincoln in 1331;[220] and John de Sutton (mayor 1385/86), who purchased six messuages, four tofts, twelve bovates of land, fourteen acres of meadow and 100 acres of woodland in Newball by Langworth, Langworth and Maidenwell for 200 marks in 1375.[221] Others, including William de Thornhagh (mayor 1362/63) and Hugh Wake (bailiff 1358/59), also came to own meadowlands and sheep flocks through defaulted debts,[222] highlighting the types of individuals with whom they did business.

The evidence demonstrates how wool remained integral to the lives of many local inhabitants, including those whose primary economic interests lay elsewhere. Considered in this way, wool should be seen in much the same light as ale or grain, with many local inhabitants keeping small amounts in their homes, much of which was sold in the city's markets.[223] As Lincoln's primary export, wool also offered an effective means for Lincoln's merchants to engage with men of great standing, including William de la Pole, all the while underwriting Lincoln's status as a leading provincial town and a centre for trade. Despite the vicissitudes of the post-plague period, Lincoln's involvement in the trade actually expanded in relation to the city's competitors, much of which was funded by an increasingly small and wealthy group of individuals, many of whom served in civic office. Whilst on the face of it this success impacted positively upon the economy of the city, the singular focus by Lincoln's merchants on the wool trade eventually came to undermine the city's well-being in more difficult periods, as the evidence of credit reveals.

Credit

This final section considers the role of credit in Lincoln's economy through an analysis of the Statute Merchant and Staple certificates of debt for the period 1284–1409.[224] These records are important for two main reasons: first, they are the only surviving records of their type for the city;[225] and secondly, they 'provide a chronology for, and measurement of, economic change by indicating rising or falling levels of economic activity', thereby supplementing the evidence hitherto outlined.[226] Despite this,

219 KB 27/251, rot. 57d; KB 27/459, rot. 62; Faith, 'Structure of the Market for Wool', 685–6.

220 CP 25/1/138/100, no. 17.

221 CP 25/1/142/137, no. 35.

222 C 131/16/2; C 131/10/12.

223 For example, *BB*, fo. 230; JUST 3/32/1, m. 3; JUST 3/33/5, m. 27; JUST 3/140, m. 30; JUST 3/188, m. 138d.

224 C 241. For an excellent analysis of credit in medieval historiography, see P. R. Schofield, 'Introduction', in P. R. Schofield and N. J. Mayhew (eds), *Credit and Debt in Medieval England, c.1180–c.1350* (Oxford, 2002), 1–18.

225 Only seven debts are entered in the *Burwarmote Book*: *BB*, fos 79–79v, 142–142v.

226 Nightingale, 'Medieval York', 6.

however, it is important to state at the outset that the absence of contemporaneous debt records from the Burwarmote Court has meant that focus here falls primarily upon high value transactions and the activities of a wealthy elite. This is an unavoidable problem, as it was in the civic courts where the bulk of smaller debts were enrolled.[227]

Established in 1283 following the introduction of the Statute of Acton Burnell, and refined later by the Statute Merchant of 1285 and Statute Staple of 1353, the debt registries in many principal towns across England, including at Lincoln, emerged to provide creditors and debtors with a secure and efficient means of recording their transactions through the enrolment of a recognisance.[228] According to law, the recognisance detailed both the amount of money borrowed by the debtor (or the value of goods) and the date at which repayment was to be made; a copy was given to the creditor.[229] In the event of default, the creditor returned to court where he produced the recognisance. If it matched the enrolled copy he was then issued with a Statute Merchant certificate (or a Statute Staple certificate after 1353), which instigated proceedings for the recovery of the debt. This resulted in a writ being issued to the sheriff who was ordered to imprison the debtor and seize his goods until satisfaction of the debt was made.[230] Unsurprisingly, given the nature of this process, the surviving certificates represent only bad debts, or, to put it another way, only those debts which were never repaid, an important consideration when drawing conclusions from this evidence. Despite the limitations of this evidence, it has been estimated that the surviving certificates account for approximately one fifth of all enrolments,[231] meaning that the total value of debts and the number of certificates discussed here should be multiplied by five to get a more accurate representation of the volume and value of lending taking place.

Of the 1,969 surviving certificates issued at the registry at Lincoln between 1284 and 1409, 1,713 involved individuals from Lincolnshire (87 per cent), a pattern of borrowing replicated throughout the country to varying degrees.[232] Of this number 882 involved Lincoln creditors or debtors, over two fifths of the overall total (44.8 per cent) (figure 3). Notwithstanding the relatively localised nature of credit issued at Lincoln's registry, these certificates serve to highlight various national and international economic links, including how trade was conducted between inhabitants of Lincolnshire and merchants from York, London, Salisbury and Coventry,[233] as well as foreign merchants from Gascony, Italy, Germany and the Low Countries, for

227 For example, Britnell, *Colchester*, 98–115, 206–17; Kowaleski, *Medieval Exeter*, 279–93.

228 For background to these developments, see R. Goddard, *Credit and Trade in Later Medieval England, 1353–1532* (Basingstoke, 2016), 1–48; and P. Nightingale, 'Monetary Contraction and Mercantile Credit in Later Medieval England', *Economic History Review*, 43, 4 (1990): 560–75.

229 C. McNall, 'The Business of Statutory Debt Registries, 1283–1307', in Schofield and Mayhew, *Credit and Debt*, 68, 77.

230 Goddard, 'Commercial Contraction', 17.

231 Nightingale, 'Monetary Contraction', 564–7; McNall, 'Statutory Debt Registries', 79.

232 McNall, 'Statutory Debt Registries', 81. Note that between 1284 and 1307 this figure was as high as 90 per cent; by the 1370s it stood at 69 per cent.

233 For example, C 241/22/120; C 241/62/18; C 241/145/71; C 241/159/13.

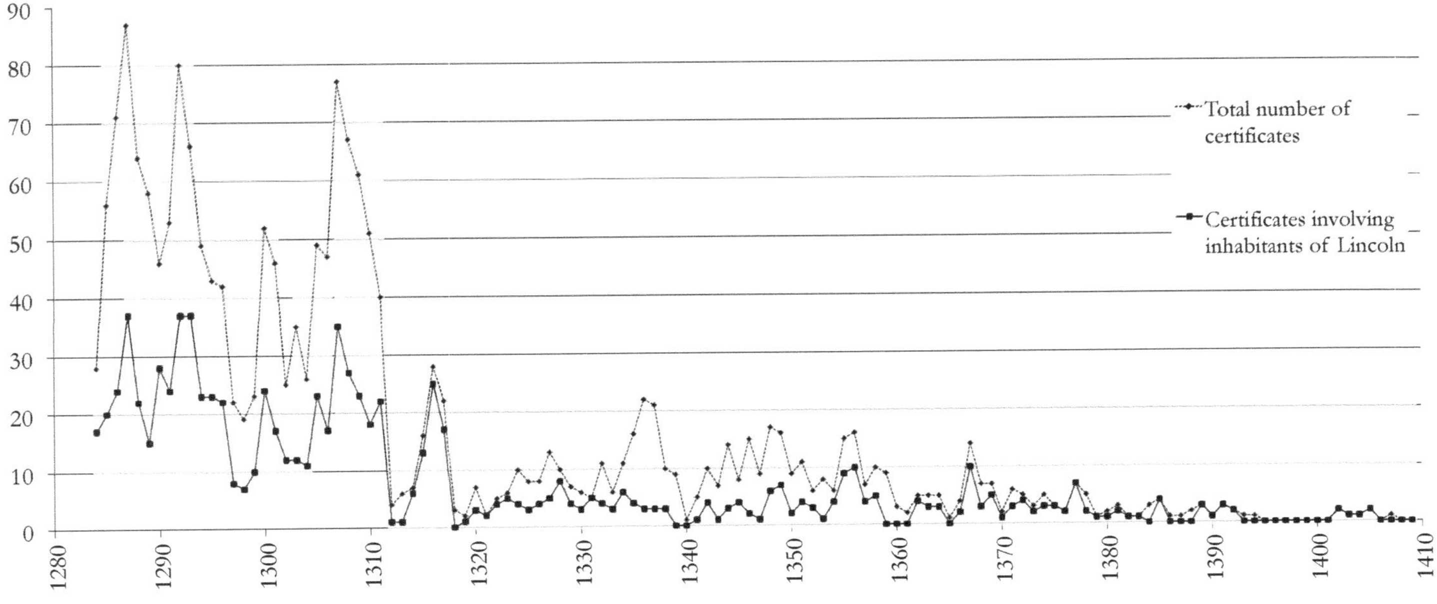

Figure 3 Annual number of defaulting Statute Merchant and Statute Staple certificates recorded at Lincoln (1284–1409)
Source: National Archives, London, Public Record Office, C 241

example.[234] Nonetheless, over the course of the second half of the fourteenth century a gradual shift in the pattern of lending for the Statute Merchant and Staple registries saw credit move away from provincial towns towards Westminster, which saw its share of certificates rise from 33.6 per cent in the 1360s to 53 per cent in the 1390s,[235] a development that had important consequences for Lincoln as a centre for credit.

The most obvious conclusion to draw from the evidence presented here is that from approximately 1309 onwards the number of certificates enrolled at Lincoln's registry fell dramatically. Yet, despite the broader changes in lending highlighted in the previous paragraph, it is important to recognise that this decline was nevertheless indicative of national trends. For example, whilst the number of certificates involving Lincoln creditors fell from 163 for 1300–09 to ninety-one for 1310–29 (a fall of 45 per cent), over the same period the national average dropped by 42 per cent. This decline has been attributed to three main factors: the strife of Edward II's reign; the sudden drop in the amount of wool exported nationally; and the fact that between 1311 and 1322 only merchants were allowed to use the Statute Merchant court.[236] Undoubtedly the most significant of these three reasons was the last, which over time reduced the accessibility of credit facilities for traders of more modest means. In particular, whereas between 1284 and 1329 53.5 per cent of all certificates enrolled at Lincoln were valued at £10 or less, after 1330 this fell to approximately 18 per cent until 1389, after which time the number of certificates enrolled at Lincoln fell into single digits (table 11). In other words, over time the Statute Merchant and Staple court came to be used primarily for high finance,[237] a noticeable shift away from the practices of the earlier period.[238] This is further emphasised by the increasing number of certificates valued at £50 or more, which stood at only 6 per cent for the period between 1284 and 1329 rising to 21 per cent between 1330 and 1389, as well as by the average and lowest transaction values. Extrapolating these findings across England would thus explain what appears at first glance to be a 'flood of credit' in the early fourteenth century but which actually represented a less privileged system of credit than that which would ensue.[239]

Considered in this way, it is likely that the steep decline in credit across England indicated by the Statute Merchant certificates was largely illusory, with different mechanisms of finance becoming employed on a more frequent basis.[240] Certainly,

234 C 241/9/254; C 241/7/37; C 241/46/211; C 241/77/8.

235 P. Nightingale, 'The Growth of London', in R. Britnell and J. Hatcher (eds), *Progress and Problems in Medieval England* (Cambridge, 2002), 101.

236 Nightingale, 'Medieval York', 12; Nightingale, 'Growth of London', 99; Nightingale, 'The Lay Subsidies', 12.

237 Goddard, 'Commercial Contraction', 19–20; J. Kermode, 'Money and Credit in the Fifteenth Century: Some Lessons from Yorkshire', *Business History Review*, 65, 3 (1991), 488.

238 McNall, 'Statutory Debt Registries', 75, 77–8.

239 Goddard, *Credit and Trade*, 130–1.

240 For example, the Court of Common Pleas grew threefold between 1275 and 1390, an observation based upon the size of individual records and their number of entries. See also D. Keene, 'Changes in London's economic hinterland as indicated by debt cases in the Court of Common Pleas', in Galloway, *Market Integration*, 59–81.

Table 11 Trends in Lincoln's Statute Merchant and Staple certificates (1284–1409)

Years	Total value of credit^	Approx. av. trans. value	Highest trans. value	Lowest trans. value	No. of trans.	Breakdown of transaction values					
						< £5	< £10	< £25	< £50	< £100	> £100
1284–89	£1,181	£8 17s 8d	£72 13s 9d	3s 8d	133	69 (52%)	30 (22.5%)	27 (20%)	6 (4.5%)	1 (1%)	0 (0%)
1290–99	£2,960	£13 15s 5d	£195	20s	215	85 (39.5%)	50 (23%)	59 (27.5%)	15 (7%)	4 (2%)	2 (1%)
1300–09	£3,129	£15 8s 4d	£100	25s	203	57 (28%)	41 (20%)	69 (34%)	22 (11%)	6 (3%)	8 (4%)
1310–19	£2,176	£20 2s 10d	£180	40s	108	26 (24%)	21 (19.5%)	35 (32.5%)	12 (11%)	11 (10%)	3 (3%)
1320–29	£987	£23 10s 1d	£200	40s	42	2 (5%)	14 (33%)	17 (40.5%)	6 (14%)	1 (2.5%)	2 (5%)
1330–39	£1,910	£54 13s 6d	£300	40s	35	3 (8.5%)	3 (8.5%)	15 (43%)	7 (20%)	1 (3%)	6 (17%)
1340–49	£735	£23 14s 3d	£100	£4	31	2 (6.2%)	7 (22.5%)	13 (42%)	4 (12.9%)	3 (10%)	2 (6.2%)
1350–59	£1,502	£36 12s 9d	£200	50s	41	7 (17%)	6 (14.6%)	12 (29.2%)	6 (14.6%)	6 (14.6%)	4 (10%)
1360–69	£1,132	£37 14s 9d	£200	£5	30	1 (3%)	2 (7%)	15 (50%)	6 (20%)	3 (10%)	3 (10%)
1370–79	£1,407	£50 5s 1d	£300	£5	28	0 (0%)	2 (13%)	13 (43%)	5 (17%)	4 (13%)	4 (13%)
1380–89	£953	£68 1s 6d	£380	£6 13s 4d	14	0 (0%)	1 (7%)	6 (43%)	4 (28.5%)	0 (0%)	3 (21.5%)
1390–99	£222	n/a	£200	£6 13s 4d	4	0 (0%)	2 (50%)	1 (25%)	0 (0%)	0 (0%)	1 (25%)
1400–09	£329	n/a	£200	40s	5	1 (20%)	1 (20%)	1 (20%)	0 (0%)	0 (0%)	2 (40%)

Source: C 241

NB: the 'Total value of credit' column is higher here than in figure 4 as it includes all credit given by or to Lincoln traders. Debts worth £1,000 are excluded from these figures as they appear to be penal bonds. For more on this, see M. M. Postan, 'Private Financial Instruments in Medieval England', in *idem*, *Medieval Trade and Finance* (Cambridge, 1973), 30. This table only records Lincoln creditors and debtors. Key: ^ = entry rounded to the nearest pound.

after the Black Death local borough courts came to be used with greater alacrity than ever before in places such as Colchester and Exeter, and it is likely that a similar pattern was experienced at Lincoln, despite the absence of evidence for this.[241] Two possible reasons for this exist, namely that it may have been cheaper to enrol debts outside of the Statute Merchant system,[242] and culturally it may have been seen as a more elite or formalised system than other courts. Whilst it is true that one of the main benefits of the Statute Merchant system was that it ensured debts were repaid speedily through the forfeiture of lands or properties, it is also possible that some borrowers remained wary of this course of action.

Throughout the early years of the Statute Merchant system (1284–1309), several of Lincoln's leading inhabitants engaged in transactions for wool.[243] For example, in 1284 Roger son of Benedict, a former mayor (1274–77, 1280), credited Alan Bouche and Philip son of Davy of Kirkby-next-Bolingbroke in Lincolnshire nine marks for one sack, whilst in 1289 Richard de Beaufou of Lincoln, another former mayor (1283–85), loaned Richard Rudd of Barton twelve marks for a sack of 'good and marketable' wool.[244] Further evidence for the proliferation of credit for wool can be seen through the high levels of credit being extended to knights, who remained leading wool growers.[245] For example, in 1302 Stephen de Stanham (mayor 1301–06, 1312/13) lent Philip de Hilley, knight and Lord of Knaith in Lindsey, £25 6s 8d during shearing season,[246] whilst several other Lincoln merchants did likewise, including Alexander son of John FitzMartin (mayor 1306/07) in 1300, John le Noyr (bailiff 1307/08) in 1301 and 1308, Peter de Thornhaugh in 1302, Walter Wrangle in 1303, Simon de Grantham in 1311, and Henry Bere (mayor 1313/14) in 1311 and 1312.[247] The prior and convent of St Katherine likewise lent £10 to John de Harrington, knight, in 1304, emphasising that these relationships were not confined solely to merchants and civic elites.[248]

High value transactions for wool were not the only types of certificates recorded during this earlier period, with lesser amounts of credit being extended to individuals for a variety of other reasons.[249] These include William de Burton of Lincoln who was owed 26s 8d for two quarters of wheat and six quarters of barley in September 1284 and Walter Wrangle of Lincoln who was owed 40s for ten quarters of barley in November the same year.[250] In 1300, too, John de Blyton (mayor 1307/08, 1315/16) lent two relatives, Walter de Appleby and William de Appleby of Ancaster, 40s as a

241 Britnell, *Colchester*, 98–115, 206–17; Kowaleski, *Medieval Exeter*, 279–93.

242 Goddard, *Credit and trade*, 34–5.

243 For example, C 241/8/31; C 241/9/112; C 241/12/56; C 241/9/340; C 241/45/181.

244 C 241/14/64; C 241/8/195.

245 *Medieval Lincolnshire*, 106–7, table 4, 126–7. P. Nightingale, 'Knights and Merchants: Trade, Politics and the Gentry in Late Medieval England', *Past and Present*, 169, 1 (2000), 38–9.

246 C 241/44/9.

247 C 241/35/326; C 241/33/61; C 241/62/145; C 241/63/254; C 241/40/103; C 241/81/1; C 241/89/7; C 241/79/80.

248 C 241/43/20.

249 For a full list of goods traded via the Statute Merchant system, see McNall, 'Statutory Debt Registries', 75.

250 C 241/7/191; C 241/16/25.

loan; whilst in 1310 Gilbert le Noyr lent Ellis Beck of Beckingham £10 on 'account of a loan'.[251] In the majority of cases, however, no reason for the debt can be determined, though occasionally the occupational details of individuals shed light on the types of transactions possibly taking place. In 1300, for example, Philip de Araz of Lincoln, mason, lent £10 to John de Gaunt of Bescaby in Leicestershire possibly for building materials or work; in 1304 Henry le Archer of Lincoln was recorded as owing Stephen de Stanham 66s 8d, perhaps with a view to buying raw materials to manufacture weaponry; and in 1307 Walter de Sewerby, tailor, extended £4 worth of credit to William de Winterton, son of Richard de Keythorpe, possibly for clothing or materials.[252]

The gradual shift away from the low value transactions that largely characterised the first twenty-five years of the Statute Merchant system did not stop Lincoln's merchants from benefiting from the crisis of famine years (1315–17). In fact, during this period they were directly involved in fifty-five of the sixty-six certificates enrolled at Lincoln's registry, their most significant involvement in chains of credit until the economic boom of the mid-1350s. It is likely that much of this credit was being extended for the purchase of staple foodstuffs, including grains, cereals and other crops; as Philip Slavin demonstrates for the south-eastern counties of England, the volatility of grain prices during famine years often encouraged vendors to buy low and sell high, thereby exacerbating an already perilous situation.[253] Towns were not unresponsive to these developments and in London, for example, brewers were prohibited from making malt so that barley and other grains were available for bread, whilst grains were imported from the continent.[254] At Lincoln the civic government ensured grains were funnelled through the correct channels by threatening hucksters with punishment if they sold breads not purchased directly from the city's bakers.[255]

In spite of such measures, Lincoln's status as a major grain centre continued to provide opportunities for profit and it is likely that the rise in the number of Lincoln merchants lending credit to fellow Lincoln merchants during these years reflects this trend (up 8 per cent), with many seeking to benefit from the crisis.[256] It is certainly notable that for the first time for the Lincoln evidence, certificates were explicitly stating that money was being lent in order to buy 'merchandise' directly from lenders.[257] This offers some context to the events of 1315 when the 'community of the town of Lincoln' petitioned the crown to complain that 'certain merchants of the same city' were buying up victuals and merchandise secretly (i.e. forestalling), so that the city's inhabitants were unable to buy 'any victuals or merchandise except from

251 C 241/71/96; C 241/84/70.
252 C 241/36/290; C 241/43/16; C 241/61/34.
253 P. Slavin, 'Market Failure during the Great Famine in England and Wales (1315–1317)', *Past and Present*, 22 (2013), 34–42.
254 D. Keene, 'Crisis Management in London's Food Supply, 1250–1500', in B. Dodds and C. Liddy (eds), *Commercial Activity, Markets and Entrepreneurs in the Middle Ages: Essays in Honour of Richard Britnell* (Woodbridge, 2011), 59.
255 *BH*, fo. 27.
256 For example, C 241/82/63; C 241/83/119; C 241/85/37.
257 C 241/82/176; C 241/84/118; C 241/83/121; C 241/82/159.

the aforementioned merchants'.[258] The king ordered these wrongs be 'corrected and put right immediately' and demanded to be informed of the 'remedies which they have applied'. Such practices persisted, however, and a year later, in 1316, Thomas de Graingham was found guilty of forestalling by the civic government, for which he was set into the stocks.[259] Such problems are reflected further still by the fact that in 1316 the lack of availability of corn in the city had become sufficiently acute that two local merchants, William de Gretton and Henry de Severby, were granted a licence by the crown to travel to Cambridgeshire and Huntingdonshire to buy corn.[260] Several others too, namely Thomas de Aton, Hugh de Edlington and Peter Blok, were successful in acquiring from the king the right of protection with a clause *nolumnus*, which effectively forbade any royal officials from carrying away their goods, as in cases of purveyance.[261] Given that the parliament of 1316 was held at Lincoln, this was undoubtedly seen as an important palliative to an increasingly difficult situation.

The most prolific lender during the famine years was John de Blyton, noted earlier,[262] who lent over £660 of unpaid credit to sixteen separate merchants and traders both within and outside the city over a three-year period. The largest sum he lent was £180 to John Skavyn of Grantham, merchant, with a further £85 being credited to Philip de Clopton, merchant of Bury St Edmunds in Suffolk.[263] Although it is likely that these particular transactions related to wholesale goods, possibly wool,[264] it is noticeable that Blyton also lent smaller amounts to traders from the local region, possibly for grains and other cereals. This included £10 to Henry de Immingham of Great Hale, twelve marks to John son of Simon Roumfare of Gainsborough, and £7 10s to Adam son of Robert FitzRoger of Carlton-next-Bassingham.[265] In 1329, following the death of John de Blyton, it was noted that his son, also John, lent £13 6s 8d to William son of John son of Thomas de Lincoln, for corn bought directly from him, suggesting that the marketing of grain may have been an active part of the family's trade.[266] Either way, the senior John de Blyton issued almost a third of all credit for the entire decade in these three years alone.

Despite the high credit yields of the early famine years, the subsequent four years saw a severe slump in lending. This reflected the continuing succession of bad harvests and livestock mortalities during these years,[267] with the Louth Park Chronicle stating that the abbey lost 'oxen, sheep, and all kinds of beast of the

258 C. Given-Wilson et al. (ed.), *The Parliament Rolls of Medieval England* (Leicester, 2005), CD-ROM version, Parliament of 1315, item 248 (*Rot. Parl.* vol. 1, 330).

259 *BB*, fo. 77v.

260 *CPR, 1313–17*, 397.

261 *CPR, 1317–17*, 375, 380; K. L. Wood-Legh, *Studies in Church Life under Edward III* (Cambridge, 1934), 25.

262 See 83.

263 C 241/82/1; C 241/82/2.

264 Blyton was a leading wool exporter, dispatching over 150 sacks of wool in 1310–12: E 122/6/7.

265 C 241/83/61; C 241/90/7; C 241/97/63.

266 C 241/106/239. For Blyton's will (1323): *BB*, fo. 93.

267 Miller and Hatcher, *Medieval England*, 426–7; I. Kershaw, 'The Great Famine and Agrarian Crisis in England, 1315–1322', *Past and Present*, 59 (1973), 41.

field, in corn and other necessaries',[268] whilst William of Wheatley, schoolmaster of Lincoln's grammar school, stated that there was such a 'great scarcity [of grain] and mortality among men and animals' in 1316, that it drove him to compose two hymns dedicated to St Hugh for a play on Christmas Day to 'comfort himself and others in their misery'.[269] Thereafter there followed a steady rise in the number of enrolments until the mid-1330s when Lincoln, like much of England, fell into recession, a problem exacerbated by a falling money supply.[270] This is seen most clearly in the reduction of the city's share of the county's creditors, which fell from 48.5 per cent for the period 1320–35 to 19 per cent during 1336–47 before returning to 45.5 per cent during the next decade (1347–58). It is likely that Lincoln's difficulties were driven primarily by its dependency upon the wool trade, which, as discussed previously, had come to be concentrated in fewer and fewer hands during this period, thereby pricing many smaller lenders out of the market. This conclusion is supported by the occupational survey of Lincoln, which records fewer merchants during this period (table 2), as well as a reduction in the number of transactions valued at £10 or less (table 11). Another factor contributing to this downturn in credit was the fact that areas of Lindsey suffered from severe flooding during this period;[271] this meant not only that Lincoln creditors began to look elsewhere for business opportunities, most notably in Kesteven in the 1330s and 1340s,[272] but that less affluent merchants working without agents would have found it increasingly difficult to purchase wools against their wealthier competitors.

Perhaps the most interesting aspect of Lincoln's credit history during this period dates from the years immediately after the Black Death, when the number of creditors actually increased from twenty-nine (1340–49) to forty-two (1350–59). What is so striking about this rise is that it stood at odds with the national trend, which saw a decline of 35 per cent as a result of the demographic crisis brought about by plague.[273] York, in particular, suffered during this period due to the re-emergence of alien merchants in the city who were successful in securing a legal monopoly on all English exports of wool between September 1352 and the summer of 1357,[274] a devel-

268 E. Venables, *The Chronicle of Louth Park Abbey*, trans. A. R. Maddison (Lincolnshire Record Society, 1891), 24.

269 *LCL VCH*, 423.

270 Miller and Hatcher, *Medieval England*, 421–25; P. Spufford, *Money and its Use in Medieval Europe* (Cambridge, 1988), 240–63.

271 *Medieval Lincolnshire*, 153; M. Bailey, '*Per impetum maris*: natural disaster and economic decline in eastern England, 1275–1350', in Campbell, *Before the Black Death*, 190; M. Livingstone, 'A Snapshot in Time: The Weather as Seen in the Record of the *Nonae* (1339–41)', in M. Kowaleski, J. Langdon and P. R. Schofield (eds), *Peasants and Lords in the Medieval English Economy* (Turnhout, 2015), 332, 345–6; William Merle, *Consideraciones Temperieri Pro 7 Annis: The Earliest Known Journal of the Weather, 1337–1344*, trans. and ed. by G. J. Symons (London, 1891). It is possible that the bovine pestilence identified for the south of England was also having an adverse effect on Lincolnshire: Slavin, 'Great Bovine Pestilence', 1239–66, esp. 1257, 1261.

272 See table 12 below.

273 Nightingale, 'Medieval York', 18.

274 Lloyd, *Wool Trade*, 205–8.

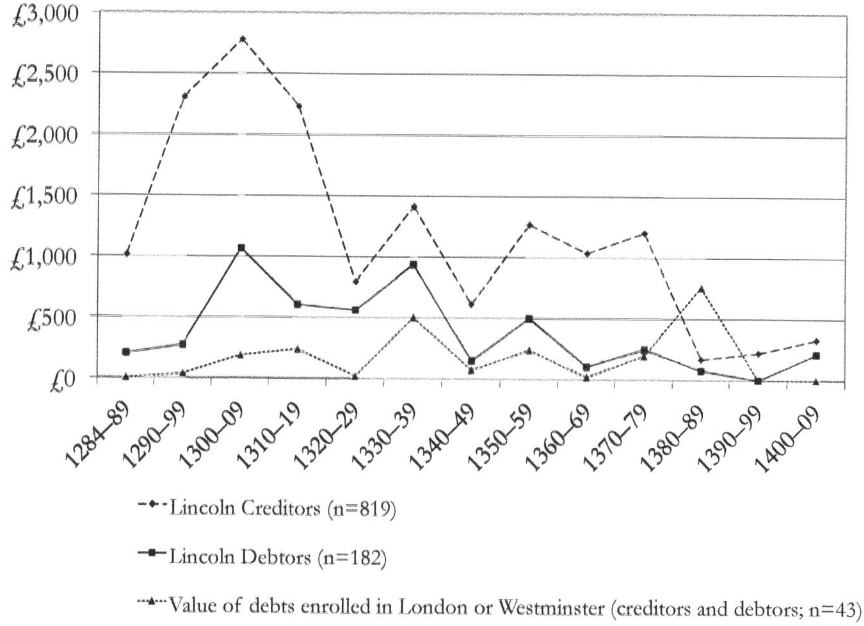

Figure 4 Value of credit and debt involving inhabitants of Lincoln (1284–1409)

opment Pamela Nightingale sees as threatening the prosperity of York's merchants.[275] The impact of this on York was a significant slump in credit during the 1350s, which fell to half the value of the 1340s. As a result, subsequent decades saw many of the city's leading merchants invest great sums into the city's burgeoning cloth industry whilst establishing what later became known as the Merchant Venturers. At Lincoln no such measures were required as, much like Coventry and Colchester, the city began to experience renewed economic growth during this decade,[276] and, unlike York, the value of unpaid credit advanced by Lincoln's merchants and traders actually doubled in comparison to the 1340s, reaching an impressive £1,268 (figure 4). Significantly, this growth was mirrored by creditors drawn from outside the city, suggesting that parts of Lincolnshire were quick to recover following the Black Death.[277]

The driving force behind this surge in credit was undoubtedly the wool and cloth trades, both of which saw an increase in national exports during the 1350s and 1360s.[278] Whilst at Lincoln alien merchants returned to the registry for the first

275 For what follows, see Nightingale, 'Medieval York', 18–23, at 18.

276 Compare Goddard, *Lordship*, 263–4, 272, fig. 8, with Goddard, 'Commercial Contraction', 18–20, fig. 1; Britnell, *Colchester*, 99–100, table 7.1.

277 £1,725 of credit was lent by non-Lincoln inhabitants in the 1340s, rising to £2,341 in the 1350s despite a decline in the number of creditors from sixty-six to fifty-seven.

278 *Export Trade*, 47–8, 76–7, 126, 128, 146, 150.

time since the 1310s following the collapse of alien credit,[279] at no stage did they ever threaten Lincoln's dominance of the region's wool trade as they did at York.[280] On the contrary, due to the introduction of new staple regulations in 1353, when it once again became a requirement for all wool hides, skins, timber and tin to be brought to Lincoln before being sold, it is likely that Lincoln's merchants simply sold their wool to alien merchants in the city until the ban was lifted.[281]

The growth in cloth exports during these two decades was driven by rapid investment by Lincoln's merchants and traders.[282] For example, in 1356 Adam Blome, spicer of Lincoln, lent Henry de Bruges, merchant of Brabant, £41, possibly to buy cloth manufactured locally;[283] in 1362 John de Hemingby and Sir Nicholas de Brantree of Lincoln, chaplain, lent £80 to Fulk de Sutton, mercer of Boston, again possibly for cloth or raw materials for export;[284] and in 1369 both John de Welton of Lincoln, draper, and Thomas de Wainfleet of Lincoln, draper, lent £10 respectively to John Clerk of Hibaldstow and John de Caythorpe of Hibaldstow.[285] The significance of the final two transactions relates to the fact that Hibaldstow lay on the fringes of Hull's economic hinterland on the southern side of the Humber, an area Jennifer Kermode postulates experienced a fourfold growth in cloth manufacture between 1350 and 1368.[286] It is possible therefore that Lincoln's drapers were attempting to expand their sphere of influence by buying or selling cloth and/or raw materials to manufacturers on credit in this area.

Despite the downturn in credit issued in the 1360s, almost certainly due to repeated bouts of plague,[287] Lincoln's Statute Merchant and Staple court continued to provide credit facilities until c.1380 when two significant economic changes occurred. The first was the decreasing output of English mints, which had begun to fall during the 1370s but shrank increasingly throughout the decade.[288] This affected the availability of credit as cash reserves dried up and lenders became more reluctant to lend for fear of not getting their money back, all the while becoming more liable to default on their own debts.[289] This explains, at least in part, the rise in the number of local merchants making their way to Westminster to seek out credit; as the emerging financial centre of England after 1350, it was able to withstand the lack of available cash more readily than provincial towns.[290] Take, for example, Thomas Elveley of Lincoln, merchant, who borrowed £220 from John More, citizen and

279 For example, C 241/136/155, C 241/135/148. See n. 151 above.

280 Lloyd, *Wool Trade*, 208.

281 As in the case of Richard Prentis of Newark cited earlier: see 73.

282 For the 1340s, see 25.

283 C 241/136/155.

284 C 241/142/19.

285 C 241/150/9; C 241/157/89.

286 Kermode, *Medieval Merchants*, 171.

287 There were no certificates enrolled in 1360–61 and only one in 1369, three plague years: Bolton, 'The World Upside Down', 27.

288 Nightingale, 'Monetary Contraction', 560–2.

289 Goddard, *Credit and Trade*, introduction.

290 Nightingale, 'Monetary Contraction', 565.

merchant of London in 1380,[291] or John Bate of Lincoln, merchant, who borrowed £380 from John FitzWalter of Dunham-on-Trent and Isabel, his wife in 1383.[292]

The second change was the failure by Lincoln's leading merchants to continue their investment in the cloth industry.[293] This almost certainly occurred during the mid- to late 1370s, a few years after the city and county had registered the highest annual cloth farm (£22) of all those listed.[294] Evidence for this shift comes from two main sources: first, the changing pattern of cloth exports at Boston, which saw the share of denizens' exports fall by over half compared to the late 1360s and early 1370s,[295] during which period there was a significant rise in exports by Hanseatic merchants;[296] second, the subsequent decline in the value of Lincoln's cloth farm, which fell to a tenth of its 1370 figure by the first decade of the fifteenth century, emphasising the sharp downturn in the volume of manufacturing and the shift towards small units of production.[297] Although on the face of it the decision to discontinue investment in the cloth industry can be seen as a logical one, in part due to the relative scarcity of coin and the continuing success of Lincoln's merchants as wool exporters, it nevertheless proved to be a miscalculation for Lincoln's status as a financial centre because the majority of credit being issued in Statute Staple courts during this period was for funding the burgeoning cloth industry.[298] This can be seen both at Salisbury and Coventry, for example, which saw substantial growth from the 1370s onwards.[299] The significance of this was that those seeking out credit for cloth or raw materials for manufacture had little reason to go to Lincoln, there being better provisioned towns elsewhere. It is seemingly no coincidence either that the 1370s was the decade which saw Coventry finally overtake Lincoln as the leading debt registry in the Midlands. The knock-on effect was that Lincoln's reputation as a centre for credit experienced a blow from which it was unable to recover, with only a handful of certificates being issued thereafter.

The final indication of Lincoln's decline as a fiscal centre can be seen by reviewing the geographical distribution of debtors borrowing directly from Lincoln creditors (table 12). Despite the vicissitudes of famine and plague, throughout much of the period here the smaller regions of Holland and Kesteven contributed between roughly a third and a half of all debtors. Only during the 1330s, when areas of Lindsey underwent severe flooding, did they account for 60 per cent. However, by the 1370s, the proportion of debtors from Holland and Kesteven had fallen to approximately a fifth, at a time when traders from these areas began to seek out credit in the capital in greater numbers than previously, including John son of Walter Bret of Wrangle, Richard Wilsford of Welbourn, Gilbert Alkborough of Pinchbeck, William Sutton

291 C 241/166/109.

292 C 241/171/128. See also, for example, C 241/178/134; C 241/175/31; Thomas, *Plea and Memoranda Rolls*, 63, 111–13, 164, 216.

293 For two possible exceptions, see C 241/173/96, C 241/159/13.

294 *CCR, 1369–74*, 172.

295 *Export Trade*, 78–97.

296 M. M. Postan, 'England and the Hanse, 1400–75', in *idem*, *Trade and Finance*, 291–4.

297 See 24–9.

298 Nightingale, 'Monetary Contraction', 569; Goddard, 'Commercial Contraction', 14.

299 Goddard, 'Commercial Contraction', 17–24; Hare, 'Salisbury', 3–8.

Table 12 Known locations of debtors recorded in Statute Merchant and Staple certificates

Dates	Holland	Kesteven	Lindsey
1284–89	7	11	39
1290–99	8	28	72
1300–09	20	32	50
1310–19	9	14	18
1320–29	1	3	7
1330–39	2	10	8
1340–49	2	5	10
1350–59	2	5	17
1360–69	4	3	11
1370–79	1	1	7
1380–89	0	1	3

NB: this table excludes traders from outside of Lincolnshire.

of Boston and John Pound of Grantham,[300] all of whom could have borrowed credit in Lincoln but chose not to.

The disappearance of widespread credit facilities at Lincoln was undoubtedly a blow to the city's prestige as a fiscal centre. Whilst it is true that the court remained in operation, albeit on a much reduced scale, it no longer drew wealthy merchants and traders from outside the city with as much regularity as it had previously, as many sought out credit elsewhere. This was not without significance and, as Kermode argues, access to foreign markets created credit opportunities for trade; as they declined, so did these opportunities.[301] This certainly explains the growing trend for Lincoln's merchants, much like those of many other towns and regions, to register their debts at Westminster.[302] Considered in this way, it is clear that the growth of London as a financial centre became too strong for towns like Lincoln which failed to capitalise on the burgeoning cloth industry, perhaps surprisingly given its earlier position of strength. It is certainly notable that Salisbury, Coventry and York, all staple towns with strong cloth industries, withstood the centripetal pull of the capital for longer.[303]

300 C 241/133/64; C 241/146/23; C 241/143/119; C 241/157/131; C 241/164/123.

301 Kermode, *Medieval Merchants*, 447.

302 C 241/175/31; C 241/214/29; C 241/228/10; C 241/232/5. Debts were not always recorded through the Statute Staple system, for example: CP 40/468, mm. 8, 32, 37, 52, 80.

303 J. Kermode, 'Medieval Indebtedness: the Regions versus London', in N. Rogers (ed.), *England in the Fifteenth Century* (Stamford, 1994), 72–88, esp. table 1.1.

Conclusion

This chapter has demonstrated that Lincoln, like many other provincial centres, played an important role within the regional economy between the late thirteenth and early fifteenth centuries.[304] As the leading market and financial centre, it drew merchants and traders from up to thirty-five miles away on a regular basis, many of whom sought out credit, goods and raw materials. Many of those travelling to the city also brought with them a variety of goods for sale, thereby establishing bonds of mutual interdependence between the city and its hinterland. Foremost amongst these goods were grain and wool, much of them redistributed throughout the region, at times at the behest of royal demands. These commodities were accompanied by an array of luxury goods brought to Lincoln by local merchants from the continent, many of which, prior to 1300, were available only at international fairs. Claims that Lincoln was a 'peripheral market' for the county's wool after the thirteenth century is not supported by the evidence,[305] and by at least the late 1330s Lincoln's merchants had come to control almost two fifths of all the county's wool exported through Boston, much of which passed through the hands of Lincoln's manual labourers and warehouses for sorting and packing. To this must also be added the unspecified volume of wool used in domestic cloth manufacture, which grew most rapidly after the Black Death but tailed off again by the close of the century.

This period was not without difficulties, however, with a series of natural disasters impacting upon established bonds of trade. Whilst Lincoln's elites undoubtedly benefitted from the famine years (1315–17), as vendors sought to purchase grains and other foodstuffs on credit, this was followed by a sharp decline as the county reeled from its losses. During the 1330s, too, patterns of lending shifted southwards as Lindsey, Lincoln's main supplier of goods and debtors, underwent flooding. Lindsey also experienced further difficulties in the years immediately after the Black Death when it recorded a proportionally high number of deserted villages compared to the figures for Holland and Kesteven,[306] all of which, over the long term at least, served to reduce the volume of trade coming into Lincoln. Furthermore, as debtors from the two southern regions of Kesteven and Holland began to look to Westminster for credit, capital drained away from the city, especially during the 1370s and 1380s, a development helped little by the falling money supply and the decision of Lincoln's leading merchants to cease their investment in the cloth trade.

By the opening decades of the fifteenth century Lincoln sat at a crossroads. It had little more than a domestic cloth industry, no longer acted as a major financial centre, and its economic raison d'être, the wool trade, saw a declining number of exports. Yet it was not all doom and gloom. Lincoln's merchants still controlled roughly a third of the county's wool, which provided employment for many local workers, all of which continued to be shipped through Hull and Boston.[307] By the 1430s, too, the mayor and burgesses were also exporting wool on behalf of the

304 Kowaleski, *Medieval Exeter*, 327–30.
305 Bischoff, 'Economic Change', 202, 264.
306 *Medieval Lincolnshire*, 160, fig. 56.
307 For example, SC 8/124/6178; E 122/59/16.

civic government in order to boost revenues, an innovative approach to fiscal management,[308] as a means to offset the loss of trade. As seen in the previous chapter, Lincoln also began to draw visitors to its courts in hitherto unprecedented numbers following its elevation to county status. Hence whilst these visitors did not necessarily fill civic coffers in the way that traders had in years past, they nevertheless ensured that Lincoln's administrative, professional, service and victualling trades continued to prosper.

308 SC 8/122/6083. For a detailed discussion of this point, see 118.

3

The Crown and the Fee Farm

The concept of 'urban decline' in the later Middle Ages, and in particular during the period between 1420 and 1560, has been debated at length by historians, although the extent to which it has been deemed characteristic of all towns is, as of yet, far from settled.[1] Whilst some towns seemingly thrived, including Salisbury and Exeter, for example,[2] others, like Boston and Lincoln, purportedly declined.[3] Unsurprisingly, broad generalisations over the relative success or failure of all English towns remain problematic and, as Palliser notes, 'there was much variation at a short-term level',[4] meaning that it becomes necessary to consider the longer-term fortunes of towns if any accurate conclusions are to be drawn. For example, whilst Coventry and Colchester are typically characterised as flourishing in the years immediately following the Black Death, both undoubtedly underwent decline in the latter stages of the fifteenth century;[5] thus at what dates should any analysis of these particular towns, or indeed any town, begin and end? As Alan Dyer asks, 'Should losses be absolute, or relative to other towns or the countryside?'[6]

An equally pressing problem is that of evidence. Whilst previous studies have drawn upon four main types of statistical records in discussions of urban decline, namely freemen admissions, customs records, rent values and taxation assessments, alongside other non-statistical data, including petitions for fiscal relief, the alleged 'flight from office' by civic officials and archaeological evidence,[7] more recent studies have begun to consider an even broader corpus of evidence, including networks of credit and urban occupational structures, both of which have been used to identify aspects of urban decline and vigour.[8] Therefore the evidence by which towns are said to grow or contract is extremely varied and, in many cases, not comparable, given the limited survival of many civic records.

Of this evidence, however, the most controversial still remains the frequent

1 For an excellent review of the early debates, see Dyer, *Decline and Growth in English Towns*; and Palliser, 'Urban Decay Revisited', 1–21. For more recent work discussing this issue: Nightingale, 'Medieval York': 3–42.

2 Goddard, 'Commercial Contraction', 22–4; Kowaleski, *Medieval Exeter*, 81–93.

3 For example, Rigby, 'Boston and Urban Decline', 47–61; *Medieval Lincoln*, 251–6, 270–3, 286–8.

4 Palliser, 'Urban Decay Revisited', 16.

5 Phythian-Adams, *Desolation of a City*; Britnell, *Colchester*.

6 Dyer, *Decline and Growth in English Towns*, 53.

7 Palliser, 'Urban Decay Revisited', 3–8.

8 Goddard, 'Commercial Contraction', 22–4; Nightingale, 'Medieval York', 3–42.

'complaints of poverty made by burgesses attempting to obtain fee farm relief',[9] otherwise an annual tax paid to the crown by civic governments in return for the right of self-governance. As evidence dictates, such complaints were made most vociferously in the period between c.1430 and c.1480 when the crown remitted approximately £13,000 in relief for this payment,[10] with towns including Oxford, Cambridge and Chester successfully claiming aid, though they were by no means the only ones. Despite this, such evidence remains controversial as the remission of taxes did not necessarily reflect urban-wide decline, arguably only a downturn in traditional revenues associated with the payment,[11] a conclusion given some credence by the evidence of Beverley, for example, whose civic government sought out aid from the crown whilst simultaneously pressing ahead with its plans to build a new guildhall – hardly the actions of a bankrupt government.[12] Dyer also points out that whilst fee farm petitions seemingly point to 'extensive decline', they were often very repetitive and replete with hyperbole, being motivated by political reasons, thereby not fully reflecting reality.[13]

In spite of the often contradictory nature of evidence, a number of broad generalisations have been made regarding the payment. In particular, Palliser notes that 'reliefs and abatements' from royal taxes were invariably 'granted to decayed towns';[14] whilst R. B. Dobson, drawing upon the work of M. M. Postan, argues that complaints over payments of the fee farm actually say more about the 'vigilance of the English government' than the veracity of the petitioners, with royal fiscal concessions during the fifteenth century being 'best interpreted as a reluctant recognition of reality, an acknowledgement that any attempt to enforce payment would produce "no profit to yor [the king's] gode grace"'.[15] Whilst such assessments are indeed valid up to a point, the problem remains that for too long petitions seeking out aid have been considered in isolation, therefore not reflecting as fully as they might the urban experience in the post-plague economic environment.

It is the purpose of this chapter to pick up the baton at this point and to analyse the Pipe and Memoranda Roll accounts for the city and to consider how successful it was at paying its annual fee farm debt to the crown. Whilst it is true that this particular focus is earlier than the classic period of 'urban decline' (1420–1560), its significance lies in the fact that Lincoln has, ever since the publication of Francis Hill's *Medieval Lincoln*, been largely characterised by physical decay and contraction,

9 Rigby, 'Boston and Urban Decline', 48.

10 To reach this figure, subtract the £60,000 Dobson identifies as being remitted 'on tenths and fifteenths alone' between 1433 and 1472 from the £73,000 Palliser cites as being remitted on 'fee-farms and other tax reliefs' between 1433 and 1482. Dobson, 'Urban Decline', 275; Palliser, 'Urban Decay Revisited', 4.

11 Bridbury, 'English Provincial Towns', 4.

12 Palliser, 'Urban Decay Revisited', 5.

13 Dyer, *Decline and Growth in English Towns*, 39–41. For an example of the political link, see L. Attreed, 'The King's Interest: York's Fee Farm and the Central Government, 1482–92', *Northern History*, 17 (1987): 24–43, at 43; *idem*, 'Medieval Bureaucracy and York's Fee Farm during the Fifteenth Century', *York Historian*, 6 (1985): 24–31.

14 Palliser, 'Urban Decay Revisited', 4.

15 Dobson, 'Urban Decline', 275–6.

financial hardship and poverty in the period immediately after the Black Death,[16] a view which has largely persisted in secondary literature.[17] In so doing, this will not only shed light upon the organisation and development of civic fiscal practice in the city but will highlight how the payment was a means by which the civic government perpetuated an image of reliability, good governance and competency to the crown in an effort to justify its status as one of the king's leading towns. It will also seek to answer three broader questions: to what extent is the fee farm a useful indicator of the commercial and economic vitality of medieval boroughs? What was its relationship to the more intermittent lay subsidies? And how truthful were Lincoln's claims of urban poverty during the fourteenth and fifteenth centuries? The result will be to develop the current understanding of the fee farm payment and its centrality to civic government, all the while revealing new insights into the issue of urban decline.

The Fee Farm

The fee farm (*firma burgi*) was a fixed annual payment made to the crown by urban communities as a substitute for various dues and tallages in exchange for self-governance.[18] Whilst originally this grant served to establish certain economic rights and privileges in urban areas, over time it saw many towns achieve the right to elect their own mayor and bailiffs.[19] Typically the fee farm was drawn from the collection of rents and tolls 'levied on merchandise entering the town and sold in its markets',[20] and its origins date back to before the Conquest.[21] Whilst initially many boroughs were granted a fee farm for only a fixed period, Lincoln, alongside London, was the earliest known borough to gain a fee farm in perpetuity, as well as the earliest to be farmed by its own burgesses (1130), not the sheriff. In fact it was not until the reigns of Henry II and Richard I that perpetual fee farms became common for English towns, thereby paving the way for increased urban autonomy during the twelfth and thirteenth centuries.[22]

The value of Lincoln's fee farm was originally set at £140 before rising in 1156 to £180,[23] which saw it ranked third behind only London (£400) and Southampton (£200).[24] As such, it stood much higher than the smaller towns of Exeter (£20),

16 *Medieval Lincoln*, 251–6, 270–3, 286–8.

17 See 9–10.

18 For a basic, but at times inconsistent, reading of some of the issues presented here, see *Medieval Lincoln*, 184–5, 243, 246, 261–8.

19 For an excellent introduction to the topic, see J. Tait, *The Medieval English Borough: Studies on Its Origins and Constitutional History* (Manchester, 1968), 139–93.

20 Attreed, *The King's Towns*, 145.

21 Tait, *Medieval English Borough*, 140–8; *Medieval Lincoln*, 63.

22 Tait, *Medieval English Borough*, 184. For this development, see Reynolds, *English Medieval Towns*, chapters three–six; Miller and Hatcher, *Medieval England*, 290–322.

23 *Medieval Lincoln*, 185.

24 London's farm fluctuated between £150 and £500 throughout the twelfth and thirteenth centuries, settling at £400 by the early fourteenth. S. Reynolds, 'The Farm and Taxation of London, 1154–1216', in *idem*, *Identities and Solidarities of the Medieval Laity* (Aldershot, 1995),

Nottingham (£52), Gloucester (£65), Oxford (£58 0s 5d), Winchester (£80) and Chester (£100), and higher than the provincial towns of Norwich (£113 8s), Bristol (£80–£120) and York (£160).[25] Unlike for Bristol, Oxford and Chester, moreover, at no stage was Lincoln's fee farm ever reassessed, despite appeals for relief at the end of the fourteenth century,[26] and it is likely that had it been it would have been lowered.[27] Despite this, it seems likely that the high value of Lincoln's fee farm was the cause of some pride in the city, reflecting both its early political and economic strength and its centrality to royal finances. For example, during the reign of Henry I the civic government successfully attained a number of royal grants compelling all foreign merchants trading in Lincolnshire to come to the city and to join the merchant guild, all of whom were to pay tolls and dues as if they were citizens.[28] In 1447, too, the city described itself as the 'thrid cite … in this noble reaume', a fact possibly linked to the level of its annual payment.[29]

Irrespective of the symbolic association between the payment and the city's well-established privileges and liberties, Mark Ormrod argues that a more accurate indication of the economic strength of late medieval urban towns (c.1300 onwards) remains the value of lay subsidy payments, an intermittent tax on the moveable goods of individuals, even if this did not adequately reflect a town's overall wealth.[30] Lincoln's lay subsidy payment was, like those of other towns, fixed in 1334, where it stood for the remainder of the Middle Ages,[31] a move which effectively shifted the responsibility of payment from individual contributors to the civic government itself, an important practical development and one explored in due course. The value of Lincoln's fixed payment, £100, was presumably based upon its previous contributions – in 1327 it contributed £51 8s 6d (a twentieth) and in 1332 £91 9s 2d (a tenth) – being rounded up for ease.[32] Even so, this was considerably less than

211–28; T. Madox, *The History and Antiquities of the Exchequer of the Kings of England*, vol. 1 (London, 1769), 402.

25 Attreed, *The King's Towns*, 13, 16, 21; Holt, 'Gloucester', in Holt and Rosser, *The Medieval Town*, 154; Liddy, *War, Politics and Finance*, 62–80; J. Laughton, *Life in a Late Medieval City: Chester, 1275–1520* (Oxford, 2008), 109; Keene, *Medieval Winchester*, vol. 1, 94–8; W. H. Stevenson (ed.), *Records of the Borough of Nottingham*, vol. 1: *1155–1399* (Nottingham, 1882), 8, 22; Palliser, 'Urban Decay Revisited', 4. For a list of early boroughs paying farms up to and including the reign of Richard I, see Tait, *Medieval English Borough*, 184; for the thirteenth century: Ballard and Tait, *British Borough Charters*, 303–25.

26 Liddy, *War, Politics and Finance*, 71–80, at 80; Palliser, 'Urban Decay', 4; Laughton, *Chester*, 35, 38, 120.

27 See main text below.

28 *Medieval Lincoln*, 185–6; L. Attreed, 'Poverty, Payments, and Fiscal Policies in English Provincial Towns', in S. K. Cohn and S. A. Epstein (eds), *Portraits of Medieval and Renaissance Living* (Ann Arbor, 1996), 330; Vince, 'High Medieval Era', 166.

29 SC 8/122/6083. My thanks to Gwilym Dodd for this reference.

30 Ormrod, 'The Crown and the English Economy', 157–8; J. F. Hadwin, 'The Medieval Lay Subsidies and Economic History', *Economic History Review*, 36, 2 (1983), 201–2; J. F. Willard, *Parliamentary Taxes on Personal Property, 1290–1334* (Cambridge: Massachusetts, 1934).

31 Hadwin, 'Medieval Lay Subsidies', 201.

32 E179/135/12, 16. Lay subsidies were typically a tenth of the value of all moveable goods in towns and a fifteenth in agrarian areas. The figure for 1327 is doubled for the purposes of this discussion (£102 7s).

the fixed quotas for London (1,000 marks (£666 13s 4d)), Bristol (£220) and York (£162), demonstrating how by this date the value of Lincoln's fee farm was almost certainly out of kilter with its annual revenues (given that lay subsidies were based on population). This remains a significant point which offers vital context to many of the developments discussed below.

Responsibility for the payment of the fee farm fell to the bailiffs, though they were originally termed 'provosts' in a charter dated 1194, the earliest surviving municipal document mentioning the payment.[33] According to the charter it was the duty of a provost to ensure 'that the farm of the town was paid', yielding 'nine score pounds ... at our Exchequer at the two terms that is to say at Easter and at the feast of Saint Michael',[34] as was the common practice for English towns.[35] This agreement was later confirmed in royal charters dating from 1200, 1227 and 1330.[36] One notable change to this procedure, however, took place during the middle decades of the fourteenth century when the city's bailiffs began to delegate the responsibility of making the payment at the Exchequer to local attorneys (*attornatus*). For example, the Pipe Rolls record the names of the following Lincoln attorneys: John de Keleby (1348/49), Roger Gunneys (1349/50) and William Wyum (1359/60);[37] whilst the Memoranda Rolls record William Alisaundre (1342/43), Adam de Merston (1345/46) and Ralph Thresk (1355/56).[38] Such evidence not only contests Francis Hill's observation that it was only during the second half of the fifteenth century that lawyers and attorneys began to represent the city in an official capacity,[39] but also indicates that an increasingly professional attitude towards civic financial affairs began to emerge around this time.

Much like the payment of the fee farm, the physical collection of monies also fell to the bailiffs and their deputies, who, in 1267, saw monies drawn from the 'tronage of the liberty of Lincoln in the fair of Boston' and 'stalls near the bridge of Lincoln'.[40] In 1322 revenues were also recorded being raised through 'cognisance of pleas of lands and tenements within ... [the] city and suburbs ..., trespasses and contracts made there, amends of the breach of assize of bread and ale, gabel, toll, and other such customs and services and amercements arising there'.[41] Additional revenues were also recorded in the charter of Edward III in 1330, being drawn from 'infangthief, outfangthief [both of which relate to the right to hang thieves] and the chattels of felons and fugitives within the said city',[42] as well as from the city's annual fair, which ran from the feast of Saint Botolph (17 June) until the feast of

33 For an earlier ecclesiastical charter see the main text below: Tait, *Medieval English Borough*, 271.
34 *Royal Charters*, 5.
35 *Royal Charters*, 5; Liddy, *War, Politics and Finance*, 60–2.
36 *Royal Charters*, 7–8, 11, 58.
37 E 372/194, rot. 16; E 372/195, rot. 15; E 372/205, rot. 15.
38 E 368/115, rot. 1; E 368/118, rot. 7; E 368/128, rot. 6.
39 *Medieval Lincoln*, 279–80.
40 *CPR, 1266–72*, 270; *Royal Charters*, 50.
41 *CPR, 1321–24*, 150–1. For these customs, see table 1.
42 *Royal Charters*, 55.

the Apostles Peter and Paul (29 June).[43] Individuals also found guilty of breaching the *Constituciones Civitatis Lincolnie* (c.1291/92) – otherwise ordinances for the wool trade – were liable to forfeit their goods to the fee farm.[44]

Another reliable source of revenue came from a payment known as *landtolpeny*, an annual tax of 1d on all lands or tenements 'held of the king as parcel of the city'.[45] In 1297/98 this raised exactly 60s, the equivalent of 720 properties,[46] though this figure did not include money owed by the Dean and Chapter, whose properties within the city contributed 5s 3d in 1319.[47] Finally, monies for the farm were raised through 'certain rents' (*certi redditus*), which averaged £9 8s in the 1290s.[48] Of course, it is likely that many of these revenues were established much earlier than the dates cited here, though they remain the earliest examples of them.[49]

In addition to fixed revenues, temporary measures were also employed, such as in October 1339 when tolls were ordered to be collected from Docdyke until the following Michaelmas (29 September).[50] Docdyke, or Dogdyke, was the part of the river Witham that was joined by the rivers Bain and Slea, lying some fifteen miles south-east of Lincoln, which controlled access to the city by ship,[51] thus highlighting how far civic authority could reach.[52] The temporary nature of this payment can be confirmed by earlier and later instructions in 1265 and 1375.[53]

The significance of this lengthy list of collection practices was that it required a large and organised municipal administration to manage it effectively. This can be seen through the appointment of collectors, also known as keepers (*custodes*), who worked for the city's bailiffs, some of whom are known by name having been recorded in the margins of the *Blickling Homilies*, one of the city's surviving civic registers.[54] In c.1350, for example, Robert Chapman was named as keeper of the keys (*clavium*) of *westbarregate*, along with William de Wallyngton for *neulandgate* and William de Jelund for *le posternel iuxta estbarrgate*, three fixed entry points into the city.[55] Interestingly, however, when these details are set alongside earlier evidence it is clear that

43 *Royal Charters*, 54.
44 *Royal Charters*, 34–7. For more on the *Constituciones*, see 75–8.
45 *CPR, 1367–70*, 247.
46 E 101/505/24, m. 1. Note for comparison that in 1525 revenues for *landtol* stood at 24s: LAO L/1/1/1, fo. 186v.
47 Recorded under the heading *redditus resoluti*: LAO, Bj 2/6/2, fo. 63v. For a later payment at this rate (1394): LAO, Bj 2/8, fo. 115. This amount was consistent throughout the century.
48 See table 9 for references.
49 For earlier less detailed references to the farm, see *Royal Charters*, 5, 7–8, 11. See also *CPR, 1216–25*, 518, for a list of tolls contributing to the fortification of the city (*ville Lincolnie claudende*). Masschaele, 'Tolls and Trade', 146–83.
50 *BB*, fo. 142.
51 *Medieval Lincoln*, 215–16.
52 For similar tolls, purportedly collected illegally, during the thirteenth century at Dunham and Torksey, see *Rot. Hund.*, 320.
53 E 159/39, rot. 5d; KB 29/28, m. 33. Note that tolls collected at Dogdyke were traditionally owed to the Honour of Richmond: KB 29/28, m. 33.
54 See 135–7.
55 *BH*, fo. 39. This date is based on the fact that Robert Chapman appeared on the jury of assize in 1352/53 and was named in a plea of *writ de recto* in 1351: JUST 1/523, m. 15; *BB*, fo. 215v.

the city's toll points actually changed over time, with *Le Barregate*, *Loufemarket* and *Claxedgate* all being noted in 1294 and 1298, for example.[56] Further evidence of this comes from the fact that a messuage named 'la tolboothe' located in the parish of St Peter at Arches was noted in 1297 as the domicile of Robert de Brughton and his wife Alice.[57] It thus seems likely that changes were made to the process of collection in the hope of establishing a more efficient means of raising revenues.

Despite the considerable time and effort expended on the collection of the fee farm, it was, as Christian Liddy notes, a common practice for 'very little of the revenue owing from a town's fee farm that could have been paid directly to the king's Exchequer to reach the crown'.[58] This was due primarily to the fact that the king drew upon these revenues as a means of patronage for crown servants, religious institutions and members of the royal family, thereby creating something known as an 'assignment'.[59] Such practices can be seen at Bristol, for example, where from 1275 the city's fee farm was assigned in its 'entirety to successive queens' as part of their dower;[60] in Exeter from 1337 when the full cost of its farm was granted to Edward, the Black Prince, as duke of Cornwall;[61] and in York where, by 1351, it was split amongst three separate assignees.[62] Lincoln was in this regard no different, and by the mid-1340s the full cost of the fee farm (£180) was accounted for by four separate assignments.[63]

The earliest of these was recorded in a charter dating from the reign of King Stephen (c.1140–47) and was one of two assignments established by the crown for pious reasons. According to the charter, the king ordered that a tenth of the fee farm (£14 as it was then) be granted to Alexander, bishop of Lincoln, on behalf of the mother church (the cathedral) as tithe.[64] When the fee farm increased to £180 in 1156, the tithe increased accordingly to £18, where it remained until the remission of the payment in the sixteenth century.[65] The second pious assignment was for the relatively small sum of £2, which was granted towards the sustenance of a chaplain performing mass at the chantry of Edward II and Isabella founded in the cathedral in 1316.[66]

The two remaining assignments can be identified as pre-payments or rewards to individuals providing support to the crown during the Anglo-Scottish wars, the largest of which was made to the Roos family of Helmsley in return for their castle

56 E 101/505/24, m. 1; E 101/505/28, m. 1; E 372/140, rot. 3d; E 372/144, rot. 10d.

57 LAO Dij 80/3/34, 71.

58 Liddy, *War, Politics and Finance*, 60–3, at 61.

59 A. Steel, 'The Practice of the Assignment in the Later Fourteenth Century', *Economic History Review*, 43, 170 (1928), 172–3.

60 Liddy, *War, Politics and Finance*, 62.

61 Kowaleski, *Medieval Exeter*, 62.

62 Liddy, *War, Politics and Finance*, 61.

63 For earlier temporary assignments, see, for example, *CLR, 1260–7*, 181, 195, 206, 219, 249, 263, 269, 286, 296.

64 *Reg. Antiq.*, vol. 1, no. 88.

65 J. Hunter (ed.), *The Great Rolls of the Pipe for the Second, Third, and Fourth Years of the Reign of King Henry the Second, A.D. 1155, 1156, 1157, 1158* (London, 1844), 28; Hill, *Tudor and Stuart Lincoln*, 73.

66 *CPR, 1313–17*, 398.

at Wark-on-Tweed in 1317.[67] Whilst originally this payment stood at £146 13s 4d before being lowered to £100 in 1322,[68] where it remained for much of the fourteenth century, its value frequently fluctuated upwards (£147) and downwards (£50) depending on the will of the king, notably returning to the higher value after 1383, a point discussed in greater detail below.[69]

The final assignment was valued at £60 and was granted to Bartholomew de Burghersh, brother of the former bishop of Lincoln, Henry, in lieu of certain lands promised to him by the king after his role at the siege of Berwick in 1344.[70] Of this money, ten marks were alienated to the cathedral. In 1345, however, this figure rose to £47, with the extra monies being used to augment the newly instituted Burghersh chantry.[71] The following year the remaining £13 was granted to the Dean and Chapter, with the money being spent on the daily feeding and clothing of the poor (*cotidie victu vestitu et calciata*).[72] In all, the four assignments (£18, £2, £100 and £60) totalled £180, the exact value of the fee farm, a reality which left no room for error whatsoever in its collection. Yet, how successful was the city in raising these funds?

The following analysis (table 13) offers a sample of the payments listed in the Pipe Rolls during the fourteenth century, accounts otherwise recording the 'routine annual audit process' of the Exchequer.[73] Listed in chronological order, the evidence is divided by five-year intervals, except where noted. The analysis records the value of the fee farm raised, the total cost of the permanent assignments and the values of debt owed by the city on the payment. The latter is divided into two separate columns. The first of these ('debt recorded') outlines the fictional level of debt recorded in the Pipe Rolls noted under the heading *Corpus Comitatus*. Such debts did not take into consideration the value of the permanent assignments, excepting the tenth granted to the church, hence the need for the second column ('real level of debt'), which adjusts this value by the number of permanent assignments paid in a given year as recorded under the heading *Nova Oblata*.[74]

An example of this accounting process can be seen from an entry dated 1359/60, which records under the heading *Corpus Comitatus* that the *Cives Linc'* owed £180 from *de firma civitatis*. However, despite there being no monies paid into the Exchequer (*In thesauro nichil*), it was nevertheless acknowledged that the tithe of £18 owing to the cathedral had been paid (*Et in decima constituta canonicis beate*

67 *CPR, 1317–21*, 29. The assignment to Roos was shared by York though it was held by Bartholomew de Burghersh between 1343 and 1350 following the death of William de Roos: Liddy, *War, Politics and Finance*, 61; *CPR, 1343–45*, 126; *CCR, 1349–54*, 187.

68 *CCR, 1318–23*, 609.

69 For example, *CPR, 1317–21*, 29; *1318–23*, 18, 264; *CCR, 1323–27*, 95–6, 230–1.

70 *CPR, 1343–45*, 255.

71 *CPR, 1343–45*, 381. See also 163.

72 E 372/205 rot. 15; *CPR, 1345–48*, 141.

73 For an overview, see R. Cassidy, '*Recorda splendidissima*: the Use of Pipe Rolls in the Thirteenth Century', *Historical Research*, 85, 227 (2012): 1–12, at 2; C. A. F. Meekings, 'The Pipe Roll Order of 12 February 1270', in J. Conway Davies (ed.), *Studies Presented to Hilary Jenkinson* (Oxford, 1957), 222–53; *Introduction to the Study of the Pipe Rolls* (London, 1884), 35–52.

74 Debts under this heading were conventionalised by 1198–99, with minor interruption during the 1260s following the Barons' War: Meekings, 'The Pipe Roll Order', 238–41.

Table 13 Sample evidence of fee farm debts and payments from the Pipe Rolls (1299–1400)

Year	Fee farm paid (£180)	Assignments/tithe	Debt recorded	Real level of debt	Sources
1299/1300	£131 18s 10½d	1 mark/£18	16s 6d	16s 6d	E 372/145, rot. 16d
1305/06*	£162	1 mark/£18	£162	£0	E 372/151, rots 1–1d
1309/10	£202	–/£18	40s	£0	E 372/155b, rots 22d–23
1314/15	£115 12s 11d	£14^/£18	£46 7s 1d	£32 7s 1d	E 372/160, rots 16, 17d
1319/20	£19 9s 8d	£147/£18	£142 10s 4d	£0‡	E 372/165, rots 14, 15
1324/25	£40	£100/£18	£122	£22	E 372/170, rots 37–37d
1329/30	£56	£100/£18	£106	£0	E 372/175, rots 35, 36
1334/35	£91	£204/£36	£233	£0	E 372/180, rots 31, 32d
1340/41*	£120 5s 2d	£204/£36	£263 4s 10d	£0	E 372/185, rots 31, 32
1344/45	£0	£162/£18	£162	£0	E 372/190, rots 13, 14
1349/50	£0	£162/£18	£162	£0	E 372/195, rots 14, 15
1354/55	£0	£162/£18	£162	£0	E 372/200, rots 14, 15
1359/60	£0	£162/£18	£162	£0	E 372/205, rots 14, 15
1364/65	£0	£162/£18	£162	£0	E 372/210, rots 16, 17
1369/70	£0	£160/£18	£162	£0 (+£2)#	E 372/215, rots 15, 16
1374/75	£0	£162/£18	£162	£0 (+£2)#	E 372/220, rots 15, 16d
1379/80	£0	£162/£18	£162	£0	E 372/225, rots 17, 18
1384/85	£0	£208 13s 4d/£18	£162	£0‡	E 372/230, rots 22, 23
1389/90	£0	£208 13s 4d/£18	£162	£0‡	E 372/235, rots 23, 24
1394/95	£0	£208 13s 4d/£18	£162	£0‡	E 372/240, rots 19, 20
1399/1400	£0	£208 13s 4d/£18	£162	£0‡	E 372/245, rots 23–23d

Key: * = returns for previous year damaged or missing; ^ = money for archers and a *vintener* (commander of soldiers) sent to defend the town of Berwick; # = positive values indicate that assignees were not paid by the civic government; ‡ = the debt to the crown is zero but the value of assignments is greater than the value of the farm *marie Lincolni xviij li de hoc anno xxxiiij sicut allocatum est in rotulis precedentibus*), thus leaving a 'fictional debt' of £162 (*Et debent clxii li*). Noted beside this information were several other payments known as *minuta firma* which related to various monies owed by individuals or groups for properties or privileges held directly from the king, including, for example, the city's weavers (*telarii*) who paid £6 every year to maintain certain trading rights.[75] Whilst the *minuta firma* are not dealt with here, their significance lies in the fact that they are included under the heading *Nova Oblata*, where the direct assignments from the fee farm were recorded, all of which must be disentangled to reveal the true extent of the accounts. As such it is possible to identify how in 1359/60 the civic government made its payments to the Dean and Chapter on behalf of Bartholomew de Burghersh (£47 plus £13 *residuas*); to John Cole, vicar of the chantry of Edward II (£2); and to Thomas de Roos (150 marks, the equivalent of £100) through his general attorney John de Codyngton, thereby fulfilling its obligations – hence the entry at the bottom of the rotulet stating *et quieti sunt* ('and they are quit'). Whilst this entry is admittedly one of the more straightforward, it serves to highlight the problem of fictional debts recorded in the *Corpus Comitatus* whilst simultaneously providing a rudimentary overview of the accounting process at this time.

As the sample demonstrates, over the course of the fourteenth century the monies raised for the fee farm were typically sufficient to pay the permanent (and temporary)[76] assignments drawn from it, underlining how the civic government dealt with its obligations quickly and effectively, whilst providing financial support to individuals and institutions patronised by the crown. It also demonstrates how trade in and out of the city continued at a level sufficient to support the financial burden of the fee farm during the century, a point at odds with the claims of poverty by the civic government. Such careful management was not uncommon and the evidence for Lincoln reflects well the wider urban experience during this period, with towns and cities making the majority of their payments in full and on time.[77] Nonetheless, whilst the sample presented here is useful in providing broad generalisations it is limited in its scope, ignoring more qualitative aspects of the fee farm, its collection and payment. The sample evidence is also curious in that, with the exception of three years (1299/1300, 1314/15 and 1324/25), very few debts are recorded, whereas in reality there were twenty in the first fifty years of the century. As such, it is important to consider these issues in greater detail before offering any firmer conclusions.

75 *Medieval Lincoln*, 326–7; *CIM, 1219–1307*, 353, no. 1202.

76 For example, in 1312/13 a one-off payment of £200 was granted towards the extension of the hospital of Queen Isabella, whilst in 1290/91 £5 was given to the cathedral for repairs: E 372/158, rot. 13; C 62/67, m. 3.

77 Attreed, *The King's Towns*, 161.

Payments and Relationships

One useful means of doing so is by comparing the debts entered into the Pipe Rolls to the intermittent payments recorded in the Lord Treasurer's Remembrancer's Memoranda Rolls (E 368).[78] According to Thomas Madox, the Memoranda Rolls detail payments relating to 'the King's Writs or Precepts of many kinds, concerning revenue, tenures and other matters agitated in the Exchequer, commissions of bailiwicks, custodies, [and] farms etc. …'.[79] In theory, therefore, this should result in short payments recorded in the Pipe Rolls being offset by those in the Memoranda Rolls (though this was not necessarily the case),[80] whilst simultaneously providing some insight into the claims of assignees regarding late or absent payments (figures 5–6).[81]

Before proceeding, however, it is important to clarify that it has been necessary to narrow the chronological focus for this comparative analysis to the first fifty years of the century (1299/1300–1349/50) due to the fact that after 1344, when all monies raised for the fee farm had been set aside for the four permanent assignments, references to the fee farm in the Memoranda Rolls become increasingly uncommon, thereby making it difficult to offer any further comparisons.

There were considerable debts recorded in the Pipe Rolls during the first fifty years of the fourteenth century (figure 5), all of which totalled roughly £974. This money was real debt owed to the crown as all temporary and permanent assignments noted in the accounts have been accounted for (as per 'real level of debt' in table 13). The average value of these debts was roughly £20 per annum or the equivalent to one ninth of the fee farm payment, though this does not offer a true reflection of the fluctuating nature of the debt, with only twenty of the fifty years recording debts. As the evidence shows, the frequency of the recorded arrears, typically prefixed by the phrase *et debet*, if not necessarily its value, decreased commensurately with the rise in the cost of the permanent assignments, ceasing altogether by the early 1330s. The significance of this was that as less money was paid directly into the Exchequer – with monies being paid directly to assignees – fewer opportunities arose for arrears to accumulate. Hence going forward any short payments recorded were held against the value of the permanent assignments, not the crown. This served not only to

78 Note that the King's Remembrancer's Memoranda Rolls (E 159), which were recorded at the same time, are not dealt with here. For their differences, see J. Conway Davies, 'The Memoranda Rolls of the Exchequer to 1307', in *idem*, *Studies Presented*, 105.

79 Madox, *Exchequer*, vol. 2, 115.

80 The Pipe Rolls seldom record cumulative arrears, only those outstanding from the current financial year, hence being entered under the heading *Novo Oblata*, not *De Oblatis*. During the period 1299/1300–1349/50 there were only three counts of arrears carried over to the following year's accounts, one of which was in 1336/37 when there were arrears of £60 (E 372/182, rot. 27d). This was offset by a surplus of £60 in the following year's accounts (E 372/183, rot. 42d). The remaining two arrears are dealt with in the main text. None are included in figure 5.

81 These payments are drawn from under the heading *Adventus vicecomitum*. For an overview of these rolls, see Conway Davies, 'The Memoranda Rolls', 108–17. See also J. F. Lydon, 'Survey of the Memoranda Rolls of the Irish Exchequer, 1294–1509', *Analecta Hibernica*, 23 (1966): 51–74.

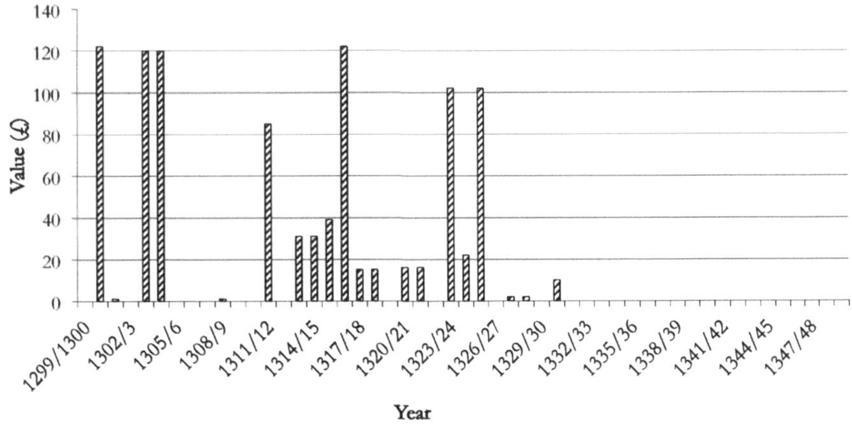

Figure 5 Fee farm arrears recorded in the Pipe Rolls (1299/1300–1349/50)
Source: E 372

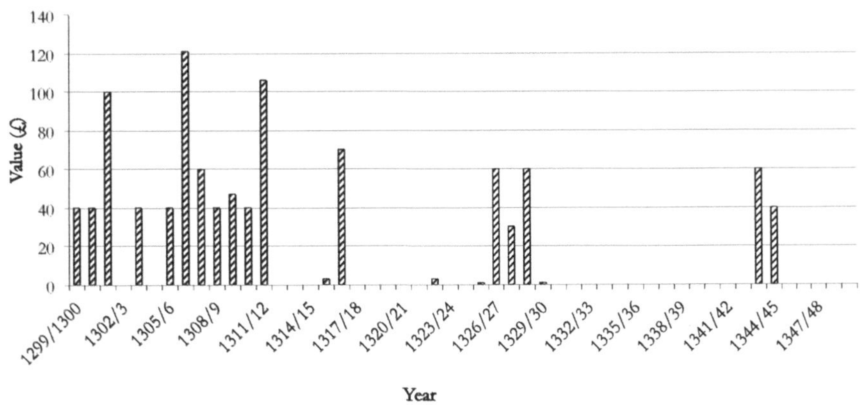

Figure 6 Additional fee farm payments recorded in the Memoranda Rolls (1299/1300–1349/50)
Source: E 368

establish a strong fiscal relationship between the civic government and the assignees but was successful in removing the burden of direct patronage from the crown to a third party. In fiscal terms this could be seen as a masterstroke of medieval administrative practice because in the long term it actually served to raise crown revenues, albeit indirectly, as complaints regarding the forfeiture or non-payment of these monies were invariably dealt with by the royal courts, usually by way of petition, all of which came at a cost to the supplicants.

Despite the value of these debts owed to the crown during this period, evidence suggests that they were nonetheless offset by additional payments recorded in the Memoranda Rolls (figure 6), all of which totalled roughly £1,002. The average of these payments was approximately £21 per annum, slightly higher than the recorded mean debt. These were recorded in twenty-one of the fifty years. Like the Pipe Rolls, this additional money was paid either at Easter or Michaelmas.

In the broadest sense, this evidence highlights three main points. The first is that the civic government was loyal to the demands of the crown, paying off its outstanding debts, if not always on time. This served to justify its ability to rule in the king's name, a significant fact given that the city's liberties had been confiscated at least three times in the thirteenth century amid claims of financial irregularities and abuse of power by civic leaders.[82] This also offers some explanation as to why the civic government was keen to conceal late payments (see below) and why it quickly paid off two substantial debts totalling £1,121 which had accumulated during the years of the suspension (1289–99),[83] with all but three years of payments being postponed (*respectus*) by the king.[84] That these debts were made personally by Stephen de Stanham in 1300/01 (as bailiff) and 1301/02 (as mayor) highlights a real concern by the civic government over its re-established fiscal relationship with the crown at this time:[85] he was only one of three mayors during the entire fourteenth century to do so personally. The two others were Alexander FitzMartin and John de Amecotes, who were noted (but not named) in 1306/07 and 1308/09, respectively, again highlighting the ongoing concern over the reorganisation and control of civic finances in the opening decade of the fourteenth century.[86] It seems likely, therefore, that the full repayment of these debts was a precondition for the restoration of the city's liberties in 1299, which was followed by a new civic charter in 1301.[87]

Of course, it is important to stress that the confiscation of urban liberties was by no means unusual during the reigns of Henry III and Edward I, though as Susan Reynolds remarks, it became increasingly uncommon from the fourteenth century onwards as towns and cities found more effective ways of maintaining political control, in particular through the comprehensive recording of local ordinances designed to minimise abuses, for example.[88] Even so, the threat of suspension lingered long in the memory and in 1338 the king warned the mayor and bailiffs to

82 C 60/11, m. 12 (1218); C 60/64, m. 2; *CCR, 1264–68*, 348 (1267); for the suspension dating from 1289, see chapter four.

83 See 126–8.

84 Farms were nevertheless collected in 1289/90, 1294/95 and 1298/99 during the suspension of liberties though they were not entirely successful, raising less than £180: E 372/135, rot. 17d (£169 14s 11½d); E 372/140, rot. 3d (£164 4s 8d); E 372/144, rot. 10d (£169 12s 3d); E 101/505/24, 28. For a similar failed experiment at Bristol in 1369/70, see Liddy, *War, Politics and Finance*, 72–80. For similarly accrued debts at Norwich, see Attreed, 'Poverty, Payments', 331, n. 11.

85 £81 was re-paid in 1300/01 and £40 in 1301/02: E 372/146, rot. 15; E 372/147, rot. 12.

86 E 372/152a, rot. 1; E 372/154 rot. 19.

87 *Royal Charters*, 18–27. The charter came at the cost of £400 towards the subsidy of 1301. The remission of the fee farm noted in the Patent Rolls of that year did not take place. *CPR, 1292–1301*, 605; E 372/147, rot. 11.

88 Reynolds, *English Medieval Towns*, 112–13.

show 'diligence in the safe-guarding of that city and its suburbs, and the preservation of the peace there' or once again forfeit the city into his hands,[89] whilst in 1351 in the foundation charter to his perpetual chantry in the parish church of St Benedict, the former mayor Robert de Dalderby recorded that it was the duty of 'the mayor of Lincoln or the keeper (*custos*) of the city if such there be' to present a suitable chaplain to the bishop on his behalf after his death.[90] Finally, despite lying within the independent jurisdiction of the Bail, between 1322 and 1331 Lincoln castle was taken into the king's hands initially by Roger Bretoun from Alesia de Lacy, whereupon a small garrison was installed, before passing through the hands of William Fraunk and Matthew Broun, something which would not have gone unnoticed by the mayor and civic officials.[91] The significance of these measures was that the civic government remained diligent in the repayment of its debts as future forfeitures would have dealt a severe blow to the prestige of the citizens and their ability to rule effectively. When this is set alongside the seriousness with which it accepted the king's demands (i.e. through the payment of a substantial fine and the restitution of monies not paid during the years of the suspension),[92] it signifies how Lincoln's civic government was ready and able to take up the organisation and management of civic affairs once again. This reflected not only upon the abilities of officials such as Stanham, FitzMartin and Amecotes, but also the new civic identity which had been established in the wake of this decision, as seen by the introduction of new procedures and reforms, many of which were written down for the first time.[93]

The second point to make is that the monies raised for the fee farm were not always ready for delivery to the Exchequer on the required dates for one of two reasons: first, delays in transportation; and second, the full amount had not been raised. Whilst there is no direct evidence of the former for late fee farm monies, that in 1322 the collectors of a tenth and a sixth in Lindsey complained they were unable to transfer £600 stored at Lincoln castle due to the perceived dangers of the road[94] offers some explanation for the absence of any returns in the Pipe Rolls for the city or the county in seven years between 1300 and 1350.[95] In each case, however, double payments were made in subsequent years.[96] This is not to suggest that poor civic organisation and administration were to blame. On the contrary, there was a robust system in place to ensure that payments were made as safely and efficiently

89 *CCR, 1337–39*, 453. For later threats: *CCR, 1396–99*, 517. For similar concerns by Londoners: Miller and Hatcher, *Medieval England*, 319–20.

90 *Chantry Certificates*, 200.

91 Whilst this was instituted initially for only three months due to the growing fears of an invasion by Dutch and German mercenaries led by Roger Mortimer, the king kept hold of the castle and the revenues of the castle for almost ten years: *CFR, 1319–27*, 101, 119; *1327–37*, 12; *CCR, 1323–27*, 28, 81; P. Chaplais (ed.), *The War of Saint-Sardos (1323–1325)* (London, 1954), 58–9, 72, nos 43–4, 54.

92 For example, in 1297 a one-off payment of £400, identified as a 'donation', was made: E 372/154, rot. 18.

93 See 128.

94 *Medieval Lincoln*, 306.

95 1307/08, 1310/11, 1331/32, 1333/34, 1335/36, 1339/40 and 1347/48.

96 See, for example, E 372/154, rot. 19; E 372/178, rot. 30.

as possible, it being stated in the royal charter of 1330, for example, that payments were to be returned alongside those of the county sheriff, thus ensuring that civic officials did not travel alone.[97] Moreover, beyond the highly organised and presumably armed journeys with the sheriff, different officials were also tasked with making specific payments to the Exchequer. For example, in 1342/43 the Pipe Rolls note that Adam de Merston, attorney, made the city's annual returns,[98] whilst the Memoranda Rolls record that an additional £60 was paid into the Exchequer by Stephen Russell, bailiff, relating to the previous year's arrears.[99] This was not an isolated case as evidence from other years demonstrates, and in 1309/10 Richard Blakeden (bailiff) and John de Castello (position unknown) were noted in the Memoranda and Pipe Rolls respectively;[100] in 1328/29 Hugh de Edelyngton (bailiff) and William le Chauntereneue (bailiff) were similarly noted;[101] and in 1342/43 William Alisaundre (attorney) and Roger de Boterwyk (bailiff) were listed.[102] This pattern was also followed in years when no additional payments or arrears were made, with officials being required to attend the Exchequer despite having nothing to declare; entries recorded in the Memoranda Rolls in these years typically read *Nichil tulit nisi brevia*.[103] Overall, at least two different officials were recorded in thirty of the thirty-nine years for which individual names can be identified.[104] Once again this reflected well upon the civic administration and it is not unreasonable to assume that Exchequer clerks were not above gossiping to their fellow colleagues (and superiors) when individuals or institutions ran into debt. Hence whilst it is clear that monies could not always be returned, negligence itself was not a problem, given that the county issues were also missing.

This evidence demonstrates how by at least the second decade of the fourteenth century there had developed a robust administrative practice at both local and national level. It is likely that these fiscal policies emerged as part of the civic reforms reflected in the *Provisions for the Government of the City* (c.1300) following the restitution of civil liberties, which stated that four men were to be elected to maintain the city's accounts, and 'that they [are to] have one chest and four keys; And that they shall render up the account to the city at the end of the year.'[105] It is likely that between 1316/17 and 1321/22, when only Roger de Totel was named as the city's official in the Pipe Rolls, or between 1343/44 and 1346/47, when only Adam de Merston, attorney, performed this role, that both of these men were one of the keepers of the

97 *Royal Charters*, 56–8.

98 E 372/189, rot. 19. Note that Merston is identified incorrectly as a bailiff. See, for example, E 368/121, rot. 1; E 368/122, rot. 2; E 368/123, rot. 4.

99 Out of £61. E 368/116, rot. 2. Note that this payment was not matched by a shortage in the Pipe Rolls in this year. See main text above for a discussion of this issue.

100 E 368/80, rot. 1; E 372/155B, rot. 23; *BB*, fo. 199.

101 E 368/101, rot. 2; E 372/174, rot. 29d.

102 E 368/115, rot. 1; E 372/188, rot. 17.

103 For example, compare E 372/166, rot. 13 to E 368/91, rot. 4 (1320/21) or E 372/178, rot. 30 with E 368/105, rot. 2 (1332/33).

104 In eleven years, the Pipe Rolls record simply 'mayor and bailiffs', 'bailiffs' or made no returns at all.

105 *Medieval Lincoln*, 403. See also 128.

chest.[106] Over time, as already identified, this development saw the introduction of attorneys being delegated the responsibility of collating the civic accounts and returning the collected fee farm monies to the Exchequer in place of the bailiffs.[107]

The third, and perhaps most obvious, conclusion to draw from the evidence is that in chronological terms the arrears and supplementary payments recorded in the Pipe and Memoranda Rolls do not match up. Whilst it might seem logical to assume that the £362 of arrears noted in the opening years of the fourteenth century (1301/02–1305/06) were repaid over the following few years at a slower rate, perhaps until 1308/09, this does not suitably explain why additional monies were then recorded in the Memoranda Rolls following their repayment. Furthermore, why were debts noted between 1314 and 1321 seemingly not repaid and why was extra money accounted for during the mid-1340s? These remain important questions, especially if a fuller understanding of the civic government's motives and attitudes towards the crown and the assignees are to be gleaned. As such, only one likely explanation presents itself: the accounts are, in one way or another, falsified.

Take as a case in point the episode involving William de Roos who, in 1323, was recorded as being owed debts of £315, which had accumulated over the five previous years.[108] Notwithstanding the fact that the money was owed in the first place, the significance of this debt is that prior to this date the Pipe Rolls can be identified as containing false information. Certainly, these debts must relate to the years from 1317 until 1322, as the Roos assignment was only instituted in 1317, during which time a reported £732 6s 8d had been paid to William.[109] However, given that there were arrears of £315 recorded in 1323 it becomes clear that this cannot have been the case, with over two fifths of the money still owing. Whether or not Roos complained about the arrears is unknown. Certainly no petition survives, though it is likely, given his later actions when money was outstanding.[110] Such evidence demonstrates how the city's officials not only misled the Exchequer clerks compiling the Pipe Rolls – especially as the money was paid directly to William – but also temporarily reneged on their duties to the crown.[111] It is likely that this subterfuge was a means to disguise the failure of the city's officials to pay off the debt, all the while maintaining an image of competency to the crown.

Despite this apparent 'fraud', it is important to stress that such administrative sleight of hand was not unknown in other towns and Lincoln's officials should not

106 E 372/162, rot. 37d; E 372/163, rot. 32; E 372/164, rot. 22; E 372/165 rot. 15; E 372/166, rot. 13; E 372/167, rot. 27; E 372/189, rot. 19; E 372/190, rot. 14; E 372/191, rot. 17; E 372/192, rot. 31.

107 See above, 97. In 1409 the keepers of the chest were described as 'treasurers' for the first time, following the granting of shire status: *CPR, 1408–13*, 137; *Medieval Lincoln*, 270–1.

108 There were five separate debts recorded in the account for 1323: E 372/168, rot. 30d.

109 He was reportedly paid £146 13s 4d in 1317/18 and 1318/19, £147 in 1319/20 and £146 in 1320/21 and 1321/22: E 372/163, rot. 32; E 372/164, rot. 22; E 372/165 rot. 15; E 372/166, rot. 12; E 372/167, rot. 27.

110 See main text below.

111 Compare this to 1377 when the city was quick to assure the king that it would pay £62 of arrears to the Dean and Chapter from a debt dating from 1373/74: *CCR, 1377–81*, 19, 32; E 372/219, rot. 20. For the petition of complaint: SC 8/85/4237.

be considered as any more corrupt than officials elsewhere.[112] In fact numerous royal and civic officials can be identified as presenting falsified accounts for a variety of different reasons, all of which were linked to local issues. For example, Jeremy Goldberg highlights how in York in 1381 tax collectors actually performed a benevolent type of fraud by ascribing money contributed by wealthy individuals to families in poorer parishes who were otherwise unable to pay.[113] Elsewhere, Stephen Rigby has argued that the lack of evidence of smuggling in the accounts of the staple port of Boston during the reign of Richard II points, however tentatively, to the 'excessive favour' of customs officials towards local merchants, meaning that they were actually given tacit permission to transport more goods than they were taxed on, possibly at a time of growing economic hardship.[114] Finally Eleanora Carus-Wilson argues that in the 1460s and 1470s the aulnage (cloth) accounts of Bristol, Wiltshire, Somerset and Dorset were either falsified or made up entirely, with the same names and payments appearing on list after list, year after year, thus offering no semblance to reality. Whilst the logic behind this 'fraud' is not certain, it is possible, as Carus-Wilson suggests, that it was either for a 'love of ease, perhaps, or of gain'.[115] Of course, whether institutional gain was the primary motive for Lincoln's civic officials in the case of the fee farm is impossible to say with any certainty, though considering their subsequent behaviour over the payment it seems unlikely; it seems more probable that they were simply unable (or unwilling) to raise the money. That said, it is also important for balance to note that the civic government was not above acting for personal or institutional profit and in 1325 the city's bailiffs were accused of 'oppressing' the 'middle citizens' by levying a tax on property called 'buscage' and of extracting ransoms from those not having 'done watches ... in the highroads opposite the doors of their houses'.[116] In 1331, they were similarly accused of 'using false weights and measures ... with impunity' for their own profit, and in 1339 several civic officials were accused of extortion.[117] Whilst such complaints or disputes were, according to Reynolds, relatively common and were 'fundamentally inherent in the situation ... between taxers and taxed, rulers and ruled',[118] it nevertheless raises a paradox between the recorded abuses of civic officials at a local level on the one hand and their willingness to embrace fraudulent practices to perpetuate an image of good governance to the crown on the other. The civic government wished if not to curry favour with the crown, then at least to perpetuate an image of loyalty and competency.

A contiguous issue to the falsification of accounts is that of omission. Take, for example, an entry recorded in the Patent Rolls dating from 1330 which ordered that £66 19s 5d be granted for life to John de Warenne, earl of Surrey (which, it seems,

112 G. Dodd, 'Corruption in the Fourteenth-Century English State', *International Journal of Public Administration*, 34, 11 (2011): 720–30.

113 Goldberg, 'Urban Identity', 204–8.

114 Rigby, *Overseas Trade*, xxiv–xxviii. See also *CFR, 1337–47*, 154–5.

115 Carus-Wilson, 'Aulnage Accounts', 114–23, at 123.

116 *CPR, 1324–27*, 236; *Rot. Parl.*, vol. 1, 433.

117 *CPR, 1330–34*, 199; *CIM, 1307–49*, 294, no. 1201; McLane, *1341 Inquest*, no. 558.

118 Reynolds, *English Medieval Towns*, 134–9.

was never paid),[119] or that of 1339 which ordered £60 be paid for six years to Robert de Dalderby in lieu of two loans worth almost £250, both of which went unrecorded in the Pipe Rolls.[120] Whilst in the latter case a payment of £100 was listed as being made several years later (1341/42) to the city's mayor, who at that time was Robert de Dalderby, it is unclear whether this was done in an official capacity or as part of the repayment for the earlier loan.[121] Although it is tempting to suggest that assignments such as these offer some explanation as to why the Pipe Roll debts were not offset by supplementary payments in the Memoranda Rolls, this is in many ways insufficient – primarily because, like assignments under the heading *Novo Oblata*, they were not accounted for, thus failing to solve the considerable arrears noted during the mid-1320s, much less why they were absent altogether. Fortunately, one final option presents itself.

As the accounts make plain, the only permissible reason for the civic government not to return the full value of the fee farm (£180) to the Exchequer was by making payments directly to crown-appointed assignees.[122] Thus after 1344, when the full value of the farm had been set aside, all recorded debts were henceforth owed to the assignees, not the crown. Hence it becomes possible by identifying complaints in the Chancery Rolls, via petitions to the crown or through the repayment of debts at a later date (as in the case of Roos already noted), to identify missed or late payments. Take, for example, a second episode involving William de Roos recorded in the Close Rolls in 1333,[123] which stated that both Lincoln and York collectively owed £433 17s 1d in arrears. If roughly half of this debt was owed by Lincoln (as seems to be the case) then this would more than adequately explain why additional payments were not enrolled in the Memoranda Rolls but were recorded as debts in the Pipe Rolls in the 1320s (they were not being offset against the fictional debt). This certainly seems the most logical outcome given that no payments were made to William in 1323/24 and 1325/26 (total value £200), despite royal instruction.[124] As such, it was only once the debts owed to William had been paid off that the fictional debt recorded in the Pipe Rolls disappeared. Further confirmation of this general practice can be identified by later additional entries recorded in the Memoranda Rolls: for example, in 1391/92 £4 was paid into the Exchequer as residue for the *quia residuum firme predicte assignatur diversis* (exactly who is not stated);[125] whilst in 1395/96 40s was paid *eo quod firma eiusdem ville assignatur domino de Roos et ecclesie*

119 *CPR, 1327–30*, 517.

120 *CPR, 1338–40*, 253.

121 E 372/187 rot. 19; *BB*, fo. 149v. It is also possible that the £337 1s 7¾d remitted from the crown to Robert de Dalderby for wool forfeited to the king in 1362 is related to this outstanding debt. However, given that this was not entered onto the Pipe Rolls emphasises the limitations of the accounting process: *BB*, fo. 254.

122 See, for example, in 1355/56 and 1356/57 when the city did not pay the Roos assignment; the remainder was duly paid to the exchequer: E 372/201, rot. 16; E 372/202, rot. 17.

123 *CCR, 1333–37*, 15. Note that a similar complaint was made by his son, Thomas, in 1359 over a debt of £28: *CCR, 1354–60*, 483.

124 E 372/169, rot. 40d; E 372/171, rot. 32d; *CCR, 1323–27*, 95–6, 230–1, 406, 461, 617; E 159/103, rot. 228d.

125 E 368/164, rot. 1.

de Lincoln'.[126] In both cases the city's debts were knowingly not owed to the crown but to the assignees themselves despite being paid into the Exchequer. Once again, it is likely that this was undertaken as a means to demonstrate to the crown that, despite being late with part of the assignments, Lincoln was making good its dues.

It is clear, then, that whilst Lincoln paid its debts it did not always do so on time, although some delays were unforeseen or unavoidable. Regardless, payments of the fee farm were organised through an increasingly sophisticated administrative network of dedicated specialists, identified from c.1345 onwards as attorneys, which reflected well upon the capabilities of Lincoln's civic government. It was, of course, in the interests of the city's officials to perpetuate this image to the crown to avoid fiscal penalties, or worse, the suspension of its liberties, and to demonstrate that the city was both a reliable source of income for the crown and an institution worthy of ruling in the king's name. Occasionally, in order to maintain this image, it became necessary for the civic government to employ an administrative sleight of hand to conceal the fact that it was unable to make its payments to assignees, albeit temporarily. Whilst it is possible that in doing so there was an attempt by the officials to avoid making these payments, it is nevertheless likely that the driving factor behind this decision was the wellbeing of civil liberties, which was tied directly to the fortunes and status of many leading citizens.

Urban Decline, Civic Conflict and Renegotiation with the Crown

Whilst the preceding analysis has not sought to explain every single recorded arrears or payment it has nevertheless highlighted several aspects of the inherent complexity of urban fiscal administrative practice during the fourteenth century and some of the methods employed in the management of these issues. Building upon these foundations, this final section will draw upon a wider corpus of evidence to explore the issue of urban decline. In so doing it will consider the centrality of the fee farm to conflicts both within and without the city and its role in the renegotiation of the city's fiscal obligations to the crown during the early years of the fifteenth century.

During the fourteenth century it was not uncommon for Lincoln's civic government to claim that the revenues contributing to the fee farm were being threatened by the actions of outsiders. This was important for two reasons: first, as representatives of the city, it served to underscore the identity and authority of members of the civic government by drawing attention to their royally sanctioned rights as a chartered borough; and second, as the fee farm payment was theoretically owed to the crown, any attacks on civic revenues amounted to an attack on royal prerogative. For example, in 1342 the civic government complained that wool was being redirected out of the county by the Cistercians, Gilbertines and 'other religious of the county' to the 'impoverishment of the city of Lincoln and other market towns of the king in the county, whereby his farms and customs are fraudulently withdrawn', a

126 E 368/168, rot. 9.

complaint subsequently upheld by the crown.[127] In 1345 a petition submitted by the civic government claimed that certain 'men of the county now hinder' the citizens of Lincoln from collecting tolls 'in certain places in the county and on things coming to the city', all of which 'have been so from time whereof there is not memory',[128] and in 1349 the 'citizens of Lincoln' were successful in their attempts to halt the bailiffs of Boston from charging tolls on pesage and tronage on their wool, profits otherwise reserved for Lincoln's fee farm.[129] Finally, in 1370 two leading citizens, Walter de Kelby and John de Suttone,[130] travelled to London and 'delivered to the Mayor and Aldermen' of the city a writ forbidding its officials from unlawfully charging tolls on the goods of the citizens of Lincoln, including John de Weltone, who 'demanded restitution of the same'.[131]

Complaints of this nature were unsurprisingly not unidirectional, there being several grievances lodged against Lincoln's officials by visiting merchants, many of whom lamented that they had been charged illegal tolls.[132] These included Peter de Savoy and the Honour of Richmond in 1361 and 1374,[133] the citizens of Salisbury in 1367,[134] and Queen Anne's men of the manor of Kirton in Lindsey in 1382.[135] The earliest of these cases in particular saw the city respond by highlighting its fiscal relationship with the crown, with the bailiffs pleading 'that they cannot put themselves on the country in any inquisition without the king, because the toll belongs to the king'.[136] It should, of course, come as little surprise to learn that the civic government was keen to uphold its own rights whilst seeking to take advantage of situations to suit itself, and in many ways these complaints were far from unique,[137] with similar grievances being raised by the burgesses of Carmarthen against Worcester in c.1313, the Queen's bailiffs of Pevensey against the Cinque Ports in 1321/22 and the burgesses of Derby against Coventry in 1375/76, for example.[138]

Nonetheless, the two most pressing claims made by Lincoln's civic government were those brought in 1375 against Oliver de Barton, constable of the castle, who was accused of perpetrating civic rights pertaining 'to the office of the market', including the assizes of bread and ale, and the trial of measures and weights, as well as illegally holding a Court Baron every eight days instead of once every three weeks as was custom, to the damage of the fee farm;[139] and from c.1376 onwards against the Dean and Chapter, who were accused of illegally permitting stalls to be erected in the Close

127 *CPR, 1340–43*, 441. This was not an uncommon complaint: Lloyd, *Wool Trade*, 302.

128 *CPR, 1343–45*, 502.

129 Pesage and tronage were fees for weighing goods and wool respectively. *CIM, 1307–49*, 521, no. 2074; *CCR, 1349–54*, 75. Lincoln made a similar complaint over the merchants of Dover (c.1370–1410); it is, however, impossible to date with any certainty: SC 8/64/3158.

130 For their roles in civic office, see appendix 2.

131 R. R. Sharpe (ed.), *Calendar of Letter Books*, Letter Book G (London, 1950), 258.

132 For Lincoln's tolls and complaints against Lincoln's merchants, see chapter two.

133 *Royal Charters*, 62–7; KB 29/28, m. 33.

134 *CIM, 1348–77*, 249, no. 663.

135 *CCR, 1381–85*, 198.

136 *Royal Charters*, 65.

137 Masschaele, 'Tolls and Trade', 173–4.

138 SC 8/6/281A; SC 8/311/15527; SC 8/333/E1085.

139 KB 29/28, mm. 34–34d, 35d; *CCR, 1374–77*, 261–2.

to the detriment of the fee farm, an accusation later found to be false.[140] Whilst it is not necessary to outline the details of both cases here,[141] it is important to draw attention to the fact that both complaints persisted until the mid-1390s, escalating to acts of violence and vandalism, all of which can be seen as a consequence of the crown's excessive fiscal demands, which made it necessary for the civic government to find new sources of revenue wherever possible (see below and table 13).[142]

One means of doing so, outlined by the Dean and Chapter in 1383, was that merchants selling their wares in the Close were threatened with pain of forfeiture and imprisonment by the civic government. Anyone found to be acting 'contrary to the proclamation' would cause 'the gate of the close ... [to] be burnt'.[143] In 1390, too, Oliver de Barton claimed that the

> late servants of the said mayor and bailiffs, and certain other evildoers have lately entered the bail, broke stalls and stakes fixed for selling merchants' wares, prevented merchants from selling the same, erected other houses and buildings in the castle dykes within the bail, for which they receive rents, and have made tenants and residents therein to come to the city court for breaches of the assize of bread and ale, and levied distresses and attached persons there ...[144]

Hence both local and visiting merchants were actively 'encouraged' to trade in areas under the jurisdiction of the civic government, thereby raising revenues directly through tolls and the perquisites of the court cases involving debts between merchants.[145]

Unsurprisingly not all recorded disputes involved the civic government and other groups and there is occasional evidence for internecine strife. Take, for example, two petitions dating from c.1316/17 relating to a disagreement between John de Leycestre (bailiff 1315/16) on the one hand and Richard de Scarle and Robert de Oxenford on the other over a £30 debt owed from the city's fee farm.[146] According to Leycestre, who appeared before the mayor and commonalty,[147] the outstanding £30 was to be paid by Scarle and Oxenford in lieu of debts owed to his father, Gilbert, though

140 *CCR, 1381–85*, 56–7, 62.

141 For these disputes, see *Medieval Lincoln*, 261–8, and Verduyn, 'Revocation of Urban Peace Commissions', 108–11. However, further analysis of extant manuscript sources relating to these disputes is yet to be undertaken. These are: LAO A/4/2/8–11, 16, 19/1–2, 21; DL 41/286; KB 29/40, m. 14.

142 *CPR, 1389–92*, 220, 270, 309; *CCR, 1392–96*, 162, 189, 319, 413–14; SC 8/21/1023A, SC 8/21/1023B; *Rot. Parl.*, vol. 3, 259.

143 *CIM, 1377–88*, 200–3, no. 376.

144 *CPR, 1389–92*, 270–1.

145 Following the conclusion of this dispute, annual revenues amounting to roughly 20s were given to the city by the Dean and Chapter as part settlement. It is likely that the Burton Rents granted as part of this agreement relate to the lands used previously to support the obit of Roger de Burton: *CPR, 1389–92*, 309; *1416–22*, 45. LAO Bj 2/7, fos 79, 146; Bj 2/8, fos 18v, 60v.

146 SC 8/71/3518–19.

147 For a discussion of the term 'commonalty', see 134–5.

this was disputed by both Scarle and Oxenford, who claimed that they had been pardoned of the debt by Gilbert.[148]

A second dispute,[149] which reached the court of the Common Pleas in 1393 but actually referred to events dating from 1388, saw John Terrington and Richard Reepham (bailiffs, 1388/89) claim that the previous year's officials, Walter de Faldingworth and William Barkworth (bailiffs, 1387/88), with the aim of 'defrauding and depriving the lord king of his farm', stole the entire fee farm (£180) and 'craftily went away'. Upon discovery of this duplicity, Walter and William were quickly arrested and placed 'safely in prison' whereupon the matter was referred to court. Predictably Walter and William, as well as another man, John de Carlton (bailiff 1387/88), noted in the surviving returns, denied this through their attorney, Robert Keele, arguing that payment had been made to the Exchequer and that the 'mayor and community' had not been 'burdened' or 'prejudiced' in anyway, the result being that 'the lord king was satisfied'. However, as all three accused agreed to handling the money, they placed themselves on the judgement of the court.

Although the outcomes of both cases remain unknown,[150] they nevertheless serve to emphasise the types of disputes which might emerge between officials.[151] They also demonstrate how, prior to the granting of shire status in 1409,[152] bailiffs were personally responsible for the payment. The origins of this arrangement most likely pre-date the *Provisions for the Government of the City* (c.1300), which stated only that elected

> bailiffs shall faithfully discharge the fee farm rent of our Lord the King at the end of the year; And if they dont [*sic*] do so the mayor and commonalty shall distrain such bailiffs by their lands and chattels until the fee farm rent of our Lord the King be fully paid; And that if any damage happens to the city thro' [*sic*] default of paying the fee farm rent of our Lord the King such damage shall be made good to the city out of the chattels of the said bailiffs ...[153]

In order to minimise the potential personal liability of the payment and to ease the 'burden' on the city's bailiffs following a 'loss of trade', Francis Hill has argued that in 1378 the number of bailiffs increased from two to three.[154] This supposition is, however, incorrect for two reasons: first, Lincoln could and did pay its fee farm on an annual basis; and second, this was not the first time the city had named three

148 SC 8/71/3518; SC 8/71/3519.

149 The following is drawn from M. S. Arnold, *Select Cases of Trespass from the King's Courts, 1307–1399*, vol. 1 (London, 1985), 58–60.

150 Though in the latter case, given that the fee farm payment was made by John Venersleye, attorney, it seems likely that this case was pursued out of malice: E 372/233, rot. 23d.

151 For a detailed and unresolved case involving suicide and the reported theft of the fee farm payment by Richard de Dalby in 1382: E 13/101, m. 9. For his will: *ELW*, 43.

152 For this development, see 118.

153 *Medieval Lincoln*, 402.

154 *Medieval Lincoln*, 254; Hill, *Tudor and Stuart Lincoln*, 26; J. W. F. Hill, 'Three Lists of Mayors, Bailiffs and Sheriffs of the City of Lincoln', *AASRP*, 39, 2 (1929), 220. Compare also to York where the fee farm was not considered a burden in the fourteenth century: J. Kermode, 'Urban Decline? The Flight from Office in Late Medieval York', *Economic History Review*, New Series, 35, 2 (1982), 187–88.

bailiffs, with three and even four bailiffs being noted in several years before this date.[155] Where Hill is undoubtedly correct, however, is that from c.1378 onwards three bailiffs became the norm.[156] Although it is by no means clear exactly what instigated this change – it is possible that the revenues lost from the removal of the Staple were a factor (see below) – Hill nevertheless pursued this idea by arguing that in 1401 the *Blickling Homilies* recorded that the city's three bailiffs requested a fourth be sworn into office 'by reason of their heavy burden' (*viz.* the fee farm),[157] though he cites no reference. Nonetheless, it seems likely that the basis for his claim relates to an entry recorded on the *verso* of folio 124 of the civic register known as the *Blickling Homilies* (it being the only entry for that year), though there is no mention of the fee farm directly.[158] In actual fact, the increase in the number of bailiffs in 1401 was the result of the excessive fiscal demands placed upon the civic government by the crown, not the fee farm, which between 1383 and 1414 saw the value of assignments increase from £180 to £226 13s 4d,[159] a rise of over 25 per cent (£46 13s 4d), a decision already identified as holding serious consequences for civic harmony.

The catalyst behind the crown's decision to raise the fee farm assignments beyond the agreed figure of £180 was the Roos payment which increased from £100 to £146 13s 4d following the purchase of a licence for 100 marks by Thomas de Roos of Helmsley (*Hamelak*), cousin and heir of William Roos, from the king in March 1383; he sought to enfeoff his wife Beatrice and his progenitors of the annual assignment.[160] That such a decision was taken without any recorded consultation with the civic government demonstrates the flagrant disregard for Lincoln's finances by Richard II's advisors at this time,[161] as his demands were contrary to the rights and privileges accorded to the city in all preceding royal charters. Even so, this did not stop the civic government making the payments, possibly in the hope that they were temporary or perhaps, once again, out of the fear of having their liberties suspended,[162] though they were not altogether powerless.[163] Such a possibility had certainly been brought to the fore once again by the fact that in 1369 the staple was removed from Lincoln to Boston, an act which undoubtedly came as a blow to the prestige of the city,[164] and shortly after in 1376 it was claimed that its removal had been perpetuated through 'corrupt means'.[165] The crown, however, remained unmoved, stating only that the staple was to 'be maintained there as long as it pleases

155 See appendix 2.
156 Although only two bailiffs can be identified for 1379/80, 1389/90, 1391/92 and 1396/97: appendix 2.
157 *Medieval Lincoln*, 254–5; Hill, 'Three Lists', 232.
158 *BH*, fo. 124v.
159 E 372/229 rot. 23 (1383); E 372/260, rot. 7 (1415).
160 *CPR, 1381–85*, 236.
161 G. Dodd, 'Richard II, Fiction of Majority Rule', in C. Beem (ed.), *The Royal Minorities of Medieval and Early Modern England* (New York, 2008), 103–60.
162 Claims for the higher amount were based upon the fact that in 1377 he was promised a like amount 'for the time being' until an annuity of 400 marks was made: *CCR, 1377–81*, 17–18.
163 For possible links between civic government and guild finance, see 190.
164 *Rot. Parl.*, vol. 2, 332–3. See also 69–70.
165 C 65/30: *Rot. Parl.*, vol. 2, 332–3.

the king'. Nonetheless, after almost fifteen years of paying additional monies on the Roos assignment, the civic government decided to employ a new tactic.

The result was two petitions submitted in quick succession to parliament in 1397 and 1399,[166] both of which stressed how the city had been 'greatly ruined' by subsequent bouts of the plague, with large areas standing 'empty and uninhabited'. According to the later plaint, the problem had grown so bad that a 'third part of the farm [i.e. £60] cannot rightly be raised, and the remaining inhabitants are on the point of leaving …'.[167] Despite these dubious claims,[168] it is interesting to note that both petitions recorded that the original fee farm of £180 was too high. Of course, whilst neither stated outright – or even mentioned – the increasingly burdensome assignments which were paid directly from the fee farm, it is important to recognise that this was almost certainly a tactic to draw attention to the finances of the city, and in particular the additional payments. The most likely reason for the lack of any direct reference to this problem was that it would have been foolhardy to state outright the full extent of the crown's unreasonable demands, for fear of further penalties. As such, this explains the overall tenor of the more detailed 1399 petition which appealed directly to the king's 'special grace … so that your said city can be relieved of its great poverty, and that it be not utterly destroyed; for the honour of your crown, and by way of charity'.[169] 'Honour' in this context almost certainly meant legitimacy and constancy, and it was undoubtedly the civic government's hope that the assignments drawn from the fee farm would be restored to the original £180. Unfortunately the request for aid was dismissed, a fact which perhaps explains the unanimous resolution by the mayor's council to introduce a fourth bailiff in 1401 following the king's decision, who was tasked with sharing the burdens of office.

Despite this failure, respite was eventually granted on 22 September 1414 following an inquisition by Peter Saltby (mayor 1404/05 and 1414/15), who confirmed that Beatrice, former wife of Thomas de Roos, lord of Helmsley, had indeed held the assignment at her death.[170] Henceforth, it was to pass to Thomas earl of Dorset during the nonage of William de Roos, her son. The most unsurprising aspect of the inquisition's findings, however, was that Saltby valued the assignment at only £100, not at £146–7 as it had been during the three previous decades – an act clearly in the interests of the civic government. That this reduction was not met with any recorded opposition from the Roos family suggests that it was done with royal consent and it is likely that the crown may finally have been persuaded of the unreasonableness of its demands.[171] This idea is given credence by the fact that only a few months later (15 December 1414) the city received a new royal charter, which stated that the king was

166 SC 8/121/6033; *Rot. Parl.*, vol. 3, 438.

167 *Rot. Parl.*, vol. 3, 438.

168 See 98 above. See also 208–9 and table 23 for a discussion of rents in Lincoln, which reached their nadir in the 1430s, not the 1390s. For claims of poverty, see Attreed, *The King's Towns*, 166–8; S. Reynolds, 'Decline and Decay in Late Medieval Towns', *Urban History Yearbook* (1980): 76–8.

169 *Rot. Parl.*, vol. 3, 438.

170 E 372/260, rot. 8. Note that this was not enrolled in the Close Rolls until 1416: *CCR, 1413–19*, 230.

171 See also the Inquisition Post Mortem entry for Beatrice de Roos which notes the value only

> willing to bestow a more abundant grace in this behalf upon the same mayor and commonalty and citizens aforesaid, we have granted to them for ourselves and our heirs that although they or their ancestors, mayors and commonalty and citizens therein hitherto have not used any one or more of the liberties or quittances or any other things contained in the charters and letters aforesaid by reason of any chance arising, nevertheless they, the mayor and commonalty and citizens and their heirs and successors mayors and commonalty and citizens of that city, may from henceforth fully enjoy and use the liberties and quittances aforesaid and the rest of the other things contained in the charters and letters aforesaid … without hindrance of us or our heirs or any whomsoever of our justices, escheators, sheriffs or others bailiffs or ministers …[172]

It seems likely therefore that over the ensuing three months the civic government had successfully renegotiated its obligations to the crown. Far from merely confirming the city's 'existing rights without adding to them', as Hill saw it,[173] this new charter re-established a fiscal status quo otherwise absent for the previous thirty-one years. Further proof of the crown's clemency in this matter was that the Roos assignment never again rose above £100.[174]

Such extensive efforts by the civic government to reduce the burden of the fee farm assignments are hardly surprising given that it was in its interests to secure the economic rights of the city through a legally binding charter, a matter seemingly sidestepped five years earlier when the city was granted shire status.[175] This served to underscore Lincoln's position as one of the leading cities in the realm, all the while conferring upon it royal favour. As such, it consolidated the identity and authority of the civic government not only with regard to the town–crown axis, but in terms of the relationship with the Roos family by signifying that Lincoln could no longer be forced to pay more than that to which it was legally bound.

Despite this careful interplay between civic and royal government, it is important to recognise that the renegotiation of the city's fee farm assignments was by no means an isolated act and following a petition in 1426,[176] which requested that the civic government be granted the right to purchase lands valued at £120 per annum to help pay for various charges due from the city including the fee farm (£180) and the otherwise intermittent royal subsidies (£100),[177] the subsidies of 1434, 1436, 1437, 1441, 1445, 1446, 1449, 1453, 1465, 1472[178] and 1482[179] were either remitted in part or in full. Whilst in some quarters this has been seen solely as evidence of urban decline,[180] there is an alternative explanation, namely that subsidy remissions were

at £100: *CIPM, 1399–1405*, no. 383.

172 *Royal Charters*, 88–9.

173 *Medieval Lincoln*, 271.

174 For example, *CCR, 1429–35*, 71; *1441–47*, 253; *1447–54*, 14.

175 *Royal Charters*, 74–87. Note that shire status was not accompanied by incorporation; this was granted during the reign of Henry V: *Royal Charters*, xxxiv, xxxvii, xlvii.

176 SC 8/121/6024. It is not known whether this request was granted.

177 See also SC 8/26/1272 (1431).

178 *Medieval Lincoln*, 271–3.

179 *CPR, 1476–85*, 521. See also the charter of Henry VI (1447) which discusses these exemptions: *Royal Charters*, 98–101.

180 *Medieval Lincoln*, 271–3.

granted to towns at least initially as a means to minimise the burden of their fee farm, which had, by the opening decades of the fifteenth century, become more acute as trade to and from them had eased due to the severe contraction of the population.[181] Certainly, that Lincoln retained the highest fee farm outside London and Southampton emphasises to a large extent how the city maintained a false economic position at this time, especially if Ormrod's theory that lay subsidies are a more accurate indication of a town's wealth is accepted.[182] As Barrie Dobson argues, the granting of shire status in 1409 was almost certainly 'a political cure for economic ills'[183] – though when drawing this conclusion he was unaware of the true extent of Lincoln's burden at this time – an outcome that explains why the civic government was also granted a new thirty-day fair, the annual farm of the weavers (£6) and several other miscellaneous payments in 1409, all of which were used to supplement fee farm revenues.[184] This also provides context to the crown's decision in 1436 to grant Lincoln's citizens the right to ship sixty sacks of wool from the ports of Boston or Hull to Calais tax free for three years with monies being used to supplement the farm,[185] perhaps yet the clearest acknowledgement of its dwindling revenues, with similar grants being issued in 1440, 1441, 1443, 1445, 1449 and 1454.[186]

It is, of course, important to provide a wider context to the idea that Lincoln maintained a false economic position in the eyes of the crown. As the accompanying analysis demonstrates (table 14), in years when subsidies were granted Lincoln paid the third highest amount in contributions to the crown out of all leading provincial towns, its position rising to second between 1383 and 1414 when the Roos assignment increased. Even when the value of the fixed subsidy is subtracted (but not from other towns), Lincoln still stood in seventh position, rising to fifth between 1383 and 1414, thereby emphasising how it was almost certainly paying too much at this time vis-à-vis its annual revenues and more than the vast majority of other provincial towns, some of which maintained more buoyant economies than Lincoln in c.1400, including, for example, Coventry, Norwich and Exeter.[187] As such this questions Bridbury's claims that remissions of taxes were 'nothing but a calculated, trumpet-tongued, and even perhaps, at times, a systematically concerted campaign to defraud the king of his meagre dues'.[188] In some cases there were undoubtedly reasonable grounds for claiming such aid and this explains why Lincoln's pleas were

181 Rigby, 'Reliability of the Non-statistical Evidence', 45; R. Britnell, 'Urban Demand in the English Economy, 1300–1600', in Galloway, *Market Integration*, 10–11. For the importance of tolls for the fee farm, see 61.

182 Ormrod, 'The Crown and the English Economy', 157–8.

183 Dobson, 'Urban Decline', 272.

184 *Royal Charters*, 74–87.

185 E 356/19, rot. 12; *CCR, 1435–41*, 20, 141; *CFR, 1437–45*, 172, 289; *WB*, fos 11v–13v; E 356/20, rots 20–20d.

186 *CFR, 1437–45*, 172, 289; *CPR, 1441–46*, 148; *1446–52*, 280; *WB*, fos, 11v–13v; E 356/20, rots 20–20d; *Rot. Parl.*, vol. 5, 38, 69–70.

187 Dyer and Slater, 'The Midlands', 628; Kowaleski, *Medieval Exeter*, 81–93; Dunn, 'Trade', 213–34.

188 Bridbury, 'English Provincial Towns', 16. See also A. Green, *Town Life in the Fifteenth Century*, vol. 2 (London, 1894), 216–17, who sees the withdrawal of civic monies from the crown as 'good business'.

Table 14 Fixed lay subsidies and annual fee farm payments for some of leading English towns

	1334 subsidy	Annual fee farm	Total
Bristol	£220	£80–£120	£300–£340
York	£162	£160	£322
Lincoln	£100	£180	£280
Southampton	£51	£200	£251
Newcastle	£133	£100	£233
Norwich	£95	£113 8s	£208
Boston	£110	£61	£171
Yarmouth	£100	£60	£160
Oxford	£91	£58 0s 5d	£149 0s 5d
Winchester	£53	£80	£133
Coventry	£75	£50	£125
Ipswich	£65	£60	£125
Gloucester	£54	£65	£119
Nottingham	£37	£52	£89
Exeter	£41	£20	£61

Evidence drawn from Hadwin, 'Medieval Lay Subsidies', 217, and sources cited throughout this chapter.

much more frequent than those of other towns. Based upon the volume and value of exports of wool and cloth, the overall population ranking of 1377 and the number of occupations recorded in the city during the late fourteenth century,[189] it is clear that Lincoln no longer ranked in the second tier of English towns, as it had in years past.[190]

Considered within a broader context of royal urban fiscal relief, which became increasingly common throughout the fifteenth century,[191] it is thus possible to see how this might be viewed as an innovative approach by the crown to the growing problems faced by civic governments in post-plague England. Quite why this aid was necessary was spelled out with remarkable clarity for Lincoln in 1447:

189 Chapters one and two.

190 See 2.

191 For example, see A. Saul, 'English Towns in the Late Middle Ages: the Case of Great Yarmouth', *Journal of Medieval History*, 8 (1982), 83; Palliser, 'Urban Decay Revisited', 4–5; Attreed, *The King's Towns*, 149, 153; Bridbury, 'English Provincial Towns', 5.

> Whereas by the petition of John Ratheby, mayor of Lincoln, and of the citizens and inhabitants of Lincoln, it appears that the king's progenitors granted the said city and the suburbs and precinct thereof with divers liberties to their predecessors at a fee farm of £180, and that the petitioners pay £100 in each tenth and fifteenth, and, though the king by advice of the council acquitted them of a parcel of their payment of tenths and fifteenths, the city is impoverished by the withdrawal of merchants and a great pestilence, so that scarce two hundred citizens stay there, of whom none can support the charge of the said farm: the king has granted licence for them to acquire in mortmain lands and rents to the value of £120 a year, and has acquitted them from the payment of tenths and fifteenths for a term of forty years.[192]

Whilst it might again be wondered to what extent the purported 'withdrawal of merchants' and the 'great pestilence' impacted upon civic finances,[193] it is difficult to see how else the crown could have dealt with the case of Lincoln at this time as all available monies raised for the fee farm had been set aside in permanent assignments. It was therefore far more cumbersome for the crown to find monies from other sources through which to pay the assignees than it was simply to remit the otherwise intermittent lay subsidies, thereby (theoretically) ensuring that the civic government was able to continue its payments and avoid a considerable administrative and fiscal headache. This reading of the evidence offers some explanation for the paradox raised by Bridbury who questioned the extent of Lincoln's poverty when set against its ability to purchase new lands in 1447,[194] and whilst it is clear that Lincoln was not bankrupt by this stage, it was almost certainly struggling in years when subsidies were granted.[195] Thus by using monies which would have otherwise been set aside for subsidies, the civic government was (again theoretically) free to purchase lands to safeguard the future revenues of the crown and by extension the permanent assignments.[196] Whether the experience at Lincoln was echoed elsewhere is not altogether clear, though it is possible that something similar was occurring at Beverley as cited at the outset of this chapter. It must also be remembered that Lincoln, too, rebuilt its guildhall during the 1390s when its initial claims of poverty were made, a period during which the mayor was being paid approximately 15 per cent of annual civic revenues.[197]

Of course, it is important to recognise that the fee farm was not always considered a burden, and at Norwich, for example, between 1443 and 1447 when the city's liberties had been seized by the crown and the civic government accumulated debts of over £440, the citizens were extremely unhappy. This was seen as a time of growing prosperity and many of the benefits associated with political autonomy had been denied to them.[198] Under-assessments were also significant, and it is little wonder

192 *CPR, 1446–52*, 80; see also *Royal Charters*, 98–101.

193 Attreed, *The King's Towns*, 166–8; Dyer, *Decline and Growth in English Towns*, 39–41; Bridbury, 'English Provincial Towns', 8–10.

194 Bridbury, 'English Provincial Towns', 10.

195 This grant almost certainly followed the city's petition of 1447: SC 8/122/6083.

196 For comparable developments at Winchester: Keene, *Medieval Winchester*, vol. 1, 96–7.

197 See 130.

198 Attreed, *The King's Towns*, 146.

that Exeter, which paid a modest subsidy of only £41 and a fee farm of £20, did not complain to the royal authorities about its payments. As is clear, not only did the value of the fee farm and lay subsidies payments not fully reflect the changing economic situation of the post-plague period, with some towns being taxed more onerously than others, it did not consider the more general experiences of individual towns. Considered in this way, is it not possible to argue that the successful payment of Lincoln's annual fee farm – and more between 1383 and 1414 when the crown's demands were at their most onerous – was in fact a sign of, if not economic vigour, then, certainly, resilience until at least the middle of the fifteenth century?

Conclusion

As this chapter has demonstrated, the fee farm was a complex and highly symbolic payment which reflected well the overall economic wellbeing of the city and its status as one of the king's leading towns. Beginning with its introduction in the twelfth century, when it symbolised the birth and growth of civil liberties and the city's early economic and political strength, through to its re-establishment in the opening years of fourteenth century, when it came to represent the rights of the new civic administration, and the granting of urban county status in 1409,[199] it provided a platform through which the city perpetuated an image of responsibility and reliability to the crown, all of which was funnelled through an increasingly sophisticated civic administration. Even so, despite these developments, concepts of civic power and authority were revealed at times to be extremely fragile. This explains why the civic government was willing to make false returns to the Exchequer in the 1320s, all the while providing vital context to the actions of local officials towards the increased Roos assignment following the removal of the staple in 1369. The timing of this event meant that the civic government was reluctant to openly criticise the demands of the crown for fear of further reprisals. Ultimately this led to the adoption of a rhetoric of poverty which eventually saw fiscal parity restored in 1414.

Given these conclusions, it is worthwhile returning to the three questions posed at the outset of this chapter. Of the first, it is clear that the fee farm undoubtedly remains a useful indicator of the commercial and economic vitality of medieval boroughs, given how the money was raised. Certainly, as the majority of towns collected monies primarily through trade, it is clear that by using the evidence of fee farm payments recorded in the Pipe and Memoranda Rolls it is possible to gauge how successful towns were at attracting merchants and petty traders from the surrounding areas. The fee farm records also remain useful for exploring the extent to which towns survived the changing economic landscape brought about by the Black Death, by showing how complaints and petitions may have been submitted for more complex reasons, not simply poverty. Although accounts of monies collected at Lincoln are scarce, with only the overall totals being recorded, they nevertheless

199 This resulted in the city being granted its own heading in the Pipe Rolls, thereby severing it from its surroundings in both a physical and an administrative sense. For the first: E 372/255, rot. 7.

allow general trends or patterns to emerge over a longer period of time and it was only after 1438 that the civic government began regularly to fall into arrears,[200] at a time of low rental income in the city, suggesting broader economic problems.[201]

The second issue, which questions the contemporary links between the fee farm and lay subsidies, is equally significant, as it demonstrates how despite the former being a tax on moveable goods, the responsibility for the payment shifted from individual tax payers to the civic government following the introduction of fixed quotas in 1334. Whether or not this ever resulted in monies raised for each 'tenth and fifteenth' being drawn from different revenue streams, including tolls, is not clear, though this remains a possibility given that the total cost (£100) had to be returned to the Exchequer whatever the economic situation of the city; as Lorraine Attreed notes for York in the late fifteenth century, whilst parishes were often assigned fixed quotas to contribute to the overall total, how hard collectors 'pressed their own friends and neighbours for payment' is unclear.[202] Hence they may have looked elsewhere for available monies, a possibility underscored by the fact that both payments were often complained of in the same petitions. This admittedly tentative conclusion highlights the need for further work on lay subsidies between 1334 and 1500, which, at present, are skipped over in favour of the more detailed early lay subsidies (c.1290–34), the 1377–81 poll tax records and the Tudor subsidies (1522–25), most likely due to the fact that they have been considered to be of limited value.[203] Yet as the evidence here shows, it is only by revealing how towns perceived and dealt with these payments during periods of economic difficulty that a more nuanced account of urban fortunes and the issue of decline can be revealed.[204] In many ways this conclusion echoes that of Dobson, who argues that royal fiscal concessions during the fifteenth century should be 'best interpreted as a reluctant recognition of reality',[205] though the reasons behind this are more complex than first meets the eye.

The third question relates directly to the feasibility of Lincoln's pleas of poverty from 1397 onwards. As argued here, the initial pleas were based primarily on the unreasonable demands of the crown, not upon any dramatic economic downturn affecting the city,[206] and whilst it undoubtedly shared many of the problems experienced by other towns following successive bouts of plague, including empty plots and physical decay, Hill's focus upon the plaintive evidence, not the accounts themselves, has misrepresented the city's overall fortunes.[207] The evidence for Lincoln echoes the sentiments expressed by Rigby, who argues that only once historians accept that ideas of urban decay are 'compatible with the resilience of municipal administration and even the personal prosperity of individual town inhabitants, will our debate

200 For example, E 372/283, rot. 4; E 372/284, rot. 10; E 372/285, rot. 4; E 372/286, rot. 5.

201 See 208–9.

202 Attreed, *The King's Towns*, 150.

203 See, for example, Nightingale, 'The Lay Subsidies', 2–9; Rigby, 'Urban Population', 393–417; Dobson, 'Urban Decline', 282; Phythian-Adams, *Desolation of a City*, 62–3.

204 For example, Dobson, 'Urban Decline', 276.

205 Dobson, 'Urban Decline', 275–6.

206 See chapters one, two and six.

207 *Medieval Lincoln*, 253–5, 270–3, 281–8, esp. 286.

go beyond the sterility of polarised opposition'.[208] Lincoln, then, like many other towns, faced its fair share of difficulties during the second half of the fourteenth century as it readjusted itself to the new economic climate but it persevered, even in the face of excessive royal demands, managing debts on an unprecedented level vis-à-vis its population. Whilst this may not point directly to a buoyant economy, to characterise the plaintive evidence as an indication of decline is to ignore not only the evidence of the Exchequer but also the city's political motives and resolve to maintain its status as one of the king's leading towns. As chapters one and two have demonstrated, Lincoln's awareness of its role as an administrative and service centre, especially in the years after the loss of widespread credit facilities and a shrinking textile industry, meant that it remained central to royal needs despite its overall lack of a specialised economy. Whilst it is true that the city nevertheless retained a large and integrated wool economy, this employed fewer workers than other industries, in particular cloth.[209] The strength of its administrative functions therefore offset these losses initially, though they could not stimulate growth in the same way as industry could. The undoubted decline of the city was therefore a much more drawn out affair, and it was perhaps only in the sixteenth century that Lincoln finally fell into the slumber from which it only awoke during the industrial revolution.

208 Rigby, 'Boston and Urban Decline', 58.
209 See 24–9 and appendix 1.

4

The Growth of Civic Government

In 1948 Sir Francis Hill published his most famous work, *Medieval Lincoln*, which provided a full and rich narrative of the city's growth from the period of the Conquest to its late medieval decline, an account which to this day remains the standard text for the city.[1] As part of his narrative, Hill described the emergence of Lincoln's civic government from the mid-twelfth century,[2] arguing that since at least that time there had existed in the city a 'court of burwarmote' presided over by a bailiff or reeve, where all the city's pleas were heard.[3] He charted how, from at least 1219 onwards, constitutional developments saw the introduction of a council of 'twenty-four' members headed by the newly instituted mayor (c.1206), a development seen in many other urban centres including Winchester, Dublin, Leicester and Exeter, all of whom were responsible for overseeing the laws and trading rights of the civic jurisdiction.[4] From the 'twenty-four', or 'mayor's council' as it was also known, the incumbent mayor and two bailiffs were chosen. Hill highlighted that by a relatively early stage the 'twenty-four' were divided into two groups of twelve, representing the *majores*, or ruling citizens, on the one hand and the *secondarii*, or middling citizens, on the other, though he stressed that these two groups were not exclusive, with 'the same kind of people' on either side of the divide, there being 'men who will later rise to civic office and men of professional standing … among the *secondarii*',[5] a situation, he concluded, which continued well into the fourteenth century. Hill also highlighted how the council of 'twenty-four' stood as little more than a symbolic title, with membership fluctuating throughout the fourteenth century between eighteen and thirty, which led him to claim that it was very much like a 'modern committee not unduly fettered by a constitution'.[6] Nonetheless, Hill also stated that the 'twenty-four' underwent a decline after the Black Death, when it became increasingly difficult to maintain their number; they were recorded for the final time in 1392.[7]

Despite the apparent decline of the mayor's council, Hill nevertheless identified how in 1422 the 'whole commonalty' congregated to decree a 'change in the

1 J. F. W. Hill, *Medieval Lincoln* (Cambridge, 1948; reprint, Stamford, 1990). See also 9–10.

2 *Medieval Lincoln*, 183–7.

3 *Medieval Lincoln*, 293.

4 *Medieval Lincoln*, 99, 153, 261–8.

5 *Medieval Lincoln*, 297.

6 *Medieval Lincoln*, 299.

7 *Medieval Lincoln*, 301.

civic body' in all matters regarding the good of the community, which effectively introduced new rules regarding the use of the common seal.[8] The impact of this change was that the number on the 'mayor's council' swelled significantly, reaching over eighty members, a total he claimed constituted an impractical and unworkable number. This development was later abandoned in 1449. From this date onwards, Hill claimed that the council struggled to find members to serve, it being declared that 'for all acts made in the common council "twenty-four" persons should be chosen by common assent with the twelve aldermen to have full authority to make ordinances for the common weal of the city'.[9] This saw twenty-two members being recorded in 1514, fifteen in 1520 and twenty-four in 1530.

In addition to Hill's narrative of the overall structure of the city's government, he also outlined how there was, since at least the reign of King John, a 'large civic establishment' which included four coroners, two city clerks and four beadles. This, he argued, grew following the introduction of the *Provisions for the Government of the City* in c.1300 after the restitution of the city's liberties in 1299, and, in addition to two bailiffs, who were tasked with selecting the two aforementioned clerks and four sergeants (beadles), there was henceforth an official weigher of goods, four men entrusted to oversee the city's accounts, and two constables for each parish, all of whom were entrusted with keeping the peace. All were presented at Michaelmas (29 September).

Finally, Hill detailed the process of election for the city's mayor by drawing upon evidence from a manuscript known as the *Blickling Homilies*,[10] an Anglo-Saxon manuscript with extensive marginalia relating to government of the city.[11] According to an entry dated Michaelmas 1360, six names were submitted to the council of 'twenty-four', one of whom was chosen as the new mayor.[12] Even so, this straightforward process was substituted at some stage during the fifteenth century, certainly by 1483 when Lincoln's custumal was written down,[13] with the mayor being thereafter chosen from those who had previously served as sheriff and who now sat 'within the chekyr'.[14] The names of four men, none of whom were permitted to have served as mayor during the previous seven years, were to be given to the 'commons' who were to choose two names. Both of these names were returned to the outgoing mayor and former sheriffs who selected one as the new mayor. Whilst Hill questioned the practicality of this process, he subsequently drew attention to the fact that it served to devolve mayoral elections over time into fewer hands, moving it away from the *secondarii* and towards those who had served previously as sheriff, a process he described as introducing a 'new classification of citizens'. He concluded his analysis

8 *Medieval Lincoln*, 276–7, 301.

9 *Medieval Lincoln*, 302. On the shift from commonalty to aldermen, see main text below.

10 *Medieval Lincoln*, 300.

11 For details of these marginalia, including a basic calendar, see Willard, *Blickling Homilies*, 47–65; R. J. Kelly (ed.), *The Blickling Homilies: Edition and Translation* (London, 2003), xliii–xlv.

12 Hill's date of 1361 is mistaken, as is his suggestion that there were seven individuals. Roger Tatersale is noted twice: *BH*, fo. 13v.

13 *WB*, fos 46v–59.

14 *Medieval Lincoln*, 270–1.

by saying that 'The oligarchic character of the corporation ... [had been] firmly established by the end of the medieval period.'[15]

There is indeed much to admire in this interpretation of Lincoln's civic structure and it remains an extremely useful platform for any study of the city's government during the later Middle Ages. Nonetheless, there are three main issues which are deserving of further attention. The first relates to the mayor's council and the extent to which its numbers declined or not, as Hill's views on this are contradictory. The second is that Hill makes no direct link between the city's coroners and the municipal government, a small but important group who otherwise played a central role in the day-to-day running of the Burwarmote Court. Thirdly, Hill says little regarding the overall hierarchy of the municipal government and its composition after the thirteenth century, and indeed less still on the day-to-day functions of the mayor and bailiffs. It is the aim of this chapter to consider these issues before analysing the wealth, occupations and residential patterns of civic officials between the suspension of the city's liberties in 1289 and the granting of shire status in 1409 in order to gauge the centrality and influence of this group in civic life during a period of unprecedented demographic upheaval.

The Re-emergence of Civic Government

According to the *Provisions for the Government of the City* (c.1300),[16] by the beginning of the fourteenth century it was customary on Holy Cross Day (14 September) for the common council to elect a new mayor who, as the most senior civic official, oversaw justice and peace in the city and maintained its many laws and customs;[17] once elected he was to 'remain in his mayoralty so long as it please him and the commonalty'.[18] However, in 1306 the practice of the mayor serving for consecutive years and in many cases on multiple occasions came to an abrupt end, with the office henceforth being held for single annual terms.[19] In fact following the mayoralty of Stephen de Stanham, which ended in 1306 after five consecutive years in office, only John de Outhorp (1348/49–1349/50) and Peter Belasis (1358/59–1359/60) held the post for two consecutive years, the former almost certainly due to the impact of plague.[20] In addition to these two individuals, only John de Blyton (1307/08 and 1315/16), Alexander son of Martin (1306/07 and 1310/11) and Roger de Tyrington (1347/48 and 1368/69) ever served as mayor on more than one occasion before the grant of shire status in 1409, though their terms were usually some years apart.[21]

One of the catalysts for this development was the reinstitution of the city's liberties in 1299, which had been forfeit to the crown since Easter 1289 following a series

15 *Medieval Lincoln*, 302.
16 Reproduced in *Medieval Lincoln*, 402–5.
17 The term of office began at noon on Michaelmas (29 September). *WB*, fo. 47.
18 *Medieval Lincoln*, 402.
19 Compare to the thirteenth century: *Medieval Lincoln*, 380–3.
20 Appendix 2.
21 For Lincoln's civic officials after 1409, see Hill, 'Three Lists', 232–47.

of fiscal abuses by the city's leading officials, many of whom were drawn from a select group of families who had in the recent past monopolised the office of mayor.[22] Evidence for the significance of this event can be found in the much better documented case of London, which was deprived of its liberties following a series of violent factional disputes in 1285, culminating in the homicide of the goldsmith Laurence Duket.[23] As in Lincoln, a protracted period of royal control ensued and it was not until 1299, following the payment of a fine of 2,000 marks, that the mayoralty and its incumbent rights were finally restored.[24] Nonetheless the powers re-granted to the civic authorities in London were in many ways unrecognisable from those seized fourteen years earlier, and during the suspension of the capital's liberties, crown-appointed officials effectively overhauled civic government by introducing new laws regarding trade, the political status of aliens, and even the basis upon which individuals gained access to office; in the words of Gwyn Williams, 'the patriciate was, quite abruptly, thrown wide open'.[25] Hence in some ways the institutional developments identified in London set the tone for the changes at Lincoln with the only difference being that for Lincoln the king was more or less willing to allow an autonomous civic policy to be pursued.[26] This is seen most clearly in the opening statement of the *Provisions* which proclaimed that they were made 'by the mayor and whole commonalty of the city of Lincoln for keeping the peace of the Lord the King and for the perpetual observance of the liberties and improvements hereunder mentioned'.[27]

Despite the restitution of civil liberties, the introduction a single annual mayoral term was in many ways surprising, more so given its early date. For example, Oxford did not adopt similar measures until well after the Black Death, whilst it was not until 1372 that York did so, though this was not always adhered to.[28] Even London, after the restitution of its own liberties, did not adopt a similar practice until at least the 1380s.[29] Nevertheless, when it is considered that the *Provisions* were written in order to 'faithfully restrain the mayor and bailiffs within their own liberties of the said city', then it is somewhat less surprising; surely it was a reference to the fiscal abuses that triggered the suspension in the first place.[30] Although the introduction on an annual term undoubtedly reflected what Reynolds sees as the 'medieval desire

22 E 159/63, rot. 2. The city was thus seized prior to the indictments of 1290 (*CPR, 1281–92*, 404, 451). Note this pushes back the date of the forfeiture cited by Hill: *Medieval Lincoln*, 212–16. See also *CIM, 1219–1301*, 353, no. 1202, for an earlier complaint (1280) against the 'mayor, bailiffs, and more powerful citizens'.

23 For the following, see Williams, *Medieval London*, 243–63.

24 See 105 and n. 87 for the fiscal penalties imposed on Lincoln.

25 Williams, *Medieval London*, 259.

26 For the ideology of crown seizures, see Reynolds, *English Medieval Towns*, 176.

27 *Medieval Lincoln*, 402.

28 P. J. P. Goldberg, *Medieval England: A Social History, 1250–1550* (London, 2004), 38; S. Rees Jones, 'York's Civic Administration, 1354–1464', in *idem* (ed.), *The Government of Medieval York: Essays in Commemoration of the 1396 Royal Charter (York, 1997)*, 131–2; Kermode, *Medieval Merchants*, 323–6.

29 C. Barron, *London in the Later Middle Ages: Government and People 1200–1500* (Oxford, 2004), 311–55.

30 *Medieval Lincoln*, 403.

to avoid domination either by cliques or the mob, to procure representatives of weight and standing, and to achieve a harmonious consensus in conformity with custom and contemporary ideas of justice',[31] it is unlikely that Lincoln's government saw itself as more democratic than other urban centres, partly due to the continuity of members of the mayor's council, but equally because the process of elections in towns in the Middle Ages 'bore little resemblance to modern democratic procedures', with those eligible to vote being a minority of the enfranchised population.[32]

Alongside the introduction of the yearly mayoral term came several new constitutional and commercial developments, including new laws regarding public disturbances, foreign merchants trading in the city, forestalling, rights of common pasture, dyeing and weaving, mercantile debts, fishing rights and the sale of false goods, including wool, cloth, shoes and tanned leather.[33] In 1301 the city was also granted a new royal charter, which inspected and confirmed the rights of existing charters and granted anew exemptions for its citizens from 'murage, pavage, pontage, wharfage, stallage and terrage' throughout England.[34] Several years later, in 1303/04, the civic government also introduced the practice of recording the names of the mayor's council in the margins of the *Blickling Homilies*,[35] whilst in 1308 a new register of lands and properties, known as the *Burwarmote Book*, was adopted by the court in order to minimise disputes relating to the civic jurisdiction.[36] Such changes enshrined the city's new practices and inculcated a new civic identity, a shift underscored by the fact that those holding the keys to power were for all intents and purposes 'new' men who maintained strong links to the wool trade, a marked shift from the period before the suspension.[37] It is likely that the introduction of these developments at incremental stages also explains the delay of Stephen de Stanham in relinquishing his position as mayor in 1306, as it is likely that he oversaw many of these changes personally. He was certainly integral to civic finances at this time, lending money to the crown on behalf of the city and returning civic monies to the Exchequer.[38] Whilst it is clear that these measures were a direct response to the suspension of the city's liberties, they also served to establish a culture of the written word in the city on a hitherto unrecognisable scale,[39] all the while satisfying the

31 Reynolds, *English Medieval Towns*, 122–3.

32 Miller and Hatcher, *Medieval England*, 316.

33 *Medieval Lincoln*, 403–5.

34 *Royal Charters*, 18–27, at 26. These are taxes relating, respectively, to walls, roads, bridges, storage, rents for market stalls and rents for shops.

35 This development is discussed in greater detail below.

36 Brooks, Lincoln Court of Burghmanote', LAO FL/Transcripts/U/28. For the *Blickling Homilies*, main text below.

37 See, for example, William Brand (bailiff 1248/49) and Henry Gupil (*viz.* Gopyl) (mayor 1288/89), mercers, who sold cloths widely at the fairs of Boston and St Ives: Miller and Hatcher, *Medieval England*, 230. For their official status, see *Reg. Antiq.*, vol. 8, nos 2271, 2359; LAO Dij 78/3/90.

38 Moore, *Fairs of Medieval England*, 63–7. See also 105–6.

39 Prior to this date the only known civic records were the now lost mayoral rolls referred to in 1269 and the *Constituciones Civitatis Lincolnie. Reg. Antiq.*, vol. 9, no. 2435. For the latter, see 75–8.

growing demands of 'the royal courts and administration'.[40] Equally they also represented the power of civic government to regulate trade in a more effective way than hitherto, thereby reflecting the broader trend for European towns to restrict unfair commercial and industrial practices by minimising competition to their authority.[41]

As the civic head, it was customary for the mayor by c.1300, if not before, to undertake one of the lesser roles of bailiff or coroner prior to his accession, though like in many other towns there was no explicit declaration of this.[42] For example, of the ninety-three mayors recorded between 1300 and 1409 only a sixth (fifteen) failed to do so, thirteen of whom did so after 1349, suggesting that there were greater opportunities for rapid municipal advancement in the post-plague environment.[43]

Unsurprisingly, not all candidates putting themselves forward for mayor were successful; evidence dating from Michaelmas 1360 reveals that of the six named candidates – William Belle, John de Bole, William Thornhagh, John de Rodes, Roger de Tatersale and William de Fynchingfeld (with Tatersale being named as victor) – only two, Belle and Fynchingfeld, did not go on to become mayor in the future.[44] In fact, Bole, Thornhagh and Rodes were named as the three successive mayors to Tatersale, suggesting that there may have been some tactical voting at work. Thus failure in one year did not necessarily hinder future success. Unfortunately neither the final tally of votes nor the names of those eligible to vote were provided, unlike in the sixteenth century,[45] meaning that the actual process of election at this time is unknown.[46] Of the 313 unique civic officials known to have served between 1289 and 1409, less than three tenths (ninety-three) served as mayor, a figure lower than at Winchester, where it stood at roughly 40 per cent,[47] and lower still than at Colchester, where at least 50 per cent of all councillors never served as bailiff (the highest civic office in the town),[48] thereby demonstrating how Lincoln maintained a wider base of office holders after the municipal reforms of the early fourteenth century than many other towns.

The position of mayor was not without its benefits, and, according to the city's *Provisions*, those successfully elected were exempted from all 'taxes, dues and talliages [*sic*] and of all other customs belonging to the city so long as he shall be mayor (saving the precept of our Lord the King in all things)'.[49] The mayor also maintained the right to take 'hansels' (the right to trade in the city without paying tolls) within the city from 'all those who pay scot and lot' (individuals eligible for office and liable to contribute to taxes) and all those who 'ought not to be ansellled [given exemption

40 Rees Jones, 'York's Civic Administration' in *idem*, *Government of Medieval York*, 109–10; See also Clanchy, *From Memory to Written Record*, 49–57, 71, 74–5.

41 G. Rosser, 'Big Brotherhood: Guilds in Urban Politics in Late Medieval England', in I. A. Gadd and P. Wallis (eds), *Guilds and Association in Europe, 900–1900* (London, 2006), 36.

42 Attreed, *The King's Towns*, 47.

43 These are noted in appendix 2.

44 Belle acted as both bailiff and coroner, Fynchingfeld as bailiff: appendix 2.

45 For example, LAO L/1/1/1, fos 19v–20.

46 For a similar election for tax collectors in 1352: *BH*, fo. 83v.

47 Keene, *Medieval Winchester*, vol. 1, 427–8.

48 Britnell, *Colchester*, 128.

49 This was revoked by 1483: *WB*, fo. 47.

from tolls by way of charter] within the county of Lincoln'.[50] He was also granted the use of a servant and a clerk,[51] which by 1422 had increased to two servants, a macebearer, a clerk, three minstrels (an allowance of 8s was made for each, along with their livery) and a common messenger (for whom a further 8s was granted).[52] Exactly when this extension of personnel took place is not certain though it seems likely that it occurred after 1400, and most likely following the grant of shire status in 1409.[53] As in many other urban centres, Lincoln's mayor was also the beneficiary of a bi-annual procession, though evidence for this only dates from 1515.[54] In that year it was stated that according to 'the laudable and ancient custom of the city', all of the city's aldermen were to wear a gown of crimson and be attendant 'on the mayor in Advent and Lent from his house to the Minster, and then home to his house again', with fines being imposed on those not doing so. It is likely that this custom dated from the visit of Richard II in March 1387, if not before,[55] when the mayor was permitted to have a sword borne before him on official occasions,[56] though the procession undoubtedly became more elaborate following the city's emergence as a county in its own right: as both Sarah Rees Jones and Ruth Frost have identified for York and Norwich respectively, such developments were often a catalyst for increased civic ceremonial practices.[57] Whatever the exact chronology of these changes, it is clear that the costs associated with civic office grew commensurate with its size and status, a conclusion which has important implications for framing complaints over falling civic revenues from c.1390 onwards.[58] In particular, by 1398 the mayor was being granted forty marks (almost £27) out of the common fund for his services,[59] a figure higher than that for Exeter (£5, which rose to 20 marks (£13) in 1469–70), but less than that for the mayor of York (£50 in 1393),[60] the equivalent of 15 per cent of the annual fee farm payment. This rose further still when the costs of the mayor's retinue and other civic officials are factored in.

The final point to note with regard to Lincoln's mayor was that he also became the de facto head of the statute merchant court, later known as the staple court.[61]

50 *Medieval Lincoln*, 402.

51 For example, *BH*, fos 35v, 45v, 57v, 63v, 77v, 78, 108v, 118v; *Medieval Lincoln*, 402.

52 *WB*, fo. 4v.

53 The mayor was still recorded as having only a single clerk in 1399/1400: *BH*, fo. 118v.

54 *Historical MSS*, 25, 26. For similar processions, see K. Kleineke, 'Civic Ritual, Space and Conflict in Fifteenth-Century Exeter', in F. Andrews (ed.), *Ritual and Space in the Middle Ages: Proceedings of the 2009 Harlaxton Symposium* (Donington, 2011), 169–70.

55 For example, scarlet cloth was provided for the mayor in c.1350: *BH*, fo. 70.

56 Hill, 'Three Lists', 230. On the visit, see Ferris, 'Chaucer at Lincoln', 296, 304, 312.

57 Rees Jones, 'York's Civic Administration', in *idem*, *Government of Medieval York*, 119; R. H. Frost, 'The Urban Elite', in Rawcliffe and Wilson, *Medieval Norwich*, 238. For the growth of civic pageantry after 1389, see Stokes, *Early English Drama*, vol. 2, 407–19.

58 See 116, 122–3.

59 *BH*, fo. 29v. This had fallen to £11 14s 4d by 1512: Ross, *Civitas Lincolnia*, 59.

60 Attreed, *The King's Towns*, 65, n. 50; Rees Jones, 'York's Civic Administration' in *idem*, *Government of Medieval York*, 133–4.

61 E. E. Rich, *The Staple Court Books of Bristol* (Bristol, 1934), 28; A. Beardwood, *The Statute Merchant Roll of Coventry, 1392–1416* (Oxford, 1939), vii–x. See also 78–81.

Even following the introduction of a dedicated mayor of the staple in 1353,[62] the city's mayor continued to oversee many of the debt cases heard at the registry, emphasising his position as the political and economic figurehead of the city.[63] Such developments were by no means unique to Lincoln and in Bristol by 1379, for example, the staple was 'absorbed into the town's governing structure'.[64]

After the mayor, the second most senior civic official was the bailiff, or sheriff following the granting of shire status in 1409, though he theoretically remained an officer of the crown.[65] Elected annually in the guildhall by the citizens on Holy Cross Day,[66] his primary responsibility was to make the payment of the 'fee farm rent to our Lord the King at the end of the year'.[67] Typically two bailiffs were sworn into office though in some years there were as many four. Like the mayor, bailiffs usually served only once and for a single term though there were some who served twice, including Hugh Bacon (1311/12 and 1316/17) and John Derfeld (1347/48 and 1368/69), whilst Thomas Hauke served in two consecutive years (1381/82–1382/83), though he was the only individual ever to do so. Nonetheless, despite the absence of any prescriptive rules regarding the number of times a bailiff could serve, no individual ever served more than twice. Such a practice differed at least in theory from that employed in other towns such as Norwich, where it was normal for citizens to choose four bailiffs each year, 'rotating the office so that no man served more than once in four years'. Irrespective of this, the policy at Norwich was seldom adhered to, with greater numbers being recorded than might otherwise be expected.[68] The evidence for Lincoln and Norwich therefore suggests that ordinances were effectively guidelines to customary practice, not indissoluble rules.

Unlike the growing retinue of staff for the mayor, the bailiff retained only two clerks and four sergeants (also known as *sub-ballium*) throughout the fourteenth and fifteenth centuries, even following the granting of shire status,[69] though he was almost certainly in charge of various minor officials including wine tasters and the keepers of the *pixis*, or money-box.[70] Of these subordinates little is known, though their names are occasionally recorded in the margins of the *Blickling Homilies*,[71] including John Faukes and Alexander de Longes, bailiff's clerks, and John de Wylingham, Henry Kempe, Richard Cokerell and Henry Draper, bailiff's sergeants (*servientes*), in 1326/27.[72] It is interesting to note that all four sergeants recorded in this year went

62 E. E. Rich, 'The Mayors of the Staples', *Cambridge Historical Journal*, 4, 2 (1933): 120–42; C 267/7/1–9, C 241/134/105.
63 For example, October 1356: Walter de Ouresby (C 241/138/13); March 1358: Robert de Holm (C 241/138/171); March 1362: John de Bole (C 241/153/135).
64 Liddy, *War, Politics and Finance*, 123–5.
65 *Royal Charters*, 78; Reynolds, *English Medieval Towns*, 109.
66 Like the mayor, his term began at Michaelmas. See n. 17 above.
67 *Medieval Lincoln*, 402. For the fee farm, see chapter three.
68 B. McRee, 'Peacemaking and its Limits in Late Medieval Norwich', *English Historical Review*, 109, 433 (1994), 836.
69 For exceptions to this rule: *BH*, fos 48v, 49, 78v. See also 118.
70 *BH*, fos ix, 59v, 107v. See main text below for the bailiff's additional duties.
71 For example, *BH*, fos 37v, 45v, 55v, 58v, 62v, 74v, 118v.
72 *BH*, fos 50v, 57v.

on to become bailiffs themselves over the subsequent decade, suggesting that there was a clear structure to municipal government whereby advancement could and did take place. An entry dating from 1323/24 tells a similar story, with William de Blyton, Walter de Ebor and Hugh de Edelyngton, clerks, and William Ryvet, John Mody and Richard de Kele, chamberlains (*camerarii*),[73] all achieving one of the three main civic posts in subsequent years (mayor, bailiff, coroner). Such evidence thus echoes that of Coventry, where officials were required to pass through the ranks of the Corpus Christi guild before joining the Holy Trinity guild, an institution synonymous with municipal government, as a means to gain experience.[74]

Although the importance of the bailiff's position stemmed primarily from his duty to collect the annual fee farm, it was nevertheless also his responsibility to maintain the city's prison at Claxledgate (*prisone de claxledgate; Oldeclaxlet*),[75] a large fortified building leading out into the suburb of Butwerk known locally by several titles including *Hawardeby*, presumably after the road lying adjacent to it; the 'gaol of the lord king in the city of Lincoln, called *Claxflet*'; the *gaola civitatis Linc*'; and, more disparagingly, as *claxletpit*.[76] Here felons arrested within the civic jurisdiction were held. Bailiffs also oversaw trade coming to and from the town through the collection of tolls;[77] made summonses to court;[78] witnessed charters and wills;[79] seized illegal goods;[80] enrolled writs and pleas;[81] submitted accounts;[82] communicated with the crown on the city's behalf;[83] and conducted public works and surveys of lands,[84] thereby performing an indispensable role for the civic authorities.[85] By the early sixteenth century the city's sheriffs (bailiffs) received an annual wage of £5.[86]

The third ranking official was the coroner, who, like all other civic officials, was elected in the guildhall, though this took place in January or February not September as was custom for other officials.[87] Like the bailiff the coroner was, in principle, a representative of the crown not the city.[88] The importance of this position relates not to the city's *Provisions*, where it is not mentioned at all, but to the fact that the city's

73 *BH*, fos 65v–66.

74 Phythian-Adams, *Desolation of a City*, 118–24.

75 JUST 1/520, m. 12d; KB 29/3, m. 3d; E 13/110, m. 14d. For an image, see *Medieval Lincoln*, plate 13.

76 JUST 3/188, rot. 126; JUST 2/67, rot. 48; JUST 2/80, rot. 2; E 13/110, mm. 14d–15.

77 See chapter two.

78 Either themselves or through their sergeants: for example, *BB*, fos 98, 108v, 115, 128v.

79 *BB*, fos 110, 249

80 KB 27/185, m. 34.

81 *BB*, fos 231v, 240v, 264.

82 E 101/334/14.

83 *BB*, fos 254, 269v.

84 C. T. Flower, *Public Works in Medieval England*, vol. 1 (London, 1915), 276–7; LAO A/1/13.

85 For additional duties of bailiffs not identified at Lincoln, see E. T. Meyer, 'Boroughs', in J. F. Willard, W. A. Morris and W. H. Dunham (eds), *The English Government at Work, 1327–1336*, vol. 3 (Cambridge, Massachusetts, 1950), 107–8.

86 Ross, *Civitas Lincolnia*, 59.

87 For example: *BH*, fos 24v, 87v. This had changed to September by 1483 at the latest: *WB*, fo. 47v.

88 R. Hunnisett, *The Medieval Coroner* (Cambridge, 2008), 3. For thirteenth-century elections, the process of which is not explicitly recorded, see *CCR, 1242–47*, 82; *1251–53*, 315.

coroners maintained a strong presence in local affairs.[89] As numerous entries of the *Burwarmote Book* record, pleas, wills, deeds and writs were frequently heard before the mayor, bailiffs and coroners, such as in 1337 when an inquisition was heard to ascertain the age of Ralph, son and heir of Thomas Broud;[90] in 1345 when Phillip Belle de Raiston and Emma his wife were questioned in the guildhall as to what status they claimed in a messuage in the suburbs;[91] and in 1362 when, following some confusion over the contents of the will of William de Burgh, the testator's executors, Nicholas de Bautre and Robert de Muston, were examined.[92] In fact the centrality of coroners to civic affairs was marked out most clearly in the fifteenth century when it became a requirement that

> no man be chosyn & put in offys of coroner of this cite w*ith* owte y*a*t thay haue beyn in ye offys of scheryschyp or borne charge for yt. Or els yf he y*a*t hathe not borne ye office of scheryfschyp be chosyn coroner may spend of yeyrly rent in lyfflode w*ith* i*n* this cite to ye walw [value] of 40s.[93]

This provision therefore ensured not only that the role of coroner was available to only a select group of wealthy citizens but that it actively sought out individuals of experience in multiple fields of government.[94]

Aside from their municipal duties, coroners also undertook responsibilities traditionally associated with their role, including holding inquests over the dead, hearing the confessions of felons, including those seeking sanctuary, and evaluating and listing stolen or seized goods. Much of this activity still survives in the city's extant coroner's rolls.[95] Given the broad variety of tasks demanded of the coroner it is likely that a careful division of labour was required, and it is of little surprise to find that only one of the coroners, Simon Levelaunce, was recorded as performing civic duties in 1375, though he was one of four men listed in the surviving coroners' rolls of that year.[96]

One area where the city's coroners differed from the office of mayor and bailiff was in the term of office. As Roy Hunnisett remarks, the position was typically entered into for life, though this was not always possible, with coroners frequently being replaced through 'sickness and/or old age, engagement upon other business, and unfitness or insufficient qualification'.[97] The evidence for Lincoln is no different, with only William de Hackthorn and William de Humberstone being identified as having held the post until their deaths.[98] More typical were individuals such as

89 For similarities at Oxford and Salisbury, Hunnisett, *Medieval Coroner*, 56, n. 8.

90 *BB*, fo. 138v.

91 *BB*, fo. 173.

92 *BB*, fo. 249.

93 *WB*, fo. 51v.

94 See 41 for the case of Simon Levelaunce, for example.

95 See appendix 1 for references. For a comprehensive list of coroner's duties, see Hunnisett, *Medieval Coroner*, *passim*; and H. E. Cam, 'Shire Officials: Coroners, Constables, and Bailiffs', in Willard, Morris and Dunham, *English Government*, 149–65.

96 *BB*, fo. 101; JUST 2/67, rot. 46.

97 Hunnisett, *Medieval Coroner*, 167.

98 Hackthorn died in 1347, being noted for the final time in 1346: *BB*, fos 176v, 178v. Humberston

Thomas Boteler who was forced to step down after being named as constable of the castle in 1330/31;[99] Thomas de Horncastre who, beside being noted as the county coroner, was forcibly retired for being old and sick after a decade in service;[100] and Richard Lunges who served as coroner for nine years before accepting the mayoralty. Others either enjoyed their work as coroner or accepted it as part of their municipal duty, and both Thomas de Thornhagh and Thomas Elsham returned to the role following their tenure as mayor. Of course, not all coroners succeeded to the mayoralty, including John de Dunham and Nicholas Werk, though there were others, including William de Humberstone and Robert de Holm, who held at one stage or another all three major civic posts. From this evidence it is clear that those undertaking the role of coroner were frequently the same men as those acting as bailiff and mayor. Not only does this reflect an integrated system of civic governance but it highlights how individuals were actively encouraged to demonstrate their usefulness to civic governance by amassing as much experience in different roles as possible.

It is unfortunate that in spite of the centrality of coroners to the make-up of civic government, the names of these men were not always recorded in surviving records; they certainly feature less prominently than the mayor and bailiffs, with many often being identified by their official title only.[101] As such, it is often difficult to identify not only those who held the post, especially in the opening decades of the century, but exactly when one tenure ended and another began. Fortunately the survival of several coroners' rolls from 1344 onwards provides additional evidence to suggest that Lincoln continued to maintain as many as four coroners throughout the fourteenth century,[102] a tradition continuing into the sixteenth century.[103] Whilst this high number was by no means uncommon, with Ipswich, Northampton, Gloucester and Berwick all having four coroners, it was increasingly so after 1300, with only Lincoln and York retaining more than three.[104]

Having considered each of the three key positions, it is necessary to turn to the 'twenty-four' or 'mayor's council' to elucidate the foundations of local government, an assembly tasked with advising the mayor, bailiffs and coroners in civic matters.[105] The first thing to note is that despite several key changes to municipal practices following the restitution of the city's liberties previously discussed, the overall composition of the council itself changed very little after the thirteenth century with the fundamental structure already in place being maintained. In practical terms, this meant that the membership of the council was made up primarily of the city's wealthier inhabitants, all of whom were admitted to the freedom of the city.[106] Even

in 1349, noted finally in 1348: *BB*, fos 186v, 206v.

99 He later returned to the post. *CCR, 1330–33*, 371; *BH*, fos 11v, 21v. See appendix 2.

100 *CCR, 1381–85*, 371, 473; *1389–92*, 471.

101 For example, JUST 3/142, rots 47, 51d; *BB*, fos 119, 128v.

102 Not three as suggested by Hunnisett: *Medieval Coroner*, 141.

103 For example, LAO L/1/1/1, fo. 21v.

104 Hunnisett, *Medieval Coroner*, 141.

105 The role of such councils was seldom defined: Reynolds, *English Medieval Towns*, 121; K. D. Lilley, *Urban Life in the Middle Ages, 1000–1450* (Basingstoke, 2002), 58–9.

106 There is only one extant list of newly admitted freemen for Lincoln before the sixteenth century (1297/98): E 101/505/28, m. 17. Compare to York or Exeter, for example: R. B.

so, as Hill identifies, there remained two distinct halves to this group, the *majores* and *secondarii*, though by the beginning of the fourteenth century these terms had fallen out of use being replaced by *commonalty* and *juratores* respectively.

According to the city's *Provisions* 'twelve fit and discreet men' were to be chosen each year as 'judges' by the 'commonalty' with the good advice of the mayor, a practice which continued well into the fifteenth century, albeit with the term *commonalty* being replaced by 'aldermen' following the grant of shire status.[107] Whilst the so-called 'judges' were undoubtedly the equivalent of the *secondarii*, the term is, as Hill rightly points out, problematic given that the original Latin text is lost.[108] Nonetheless, contemporaneous evidence describes this second tier of officials as *juratores*, which can be translated to mean 'municipal officer' or 'jurat'.[109] This can be seen from marginalia in the *Blickling Homilies* dating from 1316/17, which lists *nomina xxiiij juratorum ad consilium Gilberti de Atherby maioris* and contains the names of twenty-two individuals, all of whom are followed by the abbreviated word *jurator'*.[110] However, interspersed with these names are those of ten other men who were almost certainly members of the 'twelve', or *commonalty*. None of these are described as *juratores*, though many appear in other lists around this time, confirming their status as the dominant group.[111] Much like evidence for other urban centres, it seems that once individuals were elected to the *commonalty* they held the position for life, though there is no explicit declaration of this.[112] As such, it is unclear as to whether this division remained constant throughout the fourteenth and early fifteenth centuries as only eight lists recording the names of the *commonalty* survive.[113]

Of the twenty-five extant lists dealing with the 'twenty-four,'[114] thirteen date from between 1303/04 and 1325/26, with only one other (1335/36) appearing before 1349; the remaining eleven were all recorded between 1349/50 and 1372/73. The significance of these dates seems to be – at least in terms of administrative protocol – that it was custom for the names of the mayor's council to be written in the margins of the *Blickling Homilies* for approximately twenty years after the introduction of the city's *Provisions* as a means of consolidating the newly instituted civic identity and for a similar period after the Black Death. Similar practices can be seen at York, Faversham and Sandwich,[115] where written documents, including chronicles and lists, were used as a means to record the collective memory and identity of the town

Dobson, 'Admissions to the Freedom of the City of York in the Later Middle Ages', *Economic History Review*, 26, 1 (1973): 1–22; Kowaleski, *Medieval Exeter*, 84–6, 95–100.

107 *Medieval Lincoln*, 302, 402.

108 *Medieval Lincoln*, 209–1, 297.

109 R. E. Latham (ed.), *Revised Medieval Latin Word-List from British and Irish Sources* (Oxford, 2008), 264.

110 *BH*, fo. 19v.

111 For example, compare *BH*, fos 2v, 20v, 34v, 111v.

112 Reynolds, *English Medieval Towns*, 173–4; Kermode, *Medieval Merchants*, 44–5.

113 Their numbers fluctuate between ten and thirteen: *BH*, fos viii, 24v, 54v, 67, 81v, 90v, 137v.

114 *BH*, fos 1, 2v, 5v, 7v, 9, 19v, 20v, 34v, 38v, 42v, 51v, 60v, 63v, 64v, 65v, 68v, 69v, 71, 75v, 81v, 82v, 86v, 101v, 111v. See also *Medieval Lincoln*, 400–1, for the names of council members, c.1303–14.

115 Rees Jones, 'York's Civic Administration' in *idem*, *Government of Medieval York*, 110–11; S. Sweetinburgh, 'Kentish Towns: Urban Culture and the Church in the Later Middle Ages', in *idem* (ed.), *Later Medieval Kent* (Woodbridge, 2010), 153–8.

council;[116] as Brigitte Bedos-Rezak argues, such practices served to inscribe in real and symbolic terms the names of the officials in the 'ongoing narrative of the city's history', thereby establishing or consolidating custom.[117] It is clear that something similar was happening at Lincoln. That these lists were compiled (most likely) in the guildhall under the auspices of the council served only to heighten the 'sanctity' of the 'civic liturgy' for its participants,[118] thus complementing not only public expressions of civic identity – mayoral processions, elections, the swearing of oaths – but more mundane events, too, including the enrolment of deeds and charters, for example, all of which served to underscore the government's own status and importance. That these lists emerged in the years immediately after the resumption of civil liberties highlights how this practice was one of several catalysing forces used to express and establish a new set of civic values and ethics, free from past indiscretions.

Nonetheless, despite the introduction of recording the names of the council, after roughly twenty years the practice ceased until the catastrophe of the Black Death stimulated its reintroduction, at which point a type of institutional posterity can be identified. Prompted almost certainly by the deaths of so many former officials,[119] many of whom were in danger of being forgotten, the council decided to begin recording the names of its members once again, perhaps as a means to consolidate their own status and identity but equally to reassure themselves that not everything had changed following the disaster.[120] This stimulus predates a similar development at London where in 1419 John Carpenter reportedly compiled the *Liber Albus* for 'younger, inexperienced persons elected to office in the place of older men carried off by plague'.[121] Notwithstanding, the practice once again declined after roughly another twenty years (1372/73). Quite why it did so at this stage is unclear, although there are several possibilities. One is that the recording clerk died or that the city's clerks began to record the information in a manuscript now lost. Certainly, the absence of other records, including court rolls, accounts and council minutes, from this period suggests that different administrative practices may have been employed at this time, though this fails to explain why the names of clerks and civic officials were intermittently recorded throughout the fifteenth and sixteenth centuries.[122] Certainly, similar administrative changes occurred elsewhere following the Black Death, such as in Norwich, where the city's 'Old Free Book' was altered significantly in style emphasising a type of administrative discontinuity.[123] In Winchester, too,

116 B. Bedos-Rezak, 'Civic Liturgy and Urban Records in Northern France, 1100–1400', in B. A. Hanawalt and K. L. Reyerson (eds), *City and Spectacle in Medieval Europe* (London, 1994), 42.

117 Bedos-Rezak, 'Civic Liturgy', 43; Clanchy, *Memory to Written Record*, 231–2.

118 This was never explicitly stated in the *Blickling Homilies*: Sweetinburgh, 'Kentish Towns', 155.

119 Twelve former civic officials are known to have died in 1349, though not all had their wills enrolled, meaning this number was doubtless higher. See appendix 2.

120 Rubin, 'Identities', 405–6.

121 S. H. Rigby, 'Urban 'Oligarchy' in Late Medieval England', in Thomson, *Towns and Townspeople*, 65.

122 For example, fos 56v, 96v, 44, 134, 62, 126v, 110v.

123 Britnell, 'Black Death', 208.

the pestilence resulted in the specialisation of certain civic administrative practices, including the introduction of separate bills for recording pleas; though as Derek Keene argues, this actually saw the deterioration in the overall quality of the written record.[124] A final possibility, and one already identified for the earlier period, is that it simply fell out of favour again.

This interpretation of the evidence differs considerably from Hill, who sees the onset of plague as the death knell for the council of 'twenty-four'. Yet his position is difficult to maintain as the surviving evidence points to the fact that the mayor's council continued successfully, albeit with fluctuating numbers, until the early sixteenth century.[125] The conclusion drawn here, therefore, is that the recording of names in officially sanctioned documents actually says much more about the institutional identity and collective memory of the city's municipal government in times of difficulty than it does about constitutional structures or developments.

Moving away from the symbolic meaning of these lists, it is possible to make several observations regarding the council's composition, with the minimum size being nineteen (1321/22 and 1335/36), the maximum thirty-three (1314/15 and 1325/26),[126] with an average of twenty-five to twenty-six and a mode of twenty-four. Nonetheless, there is an important caveat to these figures: not all individuals expected to appear in these lists are actually recorded. Take, for example, the list relating to the mayoralty of Walter de Kelby recorded in 1350/51.[127] In that year none of the bailiffs (William de Herpeswelle, Walter de Ouresby and William Jolyf) appear as part of the council, though Roger de Laun, one of the coroners, does. When this is compared to the list of 1361/62 where all known officials are recorded,[128] it seems clear that there was in fact no clear protocol for recording the names of elected officials. A potential solution to this problem is offered by the list dating from Michaelmas 1317, which omits not only the names of the bailiffs and the coroners but also the mayor, John Pinson, too.[129] This suggests that the leading civic positions were at times taken for granted and were not required to be recorded. Hence the mayor's council was often actually larger than the lists themselves suggest, by at least seven officials (one mayor, two bailiffs and four coroners).

Of the council members themselves, the vast majority went on to hold one of three main civic posts, a position which remained constant throughout the fourteenth century, so far as the evidence allows.[130] This indicates a practical continuity from the earlier period, despite the most senior offices being restricted to individuals from the *commonalty*. In essence this meant that gaining access to the council was a vital stepping stone for those wishing to attain civic office.

124 Keene, *Medieval Winchester*, vol. 1, 20.

125 For example, LAO L/1/1/1, mm. 21v, 32v, 46v.

126 Not eighteen and thirty as Hill notes: *Medieval Lincoln*, 299. *BH*, fos 64v, 68v, 81v, 111v.

127 *BH*, fo. 69v.

128 *BH*, fo. 86v; appendix 2.

129 *BH*, fo. 34v. For other years where officials are omitted: *BH*, fos 1, 34v, 67, 69v.

130 For example, in 1364/65 eighteen out of twenty did so, in 1367/68 twenty out of twenty-two: *BH*, fos 42v, 82v.

Another aspect of this evidence is the clear association between members of the council and individual wealth. This can be seen by comparing the lists of 1325/26 and 1335/36 to the lay subsidies of 1327 and 1332, two taxes on moveable goods (table 15).[131] From this it is possible to identify how only two of the forty-six different individuals recorded did not contribute to either subsidy, pointing to the fact that they may have owned few movable goods or, perhaps more likely, evaded the tax.[132] Despite this the average value of tax paid by the members of the mayor's council stood at an impressive 7s, whilst over a quarter (thirteen) paid upwards of five times the city's average tax (10s or more). This dwarfed the city's average of 2s, which stands in line with regional and national trends.[133] The disparity in wealth of civic elites was not uncommon and in Exeter, for example, the city's highest ranking civic officials (mayor, steward and councillors) paid on average almost four times as much as other citizens eligible for the tax.[134] In York, Beverley and Hull, too, the largest proportion of recorded civic officials during the fourteenth and fifteenth centuries were wealthy merchants.[135] In many ways this is unsurprising given that the prevailing political theory of the time held that the 'more prosperous and able' men were to rule for the good of the community in an Aristotelian fashion; all of them were (at least theoretically) less likely to succumb to corruption.[136]

Of the eight men who appear in both lists, all were members of the *commonalty*, once again underscoring the practical continuity of the council previously identified. In fact, with the exception of Hugh de Carleton, who became the long-serving clerk of the statute merchant,[137] the remaining seven all went on to serve as mayor. It appears therefore that despite the extensive administrative changes taking place at the beginning of the fourteenth century, civic power remained firmly in the hands of twelve leading citizens as it had done previously.[138] Quite how this was viewed by the wider body politic is not altogether clear, though tensions can be identified in the closing decade of the fourteenth century. According to the commission of Sir John de Bussy, a local knight and sheriff of Lincolnshire in 1393,[139] who was appointed to oversee the mayoral election of that year, a number of citizens were

131 Work on lay subsidies is extensive but see Hadwin, 'Medieval Lay Subsidies', 200–17; and Willard, *Parliamentary Taxes*.

132 It is nevertheless possible that they did pay in 1332; thirteen entries are illegible. E 179/135/16, mm. 26–26d. For reasons for possible omission, see S. H. Rigby, 'Urban Society in Early Fourteenth Century England: The Evidence of Lay Subsidies', *Bulletin of the John Rylands Library*, 72, 3 (1990), 172, 178.

133 B. M. S. Campbell and K. Bartley, *England on the Eve of the Black Death* (Manchester, 2006), 337–9, table 18.5.

134 Kowaleski, *Medieval Exeter*, 101–5, table 3.4.

135 Kermode, *Medieval Merchants*, 38–53.

136 Reynolds, *English Medieval Towns*, 171; S. Reynolds, 'Medieval Urban History and the History of Political Thought', *Urban History*, 9 (1982): 14–23; S. H. Rigby and E. Ewan, 'Government, Power and Authority', in *CUHB*, 304–6.

137 SC 8/56/2758.

138 *Medieval Lincoln*, 295.

139 For Bussy, see *Medieval Lincoln*, 261–2.

Table 15 Tax paid by members of the mayor's council according to the lay subsidies of 1327 and 1332

1325/26	Tax	1335/36	Tax
Robert de Oxonford (mayor)^	20s	Richard le Lunges (mayor)*	3s
William de Blyton (bailiff)*^	10s	John de Blyton	3s
Ralph de Burton (bailiff)*	10s	William de Blyton*	10s
John Pinzon†	10s	Thomas de Kele*	10s
John de Tame†	6s	Ralph de Burton*	20s
Hugh de Edelington*	20s	Richard de Kele*	10s
John de Newcastle	10s	Hugh de Edlyngton*	8s
Thomas de Carleton	2s	Robert de Tame	20s
Henry de Severby	6s	Robert Beaufowe	3s 3d
William de Hakethorn	2s	Robert Quarrel	5s
William Ryvett	8s	Robert Bristall†	10s
Hamo Permonter	8s	Ralph Jolyff	12s
Thomas de Kele*	20s	Robert de Canewyk	6s
Robert Hare	2s	Roger de Dalderby*	7s
Roger de Dalderby*	7s	Thomas Russell	7s
Robert Herre	5s	Hugh de Carleton*†	1s
Richard de Kele*	8s	William de Snartford†	20s
Hugh Bakon	3s	Thomas Boteler	6d
Adam de Misne	3s	Robert de Scarle	3s 3d
Alan de Hodelston	2s	William de Ebor	3s
Geoffrey de Frothingham	4s		
John de Beaufou	10s		
Ralph de Kyme	8s		
Robert de Welton	5s		
Hugh Tiler†	4s		
William Russell, clerk	2s		
John FitzRichard	n/a		
John de Laycestre	n/a		
John Blakeden†	20s		
Henry Bere	2s		
Richard Lunges*	3s		
Hugh de Carlton*†	1s		
Henry de Benyngton	1s (wife)		
Geoffrey de Lenne	3s		

Key: † = individual not noted in 1327 but recorded in 1332; the latter (a tenth) is halved to draw it in line with the former (a twentieth); * = individual noted in both councils; ^ = official presumed to have been listed (the manuscript is damaged).

Sources: *BH*, fos 64v, 68v; E 179/135/12; E 179/135/16, mm. 26-26d

> of contrary opinions in certain matters and affairs affecting the liberty of the city on account of fraudulent claims of liberties not hitherto enjoyed or verbal traditions (*oracula*) not founded on the solid base of clear conscience (*super dare consciencie soliditatem fundata*) ...[140]

Exactly what was meant by this is unclear, though it is likely it had something to do with the financial improprieties of those tasked with overseeing civic finances, as well as with the threats and violent actions of certain members of the civic council towards the Dean and Chapter.[141] Whether or not this was a ruse to gain some sort of foothold in government is open to question, though it ultimately failed as those instituting the complaints were imprisoned by the crown before being freed at the request of Lincoln's 'council'.[142] Nevertheless, the important fact remains that throughout the fourteenth century the office of mayor was no longer monopolised by one individual or one family, a marked shift on the practices of the previous century.[143]

Occupationally, Lincoln's civic officials were dominated by merchants. This was not only true of the two councils discussed (1325/26 and 1335/36), where twenty-one of the twenty-six individuals whose occupations are known were merchants,[144] but also the period as a whole, where they made up over half of all trades listed (table 16). Despite the obvious dominance of this group, it is significant that by the 1380s their number had, at least in proportional terms, begun to dwindle.[145] Whilst at first glance it seems likely that this decline was the result of several factors, including the growing dominance of London and the south coast ports, the redistribution of credit networks towards the capital and the reduction in the number of international exporters of wool,[146] it must also be attributed in part to changes in royal legislation. In particular, in 1363 it became a 'statutory requirement for everyone to make themselves known by the craft from which they derived the major portion of their income'.[147] This provides context to the fact that over half of all those whose occupations are identified after 1363 (34 out of 60) listed an occupation other than 'merchant', compared to roughly a third before this date (44 of 115). This is significant as it demonstrates that whilst mercantile interests were often key to attaining wealth in order to gain access to the council, civic office, and subsequently parliament, not all men followed this path, both before and after these legislative changes, maintaining an interest in specific trades.

Aside from being merchants, Lincoln's civic officials most frequently engaged in the distribution of cloth (draper/mercer) or foodstuffs (fisher, spicer, butcher), while

140 *CPR, 1391–96*, 296.
141 *CPR, 1391–96*, 240; *CCR, 1392–96*, 134–4.
142 *CCR, 1392–96*, 146, 162.
143 *Medieval Lincoln*, 379–83.
144 The remaining five were a bottler, a clerk, a currier, a dyer and a fisher/porter. See appendix 2.
145 See table 2.
146 See 69–75.
147 Swanson, *British Towns*, 30; *Statutes of the Realm*, vol. 1, 379, c.6.

Table 16 Known occupations of civic officials (1289–1409)

Occupation	No.	Occupation	No.
Attorney	4	Mercer/tanner/barker	1
Barber	2	Merchant and second profession*	16
Bottle-maker	1	Merchant	96
Bower	2	Painter	2
Butcher	2	Pewterer	1
Cardmaker	1	Saddler	2
Clerk	2	Sheather	1
Clerk/chandler	1	Shipman	1
Clerk/illuminator	1	Skinner	4
Cooper	1	Smith	1
Cordwainer	1	Spicer	2
Currier	1	Spurrier	1
Fisher	5	Tailor	1
Fisher/porter	1	Tailor/dyer	1
Fuller	1	Tanner	1
Lavender	1	Taverner/hosteler	1
Lister (surgeon)	2	Weaver	1
Litster (dyer)	1	Weaver/cordwainer	1
Mason	1	Wine merchant	1
Mercer/draper	6	Wool merchant	1
Mercer/attorney	1	Wool merchant/barker	1
Mercer/mason	1	Total	175

Key: * = baker, barker (2), bower, butcher, clerk (2), draper, fisher/fishmonger (3), fustour, hosteler, ironmonger, lavender, parchment dealer, salter. Note: this list includes both *custodes* (Robert le Venur and William Cause). For details, see appendix 2.

lesser numbers acted as attorneys (after 1380),[148] bowers and skinners, emphasising the importance of the trades more generally discussed in chapter one. Even so, the variety of trades remains impressive, demonstrating that self-made men could and did rise through the ranks of government.

Whilst little has been said thus far regarding Lincoln's MPs, of those known to have represented the city prior to 1409 (seventy-two), all but ten served as civic officials.[149] This highlights how local MPs were frequently the same men who rose through the

[148] See 41–3.

[149] Note that nine of these did so prior to 1349, suggesting that MPs became more closely associated with civic office after this date. Appendix 3.

ranks of the civic administration as chamberlains, clerks, treasurers and sub-bailiffs, before taking their place on the civic council and eventually serving as coroners, bailiffs and mayor, once again underscoring the practical continuity of government already identified.[150] As part of this process it was also custom in the city for one MP to be elected for consecutive years. In turn, he was joined by a less experienced man, including those who had recently served as mayor. It appears that this was done not only in order to allow Lincoln's MPs to forge close personal relationships with other towns and groups (local gentry, royal officials) but to provide on-the-spot training for the next generation of civic representatives. For example, between 1348 and 1372 Walter de Kelby was returned as MP nine times. During his tenure he was elected alongside Peter Belasyse (mayor 1358/59) in 1360–61, John de Rodes (mayor 1363/64) in 1362, John de Bole (mayor 1361/62) in 1364–65, John de Welton (mayor 1364/65) in 1368 and John de Sutton (mayor 1367/68) in 1369 and 1372. He himself had originally attended three parliaments with the more experienced Robert de Dalderby in 1350–51 and 1353 before handing over to John de Sutton in 1372 who took over the senior position. Whilst it appears on the face of it that such practices were not affected by the Black Death, there was nevertheless a noticeable shift away from individuals who had not served in one of the three main civic positions (mayor, bailiff, coroner) after 1349, perhaps reflecting the shrinking pool of suitable candidates for the role, but equally demonstrating how the fortunes of the city on a national stage were being increasingly reserved for those serving the commonalty.

Residential Patterns

Having determined the types of individuals constituting Lincoln's civic government, it is useful now to consider where they lived in order to establish the extent to which place of residence was affected by the advancement of municipal reforms following the restitution of civil liberties. The following analysis considers the residential pattern of those attaining one of the three main civic posts (mayor, bailiff, coroner) by identifying the parish where their capital messuage or domicile was located, an approach to which Lincoln's high number of small parishes (46 in c.1300) lends itself particularly well. Whilst a more detailed street-by-street breakdown is desirable, it is not possible here given the limited scope of the evidence being used, with the majority of data being drawn from the subsidies of 1327, 1332 and 1340, records providing only a parochial breakdown of taxpayers.[151] Supplementary evidence drawn upon throughout this section includes wills, charters and pleas, many of which are nevertheless vague in outline. Take, for example, the will of John son of Thomas of Lincoln recorded in the *Burwarmote Book*, which, in 1332, made reference to the fact that Gilbert de Atherby (mayor 1316/17) lived in and rented

150 Compare to Bristol and York where MPs were often men 'with local interests who advised the town but played no direct part in its government'. Liddy, *War, Politics and Finance*, 144–55, at 144.

151 E 179/135/12; E 179/135/16, mm. 26–26d; E 179/135/26. Note that the 1340 subsidy has been cross-checked against the records from 1327 and 1332 to establish parochial markers.

one of his properties in the parish of All Saints in Hungate;[152] the will of William de Herpeswell (mayor 1352/53), dating from 1357, which bequeathed the tenement where he dwelt (*tenemento inhabito*) in Holy Trinity in Wigford to his daughter, Alice;[153] and the charter of Richard de Coupeland in 1316 that granted to John son of Gilbert de Laycestre several lands and buildings in the parish of St Peter in Wigford which were said to be located between the capital messuage (*inter capitale messuagium*) of Richard de Bellafago (mayor 1330/31) to the north and the tenement of Alice, wife of Walter, to the south.[154]

From a methodological perspective this evidence is not without its problems. Firstly, there is a clear chronological bias towards the period 1300–60, with only four locations of officials being known before 1300 and only twelve after 1360 (the last dating from 1397). As such it is difficult to gauge whether or not there were any longer term patterns in residential status, especially in the post-plague period. A second problem is that it has been possible to identify parish locations for only two fifths (122 of 313) of all known officials for the period (1289–1409), meaning that the conclusions drawn here are impressionistic at best.[155]

The following data (table 17) is organised at ten-year intervals according to parish of residence (or approximate location in the case of Eastgate). For each of these intervals the number of officials has been counted and recorded according to the highest rank of office achieved (mayor being highest, followed by bailiff and coroner). This is listed according to the date at which this position was achieved. From the data it is clear that the highest proportion of officials (thirty-nine out of 115)[156] lived in the neighbourhood around the Stonebow, the intramural city's southern gate, which lay at the junction of Salterlane (also Soper/Saperlane or Sapergate), Walkergate and Briggate, an area spanning the entire southern wall (maps 2, 5), leading to the suburb of Wigford. Located in this area were six parishes – All Saints (Hungate), St Benedict, St Mary Crackpole, St Peter at Pleas, St Peter at Arches and St Swithun – all of which lay adjacent to at least one of these main roads. The second most common area (excluding the parish of St Benedict) was the suburb of Wigford, which stretched for almost a mile from the city gate southwards; here twenty-four officials lived. This was followed by the remaining parishes from the intramural area (seventeen), the Bail (ten), Eastgate (ten), Butwerk (eight), Newport (three), Westcastle (one), and the parish of Holy Innocents, which lay beyond the city limits to the south (one). No officials are recorded as living in the jurisdiction of the Close or in the suburb of Newland.

Of the different ranks of officials, the most popular parishes for those serving as mayor were St Mary Crackpole (five), St Benedict and St Swithun (four), followed by St Mary Magdalene in the Bail and Holy Trinity and St Peter in Wigford (three each). For bailiffs not becoming mayor, the most common parish was St Peter

152 *BB*, fo. 91.

153 *BB*, fo. 232.

154 LAO Dij 76/3/32; 77/1/33.

155 Including those known to have 'moved house', see main text below.

156 Note this figure (115) does not include the seven officials known to have 'moved house', see main text below.

Table 17 Known residential locations of civic officials (c.1289–c.1399)

Location (numbers in parenthesis relate to locations on map 5 overleaf)	1289–99	1300–09	1310–19	1320–29	1330–39
(20) St Benedict*	–	–	B	B	B, M, C
(44) St Peter at Pleas*	–	B	–	M, B	B
(42) St Mary Crackpole*	–	M, B	–	M, M, B	–
(45) St Swithun*	–	–	M	–	B, M
(38) St Martin	–	–	M, M, B	–	B
(32) St Mary Magdalene in the Bail	–	–	–	–	C, B
(4) St Peter, Eastgate	–	–	B	B	B
(11) St Augustine, Butwerk	–	B	–	M, M	B
(18) Holy Trinity, Wigford	–	–	–	–	–
(4–7) Eastgate	–	–	–	–	B
(46) St Edmund	–	M	–	B, B	–
(29) St Paul in the Bail	–	B	–	B, M, B	–
(28) St Peter, Wigford	B	–	–	–	M, M, M
(21) St Botolph, Wigford	–	–	–	B	B
(39) St Lawrence	–	M	–	–	–
(24) St Margaret, Wigford	–	B	–	M	M
(26) St Mary, Wigford	–	–	B	–	–
(2) St Nicholas Newport	B	–	–	B	–
(44) St Peter at Arches*	–	–	B	M	–
(43) All Saints, Hungate*	–	–	–	–	–
(16) Holy Cross, Wigford	–	–	B	–	B
(33) St Michael on the Mount	Cu	–	–	–	–
(27) St Michael, Wigford	–	B	–	–	–
(9) St Rumbold, Butwerk	–	–	–	M	–
(35) St Andrew	–	–	–	–	M
(19) St Andrew, Wigford	–	–	–	–	–
(3) St Bartholomew	–	B	–	–	–
(10) St Bavon, Butwerk	–	–	–	–	M
(13) St Clement, Butwerk	Cu	–	–	–	–
(37) St Cuthbert	–	M	–	–	–
(40) St George	–	–	–	M	–
(17) Holy Innocents	–	–	M	–	–
(23) St John, Wigford	–	–	M	–	–
(36) St Peter at the Skinmarket	–	–	–	–	B
Sub-total of mayors/*custodes*	2	4	5	9	8
Sub-total of bailiffs	2	7	6	10	12
Sub-total of coroners	–	–	–	–	2
Total	4	10	11	19	22

Key: B = bailiff; C = coroner; M = mayor; Cu = *custos*; * = parish located near the Stonebow. Numbers in parenthesis relate to locations on map 5. Note: this table does not include those known to have moved house; see table 18 below.

1340–49	1350–59	1360–69	1370–79	1380–89	1390–99	Mayors/ *custodes*	Bailiffs	Coroners	Total
M, B, M	–	M, M	–	–	–	4	4	1	9
B, B, C	M	C	–	–	–	2	5	2	9
B	M	M	–	–	–	5	3	–	8
–	B	–	–	M, M	–	3	3	–	6
B	B	–	–	–	–	2	4	–	6
M, B	M	M	–	–	B	3	3	1	7
M	B, M	–	–	–	–	2	4	–	6
–	B	–	–	–	–	2	3	–	5
B, M, B	M, M	–	–	–	–	3	2	–	5
B	B, M	–	–	–	–	1	3	–	4
B	–	–	–	–	–	1	3	–	4
–	–	–	–	–	–	1	3	–	4
–	–	–	–	–	–	3	1	–	4
–	–	–	–	M	–	1	2	–	3
M	–	–	–	–	B	2	1	–	3
–	–	–	–	–	–	2	1	–	3
B	–	–	M	–	–	1	2	–	3
C	–	–	–	–	–	–	2	1	3
B	–	–	–	–	–	1	2	–	3
M	B	–	–	–	–	1	1	–	2
–	–	–	–	–	–	–	2	–	2
M	–	–	–	–	–	2	–	–	2
–	B	–	–	–	–	–	2	–	2
–	M	–	–	–	–	2	–	–	2
–	–	–	–	–	–	1	–	–	1
–	–	–	M	–	–	1	–	–	1
–	–	–	–	–	–	–	1	–	1
–	–	–	–	–	–	1	–	–	1
–	–	–	–	–	–	1	–	–	1
–	–	–	–	–	–	1	–	–	1
–	–	–	–	–	–	1	–	–	1
–	–	–	–	–	–	1	–	–	1
–	–	–	–	–	–	1	–	–	1
–	–	–	–	–	–	–	1	–	1
						53	57	5	115
8	8	4	2	3	–				
11	7	–	–	–	2				
2	–	1	–	–	–				
21	15	5	2	3	2				

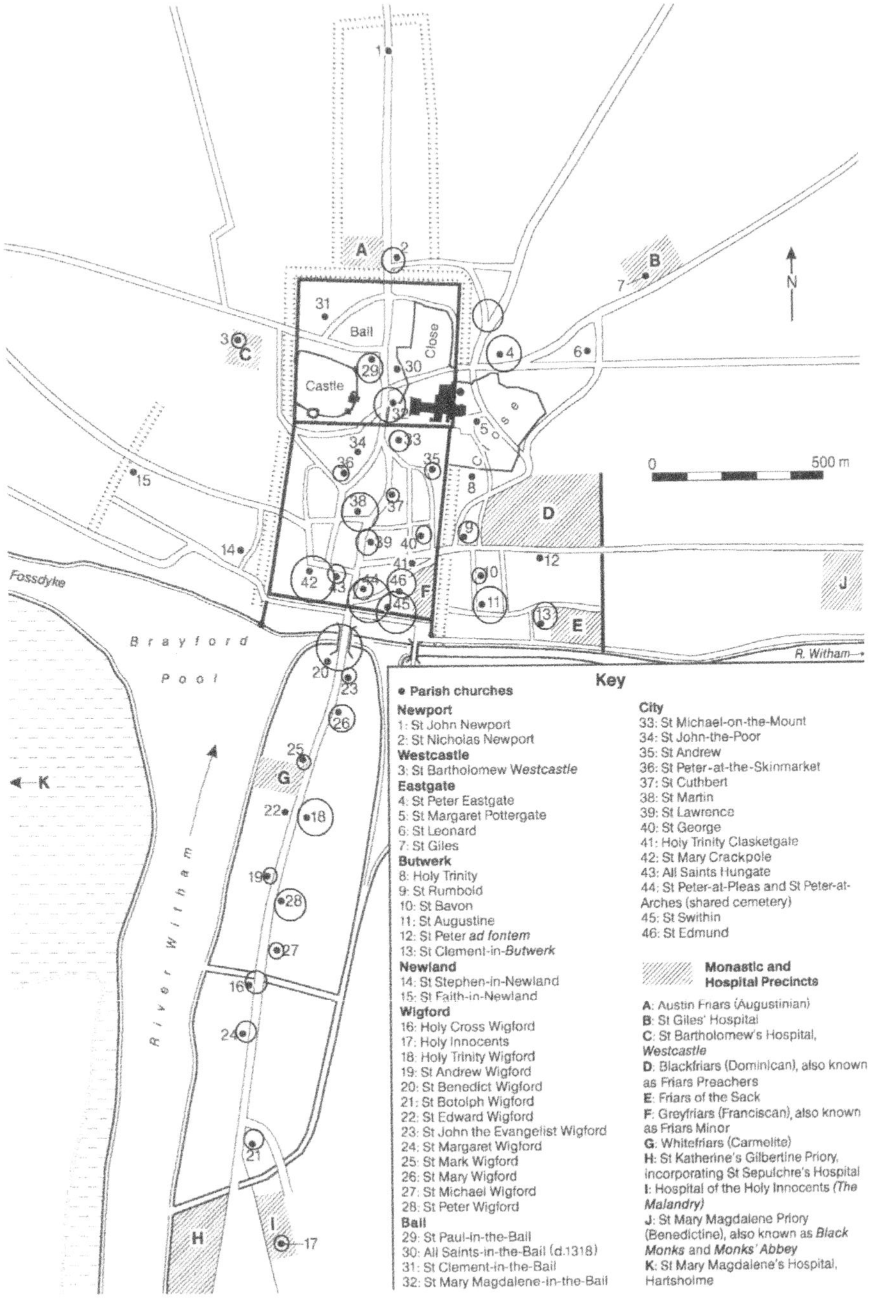

Map 5 Known residential locations of civic officials (c.1289–c.1399)

Key: the size of each circle is relative to the number of officials drawn from that parish

at Pleas (five), located near the Stonebow, followed by the parishes of St Martin, located roughly halfway up the hill in the intramural area, St Benedict and St Peter in Eastgate (all with four). Little can be said regarding coroners primarily as the majority of these individuals have been considered in the higher ranking categories of bailiff and mayor.

The clearest trend to emerge from this evidence is that the parishes of St Peter at Pleas, St Mary Crackpole and St Benedict returned the greatest number of officials between the 1320s and 1340s, a practice which continued at a lesser pace until the 1350s and 1360s, with St Mary Crackpole being popular throughout the entire period. This marked a clear shift southwards from the earlier period (1289–1319), when five out of nine mayors and one *custos* were identified as living in the parishes of St Cuthbert, St John the poor, St Lawrence, St Martin and St Michael on the Mount. A second observation is that individuals were often elected from the same parish during the same decade: for example, two bailiffs and a mayor are recorded in St Paul in the Bail in the 1320s, whilst three mayors are noted for St Peter in Wigford in the 1330s. This suggests that local connections may have been important, with mutual support being offered in elections. A third observation is that after 1350 no officials can be identified as living in the suburbs of Newport or Westcastle or the parish of Holy Innocents, thereby physically shrinking the area from where officials were elected. This is a pattern supported by the evidence of officials known to have 'moved house' (table 18).

Table 18 Civic officials known to have 'moved house'

Hugh Bacun (bailiff 1311/12)	St Edmund (1327) → St Benedict (1330)
John de Blyton (mayor 1333/34)	St Margaret, Wigford (1327/1332) → St Peter at Arches (1347)
John de Bristall (mayor 1338/39)	St Augustine (1332) → St Peter at Pleas (1349)
William de Hakthorn (coroner 1330+)	St Margaret, Wigford (1327/1332) → St Lawrence (1345)
Robert Hare (bailiff 1361/62)	St Peter, Wigford (1327) → St Michael on the Mount (1361)
Ralph de Kyme (bailiff 1333/34)	St Andrew, Wigford (1327) → St Swithun (1340)
Richard Toke (bailiff 1344/45)	St Paul in the Bail (1327) → St Swithun (1353)

From this small sample of seven officials it is clear that four relocated to one of the parishes lying adjacent to the Stonebow sometime between the 1320s and the 1340s at a period when officials from this area were being elected with greater frequency. Some of them, like John de Blyton and Ralph de Kyme, moved a considerable distance from the suburbs. Whether or not this was due to a greater propensity for officials to be elected from this area at this time or whether officials moved there in order to become more electable is not entirely clear. However, the fact that each of these officials, with the possible exception of Ralph de Kyme, served their term of office prior to their move suggests there were other contributing factors at work. Before considering what these may have been, it is first worthwhile questioning whether the two other officials who did not relocate to this area were representative of a broader trend following the Black Death to avoid more crowded areas. Certainly, a proportionally higher number of officials can be identified as living in suburbs after this date (12 from 25) compared to before 1349 (35 from 89). Recent work by Carol Rawcliffe has suggested that despite systematic measures regarding urban cleanliness being established after successive bouts of plague, processes for dealing with sanitation and pollution were nevertheless well underway before this date, albeit on something of an ad hoc basis.[157] Does the evidence of the residential patterns of Lincoln's civic officials reflect a growing awareness of the potential risks of living in crowded and less sanitary areas? Circumstantial evidence suggests it may well be the case, and following repeated complaints over the 'deep mud … dung and filth thrown in the streets and lanes, and other loathsome things lying about and heaped up' in the city's main thoroughfares in 1365, Peter Belassise and Roger de Tateshale were tasked with overseeing the repair of roads and bridges and asked to conduct a review into dumping and the disposal of dung throughout the city.[158] Even so, this fails to explain the earlier concentration of officials in and around the Stonebow, for which other reasons must be found.

Until 1237 the city's guildhall was located in the south-eastern corner of the city in the parish of St Swithun. However, at the order of Henry III the hall was granted to the newly arrived Friars Minor (Greyfriars), making it necessary for a new guildhall to be found elsewhere.[159] According to several scattered references, it is clear that by the beginning of the fourteenth century (and most likely much earlier) the guildhall, also known as the hall of pleas (*aula placitorum*), was located somewhere in the south of the parish of St Peter at Arches, which lay partially within and partially without the intramural area (its boundaries lying on either side of the wall), abutting the king's road (Briggate?) and Sapergate (map 2).[160] Later evidence dating from 1390 confirms that the guildhall was in fact located above Stonebow gate, as in that year it was knocked down and shortly after rebuilt.[161] Here the business of the Burwarmote Court was conducted, with Mondays typically reserved for disputes of land, including pleas of *writ de recto*, trespass and novel disseisin, whilst Thursdays were set aside for pleas of debt and other market offences, including forestalling and regrating.[162] In addition to civic business, after 1283 the Burwarmote Court also enrolled the business of the Statute Merchant registry (on any day) until approximately the mid-fifteenth century. The relocation of the guildhall thus drove business

157 C. Rawcliffe, *Urban Bodies: Communal Health in Late Medieval English Towns and Cities* (Woodbridge, 2013), 116–52.

158 *CPR, 1364–67*, 89; *BH*, fo. 15.

159 *CCR, 1234–37*, 495–6, 500; Robson, 'The Greyfriars of Lincoln', 113–37.

160 *BB*, fo. 81v; LAO Dij 80/3/34–6, 71.

161 Hill's suggestion that the 'new hall was still in the process of building in the early years of the sixteenth century' is incorrect as the business of the court was recorded as taking place in the guildhall by August 1394 at the latest: *Medieval Lincoln*, 254; JUST 2/93, rot. 1; JUST 1/532, m. 1.

162 Brooks, 'Lincoln Court of Burghmanmote', LAO FL/Transcripts/U/28, 2, 15.

to this area of the city unlike ever before, with merchants from all over England and the continent travelling to the city in search of credit and trade.[163]

A second catalysing force in the emergence of the Stonebow as the centre of civic life was the redevelopment of housing from c.1270 onwards. Evidence for this dates indirectly from 1330, when the charter of Edward III stated

> that the ancestors of those citizens anciently constructed upon a certain wall of that city, lying across from Newland gate as far as the manse of the Friars of the Order of Minors ... divers buildings, that is to say, chambers and houses in the dwellings adjacent to the said wall in divers places near Walkergate and Soperlane and that those buildings are for the improvement and security of the said city.[164]

Evidence for the dating of these structures comes from several sources, including a series of charters relating to the *Sancto Laudo* estate (c.1270–95), which spanned the parishes of St Mary Crackpole, All Saints in Hungate and St Peter at Arches and contained several houses, an oratory, a hall, a chapel, cellars, gardens and stables, amongst other buildings;[165] three charters dating from the 1290s that saw the future mayor, Stephen de Stanham, purchase several lands and tenements in the area, which he renovated and rebuilt;[166] and a charter from 1327 which recorded that Thomas de Carleton, future under-sheriff,[167] purchased a lane in the parish of St Mary Crackpole from the mayor and commonalty measuring 'forty-six ells [in length], and in breadth seven ells at the east end and three-quarters of an ell at the west end, at a yearly rent of 6d, with licence to enclose, build on, or work the same, as he or his heirs and assigns should think best'.[168] In addition to this, it is clear that much of this rebuilding also emerged as a result of the contracting textile industry during the second half of the thirteenth century, in particular in the parishes of All Saints in Hungate and St Mary Crackpole, where dozens of cloth workshops were formerly located,[169] it even being said in 1322 that a tenement lying in All Saints was 'waste in a waste part of the city' (*vasta et iacens in loco vasto ville Linc' supradicte*).[170] Yet, as already noted, efforts were being made to rebuild and after this date various new cottages, gardens, shops and tenements can be identified in these parishes.[171] Such evidence reflects the experience of Winchester where physical urban decay occasioned an improvement in the living conditions of its urban inhabitants by providing greater space and opportunities upon which to build.[172] Equally it also reflects the shift from a cloth industry towards that of wool.

163 See 80–1, 87–8.

164 *Royal Charters*, 55. Alterations to this translation are my own.

165 *Reg. Antiq.*, vol. 8, nos 2364–79; Vince, 'High Medieval Era', 217, figure 9.58.

166 *Reg. Antiq.*, vol. 8, nos 2353–5. See also *BB*, fos 82–82v.

167 *CCR, 1330–34*, 270, 382.

168 *CPR, 1327–30*, 19. *BB*, fos 159v–160v.

169 Bischoff, 'Economic Change', 60–72, 81–2.

170 *Reg. Antiq.*, vol. 8, no. 2362.

171 For example, *BB*, fos 151v, 175v, 185, 196, 203, 269; *CPR, 1385–89*, 415, 522; *1391–96*, 98–9; *Reg. Antiq.*, vol. 8, no. 2345.

172 Keene, *Medieval Winchester*, vol. 1, 151–5.

The emergence of the wool trade as the dominant economic force in the city in the opening decades of the fourteenth century not only resulted in an increasing number of warehouses and storage facilities being established in this area but also ensured that local and visiting merchants and traders maintained direct access to the river and overland communication and transport routes.[173] These changes were driven by the requirement for all wool traded by citizens to be brought to the local wool market in St Swithun to be weighed prior to sale. The growing importance of wool to the local economy was boosted further still in 1326 when Lincoln was named as one of nine English staple towns, which meant that henceforth all of the county's wool was to pass through Lincoln's wool market. Although Lincoln held the staple intermittently over the next half century, it nevertheless consolidated its status as the dominant centre for the wool trade in the county, a position which went unchallenged until the fifteenth century. Given the overall scale of involvement by civic officials in the wool trade at this time, it comes as little surprise to see such a high number relocating to or establishing their residences in this central area.

Whilst developments in the wool trade and the local building industry remained central to the change in civic residential patterns, socio-political reasons also played an important role too. Intermarriage, in particular, ensured that families found new ways of maintaining their wealth and status at a time when few 'survived more than one or two generations in the male line'.[174] Whilst evidence for such practices at Lincoln remains limited it nevertheless suggests that civic officials living in both the central areas and elsewhere intermarried with some frequency. For example, in the will of Ralph de Kyme (bailiff 1333/34), dated 1342, it was noted that Christine, his sister, had previously married Elias de Stubton (bailiff 1321/22);[175] whilst in 1347 the will of Matilda le Copper, widow of Roger le Copper (bailiff 1305/06) and former wife of Henry Scarle, recorded that her daughter Isobel had married Richard FitzMartin (mayor 1344/45).[176] In 1408 the will of Joanna, wife of Robert de Appulby (mayor 1401/02), her third husband, stated that she had previously been betrothed to Robert de Saltby (mayor 1384/85) and Alexander Herwey (*viz.* Herle) (bailiff 1382/83).[177] In 1315 it was noted that Hugh Russell (mayor 1319/20) was the kinsman of William son of John de Blyton (mayor 1327/28), though whether this was by marriage is not stated.[178] Lincoln thus saw developments comparable to those in York, where intermarriage helped forge new links for families in Petergate. There

173 For the following, see 67–90.

174 J. Kermode, 'Sentiment and Survival: Family and Friends in Late Medieval English Towns,' *Journal of Family History*, 24, 5 (1999), 7.

175 Kyme lived in St Andrew's parish before moving to St Swithun sometime before 1340, Stubton in St Benedict. *BB*, fos 153–153v; E 179/135/12, rot. 1d; E 179/135/26, rot. 3; E 179/135/16, m. 26.

176 Matilda lived in St John from at least 1327, FitzMartin in St Laurence. It is unknown where Roger le Copper and his wife lived. *BB*, fo. 180; E 179/135/12, rots 1d, 2d.

177 Robert de Appulby lived in St Benedict. It is unknown where Saltby and Herwey lived. *ELW*, 107–9. See appendix 2.

178 *BB*, fo. 189. Blyton lived in St Margaret, Wigford. To establish this, compare E 179/135/26, m. 1, with E 179/135/12, rot. 1, where John de Hybaldestowe and John de Wytten senior, neighbours located on either side of Blyton, are recorded as living in St Margaret. It is not known where Russell lived.

the Langton family were able to take control of the mayoralty for much of the first half of the fourteenth century, intermittently sharing office with their neighbours.[179] Whilst annual mayoral terms restricted such practices at Lincoln, it is clear that family ties, such as those evident for Blyton and Russell, were nevertheless effective in establishing informal dynasties.

Taken collectively these developments undoubtedly fostered a new mercantile identity built primarily upon the profits of the wool trade. These were in every sense of the word 'new' men, with only one civic official being identified as having dynastic antecedents from the period before the suspension of liberties,[180] a development similar to that at London.[181] Unsurprisingly, many of these men entered into partnerships with one another,[182] whilst others began to patronise local lay institutions, including chantries and guilds, thereby establishing a new civic and cultural centre in both a figurative and physical sense.[183]

Despite these changes, it is important to recognise that not all civic officials settled in this central area of the city. Wigford, Lincoln's southern suburb, was another favoured destination, which had links with wealth and status dating back at least two centuries. As David Stocker argues, during the twelfth century Wigford underwent a 'process of gentrification', which saw a number of high status buildings constructed, many of which were built in stone, thus attracting the 'social and commercial elite'.[184] It is likely that the greater availability of space within the suburb continued to attract wealthier inhabitants with designs on building grand houses,[185] some of whom kept orchards, livestock and woodlands nearby,[186] much like at Winchester and Colchester, for example.[187] The high number of parish churches in the suburb (twelve) likewise served to fulfil the pious needs of individuals and families, with numerous guilds and chantries being founded in the area.[188] Nonetheless, it remained a fact of life that the suburb was also home to a number of noisier and smellier trades, including tanning, butchery and manufacturing (tile-making, pottery), which may have discouraged some wealthier inhabitants from living there.[189] Moreover, as greater space became available in the central areas through the decay of old plots and tenements, it is possible that the suburb lost some of its appeal.

Aside from the six main parishes located around the Stonebow already discussed,

179 Rees Jones, *York*, 198.

180 This was Robert de Holm (mayor 1357/58) whose family maintained a long and distinguished lineage in the city: *Medieval Lincoln*, 386–7.

181 Williams, *Medieval London*, 115–16.

182 C 241/57/71; C 241/79/110; C 241/82/63; C 241/138/169; *CCR, 1307–13*, 452.

183 See chapters five and six.

184 Vince, 'High Medieval Era', 246; *Medieval Lincoln*, 392–3.

185 Such as St Andrew's Hall: Vince, 'High Medieval Era', plate 4.5.

186 *BB*, fos 115v, 223, 227v; LAO Bj 2/5, fos 59v, 69v, 96, 105, 111v, 119, 139v, 159v; E. G. Kimball (ed.), *Sessions of the Peace in the City of Lincoln, 1351–1354, and the Borough of Stamford 1351* (Lincoln Record Society, 1971), 3, no. 3.

187 Keene, *Medieval Winchester*, vol. 1, 143; Britnell, *Colchester*, 112.

188 Chapters five and six.

189 *BB*, fos 93, 107, 121, 179, 214; Kimball, *Some Sessions of the Peace*, 4, no. 11.

it is apparent that the other intramural parishes remained popular for civic officials, in particular St Mary Magdalene in the Bail and St Paul in Bail, both of which lay legally beyond the reach of the civic authorities.

Throughout the thirteenth and fourteenth centuries, Lincoln Castle and its surrounding walled area, known as the Bail, were held by successive constables on behalf of the earls of Lincoln, before escheating to John of Gaunt through marriage in 1362 and subsequently to the crown upon his death in 1399.[190] As an independent jurisdiction, the Bail maintained its own rights and liberties free from civic interference, with local inhabitants owing their rents and market dues to the constable of the castle.[191] This raises an important question: why did officials serving the civic jurisdiction choose to live in the Bail? Whilst it is possible that living in this area might be seen as a means to evade civic office, a pressing problem during the fifteenth century in Lincoln and elsewhere,[192] the fact that these men were civic officials serves to discount this possibility. The most likely explanation, therefore, seems to be that except within a judicial or legal context – i.e. the collection of revenues or rents, or in the management of market rights – the Bail was not in fact considered independent of the wider urban fabric, with the same types of people living either side of the 'Great Gate' (*Magna Porta*).[193] Certainly, throughout much of the Middle Ages the Bail was an area which throve due to the high number of people visiting the castle on shire business, a fact which invariably provided numerous opportunities for profit. A good example of this conceptual distinction comes from 1322 when, according to a commission of oyer and terminer, the city's incumbent bailiffs, Henry le Lavender and Richard le Little, were refused the right to collect monies in the Bail arising from 'trespasses and contracts made there, amends of the breach of assize of bread and ale, gabel, toll, and other such customs and services and amercements arising there, in aid of the farm of that city'.[194] The significance of this complaint derives from the fact that of the thirty listed men opposing the bailiffs five would go on to hold civic office.[195] These were William de Snarteford (mayor 1324/25), Roger de Dalderby (bailiff 1323/24), John de Mumby (bailiff 1326/27), Geoffrey de Frothingham (bailiff 1324/25) and Henry de Filyngham (mayor 1340/41),[196] each of whom lived in the Bail alongside the other listed men.[197] Whilst on the one hand this might seem surprising given the fact that civic rights were being opposed by those appointed, even expected, to defend the civic government's privileges, on the other it seems clear that this was a matter of principle, with the bailiffs seeking out

190 *Medieval Lincoln*, 90–1; *CFR, 1347–56*, 97; *CPR, 1361–64*, 449.

191 Table 1.

192 Kermode, 'Urban Decline?', 180; *Medieval Lincoln*, 270, 277, n. 4, 278, n. 1.

193 The 'Great Gate' was cited in the will of John Sauter, vicar in the choir of the Church of the Blessed Mary, in 1349: *BB*, fo. 203v.

194 *CPR, 1321–24*, 150–1. The commission was instituted following a petition and relates to 1318/19: SC 8/64/3155.

195 Attreed, 'Urban Identity in Medieval English Towns', *Journal of Interdisciplinary History*, 32, 4 (2002), 574–5.

196 Note also that Snarteford was a member of the civic council in 1323/24, Dalderby and Frothingham in 1325/26: *BH*, fos 65v, 68v.

197 E 179/135/12, rot. 3d. See also *BH*, fo. 18v.

monies which were not legally theirs to take. Perhaps the most significant aspect of this episode was that by opposing the city's bailiffs these men did no harm to their own civic careers, suggesting that debates could and did happen without always resorting to internecine politicking or violence.[198]

The greater availability of stone housing within the intramural area also remained a central reason for the general appeal of the intramural parishes, much less their proximity to local markets.[199] Although many of these houses were built in the twelfth and thirteenth centuries, they were nevertheless spacious and architecturally impressive, none more so than the so-called 'Jew's House' opposite the church of St Cuthbert or the 'Norman House' situated on the corner of St Michael. Of course, whether or not any stone houses were demolished and rebuilt in timber, as at York, is not clear,[200] though it is likely that many of the aforementioned new houses were constructed from timber and built upon stone foundations, a common feature of towns during the fourteenth century.[201] Such developments marked a broader urban trend for timber-framed housing at this time, primarily as it 'allowed easy expansion of building units to handle changes in circumstances, such as more functions within the domestic complex or more occupants', certainly more so than stone.[202] Nevertheless, contemporary attitudes towards domestic residence were seldom uniform, with individuals of the same rank often settling in areas according to their own economic and social needs.[203]

Such a conclusion is drawn sharply into focus when it is considered that the shifting residential pattern of Lincoln's civic officials was influenced, at least in part, by the expulsion of the city's Jewish population in 1290. Specifically, in the ensuing twenty years after the departure of the Jews, the previously heavily populated parishes of St Cuthbert, St Lawrence, St Martin and St Michael on the Mount came to house at least five civic officials, four of whom held the office of mayor.[204] These included Gilbert de Atherby (mayor 1316/17), who purchased the lands and properties of Hagin the Jew in St Martin from Stephen de Cheynduit in 1299, and John de Amecotes (mayor 1308/09), who purchased a 'good house with two shops and a magnificent passage' (*optima domus cum duabus shopis et pulcro exitu*) in St Cuthbert, formerly the property of Floria, daughter of Josce, in January 1299 from William de Tame, cordwainer.[205] Although this was a relatively short-lived trend, it nevertheless demonstrates how leading civic figures were keen to re-appropriate and proselytise this area after the expulsion of the Jews. This can be seen through

198 For example, McLane, *1341 Inquest*, no. 720.

199 Vince, 'High Medieval Era', 214–16.

200 Rees Jones, *York*, 291.

201 J. Schofield and G. Stell, 'The Built Environment', in *CUHB*, 389–91; Vince, 'High Medieval Era', 216.

202 Schofield and Stell, 'The Built Environment', 390.

203 J. Rimmer, 'The Language and Property: Vernacular in the Context of Late Medieval Urban Identities', in E. Salter and H. Wicker (eds), *Vernacularity in England and Wales, c.1300–1500* (Turnhout, 2011), 269–94.

204 Mundill, 'Jews in England', 293–7.

205 *BB*, fo. 91; *Chantry Certificates*, 201; Johnson and Jones, *Steep, Strait and High*. My thanks to Chris Johnson for allowing me to read this in advance of publication.

the foundation of three early religious institutions: the guild of Cordwainers in St Lawrence in 1307, and the perpetual chantries of Alexander FitzMartyn, also in St Lawrence in 1303, and Beatrice Colet in St Michael on the Mount (1301).[206] As late as 1363, parishioners of St Cuthbert and St Andrew founded a guild in honour of St Mary, making special reference to the tomb of 'St Hugh Junior',[207] a local Christian boy purportedly murdered by Lincoln's Jews in 1255,[208] highlighting how, despite these efforts, this area remained strongly associated with the Jews for many years.

Conclusion

The abuses which led to the suspension of the city's liberties at the close of the thirteenth century paved the way for a more homogeneous civic identity to emerge throughout the course of the fourteenth and fifteenth centuries by opening up administrative posts to a wider pool of citizens and by establishing new recording practices. Centred physically and symbolically upon the Stonebow, which housed the guildhall, the city's clear but permeable civic hierarchy and structure helped define the role and expectations of civic officials, including where they might live.[209] Over time, the residential status of officials thus helped fashion the identity of this group in a cyclical way, much like at York in the fifteenth century where officials were shunned for living in poorer suburbs.[210] Whilst at Lincoln this status reflected the growing importance of the wool trade, other socio-political and economic developments, including bonds of intermarriage and shared business interests, ensured that this new civic identity also came to reflect a new merchant class spearheaded by men with few links to the recent past. Not all civic officials pursued this course, however, with some taking advantage of the Jewish expulsion by buying up former properties and others still taking advantage of the space and traditions of the suburbs, most notably in Wigford. Whilst it is tempting to suggest that the divisions which emerged in the 1390s over the election of the mayor may have been caused by allegiances forged through shared residential space, this is at present without any firm basis in fact. Nonetheless, as earlier evidence dictated, divisions over civic policy could and did arise over such matters.

Undoubtedly one of the most significant policies to emerge from Lincoln's sweeping municipal changes in the opening decade of the fourteenth century was the adoption of single annual term for the mayor. Not only did this represent how the reinstituted government had moved away from its earlier monopolistic policies of the pre-suspension years but it also demonstrated how local government had at last heeded the warnings of the crown. An indirect consequence of these changes was that it allowed local practices to emerge which enabled the city to deal with the

206 See chapters five and six.
207 C 47/40/140.
208 *Medieval Lincoln*, 224–30.
209 P. J. Arnade, M. C. Howell and S. Walter, 'Fertile Spaces: The Productivity of Urban Space in Northern Europe', *Journal of Interdisciplinary History*, 32, 4 (2002), 540.
210 Kermode, *Medieval Merchants*, 45; Goldberg, 'Urban Identity', 197, 201, 213.

crises of the Black Death and subsequent plagues more effectively than many other towns, including Colchester and Winchester where numbers of officials rose considerably after the plague.[211] Despite this, there was nevertheless a perceptible rise in the number of individuals attaining the mayoralty without first serving as bailiff or coroner after 1349, thereby highlighting how the high death toll was liable to disrupt even the most robust practices. This was reflected most clearly by the reintroduction of recording names in the *Blickling Homilies* following almost two decades of neglect, a custom which served to remind civic leaders of their own duty, identity and history.

Further indication of Lincoln's evolving civic status was the physical and symbolic expansion of government throughout the fourteenth and early fifteenth centuries, in particular following the restitution of civil liberties and the granting of shire status. The latter, in particular, was undoubtedly a means by which the civic authorities sought to assuage any doubts over the future wellbeing of the city during a period of growing economic hardship but equally to redress the economic instability wrought by royal policy after 1383.[212] Indirectly, it may also have served to attract migrants, many of whom were lured to the city by the availability of work, particularly in agricultural and service trades.[213] Taken collectively, the experience of Lincoln highlights how the direct involvement of the crown in local political matters at both the beginning and the end of the period paved the way for a shared economic and political culture to emerge in the city which, over time, came to be matched by religious and cultural developments.[214] Although it remains true that day-to-day dealings with the crown were minimal,[215] its influence was not, and this impacted significantly on the physical and symbolic landscape of the city.

211 Britnell, 'Black Death', 208. See also Goldberg, *Medieval England*, 38–9.

212 D. M. Palliser, 'Urban Society', in R. Horrox (ed.), *Fifteenth-Century Attitudes: Perceptions of Society in Late Medieval England* (Cambridge, 1994), 144–9. See also chapter three.

213 See 33–4, 48 and n. 258.

214 Chapters five and six.

215 H. Carrel, 'The Rituals of Town–Crown Relations in post-Black Death England', in Andrews, *Ritual and Space*, 148–64.

5

Fraternity, Orthodoxy and Communal Cooperation

By the end of the fourteenth century there were at least thirty-two religious and craft-based guilds in the city and its suburbs.[1] Over 90 per cent of these institutions were established after 1275, which suggests that, despite an earlier legacy of guilds in medieval England, a specific need for them developed over the following 125 years.[2] According to existing historiography such a need stemmed from three main factors: first, as individual fears over not being decently buried grew, guilds effectively performed the role of a 'burial society'; second, the demographic upheaval of the Black Death prompted guilds to take the place of dislocated kinship structures; and third, guilds developed as a means to transcend the limitations of the parish; or, in other words, the changing needs of communities came to be better served through their involvement with voluntary associations as opposed to the often fixed and impermeable structures of the parish, a phenomenon influenced significantly by the growing involvement of the laity in local religious matters.[3] However, when these theories are set beside the evidence for Lincoln they are not altogether satisfactory. In fact, it becomes necessary to pose a number of questions: why did only some parishes establish guilds and not others? What were the founders' motivations and aims in establishing a guild? How should guilds established prior to the Black Death be considered – were they in fact different to those established after 1349? – and what was the significance of their foundation? Finally, when was the greatest growth of guild foundations in the city and how does this compare to other towns? It is the aim of this chapter to consider these questions. In so doing, it will analyse the impact of guilds upon the collective devotional and spiritual needs of their members, consider the importance of inter-guild cooperation in the city and detail how secular and religious ordinances recorded by guilds remain an important source not only for what

1 No exact figure can be given due to (a) the fluctuating number of guilds; and (b) the possibility that the returns submitted to Chancery in 1389 are incomplete (see main text below).

2 For early guilds, see, for example, D. J. Keene, 'English Urban Guilds, c.900–1300', in Gadd and Wallis, *Guilds and Association*, 3–26; G. Rosser, 'The Anglo-Saxon Guilds', in J. Blair (ed.), *Minsters and Parish Churches: The Local Church in Transition, 950–1200* (Oxford, 1988), 31–5.

3 The literature on this topic is substantial but see G. Rosser, 'Communities of Parish and Guild in the Late Middle Ages', in S. J. Wright (ed.), *Parish, Church and People: Local Studies in Lay Religion, 1350–1750* (London, 1988), 29–55; Westlake, *Parish Gilds*, 19–20; C. Barron, 'The Parish Fraternities of Medieval London', in Barron and Harper-Bill, *The Church in Pre-Reformation Society*, 13–14, 23–5.

they reveal about late fourteenth-century attitudes towards the crown, orthodoxy and organisation, but for local beliefs too.

Throughout this chapter particular focus will be placed on the growth and proliferation of guilds within the physical environment before 1389. This differs from existing studies which have largely prioritised the later fifteenth and sixteenth centuries over the earlier period and have considered such themes as charitable bequests, reputation and status, links to local and regional political elites, fraternal piety and processions.[4] This is not to say that the approach adopted here will not consider some, though by no means all, of these themes, only that its focus is for the most part different. The outcome of this approach is to demonstrate how in cases such as Lincoln, where the surviving evidence is almost exclusively limited to the guild certificates recorded in 1389, more can be revealed about the development of local socio-religious practices than was hitherto considered possible.[5]

Throughout, the singular terms of 'guild', 'fraternity' and 'confraternity' will be used whenever discussing specific institutions which, in their ordinances, describe themselves as such. However, the plural 'guilds' will be used when describing groups of institutions, whatever their title. This is consistent with Virginia Bainbridge's assertion that the plural 'guilds' was 'used by contemporaries interchangeably with other terms to describe a variety of institutions',[6] all the while maintaining the individuality of each institution. The final point of note is that the religious dedications of so-called 'craft' guilds are noted in parenthesis throughout.

Evidence

Existing scholarship on Lincoln's guilds is extremely limited. They have received little more than a cursory mention in many of the key works on the city and county.[7] Whilst this is almost certainly due to the paucity of material – for example, there are no surviving guild lists or bede rolls, and no accounts before the sixteenth century[8] – it underplays the centrality of guilds in the city from the late thirteenth century onwards. Almost all of the available evidence for these institutions derives from the certificates submitted to Chancery in 1389, though these are occasionally

4 For a historiographical review of this material, see D. Crouch, *Piety, Fraternity and Power: Gilds in Late Medieval Yorkshire, 1389–1547* (York, 2000), 4–8; K. Farnhill, *Guilds and the Parish Community in Late Medieval East Anglia, c.1470–1550* (York, 2001); C. Rawcliffe, 'Dives Redeemed? The Guild Almshouses of Late Medieval England', in L. Clark (ed.), *The Fifteenth Century VIII: Rule, Redemption and Representations in Late Medieval England and France* (Woodbridge, 2008), 1–27. See also K. Giles, *An Archaeology of Social Identity: Guildhalls in York, c. 1350–1630*, BAR British Series, 315 (Oxford, 2000).

5 *Medieval Lincoln*, 327.

6 V. Bainbridge, *Gilds in the Medieval Countryside* (Woodbridge, 1997), 6.

7 *Medieval Lincoln*, 164–6, 208, 228–9, 298, 326–7, 388; *CSML*, 95, 127, 129. There are no references in Stocker, *City by the Pool*. For the sixteenth century, see Stokes, 'Staging Wonders', 197–212.

8 The extant Cordwainers accounts begin in 1525: LAO FL/MISC/1/1/6. See Kahrl, *Records of Plays and Players*, viii–x, for details.

supplemented by references in surviving wills, charters, deeds and other miscellaneous records. Such evidence forms the backbone to this chapter.

During the Cambridge parliament of 1388 (10 September–17 October), a writ was issued by the crown ordering all guilds in England to submit to Chancery by 2 February 1389 all information regarding their foundation, government, meetings, oaths and feasts, privileges, ordinances and statutes and whether or not they held any lands in mortmain.[9] Whilst according to the *Westminster Chronicle* this demand was driven by the Commons, who wished to dissolve the guilds and confiscate their goods, lands and chattels, all of which were to aid in the war with France,[10] on the whole it was received with some confusion by contemporaries.[11] The problem is exacerbated by the lack of any surviving parliamentary roll for this year, hence it is unknown whether the Commons presented a petition on the issue or not. The writ itself contained no mention of the Commons or their aims, which has subsequently led historians to consider two further possibilities: first, that mortmain licences were to be extended to include guilds, thereby raising revenues for the crown (thus indirectly benefiting the war effort); and second, that since 1381 the fear of subversive and seditious groups had grown, with guilds being a likely forum for such activities.[12] Whilst the effectiveness of the writ might be questioned, it served to present the crown with information it did not otherwise have, all the while providing a detailed list of groups and untapped wealth. Moreover, although this information was not subsequently acted upon,[13] it is nevertheless inconceivable that a review of the possibilities of exploiting the data was not undertaken, though the intricacies of this remain obscured from view.

The reaction by Lincoln's guilds to this demand was not inconsiderable,[14] with twenty-seven certificates being returned to London by the allotted date, a number which includes twenty-nine separate sets of ordinances.[15] The certificates themselves vary in size, scope and detail; all are written in Latin. At a cursory glance, the contents of the certificates and their ordinances seem unremarkable, recording

9 For a translation of the original and subsequent writs by the crown, see *English Guilds*, 127–30.

10 L. C. Hector and B. F. Harvey (eds and trans.), *The Westminster Chronicle, 1381–1394* (Oxford, 1982), 354.

11 Westlake, *Parish Gilds*, 36–8.

12 For further background, Westlake, *Parish Gilds*, 36–7; B. R. McRee, 'Charity and Gild Solidarity in Late Medieval England', *Journal of British Studies*, 32, 3 (1993), 199; C. Barron, 'The London Middle English Guild Certificates of 1388–9', *Nottingham Medieval Studies*, 39 (1995), 108–9; J. Gerchow, 'Gilds and Fourteenth-Century Bureaucracy: The Case of 1388–9', *Nottingham Medieval Studies*, 40 (1996), 113–17. For mortmain legislation, see chapter six.

13 See 189–90.

14 Though not exhaustive, with the guilds of St Robert, St Christopher and the Tawyers (*alutarioum*) not submitting returns. These are discussed in the main text below. Guilds founded in the city not discussed here include the Husbandmen (noted in 1453), the Plough guild (noted in 1470), the Fishers, located in the church of St Benedict (noted in 1474), St Dunstan (noted in 1505), St Thomas, located in the church of St Swithun (noted in 1509), St Luke, comprising Painters, Gilders, Stainers and Alabasterers (noted in 1525), all of which could have been founded at any time. LAO, A/2/35, fos 12v, 129v; A/2/36, fos 84–84v; *LW*, 25, 39; *Historical MSS*, 54–5.

15 C 47/40/134–50, C 47/41/151–60.

similar rules and regulations to many guilds across the country,[16] though any close reading of the evidence reveals a number of surprising omissions, suggesting that at Lincoln there was some confusion over the exact nature of the crown's demands. For example, there were a number of minor omissions, including foundation dates or details of the parish church where the guild was established, as well as more major ones, including religious provisions or, in the case of twelve guilds, the absence of any reference to lands and tenements,[17] despite this being a requirement of the crown. That a clause stating that none of these guilds held any lands was added later in a different and identical hand raises the possibility that there may have been some system of review in the city before they were sent to Chancery; either that or it was added upon their arrival. This was certainly not unknown as the evidence for Beverley demonstrates: there, the town's returns were inspected by the same lawyer, Robert de Garton, prior to submission.[18] Nonetheless, despite being given almost four months to reply, some guilds, like the fraternity of Tailors (Corpus Christi), delayed making their return, noting in their ordinances that they were 'Written at Lincoln in very great haste.'[19] This suggests that they may have deliberated over its contents and possibly even whether to submit a return at all.[20] Such delays and confusion imply that the king's writ may not have been communicated immediately throughout the city, though this seems unlikely. As evidence from London and Yorkshire demonstrates, a systematic process was put in place whereby the writ was communicated widely before Christmas 1388.[21] While no direct evidence of this exists for Lincoln, it is important to recognise that not all guilds were inconvenienced by the writ, with the guild of St Lawrence stating that their ordinances were recorded because of the power of the proclamation of the king (*virtute proclamacionis per breve domini regis*).[22] The significance of the evidence therefore seems to be that the king's writ came to mean different things to different guilds, a point more fully explored below. Yet, before doing so it is first worthwhile considering the authorship of the certificates themselves.

In an insightful article on the machinery of late medieval bureaucracy, Jan Gerchow argues that almost a third of all certificates returned in 1389 were in fact written by clerks of Chancery. As Gerchow explains, this conclusion can be reached by collating the dates of the certificates, all of which were written between 26 January and 1 February, and by exploring their textual form: many demonstrated common characteristics or 'diplomatic nomenclature' in their 'protocol, context and eschatocol'.[23] For guilds not falling into this group of Chancery returns, however, including those from Lincoln, Gerchow suggests that local chanceries were most likely responsible, though he highlights that further work is needed to confirm this.[24] In reviewing the

16 See table 20.

17 C 47/40/137, 140, 146, 149–50; C 47/41/151, 153–4, 158.

18 Crouch, *Piety, Fraternity*, 23.

19 C 47/41/159; quoted in *English Guilds*, 184.

20 Barron, 'Parish Fraternities', 20–1.

21 *English Guilds*, 127–9; Crouch, *Piety, Fraternity*, 16–23.

22 C 47/40/142. Compare with the guild of St Margaret: C 47/40/143.

23 Gerchow, 'Fourteenth-Century Bureaucracy', 120–35, at 121.

24 Gerchow, 'Fourteenth-Century Bureaucracy', 135–40.

returns for Lincoln it is clear that there was indeed some form of certified authority at work, though to describe it as an organised chancery would be incorrect, and of the twenty-nine guild ordinances which survive, fifteen were sealed by or on behalf of the dean of Christianity (*sigillum decanatus Chrisianitatis Linc'*; *sigillum Christianitatis Linc'*; *sigillum officii decanatus Christianitatis Linc'*).[25]

The dean of Christianity was a figure distinct from the dean of the cathedral; he acted as an agent for both the archdeacon and the diocesan bishop and maintained control over the city's parochial system.[26] Despite emerging sometime during the early twelfth century (*c.*1123–39), little written evidence remains of the institution itself in the city,[27] though it is known that the dean was involved in a wide-ranging number of roles within the city. These included overseeing the probate of wills,[28] enforcing penance,[29] deputing for the archdeacon or the archdeacon's official, making inquisitions over vacant benefices and inducting new incumbents,[30] preventing the grazing of animals and tipping of rubbish in city churchyards, giving permission for private chapels to be established, trying cases of debt between ecclesiastics,[31] and exhorting the city clergy to take part in the Corpus Christi procession from Wigford to the cathedral,[32] amongst other tasks. He also added his seal to authenticate a composition,[33] which suggests that it was probably the dean himself who sealed the city's guild certificates, for which he possibly received a small fee.[34]

Of the fifteen guild ordinances which bear the seal of the dean of Christianity, four are shared between two certificates, highlighting that they were almost certainly recorded by a single clerk on the same day.[35] No distinct pattern emerges from the remaining eleven single returns and, unlike the returns noted by Gerchow, there is no systematic protocol or context, with the certificates varying on a case-by-case basis in their terminology and handwriting.[36] Naturally one characteristic shared by

25 C 47/40/134, 136–41, C 47/41/151–3, 157, 159–60.

26 A. H. Thompson, 'Diocesan Administration in the Middle Ages: Archdeacons and Rural Deans', *Proceedings of the British Academy*, 15 (1943): 153–94; B. Kemp (ed.), *Twelfth-Century English Archidiaconal and Vice-Archidiaconal Acta* (Canterbury and York Society, 2001); B. Kemp, 'The Acta of English Rural Deans in the Later Twelfth and Early Thirteenth Centuries', in P. Hoskin, C. Brooke and B. Dobson (eds), *The Foundations of Medieval English Ecclesiastical History: Studies Presented to David Smith* (Woodbridge, 2005), 139–58.

27 *CSML*, 35–6, 117–18; K. Major, 'The Chronology of the Archdeacons of Lincoln in the Twelfth Century', in *Reg. Antiq.*, vol. 8, appendix 1, 201–8.

28 *Reg. Antiq.*, vol. 10, no. 2907; Hill, *Bishop Oliver Sutton*, vol. 5, 162; M. Archer (ed.), *The Register of Bishop Philip Repingdon, 1405–19*, 3 vols (Lincoln Record Society, 1963–82), vol. 1, 145.

29 Hill, *Bishop Oliver Sutton*, vol. 3, 20–1.

30 Bennett, *Bishop Henry Burghersh*, vol. 1, nos 30, 336, 538.

31 Hill, *Bishop Oliver Sutton*, vol. 5, 67, 139, 200.

32 Archer, *Philip Repingdon*, vol. 3, no. 521.

33 Hill, *Bishop Oliver Sutton*, vol. 6, 135–7.

34 *CSML*, 35. Owen notes that this was not uncommon though there is no direct evidence of this.

35 These were the guilds of St Anne (founded 1344), the Holy Sepulchre (1366), St Edmund of Pontigny (1276) and St Mary (1363): C 47/40/137, 140.

36 For example, some begin *Hec est fraternitas facta in honore* (C 47/40/136–7), others *Certificacio fraternitatum gildarum infrascriptarum* (C 47/40/140), others still *Certificacio gracemanni et*

all fifteen ordinances is the reference to the seal of the dean of Christianity, which is always located within the eschatocol. Typically this is inserted within a much longer passage emphasising the benefit and role which the dean of Christianity performed in the recording of the ordinances. For example, the guild of the Holy Sepulchre recorded that the *rogatu confratrum predictorum sigillum Christianitatis Lincoln' presentibus est appensum in roboracionem et testimonium omnium.*[37] The guild of St Mary likewise stated *Et ad roborationem maiorem omnium articulorum premissorum ad specialem rogatum gracemanni et confratrum predictorum sigullum Decanatus Christianitas Lincoln' presentibus est appensum.*[38] Given the context of these statements, it seems likely that these guilds drew upon the authority of the dean as a means to reaffirm their orthodoxy and loyalty to the church, a motive clearly identifiable in the ordinances of the guild of Fullers (Holy Cross), which were written according to church law (*secundum legem ecclesie*).[39] Such measures were not unique to Lincoln and the guild of the Holy Trinity in Cambridge, for example, had its ordinances 'most diligently examined by the advocates of the consistory of Ely' to ensure that the contents were lawful,[40] whilst the guild of the Lord's Prayer in York similarly requested that the seal of the vicar general of the archbishop be appended 'in witness to the truth of the return'.[41] Such concerns underscore the variety of responses by guilds towards the contents of the royal writ, with some placing greater emphasis on the lawfulness and orthodoxy of their institution than others. As already identified, it is possible that this attitude was driven by fears over accusations of heterodoxy which had grown since the denunciation of Wyclif and his followers ('Lollards') in 1382.[42] Certainly, some chroniclers, including Henry Knighton, identified Wyclif's beliefs as one of the major causes behind the Peasants' Revolt of 1381, though studies are yet to yield any evidence in support of this view.[43] Either way there may have been some lingering doubts in the minds of those recording the certificates, however small, that heterodoxy of any kind may have been perceived by the crown in this way; as Margaret Aston writes, 'somehow, through deliberate falsification, fixed prejudice, or plausible hypothesis, the conviction seems to have become established that Lollardy was associated with the revolt'.[44] Hence this may well have been a factor in the decision of some guilds to place greater emphasis on their orthodoxy and faithfulness to the church.[45]

incorporacionis fraternitatis (C 47/41/151). The actual context and language of the certificates vary too much to be outlined here.

37 C 47/40/137.

38 C 47/40/140.

39 C 47/41/153.

40 *English Guilds*, 268.

41 *English Guilds*, 140.

42 A. Hudson, *Selections from English Wycliffite Writings* (Toronto, 1997), 5–8.

43 M. Aston, 'Lollardy and Sedition, 1381–1431', in *idem*, *Lollards and Reformers: Images and Literacy in Late Medieval Religion* (London, 1984), 6–7.

44 Aston, 'Lollardy and Sedition', in *idem*, *Lollards and Reformers*, 7.

45 The Lollard heresy was discovered to be active in Lincoln but not until the early years of the fifteenth century: J. H. Arnold, 'Margery's Trials: Heresy, Lollardy and Dissent', in J. H. Arnold and K. J. Lewis, *A Companion to the Book of Margery Kempe* (Cambridge, 2004), 79–80.

This is not to suggest that guilds not seeking out the authority of the dean of Christianity held heterodox, or even dissenting, views. Some may have been too poor to pay the necessary fees (if required), were too late in organising a visit by the dean (or one of his officials), much like the Tailors (Corpus Christi), or stood confident in their own orthodoxy and piety. That the city's two leading guilds during the fourteenth century – the guild of the Blessed Virgin Mary in St Andrew in Wigford (The Great Guild)[46] and the guild of the Purification of the Blessed Virgin Mary in St Benedict – chose not to do so certainly gives the final suggestion credibility.[47] It is also possible that a guild's refusal to have its ordinances sealed by the dean was regarded as a rejection of the church's authority by certain members of the laity; for guilds such as St Lawrence, for example, which stated that their provisions were the words of God and were given with the counsel of the brothers and sisters of the guild (*sequitur in hec verba et provisum est cum communi consilio fratrum et sororum huius fraternitatis* ...), the collective reasoning of the group was enough to make the return without ecclesiastical approval.[48] Hence, whilst there may have been no systematic chancery at work in the city (in this context),[49] there was to some extent a coordinated effort between the dean of Christianity and a large number of the city's guilds in the recording of their ordinances. Whilst on the one hand this serves to reinforce the reliability of the returns, on the other it similarly highlights the relative strength of individual guilds and their members.

Despite the effort of many guilds to seek out the authority of the dean of Christianity, it is important to stress the relatively ad hoc nature in which they did so. For example, although the vast majority of the city's parish churches were in the possession of the precentor (as part of the endowment of his dignity independent of cathedral revenues), the cathedral or religious houses located outside the city,[50] it seems that at no stage were the guilds held under their auspices ever required to have their ordinances ratified, emphasising the relatively independent status of guild from parish. Take as an illustration of this the guilds of St Bavon (located in the church of St Bavon) and St George (St George), both of which bear the seal of the dean of Christianity, and the guilds of St Nicholas (St John, Wigford) and St Anne (St Peter in the Skinmarket), which do not. All four churches were held by the precentor of

46 It is likely that the Great Guild was a later manifestation of the Merchant Guild, which was established in the city some time during the twelfth century but which lost its importance following the adoption of the mayor as the civic head in the early thirteenth century. It is possible that, like at Leicester, Lynn and Chester, for example, the alderman of the Merchant Guild was originally the early mayor. See Tait, *Medieval English Borough*, 226–32; *Royal Charters*, 1; *Medieval Lincoln*, 185–7, 195–6.

47 By the early sixteenth century both of these guilds had declined in importance, being replaced by the guild of St Anne. For more on this, see Hill, *Tudor and Stuart Lincoln*, 33–5; Stokes, 'Staging Wonders', 197–212.

48 C 47/40/142.

49 For the cathedral chancery, see Major, *Minster Yard*, 10–11.

50 For example the church of St Peter at Pleas was in the patronage of Shelford Priory, whilst the advowson of the church of St Peter ad Fontem was in the hands of St Mary's Abbey, York: *Medieval Lincoln*, 132–4.

the cathedral.[51] The same was also true of the certificates for the guild of the Blessed Virgin Mary (St Benedict), which bore the seal, and the guild of the Resurrection or Holy Sepulchre (St Cuthbert), which did not, two churches which had been granted to the prebend of North Kelsey in the cathedral.[52]

For the fourteen sets of guild ordinances not bearing the seal of the dean, there is little to suggest that they were written, at this stage, in conjunction with any other body or by a single clerk, as there is no clear protocol or context and certainly no uniform eschatocol, as in the dean of Christianity returns.[53] There are also no certificates shared by multiple guilds. Finally, the handwriting of the scribes differs considerably, thereby suggesting that they were written either by an official of the guild or a clerk on their behalf.[54]

Foundation

The foundation of a guild typically involved the collective action of a group who sought to address a specific need or requirement of the local community. This could manifest itself in a variety of ways. For example, the Poor Men's guild in Norwich was founded in 1380 to help with the upkeep of the local parish church, whilst the guild of the Annunciation in Cambridge was established in 1379 so that 'kindliness should be cherished more and more, and discord be driven out'.[55] How far such idealism reflected reality is difficult to gauge and arguably disguises divisions and ruptures in the parish and the wider 'community'; as Miri Rubin points out, 'community' remains a complex, even abstract, concept highlighting multi-layered identities which are 'negotiated and manipulated'.[56] Hence for certain groups, a guild's foundation may have been intended to provide a collective focus for its members,[57] though it obviously excluded certain individuals, notably the poor. Due to this, it is important to identify where possible the reasons for guild foundations, including their date, as this reveals much about the overall pattern of fraternal development in the city. Take, for example, the guild of Corpus Christi, located in the church of St Michael on the Mount, which was founded in 1350 by 'folks of common and middling rank'. Not only did its ordinances require that 'no one of the rank of mayor or bailiff shall become a brother of the gild, unless he is found to be of humble, good, and honest conversation', but that those unwilling to abide by their fraternal values and customs were to be barred from becoming members altogether. The guild thus maintained a

51 C 47/40/137–8, 141, 148. The endowments of individual cathedral dignities and prebends are summarised in D. E. Greenway, *John Le Neve: Fasti Ecclesiae Anglicanae 1066–1300: III Lincoln* (London, 1977), at the beginning of each dignity or prebendal section.

52 C 47/40/139, 146.

53 C 47/40/135, 142–50, C 47/41/154–6, 158.

54 For similarities at London, see Barron, 'Guild Certificates of 1388–9', 110–18.

55 *English Guilds*, 40, 270.

56 Rubin, 'Small Groups', 135.

57 For more on the cultivation of ethical and virtuous behaviour by guild members, see G. Rosser, *The Art of Solidarity in the Middle Ages: Guilds in England, 1250–1550* (Oxford, 2015), 37–87.

clear idea of exactly what was expected of its members.[58] Less explicit evidence comes from the fraternity of St Anne, which was founded in 1344 by *omnes fratres et sorores eiusdem fraternitatis in eadem parochia*, and the guild of the Resurrection which was begun (*inchoata*) by thirteen brothers and sisters drawn from the parish of St Martin in 1354.[59] That in subsequent years the membership of these guilds was extended to include those living beyond the parish boundaries seems likely,[60] again serving to highlight how pockets of local communities could and did consider themselves as independent from the wider 'community'.[61]

Other foundation details derive from guilds based upon artisanal subgroups. For example, in 1369 the fraternity of Barbers (St John the Evangelist) recorded that it was founded by *ex communi assensu omnium tonsorum Lincoln*';[62] in 1379 the fraternity of Archers (Holy Cross) was begun (*inchoata*) with the agreement (*consensum*) of all brothers of the guild;[63] whilst the confraternity of Fullers (Holy Cross) recorded that it was founded 'on the Sunday before the feast of the apostles Philip and James, [in] 1297, by all the bretheren and sisteren of the Fullers of Lincoln'.[64] Not all evidence is so straightforward, however, with some guilds failing to name their founders outright: for example the Sailors (Corpus Christi) stated that *fraternitatis fundate per nautas Lincoln*', whilst the Masons (Blessed Virgin Mary and All Saints) recorded that their rules and ordinances were 'enacted by the common consent of this fraternity' on the Feast of Pentecost in 1313.[65] Nonetheless, it seems likely in both cases that they were founded by the masters and workmen themselves.

Unfortunately, for the vast majority of guilds in Lincoln and many across England,[66] no indication is given as to why they were founded or who their founders were, with their ordinances recording only their foundation date, the details of their patron saint, and the parish church in which the guild was based.[67] Even then some guilds did not do this: for example, the Minstrels and Entertainers (no patron saint recorded)[68] and the Mercers (Blessed Virgin Mary).[69] Of course, there may have been a number of guilds, like the Blessed Virgin Mary in St Benedict, who were unaware of their origins or their founders, their ordinances stating only that 'the bretheren do not know the beginning of the gild',[70] though in most cases it seems likely that these details were simply overlooked or ignored; certainly it was not a requirement

58 C 47/40/135; trans. *English Guilds*, 179.
59 C 47/40/136–7.
60 See 184.
61 G. Rosser, 'Parochial Conformity and Voluntary Religion in Late-Medieval England', *Transactions of the Royal Historical Society*, Sixth Series, 1 (1991), 189.
62 C 47/41/151.
63 C 47/40/150.
64 C 47/41/153; *English Guilds*, 179.
65 C 47/41/158; C 47/41/154: trans. W. J. Williams, *Ars Quatuor Coronatorum*, 42 (1931): 64–7.
66 For example, *English Guilds*, 9, 54, 71.
67 For example, C 47/40/137, 142–3.
68 However, by at least 1521 the guild was associated with 'Our Lady'. *LW*, vol. 1, 102.
69 C 47/41/155–6; Stokes, *Early English Drama*, vol. 2, 649–50. Despite the absence of a date or a location it seems that the guild of Mercers was most likely founded before 1349 in St Rumbold, as a guild of St Mary was noted there in that year: *BB*, fo. 187v.
70 C 47/40/146; Westlake, *Parish Gilds*, 171.

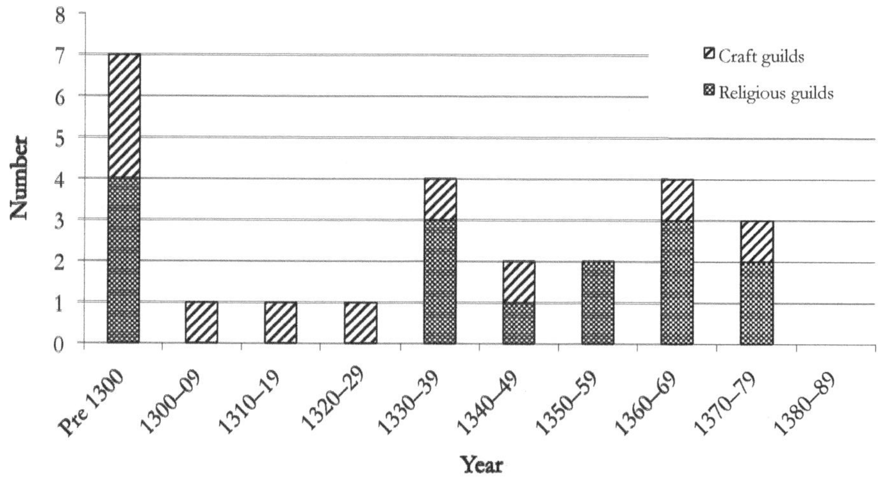

Figure 7 Known foundation dates of guilds in Lincoln (c.1250–1389)

of the king's writ to record these facts. Much like the guild of the Annunciation in Cambridge previously noted, some guilds may have been established without a clear purpose in mind. Emerging at a grass-roots level, they may have drawn their members quite informally from the local area over a period of time, recording their ordinances only when they became more firmly established;[71] certainly no guilds at Lincoln perpetuated any myths about their origins as those elsewhere did.[72] Because of this it is impossible to identify whether individuals or groups founding guilds did so on multiple occasions, like John Castre and John Trumpington in Cambridge, both of whom helped co-found the guild of the Annunciation in the church of St Mary in 1379 and the guild of the Assumption in the church of the Holy Trinity in 1384.[73] Even so, it is not unlikely as there is clear evidence for a number of leading citizens establishing multiple chantries in the city.[74]

Of the thirty-two guilds known to have existed in the city by the end of the fourteenth century only twenty provide some clue as to their foundation date (figure 7).[75] It is clear from this data that to some extent Lincoln followed the pattern that

71 For example, the Cordwainers and Fullers both added ordinances after their initial foundation: C 47/41/52–3.

72 For example, Westlake, *Parish Gilds*, 158, 199. The possible exception to this was the Great Guild which cited royal prerogative as one of the reasons for its foundation, claiming that Henry III was once a member of the guild: C 143/79/10.

73 Trumpington also co-founded the guild of St Katherine in the church of St Andrew in 1385: M. Bateson (ed.), *Cambridge Gild Records* (London, 1903), 63, 69, 77.

74 See 217 n. 120.

75 Of the guilds without ordinances, only the guild of St Robert has been included in this table (having been recorded in a will dating from 1296). The guilds of St Christopher and the Tawyers are not as they could have been founded at any time (being noted in wills dating from 1392 and 1407 respectively): *LW*, 5; *ELW*, 86, 107–8.

'in the last half of the fourteenth century gild after gild came into existence',[76] with nine new guilds being founded in the thirty years following the Black Death. Yet this must be tempered by the fact that by 1349 over half of the city's fraternal development had already taken place, there being at least sixteen guilds already established by this date. In fact, it was the two decades prior to the Black Death which saw the most significant surge in new foundations, quite possibly as a reaction to the local recession,[77] which highlights how there was an increase in fraternal values prior to 1349. However, when factoring in the relative loss of life brought about by plague, it is clear that the number of foundations made per head of population increased after this date.[78] And yet it is likely that some, if not all, of the guilds for which there is no surviving foundation date were founded in the first half of the century (or earlier). For example, whilst the guild of the Blessed Virgin Mary in the church of St Benedict admitted not knowing its foundation date, it is likely that it had been in existence long before 1349, given the fact that some of its members may have been born as early the 1320s or 1330s. This was certainly the case for the guild of Clerks (St Mary and St Nicholas), which recorded no date in its ordinances but which in 1402 was confirmed as being founded before the Statute of Mortmain (1279).[79] The fraternity of Corpus Christi, too, about which little is known,[80] may have been established prior to 1349, a date otherwise not out of kilter with other Corpus Christi foundations (1328, 1335, 1346 and 1350).[81] There is certainly no circumstantial evidence to suggest that guilds of more recent foundation were more likely to return certificates than those of earlier date.

The precocious development of guilds in Lincoln seems, at least on face value, to be explained by the city's status as one of the leading economic centres in the country.[82] The cathedral, which maintained shrines to St Hugh and the bishops Robert Grosseteste and John de Dalderby, also helped establish the city as a significant pilgrimage centre throughout the Middle Ages; in 1334/45, for example, the shrine of St Hugh alone attracted roughly 8,000 pilgrims (or 21 pilgrims per day), a figure rising as high as approximately 16,000 in 1363/64 (or 43 pilgrims per day),[83] a not

76 Westlake, *Parish Gilds*, 28; E. Duffy, 'Religious Belief', in Horrox and Ormrod, *Social History of England*, 308–9. For a breakdown of the foundations of fourteenth-century guilds where known, see Crouch, *Piety, Fraternity*, figure 1.5, 40.

77 See 86.

78 For the nine guilds founded between 1300 and 1349, there was one guild per 1,366 people (12,300 divided by nine), whereas for the nine founded between 1350 and 1400, this figure was one guild per 833 people (7,500 divided by nine). For these population figures, see 2.

79 C 47/40/149; *CPR 1401–5*, 96.

80 The certificate is very badly damaged, hence the confusion: C 47/40/134. Note that Rubin's suggestion that there was a 'patrician Corpus Christi' fraternity in the city is mistaken. The five individual Corpus Christi guilds may have counted civic officials amongst their members but none was a leading guild: Rubin, 'Small Groups', 139.

81 C 47/40/135; C 47/41/157–9.

82 For background to this point, see chapters one and two.

83 Consequently the year that the head of St Hugh was stolen from the cathedral, stripped of its jewels and thrown into a field, where it was found being guarded by a crow: *CPR, 1361–64*, 468; Venables, 'Shrine and Head of St Hugh', 140–2.

inconsiderable number.[84] Of course, such numbers would have been much higher between the months of March and September during the pilgrimage season, when the weather was generally better.[85] It is possible that these trade and spiritual links brought with them new ideas and beliefs, with some guilds being influenced by new trends of piety from the continent.[86] Some ideas may have even been brought from the continent by individuals such as Minkyn Quest, a German merchant who settled in the city around 1300 and started a family;[87] Amicie de Mecklenburg, a fellow German who owned lands in St Rumbold in *c.*1299;[88] or indeed by any number of Flemish, Italian or Brabant merchants and artisans identified as living in the city.[89] In some ways these early economic developments help explain why the city's 'craft' guilds were initially founded in greater numbers prior to the 1330s than the so-called 'religious guilds', though in truth they were hardly craft guilds at all.[90]

Surprisingly Lincoln's late thirteenth- and early fourteenth-century fraternal development stands at odds with other major urban centres, including Lynn and Norwich, which saw the majority of their guilds founded after 1349;[91] the south-western towns of Bridport and Salisbury, which recorded their greatest number of foundations at the beginning of the fifteenth century;[92] and York, and indeed all Yorkshire, which saw significant fraternal growth during the late fourteenth and early fifteenth centuries.[93] It is even possible to add London to this list: it founded only eight guilds before 1349.[94] Such evidence therefore undermines the idea that it was Lincoln's economic and spiritual hegemony which acted as the catalyst for the precocious fraternal growth because many of these towns and cities were also dominant county towns in their own right: therefore, why was Lincoln different?

One possibility put forward by Gervase Rosser is that there was an 'intense concentration' of guild foundations in the early fourteenth century across East Anglia and the West Midlands, including Lincolnshire, which he attributes to the geographical spread of high rates of population and personal mobility. The implication of this is that guilds in these areas acted 'to some degree' as substitute kinship

84 For these figures, see Nilson, *Cathedral Shrines*, 113–17, 222.

85 Nilson, *Cathedral Shrines*, 116–7; D. Webb, *Pilgrimage in Medieval England* (London, 2000), 188–9.

86 See main text below.

87 C 241/82/35, 37, 93; C 143/393/19; JUST 2/67, rot. 48; JUST 2/80, rot. 1; *BB*, fos 105v, 137–137v, 171v, 190v, 191; *CPR, 1317–21*, 112.

88 LAO Dij 74/2/18.

89 For example, Elena de Flaunders and Paul Bernard, Lombard (*BB*, fos 173v, 258v); Godfrey de Brabent (E 179/135/26, rot. 3) and Walter de Brabant (E 179/135/26, rot. 2). See also 25–6.

90 See main text below.

91 According to Westlake, Lynn had seventy-seven guilds, thirty-four of which were founded between 1349 and 1389, with only eight before; twenty-five did not record their foundation date. Norwich had nineteen, twelve of which were founded between 1349 and 1389, with only two before; five record no date. Westlake, *Parish Gilds*, 192–206.

92 A. D. Brown, *Popular Piety in Late Medieval England: The Diocese of Salisbury, 1250–1550* (Oxford, 1995), 110.

93 Crouch, *Piety, Fraternity*, appendix 1, 252–64.

94 Twenty-two guilds were established in London between 1349 and 1389, along with fourteen guilds for which there no date is given. Barron, 'Guild Certificates of 1388–9', 111–13.

families 'for uprooted migrants who were too far removed from their relations to call upon them for support'.[95] This conclusion reflects the evidence of trade and industry identified previously,[96] though does not explain why Yorkshire, another large county, did not experience similar effects.

A second more significant possibility is that guilds were organised under the auspices of civic government, much like in York in the fifteenth century, for example,[97] there being overwhelming evidence for inter-guild cooperation on a city-wide scale hitherto unidentified for other urban centres.[98] When it is considered that craft ordinances and regulations were frequently ratified by the mayor's council throughout the period, in particular during the municipal reforms of the early fourteenth century,[99] it seems likely that local civic government maintained a strong hand in the guilds' organisation and running. Not only did this ensure fairness and parity between guilds but it minimised competition for authority at a time when trade was being more effectively channelled through towns.[100] Such developments would certainly explain the absence of guilds in the Bail and the paucity of craft legislation in the surviving certificates. This evidence points towards the emergence of a system of integration whereby new guilds were actively encouraged to participate within a carefully managed fraternal network.

One means of testing this hypothesis and the apparently unique character of Lincoln's fraternal development is to consider the importance of undated certificates from towns previously identified as housing a large number of guilds after 1349. If, hypothetically speaking, half of all guilds identified for Lynn, London or Norwich which did not include a foundation date were established prior to 1349 then this would demonstrate a pattern of growth comparable to that of Lincoln. Moreover, given that there is no indication from the Lincoln data that guilds founded after 1349 were recorded with any greater alacrity than older institutions in the surviving certificates, it remains possible that the general growth of English guilds so readily ascribed to the plague is in need of reassessment.

Moving away from their foundations, one of the most striking features of guilds to emerge from the extant certificates is their recorded locations. Certainly, prior to 1349 the city's fraternal landscape was relatively widespread, with no distinct clusters of guilds (map 6). In all, four occupied the intramural area, mainly along main thoroughfares, with six being situated within the suburbs (four in Wigford, one each in Newport and Butwerk), and a single guild in the Close. Four guilds did not record a parish. Collectively, therefore, there were a large number of areas which did not house guilds, including the northern and eastern sides of the intramural city, the Bail and the suburbs of Newland and Eastgate.

95 Rosser, 'Guilds in Urban Politics', 32.
96 Chapters one and two.
97 H. Swanson, 'The Illusion of Economic Structure: Craft Guilds in Late Medieval Towns', *Past and Present*, 121 (1988): 29–48.
98 See main text below.
99 Chapter four.
100 See 128–9. For the suppression of the guild of Holy Trinity in York in 1306 for similar reasons, see Rosser, 'Guilds in Urban Politics', 36–7.

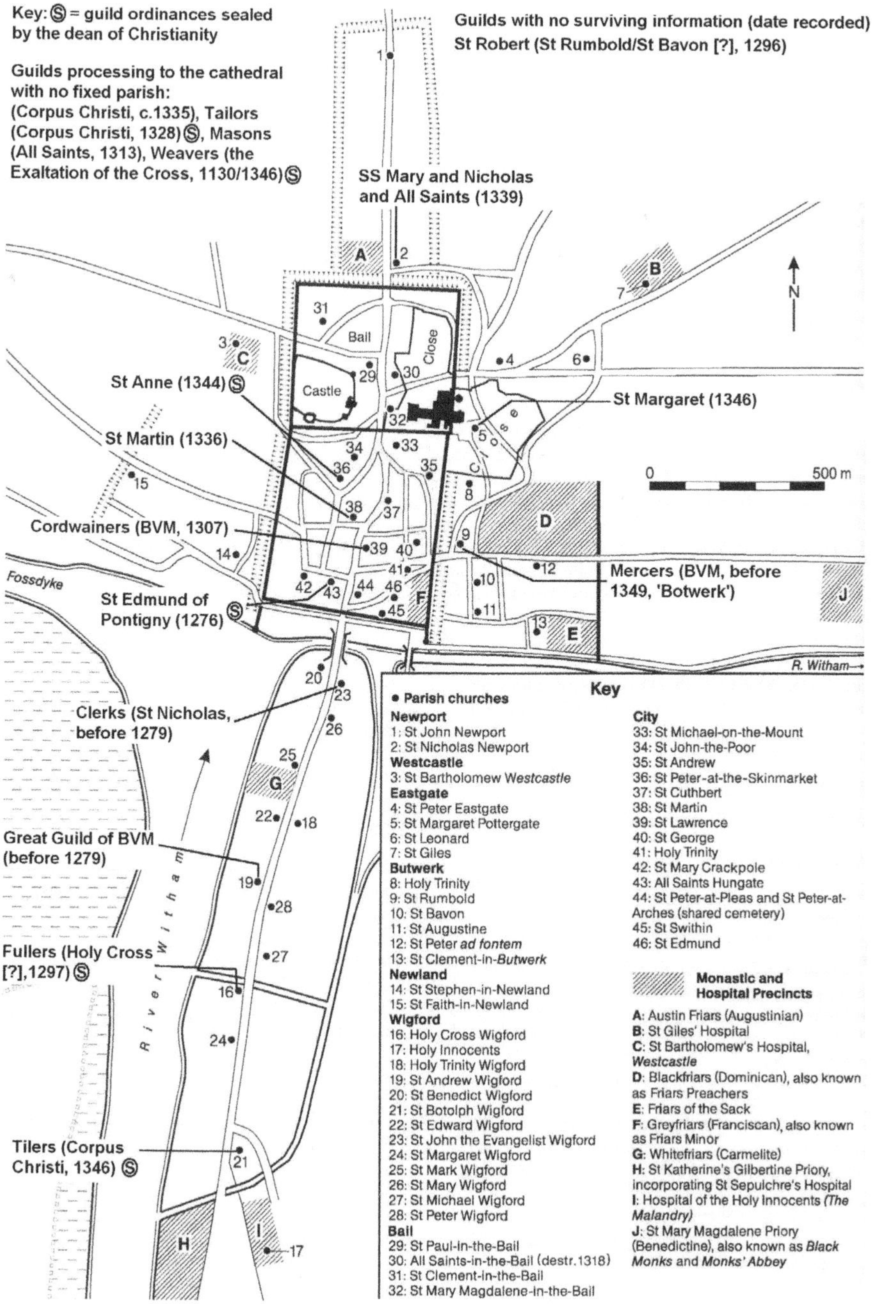

Map 6 Known guild foundations before 1349

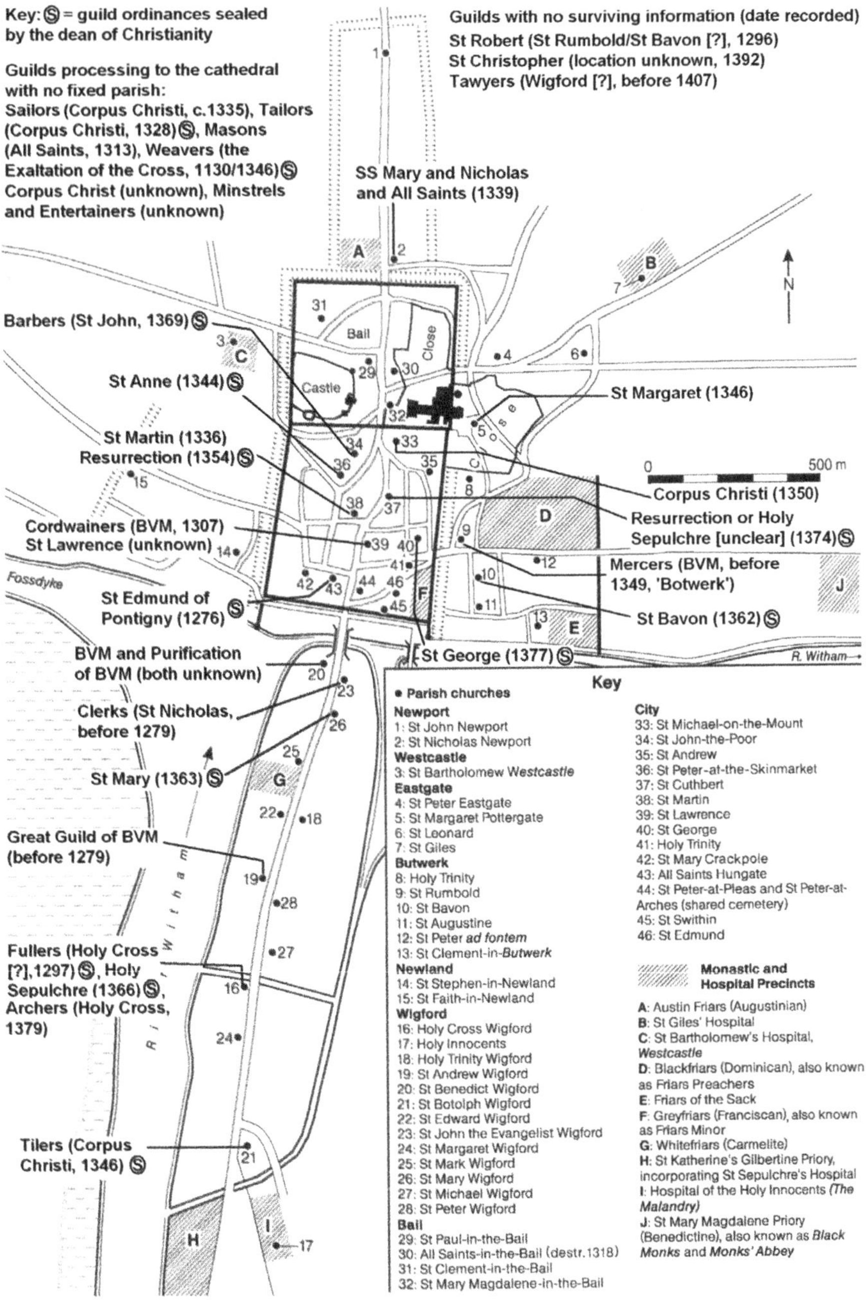

Map 7 Known guild foundations before 1410

In the forty years following the Black Death, however, the fraternal landscape changed considerably, with four new guilds being founded in the intramural area. These were situated towards the northern and eastern areas, where there had previously been none (map 7), a development mirrored to some extent in Butwerk, where an additional guild was established.[101] The suburb of Wigford, however, saw commensurate growth with both of these areas, possibly more so, where between three and six new guilds were founded, though there were no new additions to the Close or Newport. Newland, Eastgate and the Bail all remained without any guilds.

Considering the evidence from a purely spatial point of view, it is possible to identify how there existed in the city an awareness not only of the implications of the use of space but also of the opportunities available in the post-plague environment, though this is made more complicated by the fact that the foundation dates of some guilds are not known. Certainly, in spatial terms the majority of new foundations made after 1349 were established in areas where fraternities had not previously existed. It is possible that this may have coincided with a redistribution of population to areas affected most severely by the pestilence, though with few extant taxation records it is difficult to say with any certainty.[102] Even so, it is important to stress that these developments were by no means haphazard, with the majority of new guilds being established either at a considerable distance from existing ones, or, paradoxically, in the same parish church as older guilds, a trend otherwise uncommon prior to 1349.[103]

Several possibilities serve to explain these developments. The first is that in parishes where multiple guilds congregated, multiple homogeneous groups can be identified. Take, for example, the guilds of Fullers (Holy Cross), Archers (Holy Cross) and the Holy Sepulchre, all of which named Holy Cross in Wigford as their parish church, or the guilds of St Lawrence and the Cordwainers (Blessed Virgin Mary), who shared the church of St Lawrence in Micklegate. That for both churches at least one of its associated guilds was craft-based suggests there may have been a high concentration of craftsmen in these particular areas, thereby highlighting how individuals sought to interact as often as possible with friends or business associates.[104] Divisions based upon wealth can also be identified in some areas of the city, including in the parish of St Benedict where the guilds of the Blessed Virgin Mary and the Purification of the Blessed Virgin Mary congregated. The latter in particular maintained high admissions costs and fees, thereby highlighting how the guild may have been geared towards individuals of a certain social standing.[105]

101 There is a possibility that the much earlier guild of St Robert was located somewhere in Butwerk, though this is not conclusive: *LW*, vol. 1, 5.

102 See appendix 1.

103 Only two possibilities exist before 1349: one is the church of St Benedict, the other St Lawrence, although there is some ambiguity over the foundation dates of the guilds associated with these churches.

104 B. A. Hanawalt, 'Keepers of the Lights: Late Medieval English Parish Gilds', *Journal of Medieval and Renaissance Studies*, 41, 1 (1984), 36–7; R. Goddard, 'Medieval Business Networks: St Mary's Guild and the Borough Court in Later Medieval Nottingham,' *Urban History*, 40, 1 (2013): 3–27.

105 See 194–5.

A second possibility is that some guilds were in fact not particularly large or were perhaps relatively informal associations, a point explained further below. A third is that it was more cost effective to maintain an altar and its lights in the local church than to establish a guildhall, for example, with guildhalls being conspicuous by their absence in Lincoln. In fact, only the Great Guild of the Blessed Virgin Mary is known to have maintained one during the fourteenth century,[106] though it was not built by the guild, it most likely being a former hospital.[107] As such, of the nine guilds which shared a church, only four possibly shared the same altar: the Fullers and Archers (both of which venerated the Holy Cross in the church of the Holy Cross) and the Blessed Virgin Mary and the Purification of the Blessed Virgin Mary (both in the church of St Benedict).[108] This indicates that where churches were shared between guilds, the physical spaces were invariably utilised differently, thereby leading to a fourth possibility. Namely, that guilds were willing to accommodate the institutional needs of others, perhaps as part of their commitment to the parish or to the wider community more generally.[109] In fact, by considering the evidence of the key guild dates recorded in the surviving ordinances – feasts, processions and mornspeches – it is clear that this was indeed the case.

Of these three events, the most important was undoubtedly the feast, though not all guilds apparently celebrated on this day.[110] Held on the feast day of the patron saint, it was generally expected that members attend or be fined,[111] with all attendees expected to participate in services for the living and the dead. For example, the guild of the Resurrection in St Cuthbert held that 'After dinner [on the day of the feast], four candles shall be lighted, and grace shall be said, together with the antiphon *Regina caeli letare*,[112] and the Lord's Prayer; and the names of all the dead brothers and sisters of the guild shall be read over, and the *De Profundis* said for their souls.'[113] The guild of the Purification of the Blessed Virgin Mary in St Benedict, too, recorded that mass on the day of the feast was to be performed *cum nota*, though it was the only guild to record such ostentation.[114] It was also not unknown for members to be accompanied by the poor who were given bread and ale, an act of Christian and fraternal charity.[115] If a guild was particularly wealthy, guests could also be invited and, as Gervase Rosser argues, it became an occasion whereby political and social allegiances were forged, though there is no extant evidence of this at Lincoln.[116]

106 There was, however, a 'clerks' guildhall' noted in 1424 and a 'taillours hall' recorded in St Peter at Arches in 1483. Their origins are unknown: *BH*, fo. 105v; *WB*, fo. 41.
107 Vince, 'High Medieval Era', 246. See also previous note.
108 C 47/40/136–7, 142, 144, 146–7, C 47/41/150, 152–3.
109 Rosser, 'Communities of Parish and Guild', 33, 44–5.
110 Tables 21a and 21b.
111 For example, C 47/40/137.
112 *Regina celi letare* in MS.
113 C 47/40/139; trans. *English Guilds*, 177.
114 C 47/40/147.
115 For example, C 47/40/135–7, C 47/41/156–60.
116 G. Rosser, 'Going to the Fraternity Feast: Commensality and Social Relations in Late Medieval England', *Journal of British Studies*, 34, 4 (1994): 430–46.

Processions were similarly important occasions,[117] being public and communal manifestations of a guild's beliefs, though, once again, not all undertook them during the fourteenth century.[118] For those that did, however, this typically involved members making their way from their parish church (or allotted meeting point) to the cathedral where lights were offered to a dedicated altar.[119] Some, however, such as the guild of St Edmund of Pontigny, chose to process with 'joy and honour' to their own parish church, in this case All Saints, Hungate (the starting point is not noted), where they placed a candle before the saint's 'ymage',[120] whilst the Cordwainers (Blessed Virgin Mary) processed to the cathedral all the while performing a play, with members of the guild being appointed to take the roles of 'Mary, Joseph, St Blaise, and two angels'.[121]

The third event was the mornspech. Typically these events dealt with any outstanding business of the guild, including the payment of fines, expenses and subscriptions, the administration of accounts, elections for the following year's officials, the organisation of forthcoming feasts and processions, and the arbitration of disputes between members;[122] as Susan Reynolds observes, mornspeches frequently held jurisdiction independent of the courts.[123] They were therefore important events in the guild calendar. Occasionally they also witnessed a modest type of celebration, with the guild of St Edmund of Pontigny using fines from its members to pay for the day's wine.[124] Mass was also said, albeit infrequently.[125] Much like for processions or feasts, members were expected to attend these events or risk being fined in wax, which contributed towards the sustenance of the guild light.[126] In Lincoln the number of mornspeches varied widely with the guilds of the Purification of the Blessed Virgin Mary in St Benedict and Corpus Christi in St Michael on the Mount holding only one[127] whilst the Fraternity of the Holy Sepulchre held five.[128] Like feasts and processions, not all guilds held them, though it is possible that some simply did not record them.[129]

117 M. James, 'Ritual, Drama and Social Body in the Late Medieval English Town', *Past and Present*, 98 (1983): 3–29; B. R. McRee, 'Unity or Division? The Social Meaning of Guild Ceremony in Urban Communities', in B. Hanawalt and K. L. Reyerson (eds), *City and Spectacle in Medieval Europe* (London, 1994), 189–207.

118 Tables 21a and 21b.

119 For example, C 47/41/157–9. The claim by Elizabeth New that the guilds of Mercers, Sailors, Weavers, Minstrels and Entertainers and Corpus Christi were permanently located in the cathedral is not supported by the evidence, with the guilds merely being identified as processing there. E. A. New, 'Fraternities in English Cathedrals in the Later Medieval Period', in T. Thornton (ed.), *Social Attitudes and Political Structures in the Fifteenth Century* (Stroud, 2000), 34, 50, n. 7.

120 C 47/40/140.

121 C 47/41/156; trans. Stokes, *Early English Drama*, vol. 2, 650.

122 For example, C 47/40/137, 140; C 47/41/154.

123 Reynolds, *English Medieval Towns*, 119–20.

124 C 47/40/140.

125 C 47/40/149.

126 C 47/40/137.

127 C 47/40/135, 147.

128 One of which was a designated day for accounting: C 47/40/137.

129 For example, the guild of Sailors (Corpus Christi) and Confraternity of Fullers (Holy Cross)

Combining all of these dates together (processions, feasts, mornspeches), three things become clear.[130] Firstly, Lincoln's 'fraternal year' spanned the entire twelve-month period, unlike at Coventry where between 25 June and the vigil of Christmas 'there was no religious or popular symbolic coherence';[131] secondly, of all the guilds which shared the same parish church, none ever held meetings or events on the same day; and thirdly, on occasions when events did coincide, the guilds in question were always at a considerable distance from one another. For example, of the five guilds celebrating on the Sunday after the feast of the Blessed Virgin Mary (25 March),[132] one of the most popular dates in the ritual calendar, no two were situated in adjacent parishes, being at least five to ten minutes' walk away from one another. Likewise, of the three guilds celebrating on the Sunday after the feast of St Michael the Archangel (29 September), another popular feast day, all were similarly distant.[133] It seems apparent that these arrangements were by no means accidental but were the result of a high level of coordination amongst the city's guilds, both at their inception and in their ongoing development. This not only minimised competition and emphasised the importance of each individual guild's affairs but provided members with the opportunity to belong to more than a single institution.[134] In turn, this endorsed and promoted the guild within its local area, all the while firmly establishing it within the city's fraternal framework. This had important consequences for the identity of the guild, too; not only did it stress that it was an accepted institution worthy of time and investment but it appealed to and reflected local pious and social concerns, important factors in the creation of a cohesive group.

In spite of these cooperative efforts, it is nevertheless important to highlight where frictions might have existed. For example, possibly as many as five guilds processed to the cathedral on the feast of Corpus Christi,[135] an occasion which had the potential to result in open hostility, as it did in other towns.[136] Nonetheless, of the three guilds for which detailed evidence remains,[137] each took its respective candles to a distinct area of the cathedral – one to the high altar,[138] another to the choir gate,[139] the third to the altar of St John the Evangelist[140] – perhaps as a result of earlier tensions or as a means to avoid them. Elsewhere it is also possible that tensions existed between the guild of St Margaret in the Close and the civic

recorded none: C 47/41/152, 158.

130 Collated in appendix 4.

131 C. Phythian-Adams, 'Ceremony and the Citizen: The Communal Year at Coventry 1450–1550', in Holt and Rosser, *The Medieval Town*, 238–64.

132 Tailors (Corpus Christi), SS Anne, Mary, Margaret and Lawrence.

133 Tailors (Corpus Christi), St Edmund of Pontigny, and St Nicholas, St Mary and All Saints.

134 For late fourteenth- and early fifteenth-century examples of multiple guild membership, see *ELW*, 74, 107–8; *LW*, vol. 1, 23–4, 29–30.

135 C 47/40/134–5, C 47/41/157–8. The possible exception being the Tailors, which did not record a destination: C 47/41/159.

136 For example, Rubin, 'Small Groups', 143–8; A. F. Johnston, 'The Guild of Corpus Christi and the Procession of Corpus Christi in York', *Mediaeval Studies*, 38 (1976): 372–84.

137 The certificate of the fraternity of Corpus Christi is damaged (C 47/40/134). See n. 80 above.

138 C 47/40/135.

139 C 47/41/157.

140 C 47/41/158; *LCL VCH Lincoln*, 93.

authorities: this guild was the only one to hold a mornspech, or indeed any event, on the feast of St Michael, otherwise the day when the majority of civic officers were sworn into office.[141] This almost certainly resulted in members of the guild being excluded from public office as absentees were fined a pound of wax, without exception.[142] Of course, it is possible that due to the guild's location – namely outside the civic jurisdiction – it was mainly comprised of clergymen, though in the absence of membership lists this cannot be confirmed. The final possibility for tension stems from the structure of the guild, a matter to which this chapter now turns.

Form

On the composition and size of the city's guilds little can be said directly as the specific focus and function of the certificates precludes such details from being recorded. Even guilds founded by or for specific groups, such as the Archers (Holy Cross), Barbers (St John) and Clerks (St Nicholas, St Mary and All Saints), more often than not did not stipulate in their ordinances whether members were to be of that craft or profession, stating only that it was a requirement that their elected officials be.[143] In fact only the Cordwainers categorically recorded that those working in the trade must live in the city and be part of the guild,[144] thereby raising the question as to whether the guild accepted members who did not practise the craft. Unfortunately no details on this issue are forthcoming. Nonetheless, whilst office-holding was occasionally reserved for individuals of a specific status, membership was, on the whole, opened up to the wider community. Evidence for this comes, firstly, in the form of the frequent clauses recording how those who died outside the city (typically on pilgrimage) were to be celebrated for as if they had died in their *own* parish, not the parish of the guild;[145] and secondly, by the presence of the higher clergy in guilds such as Corpus Christi in St Michael on the Mount,[146] many of whom had prescribed living quarters in the Close.[147] The Great Guild, located at the church of St Andrew in Wigford, perhaps offers the best example of wide membership as it drew wealthy merchants and civic officials from across the city, evidence of which can be found in extant wills and charters.[148]

141 See 000.

142 C 47/40/143.

143 C 47/40/148, 150, C 47/41/151.

144 C 47/41/152.

145 For example, the guild of St Edmund of Pontigny recorded: *Item quod si aliquis frater vel soror moriatur in peregrinacionem vel in aliquo alio loco extra civitatem unde fratres et sorores … quantum facerent si mortuus esset inter eos in civitate in ecclesia ubi erat parochianus.* C 47/40/140; for others, see C 47/40/137; C 47/41/154, 157.

146 Geoffrey Scrope, canon, and Peter Dalton, treasurer, were both members: *LW*, vol. 1, 15; *ELW*, 97. Such diverse membership began long before 1530, as suggested by James, 'Ritual, Drama', 24–5, n. 80.

147 For the residence of the cathedral canons and dignitaries, D. Owen, 'Historical Survey, 1091–1450', in *idem*, *A History of Lincoln Minster* (Cambridge, 1994), 136–41.

148 *ELW*, 74, 139; *BB*, fos 146v, 198, 260v–261. See also C 143/79/10; C 143/349/21.

Table 19 Guild entrance fees and annual payments

Name	Parish church (foundation date)	Admission cost/annual fees (p.a.)
Fraternity of Corpus Christi	Unknown (no date)	*Illegible*
Guild of Corpus Christi	St Michael on the Hill (1350)	2s + 12d p.a.^
Guild of the Resurrection	St Martin (1354)	5d + 13d p.a.^
Fraternity of St Anne	St Peter in the Skin Market (1344)	1d p.a.#
Fraternity of the Holy Sepulchre	Holy Cross, Wigford (1366)	13d p.a.#
Guild of St Bavon	St Bavon (1362)	None but costs*
Guild of the Resurrection or Holy Sepulchre	St Cuthbert (1374)	*Illegible*
Guild of St Edmund of Pontigny	All Saints[?] (1276)	None but costs*
Guild of St Mary	St Mary, Wigford (1363)	None but costs*
Guild of St George	St George (1377)	4d p.a.#
Guild of St Lawrence the Martyr	St Lawrence (no date)	None but costs*
Guild of St Margaret	St Margaret (1336)	1d + costs p.a.#
Guild of St Martin	St Martin (1338)	1d + costs p.a.#
Guild of the Blessed Virgin Mary (The Great Guild)	St Andrew (before the Statute of Mortmain)	No information noted
Guild of the Blessed Virgin Mary	St Benedict (not known)	1d + costs*
Guild of the Purification of Blessed Virgin Mary	St Benedict (no date)	3s 4d + 3s 4d p.a.^
Guild of St Mary and St Nicholas (Clerks)	St John, Wigford (before the Statute of Mortmain)~	1d p.a.#
Fraternity of St Nicholas and St Mary and All Saints	St Nicholas, Newport (1339)	None but costs*
Fraternity of Archers (Holy Cross)	Holy Cross (1379)	1d p.a.#
Guild of Barbers (St John the Evangelist)	St John (1369)	2s 2d + 6d p.a.^
Guild of Cordwainers (Blessed Virgin Mary)	St Lawrence (1307)	*Illegible*
Confraternity of Fullers (Holy Cross)	Holy Cross (1297)	1d p.a.#
Guild of Masons (Blessed Virgin Mary and All Saints)	Unknown (1313)	4s 4d or barley + 13d p.a.^
Fraternity of Mercers (Blessed Virgin Mary [?])	St Rumbold (before 1349)†	No information noted
Fraternity of Minstrels and Entertainers (unknown)	Unknown (no date)	No information noted
Guild of Tilers (Corpus Christi)	St Botolph (1346)	3d with ¼ barley p.a.#
Guild of Sailors (Corpus Christi)	Unknown (1335)	None but costs*
Fraternity of Tailors (Corpus Christi)	Unknown (1328)	¼ barley with 12d p.a.#
Fraternity of Weavers (Exaltation of the Cross)	Unknown (1130/1346)	1d with ½lb wax p.a.#

Table 19 (notes)

Note: guilds are listed in the order they are enrolled in the TNA catalogue (C 47/40/134–50, C 47/41/151–60).
Key: * = no costs or admission fee but expenses are expected to be paid for various aspects of guild membership, i.e. payments for the candle, burial services, the poor, etc.; # = no subscription costs recorded though the lower annual fees are always accompanied by extra costs; ^ = subscription and annual fees inclusive of extra costs; ~ = for the foundation of St Mary and Nicholas: *CPR, 1401–05*, 96; † = *BB*, fo. 187v (1349).

The notion of a 'wider community' is naturally open to interpretation, and here it is useful to draw upon the evidence of admission costs and annual fees, all of which can be used to highlight possible membership trends (table 19). For example, the guild of the Purification of the Blessed Virgin Mary in St Benedict was almost certainly an institution aimed at the wealthy; its admission fee alone was the second highest in the city (3s 4d), whilst its annual fee (3s 4d) was the highest.[149] Comparable amounts were requested by the guilds of Masons (Blessed Virgin Mary and All Saints) (4s 4d or one quarter of barley three times per year) and Corpus Christi of St Michael on the Mount (2s), though their annual costs were much lower (13d and 12d, respectively).[150] This stood in contrast to the majority of guilds, including the Holy Sepulchre and St Anne, which charged no admission fees and requested much more modest sums of 13d and 1d per annum.[151] Nonetheless even guilds which recorded no admission costs or low annual fees still expected their members to contribute towards a variety of expenses, including burials, religious services, gifts for the poor, ale, the sick, pilgrims, candles and the guild feast. Guilds employing this approach included St Bavon, St Edmund of Pontigny, St Lawrence and the Sailors (Corpus Christi).[152] Overall this demonstrates that there was a wide range of membership options available for the city's inhabitants, all of which was influenced by members' ability to contribute.

Unsurprisingly, the main absentees from the city's guilds were the poor and infirm, though they played an important symbolic role in guild ceremonies. For example, it was the custom for the guild of St Margaret and the guild of Masons (Blessed Virgin Mary and All Saints) to invite as many poor as there were members of the guild to their annual feasts,[153] whilst the majority of other guilds dispensed bread, ale and coin (typically ½d).[154] The guild of the Holy Sepulchre even provided fish.[155] The Great Guild of the Blessed Virgin Mary in the church of St Andrew took such provisions a step further by establishing in the opening years of the fourteenth century a hospital for thirteen poor men (*pauperibus*) in the suburb (of Wigford?)

149 C 47/41/147; *English Guilds*, 174.
150 C 47/40/135, C 47/41/154.
151 C 47/40/137.
152 C 47/40/138, 140, 142, C 47/41/158.
153 C 47/40/143; C 47/41/154.
154 For example, C 47/40/144, 146, 148.
155 C 47/40/137.

from which 43s 5d of annual rents were drawn from plots across the city. In addition to these thirteen individuals the hospital also catered for aging brothers and sisters of the guild, suggesting that in this particular case charity and welfare were not considered mutually exclusive forms of aid.[156] Such developments reflect the broader trend for Lincoln's wealthier inhabitants to provide charity to the poor in the form of housing, victuals and clothing in a period when a number of the city's hospitals and almshouses were beginning to experience financial difficulties.[157]

Fundamentally, Lincoln's guilds were, much like those in other towns, highly receptive to female members, with all but two – the Weavers (Exaltation of the Cross) and the Clerks (St Nicholas, St Mary and All Saints) – making reference to 'sisters' in their ordinances.[158] Quite why women were absent from the Weavers' ordinances is not altogether clear, since Louise Wilkinson demonstrates there were a number of women employed in the trade in the city by the end of the thirteenth century.[159] Their absence from the Clerks' ordinances is perhaps more understandable, though this did not reflect reality as the guild did accept female members.[160] Even in guilds such as the Archers (Holy Cross), which was founded solely by men, 'sisters' were nevertheless recorded in every one of its ordinances,[161] suggesting that throughout the city there was generally no bar to female membership.

In terms of ordinances relating directly to women, however, only three can be identified, all of which arguably reflect to some extent common concerns over female behaviour. The first comes from the guild of Sailors (Corpus Christi), which noted that female members of the guild without *bone fame et honeste conversacionis* were to be fined 2d, with the profits being put towards drinks for the poor.[162] The second comes from the fraternity of St Nicholas and St Mary, which warned that any sister chattering without reason or saying anything against the constitutions or ordinances of the guild (*garulatio extra racionem vel inquiam faciat contra istas constituciones et ordinaciones*) was to be fined a pound of wax.[163] Such stereotypes can, of course, be identified elsewhere, though it is important to note that no such provisions were made for men in the city.[164] The final provision relates to working practice and the sexual allure of women: according to the ordinances of the confraternity of Fullers (Holy Cross), no man was to tread at the bar with a woman unless she was the wife of a master or her handmaid.[165] Such rules thus sought to minimise illicit sexual

156 Unfortunately the exact location of the hospital is unknown. C 143/55/6 (1302).

157 *LCL VCH*, 230–1, 234; *BB*, fos 82–82v, 84, 159–159v; C 270/23/6; C 270/23/11. For a broader context to these economic developments, see C. Rawcliffe, 'The Hospitals of Later Medieval London', *Medical History*, 28, 1 (1984), 12–15.

158 K. L. French, *The Good Wife of the Parish* (Philadelphia, 2008), 124; Farnhill, *Guilds and the Parish*, 48–9.

159 Wilkinson, *Thirteenth-Century Lincolnshire*, 98.

160 *CPR, 1401–05*, 96.

161 C 47/40/150.

162 C 47/41/158.

163 C 47/40/149.

164 B. McRee, 'Religious Gilds and the Regulation of Behaviour in Late Medieval Towns', in J. Rosenthal and C. Richmond (eds), *People, Politics and Community in the Later Middle Ages* (Gloucester, 1987), 112.

165 C 47/41/153; *English Guilds*, 180.

behaviour between unmarried members, all the while maintaining the image and respectability of the guild and trade.

Ordinances for men related primarily to fiscal matters and matters of office,[166] and there were also rules regarding disputes between members, though no sex is noted outright, in some cases.[167] Examples where this is clear, however, come from the guilds of St Anne and St Mary, both of which ordered that brothers borrowing goods from the guild and not returning them were to be fined in wax.[168] There were also rules and regulations regarding elections to the position of graceman or warden and the expectations of each role, with fines for those failing in their duties.[169] It is to be inferred from this evidence that it was only men who took up the financial and political duties of guilds, with women not being afforded that opportunity. Even so, men and women were considered equals in terms of the fees they paid and there is no evidence that women paid lower admission costs, as was the case in some London and Norwich guilds.[170]

Writing in 1870, Lucy Toulmin Smith noted with reference to the Fullers (Holy Cross), Tailors (Corpus Christi) and Tilers (Corpus Christi) that they were 'neither wholly social gilds nor wholly craft-gilds', before adding that 'only two or three of the ordinances [of Lincoln's guilds] have anything to do with the members of the gild as craftsmen'. This she thought worthy of attention, as they were 'a sort of cross between the social gild and the craft-gild'.[171] Such a view might also be extended to other 'craft guilds' as very few recorded working provisions. The Barbers (St John the Evangelist), for example, recorded only that apprentices were forbidden from seeking out their own work and that those refusing work were to be chastised (*castigari*) by the graceman and fined a pound of wax. Those who refused to pay were forced to leave the guild and presumably the craft.[172] This was certainly the case for the Cordwainers (Blessed Virgin Mary) already noted above.[173] Nevertheless, there were some guilds, like the Sailors (Corpus Christi), Mercers (Blessed Virgin Mary),[174] and even the Minstrels and Entertainers (no patron saint noted), who recorded no 'craft' regulations whatsoever, which suggests that they may have been primarily a religious guild with a specific type of membership. Considered this way it is accurate to say that there were no true 'craft guilds' in the city at this date, unlike the Fullers and Ringers in Bristol or the Tailors of Exeter, for example.[175]

166 Which was, again, typical: McRee, 'Religious Gilds and the Regulation of Behaviour', 112.

167 C 47/41/154, 158.

168 C 47/40/137, 140.

169 C 47/41/154; C 47/40/136.

170 M. Kowaleski and J. M. Bennett, 'Crafts, Gilds, and Women in the Middle Ages: Fifty Years after Marian K. Dale', *Signs: Journal of Women in Culture and Society*, 14, 21 (1989), 478; B. R. McRee, 'Religious Gilds and Civil Order: The Case of Norwich in the Late Middle Ages', *Speculum*, 67, 1 (1992), 80.

171 *English Guilds*, 179.

172 C 47/41/151. For similar provisions for the Masons: C 47/41/154.

173 C 47/41/152.

174 C 47/41/155–6, 158.

175 *English Guilds*, 283–6, 288–96, 321–3; Barron, 'Parish Fraternities', 16–17; Swanson, *British Towns*, 96–102.

In some ways this conclusion is unsurprising given that England has been regarded as 'generally slower than the more industrial parts of Europe in establishing craft guilds', with guilds becoming more 'abundant only in the fifteenth century'.[176] Another possible reason for this lack of regulation in guild ordinances has already been noted above and relates to the control of guilds by civic government. Examples of this come from 1399 when the Cordwainers acquired their own charter from the mayor and commonalty,[177] from the opening decades of the fifteenth century when new ordinances were recorded for the Barbers,[178] and from the sixteenth century when the ordinances of the Mercers, Bakers and Tanners were ratified by the mayor by way of the common seal.[179] It is clear that the civic government in Lincoln, like elsewhere, strived to oversee and control craft and trade regulations whenever possible, which explains the presence of regulations for Merchants, Weavers, Fullers, Dyers and Fishermen in the *Provisions for the Government of the City* (c.1300).[180] Such municipal control was not altogether uncommon and in Norwich, for example, four craft guilds founded prior to 1300 – Tanners, Shoemakers, Fullers and Chandlers – were suppressed by the authorities for refusing to accept the authority of the bailiffs 'over all trades and occupations'.[181] Whilst there is no extant evidence of such intervention at Lincoln, it seems likely that in the face of direct opposition a similar position would have been adopted, especially as in cases where trade regulations were broken it was the civic government who imposed fines.[182]

Aside from the more specific aspects of size, admissions and sex, it is worthwhile saying a few words on the issue of guild structure and formality. To begin with it is possible to say that two of the city's smaller guilds were only given the appearance of an 'official guild' by way of the crown's demand in 1388. The first of these was the fraternity of Minstrels and Entertainers (no patron saint), who submitted the shortest ordinances of all the city's guilds. According to their ordinances they were to meet but once a year 'in a certain, suitable, and proper place' where they were to 'set up a great candle' which was to be taken 'to the mother church, St Mary's of Lincoln, with the greatest procession, joy, and honour … on the Wednesday in Whitsun week' before they partook in 'a drinking' together. Beyond this, they noted only that the fraternity did not meet at any other time, held no assemblies, shared no oaths and owned no goods. What is immediately striking about these ordinances, apart from their brevity, is their structural informality. There is no reference to the poor or those in positions of authority – perhaps there were none – no fixed meeting point

176 Britnell, 'Town Life', 169.
177 *Historical MSS*, 53–4.
178 *WB*, fos 10v–11.
179 *Historical MSS*, 30–1. The Baker's guild was founded in 1523 and was dedicated to St Clement.
180 *Medieval Lincoln*, appendix 7, 402–5.
181 W. Hudson (ed.), *Leet Jurisdiction in the City of Norwich*, Selden Society, vol. 5 (London, 1892), lxxxviii–lxxxix, 13, 42–3; R. Holt, 'Society and Population, 600–1300', in *CUHB*, 91. For London, see Barron, 'Guild Certificates of 1388–9', 117. For a more general survey of the links between guilds and civic government: A. F. Johnston, 'English guilds and municipal authority', *Renaissance and Reformation*, 25 (1989): 69–88. For criticism of these links, Rosser, *Art of Solidarity*, 149–84.
182 For example, *BH*, fo. 26v; *WB*, fos 4, 10v.

or parish church and no references to masses for the dead or charitable provisions. Considered in this way, it is perhaps surprising that the members saw themselves as a fraternity at all, as they undoubtedly differed from other established institutions in the city. Even so, their employment of the standard nomenclature ('First it is ordered and decided among the brothers and sisters of the aforesaid fraternity ...') suggests that they may have come to see themselves as a guild due to the expectations of the crown.[183]

The second case relates to the fraternity of Mercers (Blessed Virgin Mary), which, like the Minstrels and Entertainers, noted that it held no meetings or congregations, owned no lands and processed with a great candle to the mother church on the Sunday after Pentecost, where the candle was placed before the south side of the high altar.[184] The Mercers, however, did record the name of the graceman, John Hedon (mayor 1395/96), itself an uncommon practice.[185] This is indicative of two things: firstly, that the fraternity included a number of the city's leading citizens; and secondly, how, unlike the Minstrels and Entertainers, there was at least some rudimentary structure to the guild. Even so, in the absence of religious ordinances (masses for the dead and burial services) it once again seems that this particular guild was little more than an informal association driven primarily by commercial ventures.

From these two examples it is clear that there existed within the city at least two loose associations of individuals which came to be characterised as a guild as a result of the crown's demands. This may have grown out of contemporary fears over the purpose of the king's writ, with some guilds believing it prudent to return a reply, however lacking in detail it might be; better that than be accused of heterodoxy or, worse still, sedition. Yet the importance of this evidence is that it raises the question, what defined a medieval guild? In particular, it seems that it did not necessarily have to be a highly organised or charitable institution, like many in the fifteenth century.[186] In fact, beyond offering lights – an act described by David Postles as an expression of 'popular piety'[187] – it seems that such guilds simply performed a social function for likeminded individuals.[188] That congregations of this type were recognised by local inhabitants is perhaps one of the reasons why these returns have survived; in London and Norfolk the sheriff was persuaded to ensure the ordinances for guilds were recorded,[189] and it is possible that something similar was taking place at Lincoln, perhaps under the auspices of civic government. How many other informal congregations went unnoticed or unrecorded is, of course, beyond the scope of the historian, though some, such as St Bridget and St Mary in London,

[183] C 47/41/156; trans. Stokes, *Early English Drama*, vol. 2, 649–50.

[184] C 47/41/155.

[185] C 47/41/155. Other guilds naming officials were the Weavers (though they date from their original ordinances of 1346, not 1389) and the Great Guild of the Blessed Virgin Mary: C 47/40/145a, C 47/41/160.

[186] Farnhill, *Guilds and the Parish*, 61–3.

[187] D. Postles, 'Lamps, Lights and Layfolk: "Popular" Devotion before the Black Death', *Journal of Medieval History*, 25, 2 (1999), 105.

[188] Goddard, 'Medieval Business Networks', 19–20.

[189] Crouch, *Piety, Fraternity*, 38.

stated outright in their ordinances that they did not consider themselves guilds at all.[190]

Despite the informality of these two particular guilds, the majority, including those not naming a parish church, returned highly detailed certificates, emphasising how for the most part there existed within the city a clear sense of fraternal authority, structure and formality. This is shown through the many references to the graceman and keepers, the application of fines (monetary or wax), regulations for behaviour and perhaps above all the communal feast. In a small number of cases such measures were taken a step further, with the guild of the Resurrection in St Martin, founded in 1354, recording that on the Wednesday of Easter week its ordinances would be read aloud so 'that no one may, at any time, be able to say that he has broken, unwittingly, any of the articles which all have thus heard, and to which all have bound themselves'.[191] The guild of Corpus Christi, too, founded in 1350, likewise stated that on the eve of the guild feast 'a clerk shall read and explain these ordinances'.[192] A similar provision for the guild of St Margaret has already been noted.[193] Whilst it remains true that not all guilds went to such lengths – or at least did not record them – taken independently or alongside the presence of officials, they seem to indicate a wider concern among guilds about rules and regulations, with independent formalised institutions becoming increasingly common in the city.[194]

Veneration

Eamon Duffy argues that by the later Middle Ages 'in many communities, especially rural villages, the gilds and their dedications must have seemed as immemorial as the parish church itself'.[195] So much so, in fact, that 'Devotion to the gild saint would therefore have been a "given".' Doubtless this was true of many places by the fifteenth and sixteenth centuries, though in many ways this fails to consider the guilds' origins. His contention, too, that in 'larger communities' there is evidence for innovative devotional practices by guilds such as SS Crispin and Crispianus and St Erasmus in Great Yarmouth, both of which were founded in the late fifteenth or early sixteenth century, is also to some extent deceptive, as it fails to consider how such innovative practices were also a feature of the earlier period. By using the evidence of veneration for Lincoln's guilds it is possible to demonstrate not only how collective forms of piety were equally diverse from at least the late thirteenth century onwards but also how many guilds came to be inextricably associated with the parish in which they were located as a matter of choice, not circumstance.

190 Westlake, *Parish Gilds*, 182, 184.
191 C 47/40/136; trans. *English Guilds*, 177.
192 C 47/40/135; trans. *English Guilds*, 178.
193 C 47/40/143.
194 For more on this, see main text below.
195 For what follows, E. Duffy, *The Stripping of the Altars: Traditional Religion in England, 1400–1580* (London, 1992), 163.

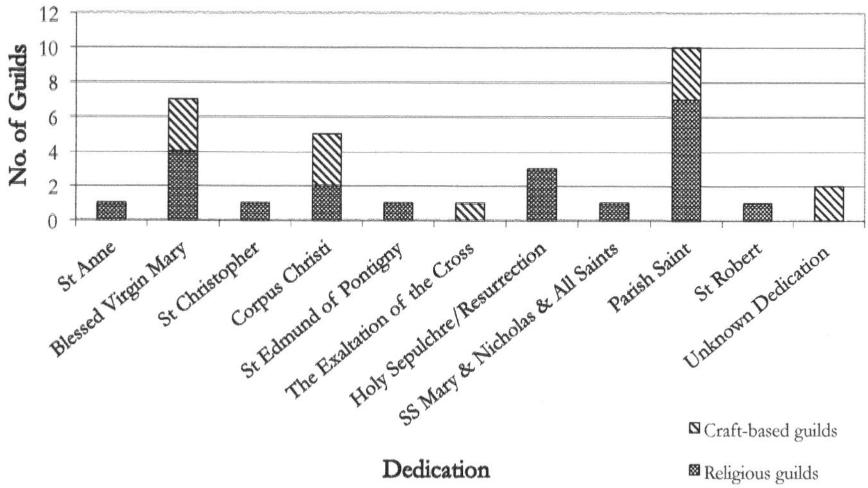

Figure 8 Guild veneration in Lincoln prior to 1410

By 1410 the most common practice in the city was for guilds to dedicate themselves to the patron saint of their local parish church (figure 8). This demonstrates the desire of the laity to take certain elements of religious life into their own hands, all the while emphasising the strong link between certain guilds and the local parish community.[196] In these instances the centrality of the high altar to fraternal practices emphasised how, despite the pious choices on offer for potential guild founders, a conscious decision had been made to increase divine worship to that particular saint. Some of these guilds worshipped in areas associated with their work, though this was by no means uniform throughout the city. For example, the Tilers' guild, which was located in the church of St Botolph in Wigford near the local tilehouse, venerated Corpus Christi,[197] whilst the fraternity of Clerks, which venerated St Nicholas, the patron saint of scholars, amongst other groups, worshipped at the church of St John in Wigford, though its appeal went far beyond that particular parish.[198]

196 Difficulties abound in ascribing guilds to one category or another. Take, for instance, the guild of St Mary, St Nicholas and All Saints (the Clerks). Whilst it was dedicated primarily to St Nicholas (the ordinances record that the guild worshipped at the high altar), it nevertheless demonstrates how corporate pieties were not singularly focused or straightforward. As such, there is some overlap between the categories 'Blessed Virgin Mary' and 'Parish Saint', meaning that there is one more guild in figure 8 than actually existed. See main text below.

197 C 47/41/157; *BB*, fo. 93.

198 C 47/40/148; *CPR, 1401–05*, 95. For the sixteenth century, see D. Hickman, *Lincoln Wills: 1532–4* (Lincoln Record Society, 2004), 150, 158, 190, 222, 282, 285, 286, 230, 349.

The second most numerous category were guilds dedicated to the Blessed Virgin Mary, the single most common focus of veneration in the city as well as nationally.[199] In total, four of the city's 'religious' guilds venerated the Virgin along with three 'craft' guilds. The likelihood is that this focus grew not only out of the earlier European practice (dating to the eleventh and twelfth centuries) of seeing her as a focus for Christ's suffering,[200] but also because she was a saint who 'performed every kind of miracle'.[201] In addition to this, there were undoubtedly local reasons too: for example, the cathedral was dedicated to the Virgin, whilst the city's mayoral seal represented the Virgin holding Christ, flanked on either side by a lion passant guardant.[202] Thus, unlike the institutions noted in the previous category, the majority of guilds venerating the Blessed Virgin Mary worshipped at dedicated side altars, not the high altar. In fact, only the guild of St Mary in the church of St Mary in Wigford used the high altar,[203] with the guilds located in the churches of St Andrew, St Benedict (two guilds), St Rumbold and St Lawrence using side altars.[204]

The third category includes guilds dedicated to Corpus Christi. In spite of the growing popularity of the festival throughout the fourteenth century, these guilds should be considered as innovative devotional practices, much like those described by Duffy – more so given that the guild of Tailors (founded 1328) was only the second guild in all England to be dedicated to the feast, ten years after its introduction (1318).[205] Three of the four other foundation dates for Corpus Christi guilds are preserved (1335, 1346 and 1350), similarly demonstrating the city's early interest in the feast.[206] Interestingly, and unlike the two preceding categories, Corpus Christi was a more favourable choice for the city's 'craft' guilds (three) than for its religious guilds (two). It is possible that the integrative power and symbolism often associated with the Corpus Christi feast was responsible for this;[207] and it should come as no surprise to find that the guild of Sailors' (Corpus Christi) was one of only two institutions to state outright that it accepted members from outside the city, in this case from Boston, emphasising the strong economic links between the two towns.[208] Hence Corpus Christi guilds, some of which did not name a parish church,[209] may have been considered more apposite to the concerns or needs of 'craft' guilds in the city, certainly more so than the more fixed parochial forms of veneration.

The final category considers guilds which, like the Blessed Virgin Mary,

199 The Blessed Virgin Mary was venerated by roughly a third of all guilds in medieval England. Hanawalt, 'Keepers of the Lights', 26–7.

200 Duffy, *Stripping of the Altars*, 260; E. Duffy, 'Mater Dolorosa, Mater Misericordiae', *New Blackfriars*, 69, 816 (1988): 210–27.

201 Le Goff, *Birth of Europe*, 75–9, at 76.

202 *Medieval Lincoln*, plate 21 ('Mayoralty Seal').

203 C 47/40/140; *LW*, vol. 1, 141–2, 149.

204 This was explicitly noted in the ordinances of St Lawrence: C 47/40/148.

205 M. Rubin, 'Corpus Christi Fraternities and Late Medieval Piety', *Studies in Church History*, 23 (1986), 100–2.

206 C 47/41/135, C 47/41/157–8.

207 Rubin, 'Small Groups', 139, 146; Rubin, 'Corpus Christi', 107–9.

208 C 47/41/158. The other being the Fullers: C 47/41/153. For the economic relationship between Lincoln and Boston, see chapter two.

209 Two certainly did not; the other is too damaged to assess: C 47/40/134; C 47/41/158–9.

worshipped at dedicated side altars. As the evidence shows, these dedications varied considerably, highlighting an array of pious interests among the laity.[210] Whilst some were more common (Resurrection/Holy Sepulchre) than others (St Christopher, St Anne), two were possibly unique.[211] The first of these was the guild of St Robert,[212] though quite which St Robert the guild venerated is unclear as no certificate survives. However, given the later trend for Lincoln inhabitants to venerate Bishop John de Dalderby, the most likely possibility is that this was in fact the former bishop of Lincoln Robert Grosseteste, there being concerted efforts in the city to have him canonised.[213] Whoever the guild was dedicated to, it appears that by 1389 it was no longer active, with no certificate being returned to Chancery. Of course, it is possible that it was rededicated to a more fashionable saint sometime during the fourteenth century, as was known elsewhere,[214] perhaps after the 1320s when interest in Grosseteste's shrine was waning.[215]

The second unusual guild dedication was to Edmund Rich, archbishop of Canterbury, who died at Soissy in France in 1240. Buried at Pontigny shortly after, he was canonised seven years later. According to Diana Webb, his tomb became a 'magnet for English pilgrims well into the next century' and several miracles were said to have occurred there; its popularity being strengthened by Thomas Becket, who spent part of his exile Pontigny.[216] Yet the power of the saint was not confined to foreign shores, with miracles reported in Catesby in Northamptonshire and Aston, which lay midway between Oxford and Banbury.[217] Whilst the origins of the guild are unknown, save that it was made (*facte*) to honour St Edmund of Pontigny in 1276, it seems likely that it may have been established by one or more zealous pilgrims at a time when St Edmund's fame and sanctity were at their strongest. This certainly fits Webb's conclusion that he influenced English pilgrims and equally with the idea that over time there were a number of inhabitants of Lincoln who were willing to embrace new pious trends.[218] This was certainly true of the guild of Sailors (Corpus

210 The guilds of St Robert and St Christopher are added to this list despite the absence of any guild certificates as there were no churches dedicated to these saints. The dedication of the Tawyers is unknown and is not considered here. For the possibility that the guild of St Christopher processed to the cathedral where there was an altar by the opening decades of the fifteenth century, see C. Wordsworth, *Notes on Mediaeval Services in England* (London, 1898), 130, 246.

211 Compare to Bainbridge, *Gilds*, 153–6; Westlake, *Parish Gilds*, 137–238; Crouch, *Piety, Fraternity*, 99; Farnhill, *Guilds and the Parish*, 172–211.

212 *LW*, 4–5.

213 M. Robson, 'Robert Grosseteste: his Memory among the Greyfriars, his Cult in Lincoln Cathedral and the Petition for his Canonisation', *Miscellanea Francescana*, 104 (2004): 306–23; and Cole, 'Canonisation of Robert Grosseteste', 1–34. See also D. Stocker, 'The Tomb and Shrine of Bishop Grosseteste in Lincoln Cathedral', in W. M. Ormrod (ed.), *England in the Thirteenth Century: Proceedings of the 1984 Harlaxton Symposium* (Woodbridge, 1985), 143–8.

214 G. Rosser, 'The Guild of St Mary and St John the Baptist, Lichfield: Ordinances of the Late Fourteenth Century', *Collections for a History of Staffordshire*, 4, 13 (1988), 19–20.

215 *LCL VCH*, 422, 436.

216 Webb, *Pilgrimage*, 63.

217 Webb, *Pilgrimage*, 67–70.

218 Such as St Etheldreda in Ely, St Simon and St Jude in Boston, St Fabian and St Sebastian in London: Westlake, *Parish Gilds*, 143, 157, 183.

Christi) who, besides venerating the host, processed each year with a candle to the altar of St John the Evangelist in memory of *sancti Iohannis de Dalderby quondam episcopi Lincoln' in ecclesia cathedrali Lincoln'* (16 January).[219] Dalderby, unlike St Edmund of Pontigny, however, was never formally canonised despite the entreaties of Edward II, though this did not prevent local inhabitants from considering him a saint.[220]

Other guilds that could also be said to have been founded upon the basis of innovative devotional practices were the three institutions honouring the Resurrection and the Holy Sepulchre, primarily because they were extremely rare.[221] In fact, so far as it is possible to tell, studies have revealed only eleven guilds dedicated to the Resurrection or the Holy Sepulchre throughout the entire medieval period, including the three from Lincoln (founded in 1354, 1366 and 1374), a proportionately high number.[222] Whilst it remains true that rarity does not automatically equate to innovation, it is significant that these guilds were established in the city as they provide a wider context through which to analyse the frequent ordinances recorded for pilgrimage by guilds.[223]

As the pattern of veneration dictates, there was an array of fraternal choice available to guild founders and there is strong evidence to suggest that some individuals were willing to embrace transient, even unofficial, pieties to reflect their own faith and devotion. Guilds such as St Edmund of Pontigny, the Tailors' (Corpus Christi) and the Sailors (Corpus Christi/John de Dalderby) certainly fall into this category. Moreover, that they did so early on in the development of these particular cults demonstrates that at times Lincoln maintained an innovative approach to sanctity and worship long before objects of devotion gained popularity elsewhere, in particular Corpus Christi. Even so, as seems to be the case with St Robert, less popular saints were, if not discarded, then perhaps supplanted by new ones as new ideas and beliefs emerged. Even so, it is impossible to forget that the vast majority of guilds were much less concerned with new expressions of piety or sanctity, seeking only additional ways of honouring the well-established parish saint through specific fraternal liturgical practices. This was equally true of those images and ideas – the Holy Cross, the Resurrection – that manifested themselves in the everyday lives of late medieval Christian thought. Such 'traditional' forms of piety, as highlighted by Duffy, were thus not always such, undoubtedly drawing upon new audiences. This is particularly important given that not every parish maintained a guild. Even so, identification with a particular saint was neither straightforward nor fixed and individual and collective fraternal identities developed within a changing urban environment as membership ebbed and flowed and local circumstances changed.

219 C 47/41/158. For the text of masses sung in honour of Dalderby, see J. F. Wickenden, 'John de Dalderby, Bishop of Lincoln, 1300–20', *Archaeological Journal*, 40 (London, 1883): 215–24.

220 Cole, 'Canonisation of John de Dalderby', 143–76.

221 C 47/40/136–7, 139.

222 J. C. Roach, 'The City of Cambridge: Religious Guilds', in *idem* (ed.), A *History of the County of Cambridge and the Isle of Ely: Volume 3: The City and University of Cambridge* (1959), 133; Westlake, *Parish Gilds*, 22, 141, 153; Crouch, *Piety, Fraternity*, 256, 262; Farnhill, *Guilds and the Parish*, 192, 199.

223 See main text below.

Ordinances

The final part of this chapter will analyse the types of ordinances recorded by the city's guilds and consider the impact of the Black Death upon them. It is the aim here to emphasise the collective piety of guilds both on an individual basis and within the city-wide framework to consider if and how these differed from fraternal practices elsewhere before assessing what this reveals about late fourteenth-century attitudes towards the crown.

The following analysis (table 20), which is based upon the methodology devised by Benjamin McRee in his study of guild charity, is structured according to whether guilds promised assistance to their members or not. Using this method, McRee was able to identify three broad trends: first, that guilds promising aid to their members 'engaged more broadly than other fraternities in a variety of social and religious activities';[224] second, that they were more conscious of their public profile than other guilds; and, third, that they used such measures as a socially binding force.[225] This led him to conclude that it was a requirement for such guilds 'to overcome the centrifugal pull of their members' varied origins' in order to 'bind them into

Table 20 Frequency of ordinances recorded in guild certificates (1389)

	All certificates		**Lincoln only**	
	GPA	**Others**	**GPA**	**Others**
Burial services	92%	58%	17 (100%)	9 (82%)
Candles	75%	74%	17 (100%)	11 (100%)
Masses	68%	40%	17 (100%)	9 (82%)
Priest (chaplains)	41%	43%	4 (24%)	3 (27%)†
Behavioural rules	38%	7%	14 (88%)*	4 (40%)†
Feast	37%	34%	16 (94%)	9 (82%)
Procession	31%	11%	8 (47%)	7 (64%)
Livery	19%	6%	0	0
Aid for church fabric	14%	18%	0	0
Totals	145	323	17	11

Key: GPA = guilds promising assistance to members; others = guilds not offering aid; † = out of 10; * = out of 16. Note this table does not include the guilds of Corpus Christi (certificate damaged), the Tawyers, St Robert or St Christopher for which no certificates survive.

224 An example of the type of aid McRee identifies can be seen for the guild of the Resurrection in Lincoln. Founded in the church of St Martin in 1354, it declared that when a member was out of work, brothers and sisters would take turns to offer him or her a meal in their homes each day: C 47/40/136.

225 McRee, 'Charity and Gild Solidarity', 201–3, at 201.

a cohesive whole'.[226] Whilst it is difficult to identify whether such measures were on the whole typical of Lincoln, given that McRee used supplementary evidence to reach his conclusions, there are three main benefits in adopting this approach: first, it allows wider comparisons to be made;[227] second, it reveals a number of local concerns which were uncommon elsewhere; and third, it demonstrates that there were in fact subtle differences between guilds offering assistance to their members and those not doing so.

As the evidence dictates, Lincoln's guilds were, if not more rigorous in the application of their faith, then certainly more judicious in the recording of their religious practices than those elsewhere, as there was typically a higher percentage in every category except 'priests', 'livery' and 'aid for church fabric', the latter two of which registered zero. For example, in Norwich the Brotherhood of Barbers (no foundation date) recorded detailed ordinances regarding lights but said nothing regarding its members' burials, feasts or processions; in Cambridge the guild of the Blessed Virgin Mary (no foundation date) likewise recorded ordinances for its members' aid and burials but nothing whatsoever for lights;[228] and in Bedale in Yorkshire, the brief return for the guild of Holy Trinity states only that it maintained a chaplain to say mass.[229] This stands in contrast to Lincoln where there are ubiquitous references to burial services, candles and masses for guilds offering assistance to their members, as well as for candles from guilds not offering aid.

Whilst it is possible that the absence of any references to the church fabric or guild livery is more indicative of clerical practice than reality, it is certainly possible that guilds did not provide monies for local churches. For example, there were six diocesan indulgences offered to penitents aiding churches in Lincoln during the fourteenth century. Out of these, only St Cuthbert, noted in 1309, ever had any established link to any of the city's guilds (the Resurrection or the Holy Sepulchre).[230] This is not to suggest that the growing insistence by the Church during the thirteenth century that parishioners contribute to church repairs was not apparent in the city, only that it was not channelled through the fraternal structure.[231] The absence of guild livery is also significant. According to the *Westminster Chronicle*, prior to the royal writ of 1388 the original request by the Commons to have guilds dissolved included a subclause which allowed them to maintain their chantries on the proviso that they did so without 'livere, confederacie, meintenaunce ou riotes en arrerissement du ley [in hindrance in law]'. Because of this, there may have been some lingering concerns

226 McRee, 'Charity and Gild Solidarity', 211.

227 At least to the extant returns which are drawn primarily from East Anglia (164), Lincolnshire (123), Cambridgeshire (60) and Suffolk (39): Westlake, *Parish Gilds*, 38.

228 *English Guilds*, 27, 269–70.

229 Westlake, *Parish Gilds*, 232; Crouch, *Piety, Fraternity*, 29.

230 The other churches were St Peter ad Fontem (1309), St Michael, Wigford (1318), St Peter at Pleas and St Bartholomew (both 1391), and St Andrew on the Hill (1395). LAO REG/3, fos 155, 384v; W. H. Bliss and J. A. Twemlow (eds), *Calendar of Papal Registers Relating to Great Britain and Ireland*, vol. 4, 1362–1404 (1902), 451, 500; *Reg. Antiq.*, vol. 2, no. 479.

231 C. D. Cragoe, 'The Custom of the English Church: Parish Church Maintenance in England before 1300', *Journal of Medieval History*, 36, 1 (2010), 27–8; E. Mason, 'The Role of the English Parishioner, 1100–1500', *Journal of Ecclesiastical History*, 27, 1 (1976): 24–5.

over recording such practices in the city as they may have been seen as potentially subversive institutions.[232] Whilst it is certainly possible that Lincoln's guilds may not have employed livery, this seems unlikely given the frequency with which guilds processed with deceased members from their homes to their local parish church,[233] with the guild of Corpus Christi founded in the church of St Michael on the Mount in 1350 stating outright that it had a 'banner of the gild', which was displayed during funerals to show 'that the dead was a brother or sister of the gild'.[234]

One surprising element to emerge from the Lincoln evidence is that in percentage terms (69 per cent, or 18 out of 26) more guilds offered aid to their members than elsewhere. In fact, the number is more than double the national average (30 per cent, or 145 out of 468).[235] By drawing upon McRee's findings, it thus follows that for the majority of the city's guilds there was great concern over fraternal regulations and public image, a point reflected most clearly in the frequency of ordinances relating to behaviour being noted by guilds offering assistance to their members, though to a lesser extent this was also true of those not offering assistance.[236] The marginally higher figure of feasts also points to the fact that guilds offering assistance to their members assembled on official business more frequently, a point which underscores these concerns (see below for the impact of the Black Death upon these practices). Hence whilst the number of processions recorded for guilds offering aid is lower than for those not doing so, it is still considerably higher than the national average, suggesting that guilds with less wealth possibly used the procession not only as a type of socially cohesive force but as the most visual and public expression of their collective identity.

If this reading of the evidence is accepted – that Lincoln's guilds recorded certain practices more readily than those elsewhere – then it once again calls into question local attitudes towards the king's writ, whilst simultaneously highlighting an idea advanced previously, namely that the city's guilds cooperated under the auspices of the civic authorities. On the one hand, this supports the idea that most guilds were concerned to express their orthodoxy, and by extension their subservience to the crown, seen either through their desire to have their ordinances ratified by the dean of Christianity or more fundamentally still through the higher percentage of pious activities recorded. On the other, it also demonstrates how the relative lack of references to guild livery or chaplains (and, by extension, access to lands and tenements from which they would otherwise have been supported) suggests that there may have been a coordinated effort on the part of guilds to mislead the crown into thinking that there was less wealth invested in these institutions than was actually the case. This was true of guilds in Yorkshire, for example; as David Crouch argues, one of the major reasons why subsequent action was not taken by the crown against guilds was that their untapped wealth (or apparent lack thereof) was simply not

232 Hector and Harvey, *Westminster Chronicle*, 356; for a discussion on this point, see Crouch, *Piety, Fraternity*, 35–7.

233 For example, C 47/40/137, 40.

234 C 47/40/135; trans. *English Guilds*, 178.

235 This figure is inclusive of the Lincoln data. McRee, 'Charity and Gild Solidarity', 203.

236 McRee, 'Religious Gilds and Civil Order', 118.

worth the trouble.[237] This may explain why a large number of guilds omitted details of their lands in their returns,[238] and may be indicative of the concentrated effort by many guilds to return a certain type of certificate, thereby underlining the high level of fraternal cooperation identified. Moreover, in maintaining an awareness of the attitude of Richard II's advisors towards the city's finances, especially after 1383,[239] guilds may have been actively discouraged by the civic government from revealing the true extent of their lands or from posing as political bodies. If true, this demonstrates the symbiotic relationship between civic government and guilds, represented most clearly through the urban-wide fraternal network and identity, which served to set apart Lincoln's guilds from those in surrounding areas and in many cases those of other towns too.

Nonetheless, it is important to recognise the possibility that the majority of Lincoln's guilds were in fact not particularly wealthy institutions, performing primarily charitable and pious functions, which is reflected by the relative absence of guildhalls and beneficed chaplains in the extant evidence. Certainly, it does not seem that they were overtly political bodies at this time, as they came to be in York in the fifteenth century.[240] This would explain the statistically higher number of guilds offering aid to their members than those not doing so (18 of 26), an idea supported by the fact that higher entrance fees did not necessarily result in greater social aid as many guilds which did not charge high admissions fees still provided aid, something McRee also identifies.[241] This suggests that civic authorities sought to control political tensions between guilds through the regulation of ritual and space, though such intervention was occasionally resented: as the provisions of the guild of Corpus Christi made plain, civic officials (who were also members of the guild) were forbidden from meddling in 'any matter, unless specially summoned; nor shall such a one take on himself any office in the gild'.[242]

Turning to the impact of the Black Death upon guild ordinances, the following analysis details twenty-four guilds for which a foundation date is known, all of which are arranged chronologically (tables 21a and 21b).

The first observation to make is that for guilds founded prior to 1349 there were proportionately more chaplains employed to say masses (one third) than for those founded after the Black Death (roughly a fifth), though this still remained well below the national average. The implication is that the majority of all guild services were performed by a hired chaplain on a temporary basis. As guild officials were all too well aware, providing monies for intercessory masses was a costly business. Take, for example, the Great Guild of the Blessed Virgin Mary which, as the only guild maintaining chaplains in perpetuity,[243] alienated £7 6s of annual rent in 1348 for

237 Crouch, *Piety, Fraternity*, 36–7.
238 See 158–9.
239 Chapter three.
240 Crouch, *Piety, Fraternity*, 158.
241 McRee, 'Charity and Gild Solidarity', 201.
242 *English Guilds*, 179.
243 No other Lincoln guild alienated properties for such a purpose, though see tables 21a and 21b.

the upkeep of two chaplains.[244] The cost of this undertaking is drawn sharply into focus when compared to the Sailors' guild of Corpus Christi, for example, which processed with a single candle to the cathedral for which each member was to pay 'one half pence and no more unless they so wish',[245] or the guild of St Mary, which also processed to the cathedral and expected nothing in return save a few pence for the upkeep of the candle throughout the year.[246] Following the pestilence, the prospect of dwindling membership for older guilds would have dealt a blow to guild revenues, which were mainly derived from annual subscriptions, fines and entrance fees. This was certainly the case for the Clerks' guild of St Mary and St Nicholas in the church of St John, which, in 1402, complained that 'all the brethren and sisters have died except Henry atte Wode', who 'is unable to support the necessary charges and works' of the guild.[247] Fortunately for the guild, the fellow guild of St Mary (presumably the Great Guild) generously purchased a licence in mortmain to grant a number of lands on its behalf thereby allowing it to survive.[248] Such problems were also exacerbated by the sharp rise in chaplains' wages, which left many of the newly founded guilds unable to hire them without risking the financial solvency of the institution.[249]

A second and equally significant change came in the form of the growing onus on members from guilds established after 1349 to play a greater role in fraternal affairs. This is demonstrated by the number of mornspeches recorded in guild ordinances, which virtually doubled from an average of less than two (1.6) before 1349 to exactly three following the pestilence. The rise was largely irrespective of whether guilds offered aid or not, though for the earlier period the majority of guilds not offering aid did not hold mornspeches, which demonstrates how this was not a pressing concern for guilds founded during the earlier period. Unfortunately whether this growth mirrored wider trends is unknown as mornspeches were not considered by McRee in his analysis, though they were undoubtedly popular as any perusal of Herbert Westlake's calendar makes clear.[250] Nonetheless, as noted previously, mornspeches were one of the three most important events of the fraternal year and it was custom for all members to attend. Following the Black Death guilds therefore began to demand more from their members in return for the social benefits they received in life and the spiritual benefits they received in death, and it seems that this demand grew as a result of the heightened fears over mortality brought about by the pestilence – fears echoed by the increased number of temporary chantries being recorded in testamentary evidence during the 1350s.[251]

One aspect of the city's guild ordinances uncommon elsewhere was the provision to go on pilgrimage, which remained to all intents and purposes unaffected by

244 C 143/349/21.
245 C 47/41/158.
246 C 47/40/140.
247 For the decline in the number of clerks recorded during this period, see appendix 2.
248 *CPR, 1401–05*, 96. No corresponding inquisition *ad quod damnum* certificate for this licence survives.
249 See 210–12.
250 Westlake, *Parish Gilds*, appendix, 138–238.
251 See 214–15 and table 24.

Table 21a Guild provisions according to foundation date (before 1349)

Name	Date	Aid	Burials
Fraternity of Exaltation of the Cross (Weavers)	1130/1346	Y	Y
Guild of the BVM (The Great Guild)	c.1250	N	Y
Guild of St Edmund of Pontigny	1276/1363	N	Y
Guild of St Mary and St Nicholas (Clerks)	before 1279	N	Y
Confraternity of the Holy Cross [?] (Fullers)	1297	Y	Y
Guild of BVM (Cordwainers)	1307	Y	Y
Guild of All Saints (Masons)	1313	Y	Y
Fraternity of Corpus Christi (Tailors)	1328	Y	Y
Guild of Corpus Christi (Sailors)	1335	N	Y
Guild of St Margaret	1336	Y	Y
Guild of St Martin	1338	Y	Y
Fraternity of St Nicholas, St Mary and All Saints	1339	N	Y
Fraternity of St Anne	1344	Y	Y
Guild of Corpus Christi (Tilers)	1346	N	Y
Fraternity of BVM (Mercers)	before 1349	N	N
Total (out of 15)		7	14

Table 21b Guild provisions according to foundation date (after 1349)

Name	Date	Aid	Burials
Guild of Corpus Christi	1350	Y	Y
Guild of the Resurrection	1354	Y	Y
Guild of St Bavo	1362	Y	Y
Guild of St Mary	1363	Y	Y
Fraternity of the Holy Sepulchre	1366	N	Y
Guild of St John the Evangelist (Barbers)	1369	Y	Y
Guild of the Resurrection or Holy Sepulchre	1374	N	Y
Guild of St George	1377	Y	Y
Fraternity of Holy Cross (Archers)	1379	N	Y
Total (out of 9)		6	9

Key: * = out of 8; note that these tables do not included guilds for which foundation dates are not known (guilds of Corpus Christi; the Purification of the Blessed Virgin Mary; St Lawrence the Martyr; Blessed Virgin Mary; and Minstrels and Entertainers); note: BVM = Blessed Virgin Mary. *Sources:* C 47/40/135–42, 144–5, 148–50, C 47/41/151–5, 157–60.

Masses	**Priest**	**Procession**	**Feast**	**Pilgrimage**	**Mornspeches**
Y	N	Y	N	N	0
Y	Y	N	Y	Y	0
Y	Y	Y	Y	N	2
Y	Y	Y	Y	Y	2
Y	N	Y	Y	Y	0
Y	Y	Y	Y	Y	4
Y	N	N	Y	Y	1
Y	Y	Y	Y	Y	4
Y	N	Y	Y	Y	0
Y	N	N	Y	N	3
Y	N	Y	Y	Y	4
Y	N	N	Y	Y	2
Y	N	N	Y	Y	2
Y	N	Y	Y	Y	0
N	N	Y	N	N	0
13	5	10	13	11	Average: 1.6

Masses	**Priest**	**Procession**	**Feast**	**Pilgrimage**	**Mornspeches**
Y	Y	Y	Y	Y	1
Y	Y	N	Y	N	4
Y	N	Y	Y	Y	3
Y	N	Y	Y	Y	3
Y	N	N	Y	Y	5
Y	N	N	Y	N	3
Y	*illegible*	Y	Y	Y	1
Y	N	N	N	Y	4
Y	N	Y	Y	N	3
9	2*	5	8	6	Average: 3

the pestilence. In fact, of the twenty-eight sets of ordinances it is possible to assess, twenty recorded guidelines for pilgrims wishing to make their way to Rome, St James or the Holy Land (seventeen in tables 21a and 21b).[252] When set alongside all guild returns from 1389, the evidence is striking. According to Westlake's calendar only two other guilds (aside from those at Lincoln) made any reference to pilgrimage in their ordinances from a total of 442 returns.[253] In an attempt to explain this, Jan Gerchow argued that it was both a reflection of 'local practice, perhaps even a competition between the Lincoln guilds in their support of pilgrimages' and an indication of clerical practice.[254] As already identified, however, it is unlikely that the latter was the case (as the handwriting and form of the city's certificates differ considerably),[255] though the former remains likely. There is also some circumstantial evidence to suggest that Lincoln's guilds occasionally took part in organised pilgrimages, much like a number of continental guilds. In Italy, for example, members were often provided financial support to go on pilgrimage with monies being used for a new standard or banner which was to be carried throughout the journey.[256] Whilst the evidence for Lincoln is in no way as explicit, members were nevertheless required to make grants of a few pence to those making the journey and to accompany them outside the city 'to the cross on the green' (*ad crucem super viridem*) near the priory of St Katherine and to meet them there on their way back (map 6).[257]

Despite the fact that evidence for pilgrimages organised directly by guilds is limited,[258] it comes as no surprise to learn that like-minded individuals from a geographically concentrated area sought to undertake such journeys together; in fact, in many ways it is surprising that such ordinances were not recorded with greater frequency elsewhere. Take, for example, a petition dating from 1350 from Robert de Dalderby (mayor 1341/42), John de Torkesay (bailiff 1345/46), Roger de Tatersale (mayor 1360/61) and Robert Hervy of Stow, which requested that they be granted permission from the crown to travel to Rome along with their four servants to seek absolution (*absolucion*).[259] Whilst it seems certain that all four men went, it

252 Of this number fourteen offered aid to their members, six did not. C 47/40/134 is too badly damaged to assess.

253 These were the Blessed Mary in Hull and Holy Cross in Lynn. Westlake, *Parish Gilds*, 193, 234. For links between guild and pilgrimage, see D. Webb, *Medieval European Pilgrimage, c.700–c.1500* (Basingstoke, 2002), 109–11.

254 Gerchow, 'Fourteenth-Century Bureaucracy', 137–8.

255 See 160–3.

256 For example, fraternities from Perugia, Bologna and Florence each undertook this practice: C. F. Black, *Italian Confraternities in the Sixteenth Century* (Cambridge, 2003), 117–21; J. Henderson, *Piety and Charity in Late Medieval Florence* (Chicago, 1997), 53–4.

257 For example, C 47/40/142–3. This cross was erected in honour of Queen Eleanor in the 1290s: *Medieval Lincoln*, 112 (n. 3), 345.

258 For links between pilgrimage and guilds founded in honour of the Resurrection and the Holy Sepulchre, see C. Morris, 'Pilgrimage to Jerusalem in the Middle Ages', in C. Morris and P. Roberts (eds), *Pilgrimage: the English Experience from Becket to Bunyan* (Cambridge, 2002), 156.

259 SC 8/239/11919.

seems that their departure was delayed until the following year by local business.[260] Less clear, however, are their fraternal ties, though it is likely that they were members of the Purification of the Blessed Virgin Mary in St Benedict.[261] Evidence for this relates to the fact that Dalderby founded two perpetual chantries in the church at the same altar used by the guild upon his return, with Tatersale establishing a second chantry sometime later in 1378.[262]

There is also coincidental evidence for a number of Lincoln inhabitants going on pilgrimage, including William de Atherby[263] and Lucy Hodelston,[264] who travelled to Jerusalem in 1350,[265] with John de Bole (mayor 1361/62) making the same journey in 1359.[266] John de Spridlington, too, who, whilst not making any journey himself, left in his will of 1349 a provision of 5s to a *certum hominem* to make the pilgrimage to St James on his behalf.[267] There were also large numbers of Lincoln citizens visiting Rome in the early fifteenth century, with many inscribing their names in the ledger kept by the English hospice located along the *Rione del Parione*, including in 1407 John son of William Blyton (mayor 1402/3).[268] As is clear, the recorded destinations of these pilgrims mirror closely the ordinances of Lincoln's guilds, pointing towards localised links between fraternity and pilgrimage.

Conclusion

Guilds in Lincoln were for the most part highly organised, both individually and collectively. From the formal structure and hierarchy of individual institutions to inter-guild cooperation, they existed within a clear framework of fraternity and collective piety, as part of a civic community. This is seen clearly through the use and understanding of urban space, including the physical separation of guilds in churches, where different saints were worshipped at different altars; the parish

260 Torkesay is recorded in the *Burwarmote Book* in June 1349 (*BB*, fo. 192v) and December 1350 (fo. 213) but not again until 1357 (fo. 230v); Dalderby was noted in 1349 (*BB*, fos 157–157v, 165, 170v, 202–202v, 205) but not again until 1354 (*BB*, fos 226v, 229v), though he had undoubtedly returned home before that as he witnessed a charter at Lincoln in April 1352 (*Chantry Certificates*, 200); Tatersale, whilst not noted until September 1353 (*BB*, fo. 223v), was most likely in the city before then (for example, in September 1350 lands were to be sold to him but he was not named as a witness; *BB*, fos 211v–212). It seems likely, therefore, that the group departed early in 1351, arriving back sometime before April 1352. Of Stow little is known, except that he borrowed £20 from Walter de Kelby in 1348 which he failed to repay: C 241/126/173.

261 Dalderby was also certainly a member of the Great Guild: C 143/287/22.

262 Chapter six.

263 Possibly a relative of Gilbert Atherby (mayor 1316/17): see appendix 2.

264 Most likely the relative of either Thomas or John de Hodelston, both of whom served as bailiff and mayor, in 1385/86 and 1374/75 respectively: see appendix 2.

265 *CCR, 1349–54*, 271–2.

266 *CPR, 1358–61*, 226.

267 *BB*, fo. 199v.

268 J. Allen (ed.), *The English Hospice in Rome* (Leominster, 2005), 18, 66, 110, 113, 117, 121, 131–2 and appendices 7 and 12.

system, where guilds were frequently established at arm's length from one another; and in the organisation of socio-religious events staged throughout the ritual year. This was cooperation in the community for the good of the community, despite its many differences and divisions, a phenomenon indicative of a clear fraternal identity. The dating of guild events – feasts, processions and mornspeches – is particularly important in understanding how this grew organically out of local needs, and Barbara Hanawalt's observation that 'patron saints were selected because their feasts fell conveniently in the planting and harvesting season' is not reflected in the evidence for Lincoln,[269] perhaps highlighting one of the major differences between the development of urban and rural guilds. In fact, concerns in the city stemmed primarily from the availability of space and the suitability of a patron saint for individual and collective devotional needs. Nowhere is this clearer than in the foundation of guilds dedicated to St Robert and St Edmund of Pontigny or the numerous Corpus Christi guilds, where it is apparent that collective acts of piety were subject to trends and changes over time.

As new guilds were founded it was important that they subscribed to the established patterns of cooperation and shared space at work in the city, as this maximised both their membership opportunities and their profits. It seems clear that the civic government played an important role in this, in particular in the recording of the rules and regulations for the so-called 'craft' guilds, thereby emphasising not only its own centrality and identity but the city's too, all of which reached the ears of the crown by way of the certificates returned to Chancery. The variety of options for payments also offered opportunities to all but the very poor, who nevertheless played a symbolic role. This had an impact on the types of guilds people were able to join, and as a result lower costs came to be associated with guilds which did not offer financial support to their members or which maintained fewer rules and regulations,[270] thereby challenging accepted notions of what a guild in the later Middle Ages actually was. All the same, yearly processions, even for groups that perhaps did not consider themselves guilds, ensured a form of social cohesion or collective identity far beyond the boundaries of the parish. The particular terms on offer for guild members therefore remained a key factor in the decision-making process. Another was, of course, expectation, and whilst only the Cordwainers explicitly stated that all those practising the craft were required to join the guild, it is likely that other pressures were brought to bear on potential members, in particular from associates, friends and family.

Although existing studies of late medieval guilds have promoted the Black Death to a level of considerable importance, usually seeing it as a catalyst for fraternal growth and development, in Lincoln its impact was muted. Prior to 1349 the city had already established a rich fraternal landscape, housing at least sixteen guilds before that date. In fact, the greatest surge in foundations was in the 1330s during a period of economic recession. This suggests that the collective representations of piety through the maintenance of lights and the growing involvement by the laity in

269 Hanawalt, 'Keepers of the Lights', 27. For these festivals, see Arnold, *Belief and Unbelief*, 113–15.

270 Compare tables 19 and 21.

voluntary associations were more pressing concerns for members than the need to repair dislocated kinship networks. It is possible that these changes were driven by the increasing laicisation of religious spaces, which followed an upturn in perpetual and temporary chantry foundations in the city during the 1310s and 1320s.[271] This is seen most clearly through the number of guilds maintaining lights in the 1330s but not providing monies to support chaplains.[272] Guilds offered new opportunities for local individuals and groups who had neither the wealth nor the means to institute private masses, thus underscoring the growing interest in salvation which emerged towards the end of the thirteenth century.[273]

Similar expressions of piety have been identified by Andrew Brown in the diocese of Salisbury, where 'Parishioners of smaller parishes perhaps found their devotional concerns better satisfied by the parochial framework; [whereas] those in larger parishes may have sought to capture the intimacy of smaller ones by founding fraternities within their parish churches.'[274] Nonetheless, in Lincoln the opposite was true and at no stage did the relatively small size of the city's parishes become a barrier to foundations. This demonstrates how the parish did not always satisfy individual or collective devotional needs and, as Jennifer Kermode points out, towns housing a high level of parish churches should be seen as 'accommodating several lay communities, rather than comprising a single one'.[275] There is no reason why this reasoning should not be extended to the parish more generally. This is perhaps nowhere clearer than in the fact that not all parishes founded guilds, hence membership invariably cut across parish boundaries. This was seen for guilds such as the Sailors (Corpus Christi), which opened its doors to men and women from as far afield as Boston, or the fraternity of Clerks (St Nicholas, St Mary and All Saints), which attracted individuals from beyond the city, along with members of the clergy.

In a roundabout way this questions whether there were any intrinsic differences between guilds established before 1349 and those founded afterwards. Whilst it is clear that following the pestilence guilds placed greater demands upon their members by requiring them to attend a higher number of official events, in particular mornspeches, it is also evident that the lower costs involved in joining a guild meant that there was an overall downturn in the number of chaplains being employed to say intercessory masses on their behalf. Despite this there were nevertheless no wholesale changes to the practices of guilds following the pestilence and the popularity and relative affordability of pilgrimages and processions continued, with the latter reaching their apotheosis in the fifteenth and sixteenth centuries when the entire enfranchised community was required to partake in the procession of St Anne.[276]

Finally, in terms of the royal writ, the attitudes revealed by guilds towards the crown demonstrate an acute awareness of contemporary social and political issues, and it is possible that there may have been some attempt to mislead the crown as

271 R. Swanson, *Church and Society in Late Medieval England* (Oxford, 1989), 255–60.

272 Table 21a.

273 See 199–200.

274 Brown, *Popular Piety*, 143.

275 Kermode, 'The Greater Towns', in *CUHB*, 461.

276 Stokes, 'Staging Wonders', 199–201.

to the number of guilds employing a livery or to the value and number of lands and properties owned by them; as Crouch argues, 'the whole political background against which the returns were made encouraged the gild officials to minimise their assets'.[277] It is certainly possible that the civic government sought to depoliticise the city's guilds during a period of financial difficulty with the crown. That said, it is highly unlikely that Lincoln's guilds maintained many assets as there were few chaplains to provide stipends for and but a single fraternal guildhall in the fourteenth century (in addition, that is, to the civic guildhall). Large amounts of capital were therefore unnecessary in the day-to-day running of Lincoln's guilds.[278] Any attempt to downplay guild assets was eclipsed only by the desire to maintain orthodoxy and to avoid at all costs accusations of sedition, which perhaps reflects the higher number of religious ordinances recorded in the extant certificates. Despite their socio-religious foundations, then, guilds could at times take on a quasi-political guise, one bound up in parochial and communal identities, through which personal and collective attitudes could be expressed. Such 'good behaviour', at least in the eyes of the crown, reflected positively upon the civic government's ability to rule effectively in the king's name, all the while tying civic and fraternal identities together in a reciprocal and consensual relationship.

277 Crouch, *Piety, Fraternity*, 36.
278 Crouch, *Piety, Fraternity*, 246

6

Chantry Founders, Commemoration and the Rental Market

Recorded in the chapter house at Lincoln cathedral on 15 April 1352, Robert de Dalderby's charter began

> I, Robert de Dalderby [mayor 1341/42], citizen of Lincoln, ordain and constitute two perpetual chantries in the church of St Benedict in the city of Lincoln and two chaplains, one who shall be warden, and the other who shall be his fellow, to celebrate at the altar of the blessed Mary in the said church. I appoint Ralph de Thymelby, chaplain, to be warden, and Sir Robert de Thymelby, chaplain, to be fellow to him, that they and their successors may celebrate for me and the souls of whom mention is made below ...[1]

Further to this short preamble, Dalderby's charter recorded extensive details of the financial provisions and living arrangements for the two chaplains, including a list of their duties, services to be performed and items bequeathed for the purpose, rules regarding the physical upkeep of the endowed lands, the right of presentment and the names of the beneficiaries of the intercessory masses. Less than ten years earlier on 19 July 1344 a similar, albeit much shorter, set of provisions recorded in the testament of Walter son of William de Launesdale (bailiff 1337/38) were ratified in the Burwarmote Court. According to Walter's will, Joan, his wife and executor, was to sell his messuage in the parish of St Peter in the Skinmarket and with the monies find two fitting and honest chaplains to celebrate divine offices in the church of St Peter for one year for his soul and those of his late wife Ellen, his father and mother and all their benefactors.[2] No other details were provided.

Both documents, whilst clearly differing in their overall content and detail, represent well the types of evidence used to explore the importance of chantry foundations in the later Middle Ages, which, from at least the beginning of the thirteenth century, grew in great popularity throughout England.[3] Based upon the belief that prayers for the dead could help ease the suffering of those in Purgatory,[4] the efficacy

1 *Chantry Certificates*, 199.

2 *BB*, fo. 167v.

3 K. L. Wood-Legh, *Perpetual Chantries in Britain* (Cambridge, 1965), 5–7, 30–64. M. H. Rousseau, *Saving the Souls of Medieval London: Perpetual Chantries at St Paul's Cathedral, c.1200–1548* (Farnham, 2011), 2–6.

4 For Purgatory, see J. Le Goff, *The Birth of Purgatory*, trans. A. Goldhammer (London, 1984), esp. chapter nine. For a critique of his work, see A. J. Gurevich, 'Popular and Scholarly

of mass was enshrined in ecclesiastical dogma at the second Council of Lyons in 1274, when it was stated that 'We believe that the intercessions of the faithful who are living help to relieve the pains [of souls in Purgatory], that is to say Masses, prayers, alms and other works of piety, which have customarily been performed by the faithful, on behalf of others of the faithful, according to the approved practices of the Church.'[5]

It is the aim of this chapter to explore this idea by analysing the growth and proliferation of chantries in Lincoln and to consider their place and function within the urban landscape from the late thirteenth through early fifteenth centuries. In so doing it will draw important links between chantries and the rental market, the role of the crown in granting licences and the influence of bishops in managing the affairs of chaplains, all the while questioning the motives behind the foundations. Given how recent scholarship on this matter is polarised, with some suggesting that chantry foundations were corporate and parochial acts of kindness or 'parish amenities',[6] whilst others have suggested they were expressions of status and wealth,[7] the evidence discussed here will offer further context to this debate by presenting the findings within the broader issue of urban space.

Before analysing the evidence, however, it is useful first to draw attention to the distinction employed throughout this chapter between perpetual and temporary chantries. Whilst it is true that in many ways they were identical institutions with the same goal and function, differing ostensibly only in their duration, it will become clear that they nevertheless varied in terms of the status and wealth of their founders, the methods by which they were established, and, perhaps most fundamentally, the way in which they were perceived by local inhabitants. Whilst this arguably oversimplifies the various 'shades' of post-obit provisions into two distinct groups, it nevertheless provides a useful platform for exploring the evidence.[8]

General Patterns: Perpetual Chantries

Whilst it is impossible to gauge the overall number of perpetual chantries founded in England during the later Middle Ages, it is nevertheless feasible to highlight patterns

Medieval Traditions – Notes in the Margins of Jacques Le Goff's Book', *Journal of Medieval History*, 9 (1983): 71–90. For Purgatorial beliefs within an English context: C. Burgess, '"A fond thing vainly invented": An Essay on the Pious Motive in Later Medieval England', in S. J. Wright (ed.), *Parish, Church and People: Local Studies in Lay Religion, 1350–1750* (London, 1988), 56–84.

5 Quoted in N. Tanner, *The Church in Late Medieval Norwich, 1370–1532* (Toronto, 1984), 92.

6 C. Burgess, 'Chantries in the Parish, or "Through the Looking-glass"', *Journal of the British Archaeological Association*, 164 (2011): 100–29, at 107; *idem*, '"For the Increase of Divine Service": Chantries in the Parish in Late Medieval Bristol', *Journal of Ecclesiastical History*, 36, 1 (1985): 46–65; Duffy, *Stripping of the Altars*, 140–1, 369–70.

7 Swanson, *Church and Society*, 296–9; P. W. Fleming, 'Charity, Faith, and the Gentry of Kent, 1422–1529', in T. Pollard (ed.), *Property and Politics: Essays in Later Medieval English History* (Gloucester, 1984), 36–58.

8 Burgess, 'Chantries in the Parish', 104.

raised through individual case studies.[9] For example, it has been estimated that between 1300 and 1402 London saw an average of twenty-eight perpetual chantries founded each decade, a number attributable both to its exceptional size and exemption from mortmain legislation.[10] Unsurprisingly the number of foundations in London dwarfs all other provincial centres, including York, where roughly 140 perpetual chantries were established (1230–1528), fifty-six of them in the Minster;[11] Norwich, where roughly sixty-three were established, including those in the cathedral (1240–1543);[12] and Bristol, which housed approximately fifty-five (1328–1514).[13] Smaller urban centres unsurprisingly recorded comparatively fewer chantries, including Durham with seventeen (c.1217–1540), though this figure excludes those located in the cathedral;[14] Hull with seven (1400–1529);[15] and Bury St Edmunds with six (1380–99 and 1439–1530).[16]

Direct comparisons with Lincoln are therefore understandably difficult as the criteria upon which these figures are based are not uniform. For example, it is clear that in all cases the general chronology is different, whilst there is the additional issue of what areas or jurisdictions are included. A further, arguably more fundamental, problem lies in identifying whether chantries receiving a licence were actually established or not; as Dobson notes, 'royal licences to amortise rents or property … frequently emerge as declarations of intent, rather than proofs of creation', meaning that such records must be used with caution.[17] This was also true of Lincoln. For example, in 1340 Ralph de Burton (mayor 1329/30) purchased a licence in mortmain from the crown for half a mark to found a perpetual chantry in the parish church of St Mary Crackpole.[18] Shortly after, however, it seems that Ralph found the prospect of establishing the chantry unmanageable for reasons unknown. This serves to explain the contents of his will, dated 1341, which ordered his executors to sell all his lands and give the proceedings to a chaplain to perform mass in St Mary Crackpole for an unspecified length of time.[19] Confirmation of his change of heart comes from a charter dated 1343, when Walter Dymmok and Alice, his wife, endowed an

9 Swanson, *Church and Society*, 45.

10 H. M. Chew, 'Mortmain in Medieval London', *English Historical Review*, 236 (1945), 13. For mortmain, see main text below.

11 R. B. Dobson, 'Citizens and Chantries in Late Medieval York', in D. Abulafia, M. Franklin and M. Rubin (eds), *Church and City, 1000–1500: Essays in Honour of Christopher Brooke* (Cambridge, 1992), 314; J. Raine (ed.), *Fabric Rolls of York Minster* (Durham, 1858), 274–306.

12 Tanner, *Medieval Norwich*, 92–3 and appendix 10, 212–19.

13 C. Burgess, 'Strategies for Eternity: Perpetual Chantry Foundation in Late Medieval Bristol', in C. Harper-Bill (ed.), *Religious Belief and Ecclesiastical Careers in Late Medieval England* (Woodbridge, 1991), 24–32.

14 M. Harvey, *Lay Religious Life in Late Medieval Durham* (Woodbridge, 2006), 155.

15 P. Heath, 'Urban Piety in the Later Middle Ages: the Evidence of Hull Wills', in B. Dobson (ed.), *The Church, Politics and Patronage in the Fifteenth Century* (Gloucester, 1984), 219.

16 R. B. Dinn, 'Popular Religion in Late Medieval Bury St Edmunds' (University of Manchester, unpublished Ph.D thesis, 1990), vol. 2, 694, table 17.3.

17 Dobson, 'Citizens and Chantries', 313.

18 *CPR, 1338–40*, 478; C 143/251/14.

19 *BB*, fo. 149.

additional 100 marks towards the annual pension (*pensio*) of Ralph's chaplain, who was to serve for a further twenty years.[20]

In spite of such problems, it has been possible to identify at least ninety-one perpetual chantries for Lincoln during the later Middle Ages (c.1170–1547), a figure second only to London and York (figure 9), though this must be seen as an absolute minimum given the general paucity of surviving records for the fifteenth century and the shifting basis upon which foundations were made.[21] Of this number almost three quarters (sixty-five) were founded by clergymen or members of the gentry and aristocracy (including the king), the vast majority of whom did not reside in the city.[22] All but six of these chantries were established in the cathedral, underlining its position as the spiritual centre of the diocese,[23] though it is unlikely that the number of active institutions ever approached this figure. For example, in 1440 the bishop of Lincoln, William Alnwick (1436–50), reduced the number of chantries from forty-one to nineteen, noting only that many had fallen into financial difficulty.[24]

Of the six known chantries founded outside of the cathedral by this group, one was established at the Hospital of St Giles by Richard son of Herbert of Newport, rector of Faldingworth, in 1253;[25] one at the chapel in Lincoln castle (c.1267–68) by Henry III, for the souls of his predecessors;[26] one at the hospital of Holy Innocents without Lincoln before 1274 (founder and beneficiaries unknown);[27] one at the Benedictine priory of St Mary Magdalene, known locally as the 'Blakemonkes' (re-founded in 1397; original foundation sometime in the twelfth century), by the abbot and convent of St Mary, York, for 'Henry, sometime king of England and his consort';[28] and one in the parish church of St Clement in the Bail by Dean John Macworth in 1412 for the souls of the benefactors of the church fabric.[29] Neither these chantries nor those founded in the cathedral are dealt with here.

The sixth chantry, which is considered here, relates to the chapel housed on the Great Bridge (*magna ponte*) founded by Henry II (c.1175) in honour of St Thomas the Martyr,[30] which, by at least the early fourteenth century, had become the responsibility of the local civic government. Certainly in 1324 it was claimed by two commissioners sent to inspect the chantry on behalf of the bishop that there were 'notable defects in the chapel of St Thomas Martyr on the bridge in Lincoln and in the books and ornaments of the same, the repair of which is the responsibility of the

20 *BB*, fos 161–161v.
21 See main text below.
22 This information has been compiled with the help of Marianne Wilson.
23 For the cathedral's chantries: H. Bradshaw and C. Wordsworth (eds), *Statutes of Lincoln Cathedral*, vol. 2 (Cambridge, 1892), 889–99; P. B. G. Binnall, 'Notes on the Medieval Altars and Chapels in Lincoln Cathedral', *Antiquaries Journal*, 42 (1962): 68–80; Wood-Legh, *Perpetual Chantries*, 112–13.
24 Bradshaw and Wordsworth, *Statutes of Lincoln Cathedral*, vol. 2, 439–42.
25 *Reg. Antiq.*, vol. 2, no. 395.
26 *CLR, 1267–72*, 43; E 372/115, rot. 9d. This was possibly on the site of an earlier chapel: 'Peter Langtoft's Chronicle', in *The Works of Thomas Hearne* (London, 1810), 26.
27 *CIM, 1307–49*, 72–3, no. 293; *LCL VCH*, 230–1.
28 *CIM, 1392–99*, 96; *CCR, 1396–99*, 156.
29 LAO Dij 50/2/18.
30 *Medieval Lincoln*, 149.

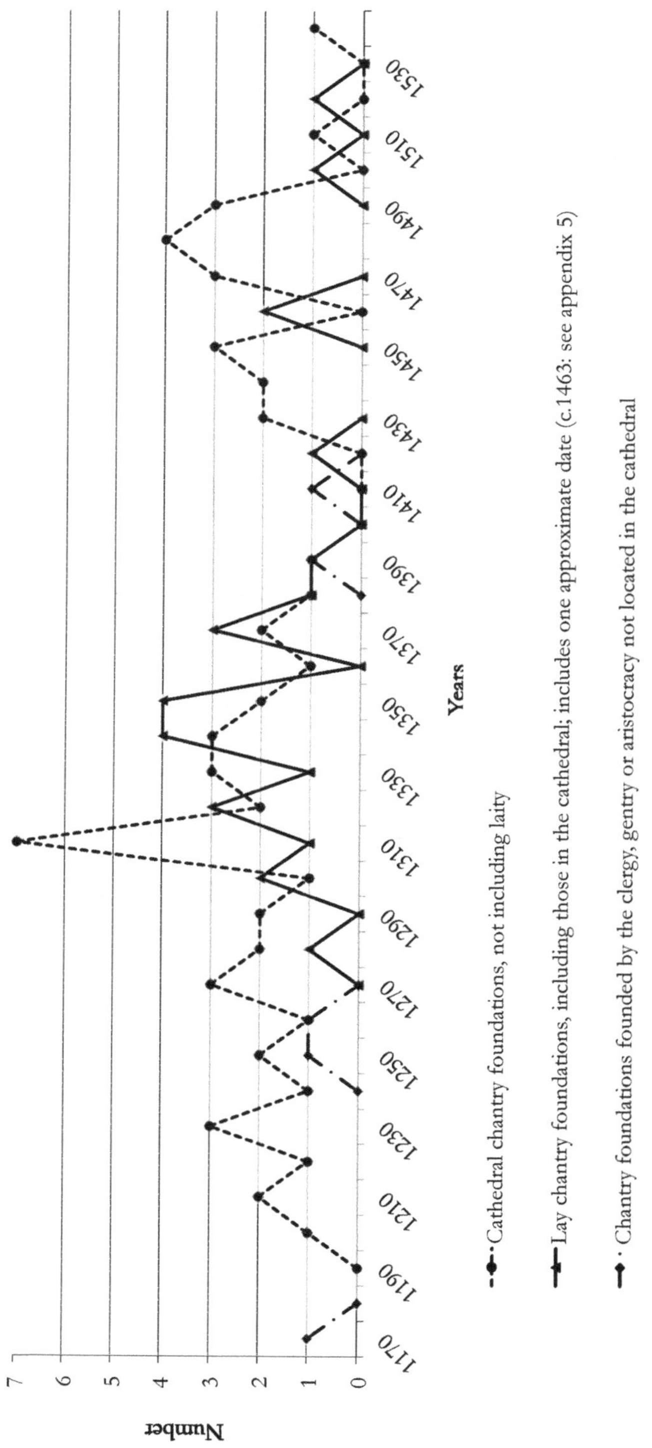

Figure 9 Perpetual chantries founded by in Lincoln (c. 1170–1547)

community of the city'.[31] As a result a mandate was issued warning the community to repair the chapel, though, according to the commission, it apparently refused. However, given that a chantry founded by Thomas de Wykford and Agnes, his wife, in 1329 was moved from the church of St Benedict to the Great Bridge sometime after 1336 suggests that this was done with the aid or advice of the civic government, thereby providing a remedy to the problem.[32] This certainly explains how by at least the early sixteenth century the chapel on the bridge was known locally as the 'Wykford Chantry'.[33]

In total, Lincoln's lay inhabitants were therefore responsible for the foundation of twenty-six perpetual chantries (including one re-foundation), the first of which was established in 1284, the last in 1521 (appendix 5). Taken independently of the chantries founded by the clergy, gentry and aristocracy not residing in the city, it is possible that this comparatively smaller figure could be seen as an indication of a relative lack of interest in permanent forms of commemoration over this period by this group. Certainly when compared to York, where nearly two thirds of all chantries were founded outside of the cathedral precinct (roughly eighty-four),[34] it might be said that the laity of Lincoln were much less inclined to establish perpetual chantries than their counterparts in the north. However, this would be misleading; as Barrie Dobson notes, in 1428 it was reported by York's 'civic jurors' that only thirty-nine of the city's perpetual chantries had actually been founded by the 'mercantile elite', i.e. the laity.[35] Therefore by using the populations of each city in 1377 as no more than a rough guide – with York having almost exactly twice the number of eligible tax payers as Lincoln[36] – it is possible to argue that the laity of Lincoln actually founded more institutions per head of population than those in York.

A second indication of the high level of interest among Lincoln's laity in perpetual chantry foundations derives from the fact that between 1320 and 1380 the number established by the laity (fifteen) actually outstripped those founded by the clergy, gentry and aristocracy combined (thirteen), highlighting the growing fashion for chantries during this period, with similar growth being identified for Bristol (1320–50) and York (1300–50).[37] Whilst it is apparent that the Black Death played only a minor role in instituting new foundations,[38] in the years immediately following the initial outbreak there was nevertheless a temporary surge in religious fervour with

31 LAO Reg/5, fo. 368v. My thanks to Nicholas Bennett for the reference and translation.

32 The exact date of translation is unknown. The claim by Venables that this occurred in 1330 is not accurate; a charter dated 1336 still refers to the Wykford chantry as being in St Benedict. Venables, 'List and Brief Description ', 334–5; *BB*, fo. 157.

33 *Historical MSS*, 26–7, 32, 35, 38.

34 Dobson, 'Citizens and Chantries', 314.

35 Dobson, 'Citizens and Chantries', 317, n. 20.

36 Dyer, 'Ranking of Towns', 758.

37 Dobson, 'Citizens and Chantries', 320; R. B. Dobson, 'The Foundation of Perpetual Chantries by the Citizens of Medieval York', in G. J. Cuming (ed.), *Studies in Church History*, vol. 4 (Leiden, 1967), 32; Burgess, 'Strategies for Eternity', 27–9.

38 Between 1300 and 1349 eleven foundations were made (in addition to one in 1284), with a further nine being established between 1350 and 1399 (with three established after 1400), thereby representing a marginal increase if they are seen within the context of pre- and post-Black Death population figures: there was one chantry founded per 1,118 people (population

four perpetual chantries being founded in only three years, a pattern similar to that of temporary chantries.[39] This is seen clearly in the case of Thomas de Kele, who began the process of establishing his own chantry in St Mary Crackpole in October 1349 during a period when plague still lingered in the city.[40] In 1352 a chantry was also founded on behalf of Robert de Chesterfeld, chandler and former mayor (1346/47). According to the latter's will, enrolled in December that year, all his lands, shops and tenements were to be given to Robert Whitwell, Peter de Dalderby and John de Bourne, canons, so long as they 'shall do what seems best for the good of my soul, Alice, my wife, and my children, Adam Moysen, his wife and children, and all the faithful departed'. They chose, under the direct guidance of Whitwell, to found the chantry at St Swithun where Chesterfeld had already established seven candles upon the high altar.[41] The final two foundations made during these three years were those of Robert de Dalderby noted at the outset of this chapter, who established two chantries following his return from pilgrimage to Rome.[42]

Given the strong tradition of founding perpetual chantries in the city both before and after the Black Death, one of the most significant aspects of the evidence to emerge is that by 1392 the demand for new foundations drew to a virtual standstill, with only five more ever being made after this date.[43] More surprising still is that all but one of these later foundations ('John Huddilston's Chaunterie') seemingly circumnavigated the Statute of Mortmain.[44] Introduced in 1279 to preserve the feudal revenues of the crown, the Statute of Mortmain forbade alienations to the 'dead hand' of the church without a royal licence; certainly there are no surviving licences (typically entered into the Patent Rolls) or *inquisitio ad quod damnum* certificates (a subsidiary document listing various details relating to the proposed foundation, including the location(s) and value(s) of alienated land(s), upon which the fine for the licence was levied) for later foundations. The means by which this legislation was bypassed was that founders enfeoffed their lands and properties not to the chantry or religious institution directly, as was more commonly the case,[45] but to a group of independent trustees who organised the stipend of the chaplain between them. When a member of this group died, the individual was replaced, thus beginning the cycle over.[46] Unsurprisingly, this practice was outlawed in 1391, resulting in an unprecedented 378 licences being issued the following year. This

12,300) before 1349; and one foundation per 833 after 1349 (population 7,500). For population figures, see 2.

39 See main text below.

40 C 143/295/7. This was not fulfilled until 1358/59 following his death between May 1350 and September 1351, however. *CPR, 1348–50*, 466; *1358–61*, 175; LAO Reg/8, fos 123–123v, 134; *BB*, fo. 210v, 234.

41 *BB*, fos 220v–221; *Liber Cant.*, fos 343v–344v; LAO Dij 51/3/6. The lands granted to the canons were seemingly alienated under a general licence: C 143/301/20; *CPR, 1350–54*, 378. The chantry was still active in 1433: LAO A/2/32, fo. 72. For Whitwell's will, see C. W. Foster (ed.), *Lincoln Wills, vol. 1: 1271–1526* (Lincoln Record Society, 1914), 7–11.

42 See 194–5.

43 See appendix 5.

44 *CPR, 1461–67*, 382.

45 Wood-Legh, *Perpetual Chantries*, 8–16.

46 Wood-Legh, *Perpetual Chantries*, 16–29.

was accompanied by threats from the king that institutions without a legal licence would be fined or possibly forfeited to the crown.[47] After 1392, and quite possibly as a consequence of this new legislation, mortmain licences became increasingly uncommon in England as a result of the shift in Crown policy.[48] This was certainly true of Lincoln where only a further three were granted to lay inhabitants after this date, two of which related to the Hodelston chantry founded in 1371 (1415 and 1465),[49] the last to the guild of St Nicholas in Newport (1402).[50]

The decline in the number of perpetual chantry foundations was not unique to Lincoln, being mirrored to a greater or lesser extent by events at Norwich, London and Bristol, especially in the first half of the fifteenth century.[51] It is the view of Clive Burgess that no new foundations were made at Bristol between 1411 and 1441 due to the alarm of prospective founders 'at the failure of early foundations', with many regarding ideas of perpetuity as 'too risky an ideal'.[52] Whilst it is possible that similar fears affected prospective founders in Lincoln, these should not be seen as the only reasons for the decline, and it is likely that difficulties within the rental market, inadequate endowments and a general rise in chaplains' wages were equally to blame.

Perpetual Chantries and the Rental Market

The importance of the rental market in the growth and proliferation of chantries during the Middle Ages cannot be underestimated. As contemporary founders were all too well aware, the successful maintenance and survival of chantries remained dependent upon the collection of annual rents from amortised lands and tenements.[53]

By the close of the fourteenth century the effects of depopulation had, like in many other urban centres, served to undermine the very existence of many chantries through a decline in the number of annual rents.[54] This has been demonstrated in two separate studies by A. F. Butcher, who assessed the extant accounts of Oseney Abbey in Oxford and Canterbury Cathedral Priory in one, and the Bursars' rolls of University College in Newcastle in the other.[55] Whilst for Canterbury Butcher found that from at least the 1420s onwards rents in the city began frequently to fall into arrears, similar difficulties did not emerge at either Oxford or Newcastle until the 1440s.[56] Butcher saw this primarily as a result of the inability of each town 'to

47 S. Raban, *Mortmain Legislation and the English Church, 1279–1500* (Cambridge, 1982), 127–9.
48 Raban, *Mortmain Legislation*, 158–9, 191–2, graphs 4–6. For this policy shift, see 212.
49 C 143/447/8; *CPR, 1413–16*, 371–2; *1461–67*, 382 (re-founded). See also, *CCR, 1454–61*, 124–5.
50 *CPR, 1401–05*, 96. See chapter five.
51 Burgess, 'Strategies for Eternity', 28. Compare to York which experienced no such decline in foundations (c.1400–30): Dobson, 'Citizens and Chantries', 327.
52 Burgess, 'Strategies for Eternity', 30–1, at 31; Tanner, *Medieval Norwich*, 93–4.
53 Wood-Legh, *Perpetual Chantries*, 40; Brown, *Popular Piety*, 97.
54 Swanson, *Church and Society*, 52.
55 A. F. Butcher, 'Rent and the Urban Economy: Oxford and Canterbury in the Later Middle Ages', *Southern History*, 1 (1979): 11–43; *idem*, 'Rent, Population and Economic Change in Late-Medieval Newcastle', *Northern History*, 14 (1978): 67–77.
56 Butcher, 'Urban Economy', 31–5, 39–40, 42–3; *idem*, 'Economic Change', 75.

sustain rent levels in the face of declining prosperity and a falling rate of immigration', problems brought about by subsequent outbreaks of plague.[57]

Direct evidence for Lincoln's rental market derives from a series of fragmented accounts recorded by the Dean and Chapter of Lincoln Cathedral, covering forty-nine years between 1318 and 1435 (tables 22 and 23). The first set of accounts, which begin in 1318/19 and end in 1375/76, list the names of individual tenants or those sub-letting the property, along with the value of any outstanding monies relating to gardens, vineyards and lands, as well as buildings according to their type: cottages, tenements, mills and cellars.[58] These records detail properties from thirty-three different parishes, underscoring the Dean and Chapter's status as the major landholder in the city.[59] For the second set of accounts dating after 1378/79, however, only the total value of money owing is recorded, including defaults on payments and the decaying value of lands and tenements.[60] The second accounts are also separated according to whether they were rents due from the Close or from other parts of the city.

Table 22 Dean and Chapter rental arrears (c.1318–c.1340)

Years	Value	Years	Value
1318/19	£10 14s	1328/29	£4 11s 10d
1319/20	£7 0s 2d	1329/30	£6 2s 4d
1320/21	£8 18s 5d	1331/32	£7 13s 8d
1321/22	£9 3s 10d	1332/33	£5 6s 1d
1322/23	£8 6s 6½d	1334/35	£4 5s ½d
1323/24	£10 11s 4d	1335/36	£4 16s 4d
1324/25	£9 17s 1½d	1336/37	£4 15s 7d
1325/26	£7 9s 1d	1337/38	£7 3s 9d
1326/27	£6 12s	1338/39	£6 3s 8d
1327/28	£5 9s 3d	1339/40	£6 3s 4d

Sources: LAO Bj 2/5, Bj 5/1–2, Bj 5/8/9, Bj 5/8/16.

As the accounts from the first half of the fourteenth century indicate (table 22), the rental arrears of the Dean and Chapter remained relatively stable over a

57 Butcher, 'Urban Economy', 34, 42–3; *idem*, 'Economic Change', 75–7.

58 *Arreragium redditus infra villam Lincoln*': LAO Bj 2/5, fo. 8.

59 Compare the value of rents cited below to those received by the civic government in the 1290s, for example: see E 101/505/24 m. 1; E 101/505/28 m. 1.

60 *Diminucionibus et in allocationibus per defaltum et decasum redditus tenementorum et gardinorum infra civitate Lincoln*': LAO Bj 2/10/13. Decayed rents were payments less than the full value of what was owed, or part payments, thereby leaving arrears: Butcher, 'Urban Economy', 22–6.

Table 23 Dean and Chapter accounts for defaulted and decayed rents (c.1359–c.1435)

Years	Value, excl. Close	Close	Years	Value, excl. Close	Close
1359/60	£21 8s 6d*	n/a	1393/94	£12 7s 3¼d	£4 18s 4d
1374/75	£11 13s 11d*	n/a	1394/95	£12 17s 7¼d	£4 18s 4d
1375/76	£6 11s 4d*	n/a	1395/96	£12 19s 11¼d	5s 5d
1378/79	£9 18s 7¼d	£1 6s 4d	1396/97	£12 12s 1¼d	5s 10d
1379/80	£8 11s 7¼d	£1 6s 8d	1399/1400	£15 5s 6½d	£5 12s 1d
1380/81	£8 17s 4¼d	6s 8d	1400/01	£14 19s 10¼d	£7 6s 8d
1381/82	£8 0s 9¼d	6s 4d	1401/02	£14 6s 5¼d	£10 4d
1382/83	£8 0s 9¼d	£1 13s 4d	1402/03	£14 12s 8¼d	£5 18s 4d
1383/84	£9 16s 5¼d	£3	1404/05	£17 3s 11 1¼d	£10
1384/85	£11 3s 2¼d	16s	1406/07	£17 8s 3¼d	£13 12s 4d
1385/86	£11 18s 11¼d	£2 3s 4d	1407/08	£16 16s 9¼d	£13 6s 8d
1386/87	£11 17s 1¼d	16s	1409/10	£17 16s 9¼d	not stated
1389/90	£11 4s 4¼d	£3 4s	1426/27	£23 4s 10¼d	£8 10s ½d
1390/91	£11 18s 9¼d	£2 13s 4d	1434/35	£26 19s 11½d	£10 11s ½d
1392/93	£13 9 ¼d	16s			

Sources: LAO Bj 2/7, Bj 2/10, Bj 5/10/3a, 3c, Bj 5/9/10/6, Bj 8/2; key: * = accounts listed individually.

twenty-two-year period, averaging £7 4s 7d,[61] with lower and upper limits of £4 11s 10d (1328/29) and £10 14s (1318/19). Whilst at first glance such figures might seem excessive, they were nevertheless not out of kilter with those of Oseney Abbey for the smaller town of Oxford, where losses of up to £5 16s 5½d were routinely recorded in the 1320s.[62] Whilst at Lincoln it is possible that the higher figures for the late 1310s and early 1320s were due to the impact of famine, with many tenants being unable to pay their rents due to difficulties in the local economy,[63] the accounts demonstrate how the city quickly recovered by the later 1320s, with the 1330s demonstrating a particularly constant value despite the recession.

Comparisons with the period after the Black Death tell an altogether different story, with arrears increasing steadily over a period of some sixty-five years (table 23). 1359/60, in particular, was a bad year, most likely reflecting the long-term impact of the Black Death.[64] However, whatever caused this particular peak, by the mid-1370s

61 LAO Bj 5/8/16, fo. 76.

62 Butcher, 'Urban Economy', 27–8. Oxford had a population roughly two thirds that of Lincoln in 1377 (2,357): Dyer, 'Ranking of Towns', 758.

63 See 85–6.

64 It certainly predated the second bout of plague of 1361/62, two years which saw eighteen wills enrolled compared to the yearly average of 2.9. See 3 n. 14.

the value of unpaid rents had begun to return to its pre-Black Death level,[65] a pattern seen in many other English towns,[66] suggesting that there had been a significant influx of migrants, with many filling empty properties.

Despite an increase in rental arrears during the 1380s, in which the average value of defaulted or decayed rents stood at £9 10s 6d (excluding the Close), the evidence for Lincoln demonstrates that the city remained highly resilient in the face of repeated bouts of plague. A similar pattern also emerges for the 1390s, although the average increased to £11 17s 5d. By the 1400s, however, it is clear that there were persistent problems filling properties, which saw the annual value of arrears increase to £15 9s 4½d. This downward trend was to continue and, if the evidence of 1426/27 and 1434/35 is anything to go by, the 1420s and 1430s were the worst affected years, peaking at £23 4s 10¼d and £26 19s 11½d respectively, suggesting that migration into the city had slowed dramatically at this time, much like for many other towns.[67]

Despite this general pattern, it seems that the jurisdiction of the Close actually underwent economic difficulties earlier than the rest of the city, with defaults and arrears increasing proportionately quicker around the turn of the century. Fortunately some indication of the cause dates from 1400/01 when it was stated that £7 6s 8d was owing from only eight properties,[68] including a hospice called Colby Place (26s 8d) and properties rented by Alice Snartford, wife of T. Neubald (13s 4d), and R[...] Filyngham (10s). This highlights that whilst arrears were owed from only a handful of properties, they were nevertheless highly expensive, suggesting that costlier properties were being rented out at a much lower rate than in previous years or abandoned in favour of more affordable accommodation elsewhere. Given how by c.1450 the annual rental income for the Close as a whole averaged between £21 and £26, it seems clear that these losses were a significant proportion of the Dean and Chapter's income from local property.[69] There is no reason to think that similar problems did not affect the city more generally.

Unsurprisingly contemporaries were not unaware of these problems, with founders and their ancestors amortising additional lands in order to secure the future for their chantries. For example, upon its foundation in 1371 the Hodelston chantry was granted rents from three messuages in the parishes of St Mary Magdalene in the Bail, St Michael on the Mount and St George, worth 60s per annum, which were later augmented in 1415 by 10s per annum from a messuage in St George.[70] The Sutton chantry, too, which was established in the church of St Andrew in Wigford in 1382, received upon its foundation rents from three messuages, one shop and a vacant plot, though over the following decade it received rents from a further six shops, a messuage and an acre of land.[71]

65 LAO Bj 5/1, fo. 9v; Bj 5/2, fo. 8.
66 Keene, *Medieval Winchester*, vol. 1, 237–8, 243–4; Butcher, 'Urban Economy', 38, 42; Rees Jones, *York*, 294–5.
67 See 61 n. 62.
68 LAO Bj 2/10, fo. 39a.
69 LAO Bj 5/11/2, unfoliated.
70 *CPR, 1413–16*, 371–2; C 143/447/8; C 143/376/22; *Liber Cant.*, fos 162v–163.
71 *CPR, 1381–85*, 96, 443; *CPR, 1389–92*, 196; C 143/399/20; C 143/408/16; C 143/412/23.

Another issue faced by chantry founders was the occasional inadequacy of individual endowments, though this was not necessarily a problem restricted to the period after the Black Death. For example, in 1309 a number of lands supporting the chantry of Roger FitzBenedict in St Peter in Eastgate had reportedly become so sterile that no one was willing to cultivate them. Fortunately this problem was resolved shortly after, with the Dean and Chapter (the chantry's trustees) granting a licence for the lands to John Kempe at a reduced rate of 60s for a fixed term of five years.[72] Similar problems beset even the most well-endowed foundations, including the Cause chantry founded in the cathedral in 1378.[73] Despite eleven messuages, 100 acres of land and a dovecote being alienated for its upkeep, the chantry was recorded in 1440 as more than £4 in arrears, suggesting that, like the FitzBenedict chantry, many of its lands went uncultivated, perhaps for a lack of workers.[74] Fortunately for the founders, the Cause chantry survived Alnwick's overhaul of 1440 and was noted as being operational as late as 1492, thus emphasising the importance of being sponsored by a powerful patron.[75]

Further financial problems arose in the form of a general rise in chaplains' wages following the Black Death, with Lincoln diocese being hit particularly hard.[76] An indication of this rise can be seen by comparing the stipend of the chaplains celebrating at the temporary chantries of John de Kirketon in 1328 and John de Bakyngton, baker, in 1352, the former of whom received 60s, the latter – for two chaplains – 12 marks or 70s each.[77] Although such anecdotal evidence does not demonstrate the overall variety of wages available to chaplains it is at least instructive of the wider experience.[78] Certainly, the Baiocis chantry, which had initially been granted nine messuages in the city and suburbs in 1342, worth 60s per annum, saw the chantry chaplain, Robert Russell, resign his post in 1449 due to the perceived poverty of the benefice.[79] The effect of these wage rises was clearly problematic and, according to Dorothy Owen, some chaplains turned to petty crime as a means to supplement their income, with the rolls of the justices of the peace being 'full of accusations of theft and violence by chaplains' in the 1370s.[80]

Such issues did not go unnoticed by the ecclesiastical authorities and in May 1350 the archbishop of Canterbury issued the *Effrenata*, the clerical equivalent of the Statute of Labourers, which capped wages at their pre-1349 level.[81] This decision was

72 LAO FL/Transcripts/J/33, 73.

73 See main text below.

74 C 143/394/18; Bradshaw and Wordsworth, *Statutes of Lincoln Cathedral*, vol. 2, 443.

75 LAO, A/3/1, fo. 80v.

76 Thompson, 'Registers of John Gynewell', 326.

77 *BB*, fos 110, 227v.

78 W. A. Pantin, *The English Church in the Fourteenth Century* (Cambridge, 1955), 29; Wood-Legh, *Perpetual Chantries*, 93–4.

79 LAO Reg/19, fo. 1v.

80 *CSML*, 133.

81 B. H. Putnam, 'Maximum Wage-Laws for Priests after the Black Death, 1348–1381', *American Historical Review*, 21 (1915), 18–25. For *Effrenata*, see R. L. Storey, 'Recruitment of English Clergy in the Period of the Conciliar Movement', *Annuarium Historiae Conciliorum*, 7 (1975): 290–313.

not welcomed in all quarters, however, especially in the diocese of Lincoln, where the then bishop, John Gynwell (1347–62), refused to implement it. In fact it was not until February 1362 that Gynwell's intransigence finally subsided and the decision was reversed. Even so, in June the following year it was overturned by the new bishop, John Buckingham (1363–98), who openly permitted chaplains 'to receive more than the usual salary "in spite of any constitution on the subject"'.[82] Nevertheless, by the 1370s the issue of clerical wages had once again reared its head – perhaps as a result of the increase in clerical crime – with some chaplains being compelled by Buckingham to serve in poorer parishes for less money than they might otherwise have earned, emphasising the issue of earlier inaction.[83]

Naturally the significance of these wage rises can only be fully appreciated when they are set alongside the rents used to fund them; as Richard Britnell argues, rents were often fixed by custom and in many cases remained 'unresponsive to all but the longest trends in prices and wages'.[84] It seems likely therefore that over time chantry expenses (wages of chaplains, general upkeep) came to outstrip income (rents from properties and lands), thus plunging a number of institutions into irrevocable debt; this was certainly a problem in London where, by the 1380s, chaplains were finding it difficult to secure suitable positions.[85] These problems possibly explain the disappearance of the Jolyff chantry (founded 1347) from the records in c.1426,[86] and the Hodelston chantry (founded 1371) which, despite being re-founded in 1465, was amalgamated to the rectory in 1484.[87] The problems of the Baiocis chantry have already been noted. With regard to the majority of perpetual chantries not recorded in surviving bishops' registers, however, it is difficult to say how they fared, as no civic charters, like those which survive for York,[88] exist. It is nevertheless likely that many continued to struggle in the 1420s and 1430s as rents fell precariously low. Certainly, when it is considered that all but five of the city's twenty-six lay-founded perpetual chantries were defunct by 1548,[89] then this confirms Robert Swanson's observation that the majority of chantries fell into decay 'within a few generations' of their foundation.[90] Unsurprisingly, similar problems affected other towns, in particular York, where the revenues of the vicars choral suffered in the years after the

82 Putnam, 'Maximum Wage-Laws', 25; R. N. Swanson, 'Universities, Graduates and Benefices in Later Medieval England', *Past and Present*, 106 (1985), 38–9.

83 P. Heath, 'Before Reform and Reformation: The English Church in the Fourteenth and Fifteenth Centuries', *Journal of Ecclesiastical History*, 41, 4 (1990), 656; Storey, 'Recruitment of English Clergy', 298–9. For potential solutions to these types of problems, see *CSML*, 97–8; *LW*, 11.

84 R. Britnell, *Britain and Ireland, 1050–1530: Economy and Society* (Oxford, 2004), 439–46, at 440.

85 R. M. T. Hill, '"A Chaunterie for Soules": London Chantries in the Reign of Richard II', in F. R. H. Du Boulay and C. M. Barron (eds), *The Reign of Richard II* (London, 1971), 242–5.

86 LAO Reg/17, fo. 2; Reg/19, fo. 1v. The chantry recorded financial problems in 1408: Archer, *Philip Repingdon*, vol. 1, 125–6.

87 Venables, 'List and Brief Description', 339.

88 Dobson, 'Citizens and Chantries', 316–18.

89 *Chantry Certificates*, 198–206.

90 Swanson, *Church and Society*, 98. For the fortunes of chantries in the sixteenth century, see A. Kreider, *English Chantries: The Road to Dissolution* (Cambridge, 1979), 71–92.

Black Death, primarily as a result of 'the fact that so much of their ancient estate had been granted to free tenants at perpetual rents that, by the early 13th century, income reflected nothing like the real economic value of the property'. [91] Their survival, like that of chantries, thus depended on a buoyant rental market.

One final point to consider is the ongoing ability of citizens to purchase a licence in mortmain. Whilst licences were traditionally obtained from the crown in order to offset the loss of feudal revenues, according to Michael Hicks by the opening decades of the fifteenth century their raison d'être had shifted, with the crown placing less emphasis on alienations to the 'dead hand' of the church and more upon their function as a form of patronage.[92] The significance of this shift was that the general cost of licences grew, especially during the reigns of Henry V and Henry VI. This is certainly true of the Lincoln evidence. Compare, for example, the licences granted to John de Blyton (1315) and Thomas Archer, John Hodeleston and Nicholas Broghton (1415), each of whom paid £5. Whilst the former was granted permission to alienate lands worth 100s (£5) of annual rent for the upkeep of his chantry, i.e. the exact value of the fine,[93] the latter were permitted to alienate lands worth only 10s per annum, the equivalent to one tenth of the fine; put another way, the fine of Archer, Hodeleston and Broghton cost ten years' worth of rent.[94] It is clear therefore that whilst the actual cost of licences did not change dramatically, their overall worth depreciated considerably on several counts, thus making it necessary for even greater funds to be invested in chantries founded (or augmented) in the fifteenth century.[95]

General Patterns: Temporary Chantries

Despite the problems befalling many of the city's perpetual chantries, temporary foundations seemingly thrived from at least the third decade of the fourteenth century onwards. Whilst this was almost certainly due to the more modest outlay of funds needed to establish them, it is possible that their rapid growth was influenced during this period by the high death toll of the famine of 1315–17, in which approximately 10 per cent of the population died;[96] certainly, rental arrears reached a peak for the pre-Black Death period shortly after in 1318/19 (table 22). Nonetheless, in the absence of earlier evidence this remains speculative.

The following analysis draws evidence from 282 fragmentary wills recorded in the *Burwarmote Book* between 1315 and 1376 which record details of the lands and properties of testators,[97] many of whom left provisions for temporary

91 Rees Jones, 'God and Mammon', 193, 198.

92 M. Hicks, 'Chantries, Obits and Almshouses: the Hungerford Foundations, 1325–1478', in C. M. Barron and C. Harper-Bill (eds), *The Church in Pre-Reformation Society* (Woodbridge, 1985), 139–41.

93 C 143/105/14.

94 C 143/447/8.

95 For gifts to Robert de Dalderby's chantry in 1431, see *ELW*, 164–5.

96 Kershaw, 'The Great Famine', 11.

97 This figure excludes thirteen wills by the clergy.

chantries.[98] Of these 282 wills, thirteen which left provisions for temporary chantries are not considered here. This is due to the fact that in each will the recorded lines of reversion are so long or detailed that the proposed chantry almost certainly never took place.[99] For example, in 1349 John de Fenton bequeathed a shop on the Great Bridge and a messuage in St Augustine's to his son Walter for his life and his heirs (should he have any); a great chamber with solar in St Benedict and a garden in Newland to Emma, his daughter, for her life and heirs (should she have any); a messuage in St Benedict's to Joan, his daughter, for her life and heirs (should she have any); and his cottages in St Augustine to Thomas, his son, and Cecilia, his daughter, for both their lives and heirs (should they have any). Accompanying each separate bequest was an additional clause stating that upon the death of any of his offspring, their lands and properties were to be passed directly to the next rightful heir in perpetuity (*predictis meis heredibus imperpetuum*). Only then, once all of his children had died without heirs, were these lands to be sold for divine offices.[100] Considering that there were five children in all and potentially many grandchildren, it seems almost inconceivable that this foundation ever saw the light of day. Therefore, cases where reversionary lines are extensive – typically two offspring and their heirs – are not considered as successful foundations here. Whilst this is by no means a foolproof method of establishing the number of temporary chantries in the city, it nevertheless serves to remove those most likely not founded. Whilst Burgess sees this type of 'reversionary practice' as a 'balancing act' between a testator's 'duty' to 'improve their parish facilities' and their responsibility toward their 'dependents and heirs',[101] it is nevertheless clear for some, such as Fenton, that chantries were only established as a last resort, the primary interest being the living.

Provisions for temporary chantries were recorded on average in 44 per cent of wills enrolled in the *Burwarmote Book* (table 24), a figure in keeping with other urban centres during the later Middle Ages. For example, it has been estimated that between a third and two fifths of all testators in Norwich (1370–1532), London (1401–49, 1479–86, 1523–25, 1529–30), Hull (1400–1529) and Bristol (1400–99) left provisions for temporary institutions,[102] figures marginally higher than for the smaller centres of Bury St Edmunds (1439–1530), Tenterden (1449–1535), Sandwich (c.1450–1539) and Colchester (1485–1529) where only a quarter of testators left

98 Note that the evidence contained in the *Burwarmote Book* reveals only two chantries being founded by monetary bequests, with a further one being instituted by charter. These are not included in the figures here (*BB*, fos 97, 161–161v, 227). The number of temporary chantries discussed throughout this chapter therefore underestimates their overall number. For further context to this problem, see J. A. F. Thomson, 'Piety and Charity in Late Medieval London', *Journal of Ecclesiastical History*, 16 (1965), 191.

99 The omissions relate to *BB*, fos 131v (Walter de Denby), 156v (Ralph le Mareschall), 185 (Henry de Laghton), 188v (Walter de Lynby), 191 (John de Fenton), 192v–193 (Robert Payntour), 199v (Robert de Maunsfeld), 206v (William de Humberstone), 218v (John son of Alexander), 233 (Adam de Dunham), 237v (Adam de Merston), 249v (Hugh Wake), 270v (Agnes Tolle), spanning the dates 1336–70.

100 *BB*, fo. 191.

101 Burgess, 'Chantries in the Parish', 111–13.

102 Tanner, *Medieval Norwich*, 100–1; Heath, 'Urban Piety', 210, 220; Burgess, 'Divine Service', 47, n. 4, 52; Thomson, 'Piety and Charity', 191–2.

such provisions.[103] This is significant as it demonstrates a remarkable stability in the number of foundations being made throughout the later Middle Ages (even accounting for the absence of monetary bequests for chantries).

Table 24 Proportion of lay wills recording temporary chantries

Date	Total number of wills	No. of temporary chantries recorded	Percentage
1310–19	16	3	19%
1320–29	29	12	41%
1330–39	15	8	53%
1340–49	133 (incl. 101 in 1349)	52 (38 in 1349)	39%
Subtotal	193	75	39%
1350–59	43	27	63%
1360–69	36	17	47%
1370–76	10	4	40%
Subtotal	89	48	54%
Total	282	123	44%

The second point to raise is that the Black Death had only a short-term impact upon the overall number of provisions made for temporary chantries, a trend which lasted throughout the 1350s. Whilst this disparity can be explained by the lower cost of establishing a temporary chantry, it nevertheless highlights heightened sensibilities towards death in the years immediately after the plague.[104] Several wills explicitly record the fears of testators (unlike in the more sober foundation charters of perpetual chantries), not only for themselves but for their friends and family, and it is conceivable that many of these feelings remained fresh in the minds of plague survivors until the 1360s when the number of provisions for temporary chantries began to return to pre-Black Death levels. For example, in September 1349 Roger de Remay sold several properties in the city and with the money directed that masses might be said for 'my soul and all faithful departed who are in pain or peril (*dolore sive periculo*)'.[105] In 1349 several individuals, including Alexander de Segrave, Robert Hodelston (mayor 1342/43) and Hugh Belger, implored God to forbid (*quod absit*)

103 Dinn, 'Popular Religion', vol. 2, table 17.1, 691; R. Lutton, *Lollardy and Orthodox Religion in Pre-Reformation England* (Woodbridge, 2006), 55.

104 Horrox, *The Black Death*, 10–11.

105 *BB*, fo. 206.

that their offspring die without heirs,[106] a motif not identifiable in wills in Lincoln before this date. Yet perhaps the most poignant fear was expressed by Thomas de Roderham, who, in July 1349, settled his lands and goods upon his wife and their unborn child 'should it survive (*illum vivere si*)'.[107] There was, then, a very real fear that plague could wipe away whole families, a fear realised in the case of John de Rampton, Joan, wife of John Barbour, and Christina de Rampton, all whom named each other in their respective wills, all of whom died within a few days of each other in July 1349. Their deaths are made yet more poignant by the fact that their wills are enrolled on consecutive folios of the *Burwarmote Book*.[108]

Unsurprisingly such fears were not always so readily expressed, and it is possible that the lengthy lines of reversion hitherto identified also emerged as a result of plague. Certainly it is no surprise to learn that eleven of the thirteen reversions omitted from the evidence here were noted in 1349 or after, including the case of Fenton cited above.[109] Such reversionary practices thus represent the desire of testators to provide for the living whilst simultaneously establishing a contingency plan for their soul through the performance of the mass. Not only did this minimise the chance of lands falling into the hands of the king, as was custom in cases where lands and properties went unclaimed or were disputed,[110] but it ensured that they were put to good spiritual use should the worst-case scenario come to pass.

Founders of Perpetual Chantries

In terms of the status of perpetual chantry founders, it is perhaps to be expected that they were not infrequently the most powerful and wealthy individuals in the city (table 25). This was due not only to the value of alienated lands, goods and properties given to each chantry but also to the general cost of acquiring a licence.[111] In Lincoln, licences ranged from 20s to £30, with an average of £8 and a mode of £5, sums beyond the means of most lay inhabitants. Moreover, when this is set alongside the fact that several individuals also built their own chapels, including William de Baiocis, Ralph Jolyff and Roger FitzBenedict,[112] with many more still making gifts and donations to their serving chaplains, such as Robert de Dalderby, who gave a missal worth 6 marks, a *portas* with musical notation worth 26s 8d and a chalice worth 26s,[113] then it is clear that the licence itself was one aspect of a much larger financial outlay.

106 *BB*, fos 191v, 192, 201, 233.

107 *BB*, fo. 199v. Identical fears were expressed by John de Qhwytgift (*viz.* Wytgift) over his unborn child in June 1349: *BB*, fo. 194.

108 *BB*, fols. 198v–199.

109 Beginning with Henry de Laghton; see n. 99 above.

110 *BB*, fos 127, 135, 141, 151, 174v; *Royal Charters*, 48–52.

111 Wood-Legh, *Perpetual Chantries*, 155–6; Dobson, 'Citizens and Chantries', 312.

112 *BB*, fo. 154v; *Liber Cant.*, fos 3, 310–11.

113 *Liber Cant.*, fo. 292. For other similar gifts to chantries, see *Liber Cant.*, fos 162v–163, 293, 310v, 343v–344v; LAO Reg/2, fos 14–15.

Table 25 Status and occupation(s) of lay perpetual chantry founders (c.1284–c.1521)

Status and occupation	**Number**
Mayor	[15]
Esquire	1
Merchant	10
Merchant/draper	1
Merchant/butcher	1
Spicer	1
Unknown	1
Bailiff (not becoming mayor)	[4]
Chandler	1
Merchant	2
Unknown	1
Woman (including wife)	4 (2)
Chaplain	4
Status unknown	3
Canon	1
Knight (and king's arrayer)	1
Cordwainer (*souter*)	1
Former clerk and under-sheriff	1
Total	34

Note: founders of multiple chantries are counted only once.

Of thirty-four identified founders, nineteen were civic officials, with fifteen serving at some stage as mayor. The vast majority of these men were wealthy merchants.[114] In addition to this, two chantries were founded solely by women, Beatrice Colet and Agnes, wife of Thomas Cause,[115] whilst two wives, Agnes de Wykford and Matilda Pinsun, were named as founders alongside their husbands. There was also a canon (Robert de Whitwell),[116] a knight and king's arrayer (William de Baiocis),[117] an under-sheriff (Thomas de Carleton)[118] and a cordwainer (Thomas de Wykford), though in the last case it is inconceivable that he was an artisan not a wholesaler.[119] Finally there were four chaplains and three individuals about whom nothing is known.

114 This figure does not include the chantry of William de Blyton or the 'Chandeler chauntere', whose founders remain unknown.

115 Whilst the *inquisitio* granted to Beatrice does not record the foundation of her chantry outright, subsequent references confirm that it was indeed founded: *CPR, 1292–1301*, 576; C 143/37/15; *BB*, fos 271, 272v; *Liber Cant.*, fo. 162v.

116 See 204–5 and n. 41.

117 *CPR, 1321–24*, 132.

118 See main text below.

119 Wykford was a member of the mayor's council in 1323/24 and paid 5s tax in the lay subsidy of 1327 and 10s in 1332: *BH*, fo. 65v; E 179/135/12, rot. 2; E 179/135/16, m. 26.

The second observation to make regarding the foundation of perpetual chantries is that despite the majority (thirteen) being established by a single individual, several were instigated by groups. Of these, six were established by two people, including the two married couples already noted, with three being founded by groups of three, four and six people respectively. In two cases individuals founded more than a single chantry.[120] Of the groups of founders, the largest relates to the Tatersale chantry founded in St Benedict in 1378; it included two former mayors (William de Snelleston, Robert de Ledes), an unknown individual (Richard de Lyndesey) and all three chaplains identified here (John de Lee, Simon de Thornton and Peter de Leggesby).[121] Perhaps the most striking aspect of this particular chantry is that none of its founders were named as beneficiaries of the intercessory masses. Whilst it is possible, even likely, that these individuals were merely overseeing the wishes of Roger de Tatersale and his family, it is important not to rule out more altruistic motives. One possible means of testing this idea is to identify those named as beneficiaries of the intercessory masses.

With the exception of the chantry of Robert de Sutton (1382), who named only himself as beneficiary, and the chantries of Beatrice Colet (1301), William de Blyton (c.1425) and the 'Chandeler chauntere' about which nothing is known save their existence, all lay perpetual chantry foundations were linked with at least one other individual by name. The chantries of Robert de Chesterfeld (1351) and John de Hodelston (1371) named six and seven individuals respectively,[122] whilst the chantry of Thomas de Carleton (1339) named an unprecedented eleven in addition to his ancestors and all the faithful departed.[123] The implication of this is that the majority of those establishing perpetual chantries were, as one potential founder put it in 1366, keen to share with their family and friends the 'benefits of everlasting glory' (*beneficia gloriam consequamur sempiternam*).[124]

Such a motive can be seen most clearly for the Carleton chantry, which reveals how lists of beneficiaries can be used to reconstruct local cliques or groups.[125] Listed alongside the founder, Thomas de Carleton, were two brothers, Walter, a clerk, and Hugh, clerk of the statute merchant;[126] another possible relative, Dulcia de Carleton; his wife Cecilia; Daniel de Grayngham, a local draper;[127] and James de Berne, a leading civic figure and wealthy merchant.[128] In addition to these individuals were

120 William de Baiocis founded both his own chantry and a chantry in the Friars of the Order of the Penance of Jesus Christ (of the Sack); whilst Robert de Dalderby founded his own chantry and co-founded a chantry for the guild of the Blessed Virgin Mary. See appendix 5 for references.

121 *CPR, 1377–81*, 157; C 143/393/19; *ELW*, 82. See appendix 2 for dates of office.

122 *Liber Cant.*, fos 343v–344v; *BB*, fos 220v–221; *CPR, 1338–40*, 301–2.

123 *Liber Cant.*, fos 162v–163.

124 This relates to Oxonford's failed attempt to establish a chantry in the cathedral. See main text below. *BB*, fo. 260v.

125 *CPR, 1338–40*, 301–2; C 143/249/15.

126 SC 8/56/2758. Hugh's relationship as brother of Walter (and thus Thomas) can be established by a charter dating from 1364: *BB*, fo. 257v.

127 C 241/109/219. Note the *inquisitio* records him as Grayngham not Gayngham: C 143/249/15.

128 Berne, who died c.1322–27, is noted in Thomas de Carleton's will as previously owning lands in St Michael on the Mount. During his life he lent, alongside several other leading citizens,

three other men, Hugh de Stokes (and his wife Etherelda), John Judekyn and Gilbert de Ledred (and his wife Joan),[129] all of whom were indicted alongside Thomas de Carleton for defrauding the city by falsely obtaining expenses for parliament in 1338, seizing municipal power and expelling the mayor and 'confederates', and stealing £300, amongst other crimes.[130] Such evidence shows how those listed in perpetual chantry foundations were occasionally demonstrative of powerful cliques, a fact which would not have gone unnoticed by local inhabitants, but also how beneficiaries of masses represent the often altruistic motives of founders towards friends and family.

A contiguous issue, and one which serves to highlight further still this link between wealth and status, is the names of witnesses recorded in extant foundation charters.[131] For example, for the chantry of Robert de Dalderby, founded in St Benedict in 1351 and noted at the outset of the chapter, witnesses included the precentor and sub-dean of the cathedral (Anthony de Goldesburgh and Hamone Belers), the incumbent mayor (Thomas de Lokton), three former mayors (William de Blyton, John de Outhorp and Walter de Kelby), the dean of Christianity (John de Wykford) and several unnamed others;[132] the chantry of Alexander FitzMartyn, founded in St Lawrence in 1303, likewise named the then bishop (John de Dalderby, 1300–20), the chancellor (Ralph Barri), treasurer (Gilbert Dervile) and sub-dean of the cathedral (Henry de Benynworth), the archdeacon of Stow (William de Okham), several canons (Richard de Hederington *cum aliis*), the incumbent mayor (Stephen de Stanham), the former keeper of the city (William Cause), two future mayors (John de Amecotes, Gilbert de Atherby), two former bailiffs (Jacob Bern, John de Normanton) and numerous others (John de Roderham, *cum aliis*).[133] The names of the witnesses to the chantry of John de Hodelston, founded during his mayoralty in 1375 in the church of St Peter at Pleas, tell a similar story and include the treasurer (John de Welborne), four canons (Thomas de Sutton, Geoffrey le Scrope, Richard de Wynewyk, John de Belvere), five former mayors (Walter de Kelby, John de Sutton, Roger de Tatershale, William de Belay, William Ingill) and several others (John de Brauncepath, John de Wykford and John de Colby, notaries public, *et aliis*).[134] The last entry in particular exemplifies the established link between civic power and expressions of piety and commemoration whilst underlining how socio-religious acts, such as chantry foundations, served to draw the secular and ecclesiastical worlds together

significant monies to the crown for the war with the Scots and was a member of the mayoral council for over a decade (1303–16). His widow, Bella, engaged in several disputes with Thomas after his death. *BB*, fos 89v, 104v–105, 134v, 135, 159v–161; *CPR, 1313–17*, 189; *BH*, fos 1, 3v, 5v, 19v, 20v, 71v, 111v.

129 He was escheator in 1332 and sheriff from May 1338 to January 1341. *List of Sheriffs for England and Wales* (List and Index Society, vol. 9) (New York, 1963), 79; A. C. Wood, *List of Escheators for England and Wales* (List and Index Society, vol. 72) (London, 1971), 7.

130 McLane, *1341 Inquest*, nos 712, 720, 867; *CPR, 1330–34*, 270; *1340–43*, 323–4.

131 For dates in office for individuals noted in this paragraph, see appendix 2.

132 LAO Reg/9, fo. 94v.

133 LAO Reg/2, fo. 15.

134 *Liber Cant.*, fo. 163.

in the pursuit of orthodox Christian values.[135] Nonetheless, there is some evidence to suggest that not all lay-founded chantries were established under the auspices of both lay and ecclesiastical authorities, and in 1347 the foundation charter of Ralph Jolyff listed only the bishop of Lincoln (Thomas Bek, 1341–47), the precentor (Peter de Dalderby), treasurer (Walter de Stauren), sub-dean (Nicholas de Tarenta) and provost of the cathedral (John de Bourne) amongst several unnamed others (*et aliis*) as witnesses.[136] The lack of surviving records for the majority of Lincoln's lay-founded perpetual chantries nevertheless suggests that they were founded with little or no input from the ecclesiastical authorities. Taken together this serves to highlight how despite the relative uniformity of many aspects of perpetual institutions, there remained a high degree of autonomy in their organisation and foundation.

Founders of Temporary Chantries

The social status and wealth of temporary chantry founders were much more diverse than those of perpetual founders (table 26). This is particularly marked by the absence of any information for almost two fifths of temporary founders identified as paying tax either in 1327 or 1332 who might otherwise be expected to appear in surviving civic records but do not (with the exception, of course, of their wills). However, for the individuals whose social status or profession can be identified, it is those holding civic office who once again played a dominant role, all of whom paid an average 3s in tax, a third higher than the general taxpaying population (2s) and the highest of all categories of temporary founders (with the exception of a single taverner). Whilst this might tentatively suggest that the establishment of intercessory masses was a marker of the homogeneity of civic officials, especially when it is set alongside the evidence of perpetual founders already discussed, this would be misleading. Of the 176 unique office holders serving between 1315 and 1376, only sixty (34.1 per cent) had their wills recorded. More importantly, of this number only twenty-five recorded provisions for temporary institutions at their death, meaning that only one sixth (14.2 per cent) of all office holders recorded provisions for temporary chantries by the sale of lands, in addition to the 10 per cent who founded perpetual chantries. Considered in this light, it seems clear that chantry foundations were not integral to the identity of civic officials, with others leaving provisions for the foundation of hospices, almshouses and gifts to the poor, for example,[137] acts similarly understood to confer spiritual benefits upon their founders,[138] although chantries undoubtedly remained the single most common *post-obit* enterprise.

135 Fleming, 'Charity, Faith', 40.

136 *Liber Cant.*, fo. 311.

137 Including the wealthy Stephen de Stanham (mayor, 1301–06, 1312/13) who left £40 for one year for the poor begging from door to door (*ad erogandum pauperibus hostiatim mendicantibus per Linc' infra primum annum*), amongst other gifts; William de Snartford (mayor 1324/25) who ordained a shop be set aside for 'the poor, freely and peacefully without any rent of any description whatsoever'; and Ralph Snelleslound who left a house 'for the poor': *BB*, fos 82–82v, 84, 159–159v.

138 S. Sweetinburgh, *The Role of the Hospital in Medieval England: Gift-Giving and the Spiritual*

Table 26 Status/occupation of temporary chantry founders, including taxable wealth recorded in 1327 and 1332

Status/profession	**No.**	**% of founders**	**No. paying tax**	**Mean tax**
Unknown	44	40.0%	24	2s
Official (mayor, bailiff or coroner)	(25)	22.8%	16	3s
Attorney	1	–	–	–
Baker	1	–	–	–
Clerk	2	–	–	–
Draper	1	–	–	–
Fisher	1	–	–	–
Merchant	6	–	–	–
Merchant and second profession:	(3)	–	–	–
Fisher	1	–	–	–
Salter	1	–	–	–
Tanner/barker	1	–	–	–
Painter	1	–	–	–
Shipman	1	–	–	–
Unknown	8	–	–	–
Women	17	15.5%	6*	2s 8d
Baker	4	3.6%	1	2s
Skin-dealer/skin-merchant	3	2.7%	3	7d
Attorney	3	2.7%	–	–
Merchant	3	2.7%	1	3s
Tanner	2	1.8%	1	2s
Other	(9)	8.2%	–	–
Barker	1	–	–	–
Cartwright	1	–	–	–
Clerk	1	–	–	–
Fisherman	1	–	–	–
Painter	1	–	–	–
Potter	1	–	–	–
Taverner	1	–	1	4s
Keeper of Hospital of Holy Innocents	1	–	–	–
Total	108	100%	55	2s 3d

Source: E 179/135/12; E 179/135/16, mm. 26–26d.

Key: * = three relate to the household (i.e. husband), not the spouse. Note that individuals appearing in more than one category are counted only once. Those drawn from the 1327 tax are not counted in the 1332 evidence, with the value of the latter being halved to keep it in line with the rate of a twentieth recorded in the former (see 96 and table 15 for more on this).

Following office holders, the second most common category of founder was women – though in proportional terms they actually established less than one sixth of all temporary chantries (15.6 per cent) vis-à-vis their male counterparts. Of the thirty-six surviving wills for women, less than half (seventeen or 47 per cent) made provisions for temporary chantries, a proportionally higher number than that for men (38 per cent or ninety-four out of 246). Although the sample size is much smaller, it demonstrates the concern of women to fulfil the obligations of their husbands and families, as well as their own pious interests.[139] Evidence for this can be seen by the fact that two thirds of this group (twelve) were widows, with the remaining five either not recording their marital status or noting an entirely different status altogether.[140] Whilst on the one hand this demonstrates that almost a third of all women making provisions for temporary chantries had access to wealth by means other than marriage, it underscores how the majority only took control of their assets once their husbands died,[141] a common practice in late medieval England.[142] The value of tax paid by women either alone or in conjunction with their husbands was 2s 8d, a figure higher than average for temporary chantry founders and taxpayers in general.

The remaining individuals and artisanal sub-groups can be considered together as in many ways they are self-explanatory. Not only do they demonstrate a sliding scale of status and wealth, particularly when compared to the more costly and prestigious perpetual institutions, but they emphasise the diverse trades and professions of temporary chantry founders, including, for example, a potter, a cartwright, several merchants and John de Carlton, Keeper of the Hospital of Holy Innocents.[143] The variety in this 'group' is evinced by the value of tax paid, which ranged (where known) from as little as 2d to 4s, with a mean of 2s, consequently the city's average.[144]

Civic office, though not unimportant, was far less significant for founders of temporary chantries than individual wealth. In fact, much like for perpetual chantry founders, it was the ready access to lands and properties, all of which could be sold to fund *post-obit* enterprises, which remained the bedrock upon which fixed-term institutions thrived. Even when chantries founded by monetary bequests alone are

Economy (Dublin, 2004); M. Rubin, *Charity and Community in Medieval Cambridge* (Cambridge, 1987). For an excellent survey of mercantile involvement in establishing and maintaining almshouses, see C. Burgess, 'Making Mammon Serve God: Merchant Piety in Later Medieval England', in Barron and Sutton, *The Medieval Merchant*, 197–205.

139 Burgess, C., '"By Quick and by Dead": Wills and Pious Provisions in Late Medieval Bristol', *English Historical Review*, 102, 405 (1987): 837–58, at 842.

140 For example, Denise (d.1349), was noted as sister of John Brayland, whilst Cecilia (d.1349) identified herself as the daughter of John son of John de Toft. *BB*, fos 185v, 196v.

141 For example it is only possible to place a value against Agnes de Hodelston through her husband Alan, who paid 2s in 1327: *BB*, fo. 165v; E 179/135/12, rot. 4.

142 Goldberg, *Medieval England*, 7–8; C. Beattie, 'Living as a Single Person: Marital Status, Performance and the Law in Late Medieval England', *Women's History Review*, 17 (2008), 334.

143 For example, *BB*, fos 84, 120–120v, 176v, 194v, 242, 243. Note that Carlton was accused of selling hospital endowments in Boultham to John de Blyton in 1331 contrary to a royally sanctioned agreement and for bargaining with 'royal alms' (*regiis elemosinam*): *CPR, 1327–30*, 519; *1330–34*, 189; *1334–38*, 168; SC 8/168/8359; *BB*, fo. 120v–121.

144 See also 138.

factored in, it is unlikely that this overall picture changed, demonstrating a strong belief in the efficacy of the mass to provide succour for the souls of those in Purgatory.

Spatial Distribution of Perpetual Chantries

Of the twelve perpetual chantries founded between 1284 and 1349, four were located within the intramural area, six in Wigford, with a further one each in the suburbs of Eastgate and Butwerk (map 8). Two notable areas where there were no perpetual chantries were the independent jurisdictions of the Close and the Bail. It is possible that their absence in the former was an indirect result of the reported acts of violence perpetrated by the laity towards the clergy from the mid-thirteenth century onwards, all of which served to encourage successive bishops to seek to enclose the cathedral precinct, an aim realised in the 1330s.[145] Whilst by this date the violence had subsided, it was commonplace in the years leading up to it for local lay men and women to bequeath their lands and properties to the Dean and Chapter for the enlargement of the Close wall.[146] Whilst on the one hand such bequests would have been considered an act of piety, with benefactors being added to the bede roll of the Works chantry,[147] on the other they served to divest many lay grantors of the very lands and properties possibly earmarked for personal foundations in the future.

The absence of perpetual chantries in the Bail is more difficult to explain, especially given the high number of civic officials living in the area.[148] It is possible that the relative proximity of the cathedral, with its numerous chantries and shrines, served to cast a shadow over any potential foundations, though this seems unlikely given that perpetual chantries were founded in St Peter in Eastgate and St Michael on the Mount, two churches lying adjacent to the Bail. A more likely explanation was the relative unsuitability of churches and the lack of available space in this area. For example, following the union of the parishes of All Saints and St Mary Magdalene in 1318[149] after a reported decline in the number of parishioners in the former – quite possibly as a result of the enlargement of the Close wall noted above – only three parish churches were left in the Bail, one of which, St Paul's, was reportedly in need of urgent repairs.[150] Of the remaining two, the church of St Mary Magdalene already held services according to the rules set down by Bishop Oliver Sutton at the end of the thirteenth century, whilst the last, St Clement, eventually saw the foundation of a chantry in 1412 by the dean of the cathedral.[151]

After 1349 the spatial dynamic of perpetual institutions in the city changed

145 For an overview of these developments, see A. Kissane, '*Manibus Violentis*: Touch and Sanctuary in Medieval Lincoln', in U. Krampl, R. Beck and E. Retaillaud-Bajac (eds), *Les cinq sens de la ville du Moyen Age à nos jours* (Tours, 2013), 317–20; Owen, 'Historical Survey', 124–5, 147–8, 152–4.

146 For example, LAO Dij 77/1/12, 15, 28–9, 35, 42.

147 See main text below.

148 See table 17.

149 LAO Reg/3, fo. 388v.

150 LAO Reg/3, fos 33, 45.

151 Bradshaw and Wordsworth, *Statutes of Lincoln Cathedral*, vol. 2, lxxii. See also 202.

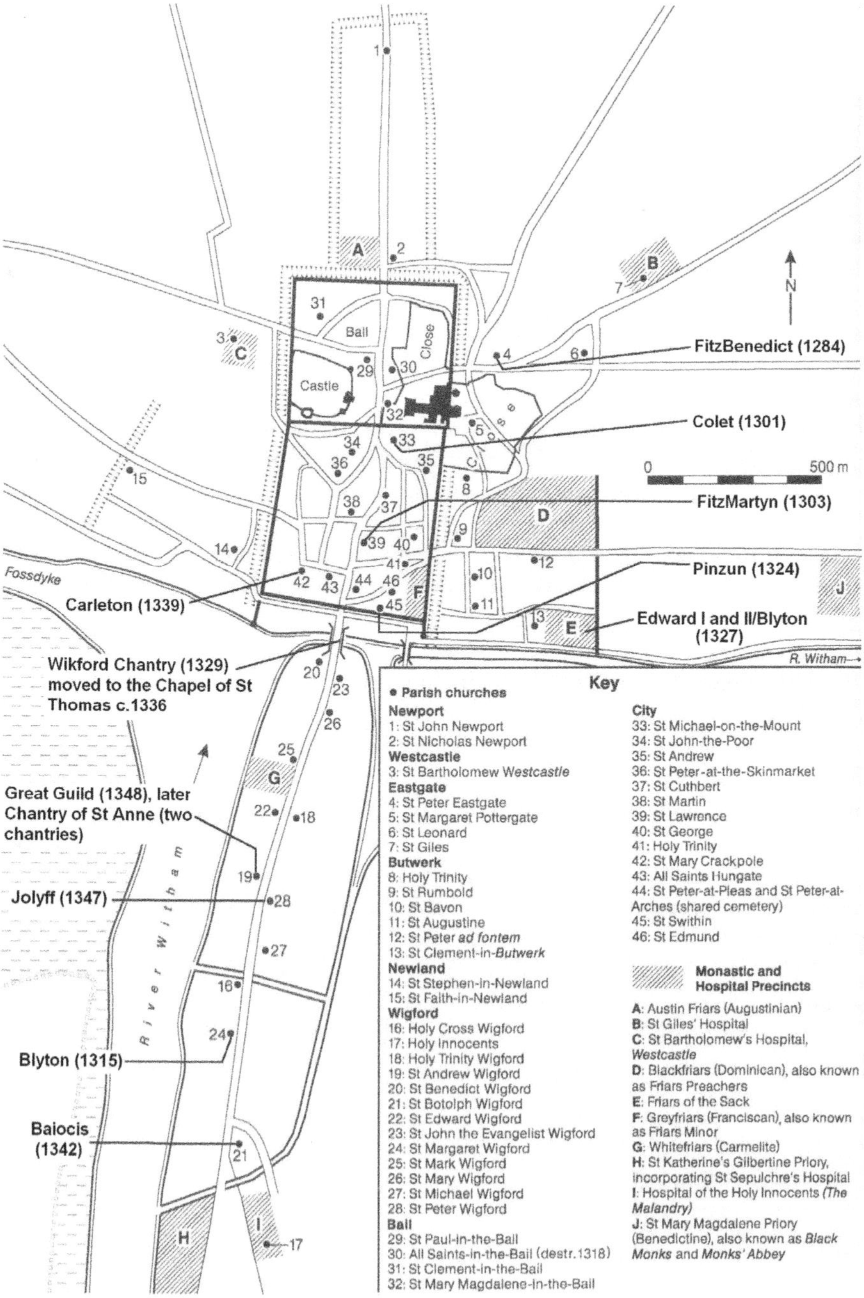

Map 8 Perpetual chantries founded by the laity before 1349

considerably with a large cluster appearing around the Stonebow (map 9). Whereas before 1349 there had only been three perpetual chantries in this increasingly important civic and social centre,[152] there were now nine, demonstrating how, despite the devastation of the pestilence, the area throve in a variety of ways, becoming not only the residential choice for many of the city's officials but the focus for an increasing array of commemorative practices.

It is within this spatial context that it is possible to identify the element of competition at both an individual and a parochial level.[153] Whilst it is possible that founders of chantries in the city sought, much like in Bristol, to provide benefits to their parish by increasing divine service,[154] that they did so as often in the same few churches suggests that there were other factors at work. Foremost amongst these was how perpetual chantry foundations became an effective means for demonstrating the wealth and status of not only a particular parish church but also, more significantly, those who patronised and worshipped in it. This view provides important context for the foundation of the guild of the Purification of the Blessed Virgin Mary in the church of St Benedict discussed in the previous chapter, one of the city's two leading guilds in the fourteenth century. Not only did the guild maintain the highest annual fees in the city but it was also the only guild recording ordinances for music during mass.[155] It thus seems likely that as the century progressed there was a consolidated effort by local civic leaders to develop the area in and around the Stonebow into a centre of patronage and piety largely free of ecclesiastical influence,[156] much like in some continental urban settings,[157] which not only reflected the commercial and financial importance of the district but underscored its links to civic power and authority.

Of course, not all perpetual chantries established after 1349 were located within this central area, with others being founded in the church of St Andrew, Wigford, in 1382 (Sutton) and the Gilbertine Priory of St Katherine in 1392 (Kelby).[158] A third chantry, established by Agnes Cause was founded in the cathedral in 1378, a location otherwise not readily sought out by the city's laity, at least at first glance.

Despite the success of Agnes in establishing a chantry in the cathedral, it is nevertheless important to highlight how this was not the first attempt by members of the laity to do so. For example, in 1366 a former mayor, Robert de Oxonford (1325/26), sought and failed to establish a perpetual chantry for four chaplains.[159] Whilst the reasons for his failure are not known, it is likely that the Dean and Chapter were not keen on permitting chantries to be founded in the cathedral by powerful members

152 See 142–51.
153 Dobson, 'Citizens and Chantries', 321–2.
154 Burgess, 'Divine Service', 50–4.
155 C47/40/147.
156 See 159, 162.
157 S. Weddle, 'Identity and Alliance: Urban Presence, Spatial Privilege, and Florentine Renaissance Convents', in R. J. Crum and J. T. Paoletti (eds), *Renaissance Florence: A Social History* (Cambridge, 2006), 394–412.
158 It is likely that this chantry was actually founded before 1392, the licence being prompted by the change to mortmain legislation. See main text above.
159 *BB*, fo. 260v.

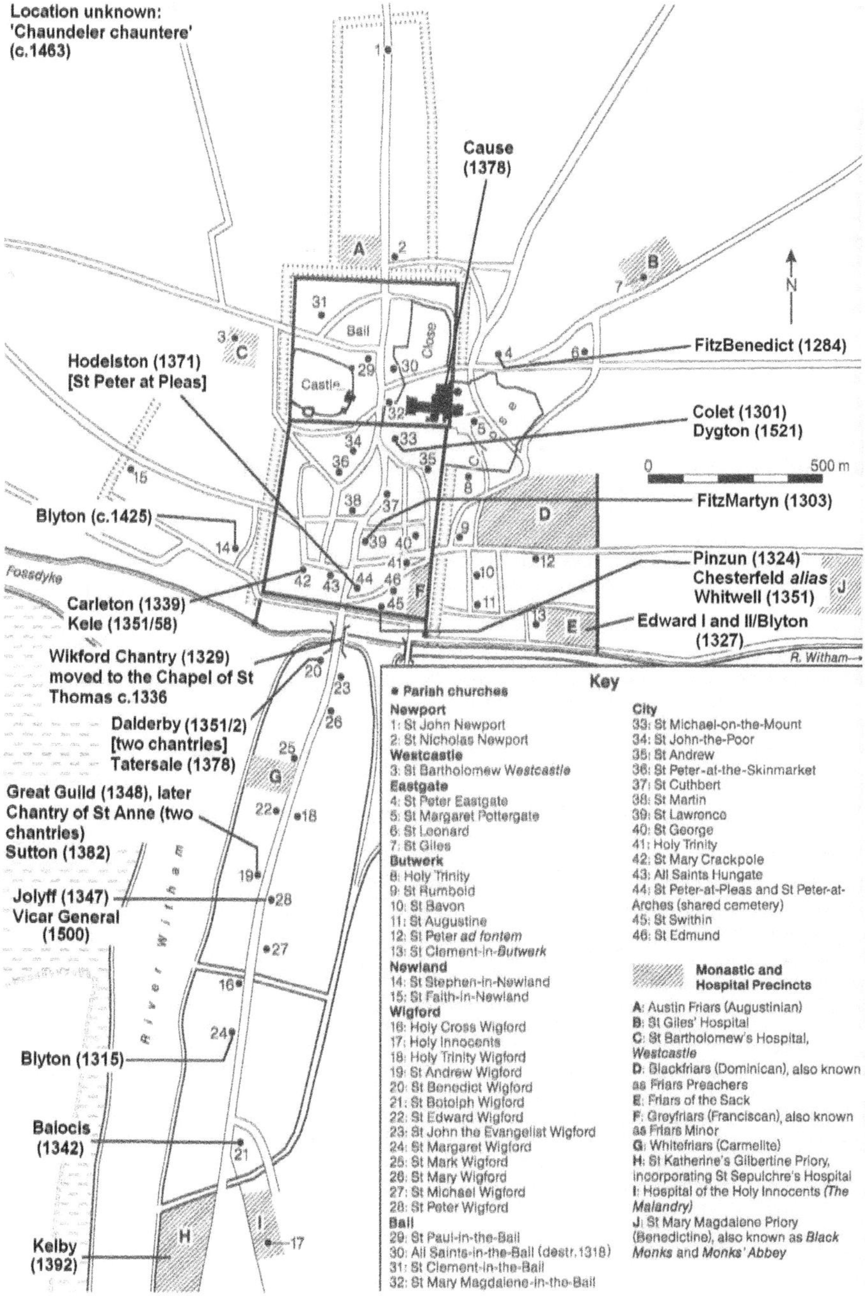

Map 9 Perpetual chantries founded by the laity (1284–1521)

of the local laity, as it may have been regarded as interfering with ecclesiastical affairs. Certainly, such attitudes have been identified at York, Norwich and Westminster, with Dobson noting for York that before the middle of the fourteenth century 'burial nor (much less) the creation of a chantry in the Minster was never a practical or indeed a particularly looked-for possibility'.[160] Given that Agnes was a woman with little or no political influence, who not only offered a generous endowment but sought to be guided 'in accordance with the ordinance of the said Master Geoffrey le Scrope',[161] suggests that her aims were on the whole more conducive to those of the Dean and Chapter.

This conclusion is also supported somewhat paradoxically by the fact that two extremely well-endowed chantries were established by non-resident laymen in the cathedral in the first half of the fourteenth century.[162] The first was established in 1332 by Bartholomew Burghersh, brother of the then bishop of Lincoln, Henry Burghersh (1320–40), a wealthy magnate and administrator, who lent over £4,000 to Edward III and owned significant lands in Devon, Kent and Sussex upon his death in 1355.[163] The second was founded in 1345 by Joan Cantilupe, wife of Nicholas de Cantilupe, a soldier, administrator and justice of the peace, who fought alongside the earl of Derby in the Hundred Years War and who possessed several residences in the Midlands at Greasley and Ilkeston.[164] Not only is it clear that these were powerful and wealthy laymen with strong links to the crown but, most significantly, they were absent from the day-to-day running of their chantries, thereby leaving the Dean and Chapter to manage their own affairs.

Despite the relative failure of local lay founders to establish perpetual chantries in the cathedral, it is important to recognise that, unlike at York, Norwich and Westminster, several individuals were nevertheless successful in establishing perpetual masses and obits at the Works chantry from at least the middle of the fourteenth century onwards. Located in 'the most northerly chapel on the east side of the great south transept', the Works chantry was established during the bishopric of William of Blois (1203×6) 'to pray for the souls of the benefactors of the Fabric',[165] including, for example, individuals gifting lands for the completion of the Close wall in the 1330s. Whilst it is certainly true that such masses were not independent foundations with their own proscribed rules and regulations or even with their own distinct space, they were still established with perpetuity in mind, a fact which serves to blur the distinction hitherto adopted here regarding the form and function of temporary and perpetual chantries. Take, for example, Roger Briddok (bailiff 1341/42) who in 1349 gifted to the master of the fabric a single plot on Skinnergate so that he would

160 Dobson, 'Chantries and Citizens', 318; Tanner, *Medieval Norwich*, 97; Rosser, *Medieval Westminster*, 260, n. 44.

161 *CPR, 1378–81*, 279. See appendix 5 for further references.

162 For a later lay foundation by Joan, countess of Westmorland, for Katherine de Swynford, duchess of Lancaster, *CPR, 1436–41*, 137.

163 *Chantry Certificates*, 207–17; 'Burghersh, Bartholomew, the elder', Oxford Dictionary of National Biography. For links between the Burghersh chantry and the fee farm, see 100.

164 *Chantry Certificates*, 220–4; 'Cantilupe, Nicholas, third Lord Cantilupe', Oxford Dictionary of National Biography.

165 Owen, 'Historical Survey', 149.

celebrate for his soul and that of Catherine, his wife, in perpetuity,[166] and Adam de Ouresby who in 1354 provided 10s of annual rents to John Cole to use for the fabric of the church so that he might celebrate for his soul and that of his wife, Alice.[167] In 1381, too, an obit worth 64s in annual rent was established on behalf of Roger de Burton by mayor, Simon de Messingham, and bailiffs, Thomas Hauk, Semans Patyner and William de Halton.[168] Considered within a broader commemorative context, it stands to reason that relations between the local laity and the Dean and Chapter were sufficiently cordial throughout much of the fourteenth century for them to feel able to make their foundations in the Works chantry, even if not strictly on their own terms.[169] To what extent the tensions which arose between the Dean and Chapter and the civic authorities from the mid-1370s onwards impacted negatively upon lay–ecclesiastical relations is not yet clear,[170] but the fact that cathedral services were known to have been interrupted on more than one occasion suggests that there was an increasing disregard for the status and rights of the cathedral at this time.[171]

Perpetual chantries at Lincoln, like elsewhere, were largely the reserve of the wealthy. Over time they came to reflect the residential and occupational status of civic leaders, two important factors in fostering a strong and centralised mercantile identity. Whilst not all merchants or civic officials followed this route to salvation, with others founding their chantries in more diverse places, including in the cathedral and local friaries, the concentration of permanent institutions at the physical and symbolic heart of Lincoln's civic jurisdiction established what Clive Burgess sees as a 'continuous and co-operative religious dynamic',[172] through which civic power, orthodoxy and piety were demonstrated.

Spatial Distribution of Temporary Chantries

The locations of the city's temporary chantries have been reconstructed here primarily through details recorded in wills. Typically these state that the testators' lands and properties were to be sold for masses to be performed in a specifically named church, before occasionally including details of the dedicated altar where these services were to be conducted.[173] In cases where these details are not provided, evidence of the individual's parish of residence is used to indicate the location of the chantry.[174] Whilst in the latter cases (twenty-six) this approach should be seen as

166 *BB*, fo. 198.

167 *BB*, fo. 225v.

168 LAO Bj 2/7, fo. 79. See also LAO Dij 74/2/35, which discusses Burton's will. Note, however, that this obit was later known as 'Burtonchaunterie', suggesting that it may have received future grants: *CCR, 1454–61*, 124–5.

169 Some, including Agnes, widow of William le Chaloner, attempted to impress their demands on the Dean and Chapter in 1350. It is unknown how successful this was: *BB*, fo. 210v.

170 See 112–13.

171 Kissane, '*Manibus Violentis*', 324–7.

172 Burgess, 'Making Mammon Serve God', 201.

173 Examples include *BB*, fos 104, 110, 129v, 146v.

174 For the methodology on establishing parish residence, see 142–3.

no more than a guide to the likely locations of individual chantries, it nevertheless provides a fair indication of their whereabouts. In particular, of the thirty-five individuals recording parish details in their wills, twenty-eight (80 per cent) followed this practice, with the remaining seven (20 per cent) making their foundations in the city's various friaries, hospitals or the cathedral.

According to the testamentary evidence, provisions for temporary chantries were established in over half (twenty-nine) of all ecclesiastical buildings in the city (table 27), more than for perpetual chantries, which appeared in only sixteen different buildings. This suggests that the lower cost of establishing temporary masses resulted in a wider distribution of chantries throughout the city. This is not altogether surprising given the broad spectrum of wealth and occupation of founders already identified, though it remains significant that almost a third (eighteen) were established in the six parishes located within the vicinity of the Stonebow, with St Benedict topping the list, again highlighting the success of the laity in establishing this area as a centre of civic and religious patronage. This area was followed by the remaining intramural parts of the city (thirteen), the suburbs of Wigford (twelve), Butwerk (five) and Newport (four), friaries (four), the Bail (three) and the cathedral (two).

Despite this general conclusion, it is clear that the testamentary evidence is not an altogether reliable measure of the distribution of temporary chantry foundations. For example, whilst the evidence points to a relative decline in the popularity of St Benedict and St Peter at Pleas during the second half of the century, this is not borne out by subsequent evidence. Nor is the fact that St Augustine and St Cuthbert were particularly popular churches in the second half of the century. Two possibilities serve to explain this anomaly. The first relates to the transient nature of chantries themselves. For example, in Lincoln temporary foundations were usually established for between one and three years,[175] periods typical of the later Middle Ages.[176] This highlights how particular churches could have had a few prominent deaths within a short space of time, thereby seeming more popular than they actually were. The second relates to the incompleteness of the evidence base itself. Whilst it has been possible to identify the locations of sixty-one temporary chantries, over two fifths (48 or 44 per cent) still remain unknown. Hence there remains a considerable margin for error in interpreting this evidence.

An arguably more accurate means of identifying patterns in temporary chantry foundations comes from analysing the ecclesiastical returns of 1377 and 1381, which record the names and rank of the clergy serving in each of the city's parish churches.[177] While this approach offers an admittedly synchronic snapshot of only a four-year period, it nevertheless provides a more comprehensive picture of commemorative practices than the testamentary evidence.

175 *BB*, fos 167v, 180–180v, 192, 195, 202, 223v, 227v, 253v, 267v; for longer: fos 161v (six years), 229 (twenty years).

176 Tanner, *Medieval Norwich*, 101; Burgess, 'Divine Service', 52.

177 A. K. McHardy, *Clerical Poll-Taxes*, 1–5, 98–100; *idem*, 'The Lincolnshire Clergy', 145–51. There are no surviving returns for 1379.

Table 27 Known locations of temporary chantries: testamentary and subsidy evidence (1327–76)

Parish church	1327–49	1350–76	Total
St Benedict*	5	1	6
St Augustine, Butwerk	2	3	5
St Cuthbert	3	2	5
St Swithun*	1	3	4
Holy Trinity, Wigford	3	–	3
St Nicholas, Newport	3	–	3
St Peter at Arches*	2	1	3
All Saints, Hungate*	1	1	2
Cathedral	1	1	2
Friars Minor	2	–	2
St Botolph, Wigford	2	–	2
St Margaret, Wigford	2	–	2
St Mary, Wigford	–	2	2
St Michael on the Mount	1	1	2
St Peter at Pleas*	2	–	2
St Martin	2	–	2
St Mary Magdalene in the Bail	2	–	2
Holy Cross, Wigford	–	2	2
Carmelite Friary	1	–	1
St John, Newport	1	–	1
St George	1	–	1
St John, Wigford	1	–	1
Holy Trinity	–	1	1
St Mary Crackpole*	–	1	1
St Peter, Wigford	–	1	1
St Paul in the Bail	–	1	1
St Peter in Eastgate	–	1	1
St Peter in the Skinmarket	1	–	1
Totals	39	22	61

Key: * = parish located near the Stonebow. Note that no locations are known prior to 1327.

For the following analysis (table 28), all clergy listed in the clerical returns have been considered, from the lowest acolyte up to and including parish priests,[178] as this remains the most effective means of demonstrating the relative popularity of individual churches, with higher numbers of clergy reflecting more services.

By the late 1370s it is clear that St Benedict was the most popular parish church for commemorative services in the city, maintaining almost double the amount of clergy of any other church and over four times the city's average of three. In second place stood St Peter at Pleas, followed by St Mary in Wigford, St Mary Crackpole and St Mark in Wigford. The least popular churches were St Stephen in Newland, Holy Trinity outside the Walls, St Nicholas in Newport and St Edward the King in Wigford, all of which averaged less than one member of clergy over the four-year period. In spite of these findings, twelve of the city's parish churches were not noted in any capacity in the tax whatsoever,[179] which suggests that some may have been abandoned following successive bouts of plague, as was the case at Norwich, Yarmouth and Winchester.[180] Even so, the absence of some, though by no means all, is in many ways unsurprising. For example, whilst it is to be expected that both St Bartholomew and St Giles were absent from this list, with each being subsumed by their respective hospitals during the thirteenth century,[181] and St Mary Magdalene in the Bail, which was part of the Close (and taxed as part of the cathedral), the absence of St Peter at the Skinmarket is somewhat puzzling, especially as it was noted in testamentary evidence (table 27). Irrespective of this, for the majority of churches in the city, and in particular those ranked from seventh to ninth (thirteen churches), there was a relative uniformity in the numbers serving in each church, with all maintaining between two and three members of clergy.

What this evidence highlights, therefore, is that whilst success bred success, failure also bred failure. In real terms this meant that the parish churches with the best facilities and experience in dealing with commemorative practices served to attract the greatest number of temporary chantries above and beyond their permanent foundations, whilst other churches floundered, attracting few, if any, private masses by the end of the fourteenth century. Even when guilds are factored into this analysis, the overall picture alters little, though there were admittedly several low-ranking churches that housed them, a finding which supports the idea not only that the majority of guilds hired chaplains on a temporary basis to perform their services,[182] but that some guilds were founded primarily in poorer parishes by less affluent inhabitants. Nonetheless, when the testamentary evidence and poll tax data are considered in tandem it is apparent that Lincoln's civic community was keen to patronise and support a whole range of churches and ecclesiastical institutions

178 For gradations of clerical office: Pantin, *The English Church*, 27–9.

179 These were St Giles, St Bartholomew, St Peter at the Skinmarket, St John the Poor, St Leonard, St Clement in Butwerk, St Stephen in Newland, St Faith in Newland, St Clement in the Bail, St Mary Magdalene in the Bail, St Andrew under the Palace and Holy Trinity, Clasketgate. This figure does not include All Saints in the Bail which was amalgamated to St Mary in 1318. See main text above.

180 Britnell, 'Black Death', 201; Keene, *Medieval Winchester*, vol. 1, 97.

181 Vince, 'Early Modern Era', 308.

182 See 000.

Table 28 Number of clergy listed in the clerical Poll Taxes of 1377 and 1381

Rank	Parish Church	1377	1381	1377/81 average	No. of guilds	No. of perp. chantries
1st	St Benedict*	13	13	13	2	3
2nd	St Peter at Pleas*	7	7	7	–	1
3rd	St Mary, Wigford	6	7	6.5	1	–
4th	St Mary Crackpole*	4	5	4.5	–	2
4th	St Mark, Wigford	3	6	4.5	–	–
5th	St Michael on the Mount	5	3	4	1	2
5th	St Swithun*	5	3	4	–	2
5th	St Margaret, Wigford	4	4	4	–	1
5th	Holy Trinity, Wigford	2	6	4	–	–
6th	St Botolph, Wigford	3	4	3.5	1	1
7th	St Andrew, Wigford	3	3	3	1	3
7th	St Martin	3	3	3	2	–
7th	St Peter at Arches*	4	2	3	–	–
7th	St Cuthbert	3	3	3	1	–
7th	St Peter, Wigford	3	3	3	–	2
7th	St John, Wigford	3	3	3	1	–
7th	St Martin in Dernstall	3	3	3	1	–
8th	St Peter, Eastgate	3	2	2.5	–	1
8th	St Lawrence	2	3	2.5	2	1
8th	St Paul in the Bail	2	3	2.5	–	–
9th	St Edmund	3	1	2	–	–
9th	St Augustine	2	2	2	–	–
9th	St George	1	3	2	1	–
10th	Holy Cross, Wigford	1	2	1.5	3	–
10th	St Michael in Wigford	1	2	1.5	–	–
10th	St John in Newport	1	2	1.5	–	–
10th	All Saints, Hungate*	2	1	1.5	1	–
11th	St Bavon	1	1	1	1	–
11th	St Peter ad Fontem	1	1	1	–	–
11th	St Rumbold	1	1	1	1	–
12th	Holy Trinity outside the Walls	–	1	0.5	–	–
12th	St Nicholas in Newport	1	–	0.5	1	–
12th	St Edward the King, Wigford	1	–	0.5	–	–
13th	St Stephen in Newland	–	–	–	–	1
			Average	3		

Key: * = parish located near the Stonebow. Data taken from McHardy, *Clerical Poll-Taxes*, 2–5, 98–100. For Lincoln's guilds, see chapter 5. This data excludes hospitals, friaries and the cathedral.

throughout the city, acts reflecting the broad range of choices open to individuals with the wealth and wherewithal to provide succour for the souls of themselves and their loved ones in the afterlife.

Conclusion

The growth and proliferation of chantries from the late thirteenth century onwards marked the broad shift towards the parish as the principal focus of lay religious piety.[183] Whilst this undoubtedly bestowed greater autonomy upon the laity, both through the elaboration and adornment of churches and the management of parish affairs, it nevertheless brought about new challenges.[184] For chantries and other institutions including guilds the most significant was undoubtedly the Black Death, which heralded both short-term and long-term changes to patterns of commemoration in Lincoln and elsewhere. In particular, this saw a temporary surge in foundations as fears over death and dying grew in the midst of the realisation that entire families and kinship networks could be wiped out by the pestilence. Such fears manifested themselves most clearly through the sharp rise in the number of temporary chantries being founded during the 1350s and 1360s, as well as through the new custom of recording detailed reversions in wills. For perpetual foundations this surge was no less marked though much shorter, undoubtedly as a result of the greater financial outlay required. This supports the evidence for guilds noted in the previous chapter and emphasises how at Lincoln there was no major shift in attitudes towards piety and commemoration following the Black Death. This conclusion has important implications for claims that there was a 'multiplication of masses which accompanied the chantry movement later in the fourteenth century'.[185] Certainly whilst it is to be expected that fears were heightened due to the severity of the Black Death and subsequent bouts of plague, as much as anything by anxiety of mass burials,[186] post-obit practices did not alter in any noticeable way, nor did they become more numerous – a fact underlined by the relative consistency in the proportion of temporary chantry foundations identified at both Lincoln and other towns throughout the Middle Ages. The changes which did occur were minor, most interestingly the emergence of the language of fear in the vocabulary of testators. Certainly, it would be worthwhile comparing the contents and form of perpetual chantry services in both Lincoln and elsewhere (temporary chantries do not record such details) to see if they altered in any appreciable way after the initial bout of plague to identify whether there was any shift in attitudes towards death, Purgatory and the afterlife.[187]

183 Swanson, *Church and Society*, 255–60.

184 Duffy, 'Religious Belief', 303–10.

185 R. N. Swanson, 'Indulgences for Prayers for the Dead in the Diocese of Lincoln in the Early Fourteenth Century', *Journal of Ecclesiastical History*, 52, 2 (2001), 219.

186 M. Aston, 'Death', in Horrox, *Fifteenth-Century Attitudes*, 204.

187 Note that while Marie-Hélène Rousseau remarks how, after 1349, services at St Paul's Cathedral, London, became 'more elaborate', she does not elucidate the point further: Rousseau, *Saving the Souls of Medieval London*, 169.

Certainly, Rosemary Horrox has identified how the fear of contagion led people to abandon the sick, leaving them to die alone, whilst others refused to carry the bodies of relatives.[188] Were these attitudes reflected in services?

One obvious impact of subsequent bouts of plague was depopulation, which served to undermine the stability of the city's rental market and, as a consequence, the basis upon which perpetual chantries were founded. This was true of the 1360s, when no foundations were made, and the 1420s and 1430s, when rental arrears reached their nadir, as migration into Lincoln, like that to many other towns, stalled.[189] Demographic problems were, of course, exacerbated by human agency, and the refusal of successive bishops to enrol the *Effrenata* failed to halt the rise in chaplains' wages, which eventually saw chantry expenses outstrip revenues. Although efforts were made wherever possible to address these problems, with founders and ancestors alienating additional lands and properties to chantries in the hope of prolonging their existence, such attempts were made all the more difficult by the crown's decision to increase the costs of acquiring a licence from the turn of the fifteenth century, thereby placing additional pressures on already stretched resources. Eventually these issues became insurmountable, resulting in the stagnation of lay perpetual foundations by c.1400, after which date only five further perpetual chantries were established by the laity, four of which contravened the Statute of Mortmain. This is not to say that interest in perpetual institutions had waned; only that during the fifteenth century bequests were more frequently made to 'augment existing chantries than to create new ones', as was the case at York.[190]

Of the founders, it is clear that social status and wealth were key determinants in the growth and proliferation of temporary and perpetual chantries, though social status, in particular access to civic office, saw the more expensive and prestigious foundations reserved for a small but select group of individuals. Overall there was a sliding scale of foundations associated with different gradations of the social ladder, all of which was bound to the availability of lands and properties. It might even be said that the 'chantry founding class' was arguably synonymous with the 'property holding class'. Even so, it is important to remember that not all wealthy testators sought to make such foundations, with some placing greater emphasis on the wellbeing of their families. Although there is little surviving evidence for Lincoln of temporary chantries being founded by monetary bequests alone, they were undoubtedly more widespread than identified here. Taken together, the evidence for Lincoln, therefore, lends support to Dobson's assertion that chantries were the 'most widespread institutional expression of late medieval society's most personal religious

188 Horrox, 'Purgatory, prayer and plague', in P. C. Jupp and C. Gittings, *Death in England: An Illustrated History* (Manchester, 1999), 97–8, 102.

189 Britnell, *Colchester*, 86–97, 193–205. Such problems were equally true of rural areas: R. H. Britnell, 'The East Midlands', in J. Thirsk (ed.), *The Agrarian History of England and Wales*, vol. 3: 1348–1500 (Cambridge, 2011), 619.

190 Quoted in Dobson, 'Citizens and Chantries', 328, n. 51. Note that virtually no evidence for Lincoln's lay-founded chantries in the fifteenth century survives. See appendix 5. For the civic management of chantries in the sixteenth century, however: *Historical MSS*, 24, 26–8, 30–2, 34.

aspirations'.[191] Not only did this benefit the churches they patronised and the laity who attended them, but it reflected the social status and standing of the founder, his family and friends. As the chantry of Thomas de Carleton demonstrates, chantries were occasionally used as political symbols representing powerful cliques, whilst others, such as that established by Robert de Hodelston, were seen as beacons of civic power and authority. Nowhere is this symbolic power made clearer than in the fact that a third of all the city's lay-founded perpetual chantries (and a fifth of all temporary chantries) were established in the parishes located around the Stonebow where the guildhall was situated, thus establishing a tangible link in the minds of the city's inhabitants between wealth, civic office and institutionalised piety.[192]

191 Dobson, 'Citizens and Chantries', 312.

192 For similar developments at London and York, see A. K. McHardy, 'Ecclesiastics and Economics: Poor Priests, Prosperous Laymen, and Proud Prelates in the Reign of Richard II', in W. J. Sheils and D. Wood (eds), *The Church and Wealth* (Oxford, 1987), 136; Dobson, 'Citizens and Chantries', 321–2.

Conclusion

When, during the reign of Richard III, the civic government of Lincoln complained that the 'decay and dystruccion of youre seyd pore Cite', which in 'aunciaunt tyme' had been frequented by 'Merchantez' who 'bought, and bartered wythin the seyd Cite with cloth, whereupon … [there] usede [to be] grete cloth makyng, and the people putt in occupation, wherby many … placez were inhabett that is nowe playne felde …', they did a great disservice to their institutional forbears.[1] Whilst it remained true that by this period the city had fewer inhabitants than in times past due to successive bouts of plague, the petition nevertheless glossed over the efforts of preceding generations to provide solutions to the decline of the once dominant textile industry. In particular, following its initial contraction in the thirteenth century, the city quickly established itself as a major centre for the wool trade, while after its re-emergence and subsequent decline in the second half of the fourteenth century, Lincoln saw commensurate growth in the service and agricultural sectors. Of course, it is to be remembered that the supplicatory tone and exaggerated nature of petitions such as this were intentional, and it would be egregious to suggest that the civic authorities were not unaware of these developments when they drafted the petition.[2] Certainly, as the evidence for the later fourteenth century indicates, the local civic authorities were highly sensitive to changes in local and national politics. Considered in this way, this episode serves as a useful analogy for reviewing the two main conclusions of this study.

The first is that the relationship between royal towns and the crown remains central not only for understanding how local attitudes towards power and authority were defined but for exploring the social and economic experiences of individual towns more generally.[3] The clearest illustration of this is the restitution of Lincoln's civil liberties in 1299, which set the tone for many of the developments of the following century. Not only did the intervention of the crown prompt the introduction of new rules for governing the town but it provided a solid platform for 'new

1 *Historical MSS*, 263–5.

2 Reynolds, 'Decline and Decay in Late Medieval Towns', 76–8.

3 For more on this relationship, see Rigby and Ewan, 'Government, Power and Authority', 291–312.

men' to emerge, many of whom, unburdened by the political follies of the recent past, held links to the growing indigenous wool trade. In turn this led to the adoption of a more robust civic administration designed to minimise the influence of groups or cliques, all the while providing a basis for a flourishing mercantile identity. Over time this came to be reflected by the residential pattern of civic officials and the patronage of local religious institutions, all of which served to establish a civic centre of benefaction and piety largely free of ecclesiastical influence, and to draw where possible tangible links between civic government and orthodoxy.

Royal policy also fuelled the local manufacture of arms for war on a scale unseen in many other smaller towns, whilst the ever-expanding royal administration prompted the growth of an important parchment industry in the city; developments linked to the availability of local resources. The business of the county and staple courts likewise brought thousands of visitors to the city annually, many of whom required food and lodging, providing an additional stimulus to the city's expanding service industry and underscoring Lincoln's status as a provincial town. The hand of the crown was also felt in the licensing of chantries and in the posthumous recording of guild ordinances. The tenor of the latter in particular was influenced greatly by the ongoing disagreement between the civic government and the crown over its fee farm payment which became overburdened in the 1380s. In terms of trade, too, the crown's influence was significant, and its decision to raise taxes on wool in the 1330s priced many local merchants out of the industry, whilst its demand for grains and other foodstuffs led to the city becoming the most important inland collection point in the county.

Whilst it is clear that much of Lincoln's economy was geared towards providing for the needs of the crown, there was nevertheless a high degree of autonomy inherent in the decisions made by individuals and civic government alike; as Christian Liddy points out, it was a widely held belief during the later Middle Ages that the relationship between crown and town should be 'broadly collaborative and consensual'.[4] Considered so, it is important that the aforementioned developments are not seen solely as a product of obligation and duty but as mutually advantageous. This stands in accord with the broader conclusions of Gerald Harriss who highlights the collaborative methods of the English state throughout the later Middle Ages as a means to develop an effective political society.[5] It was thus in the crown's interests for Lincoln to succeed; a stable and economically vibrant city benefitted the king in numerous ways, not least through loans and taxes, but equally through the manufacture of goods in times of war and peace and the maintenance of law and order.

From a local perspective, by aligning Lincoln's economic interests with those of the crown, civic leaders were not only able to provide jobs for local inhabitants but could reap great financial rewards, all of which justified their ability to rule in the king's name whilst minimising competition for authority. Whilst this approach to governance was not without its problems, least of all too much interference,[6] it

4 Liddy, *War, Politics and Finance*, 214.

5 G. Harriss, 'Political Society and the Growth of Government in Late Medieval England', *Past and Present*, 138 (1993): 28–57.

6 See 163.

nevertheless allowed a functional and interdependent civic 'community' to emerge. By identifying crown/town relations in a more organic and pervasive way than previous works, this study has sought to move the debate away from the language of dependency and ritualised performance so readily identified for towns after 1350.[7] As such, the full extent of these links can only be realised through a systematic analysis of central government records, which remain the primary source for reconstructing the city's later medieval history. Although this approach admittedly often lacks the detail of local records, it nevertheless demonstrates that for centres such as Lincoln, for which only a handful of civic records survive, individual histories are recoverable and can add nuance to our existing knowledge of the fortunes and functions of later medieval towns.

The second conclusion of this study has been to challenge the assumption that the Black Death was a major turning point in the fortunes of all late medieval English towns. Certainly, despite the severe loss of life brought about by the initial outbreak of plague, it does not appear to have induced any major changes to local pious and religious practices in the city. For example, whilst it is true that there was a rise in the number of chantries being established throughout the 1350s, this was temporary, with foundations returning to pre-plague levels by the early 1360s. Likewise, although greater onus was placed on members to play a greater role in the fraternal affairs of guilds established after 1349, foundations nevertheless continued at a similar pace to that of the two decades prior to the outbreak of plague, suggesting that famine and recession were equally important factors in the development of fraternal practices in the city. Certainly by the 1330s it is clear that the foundation of guilds was shaped primarily by a contemporary understanding and awareness of religious spaces, which, under the guidance of municipal government, limited the proliferation of these institutions according to the needs and uses of the civic community. The issue of space was equally pressing for chantry foundations, though broadly speaking these also reflected individual concerns, in particular wealth and status. The evidence put forward here therefore differs in many respects from that recorded for towns such as Norwich, Bristol, Lynn, London and York, which saw varying degrees of pious growth in the post-plague period. Nevertheless, few of these studies tackle head on the issue of undated guild certificates or concepts of religious space in the systematic manner adopted here, both of which remain central to understanding the broader trends of piety and commemoration in later medieval England.

A similar story emerges for Lincoln's trade, which saw the burgeoning cloth and wool industries draw merchants and traders to the city in greater numbers than at any time since the turn of the fourteenth century. This is seen in the rise in the value and number of certificates enrolled before the Statute Staple court during the 1350s and 1360s, but equally through the volume of cloth being exported to the continent. In terms of the civic administration, too, little changed after 1349 and the introduction of a single mayoral term at the turn of the century ensured that no great

7 Carrel, 'The Rituals of Town–Crown Relations', 148–64; L. Attreed, 'The Politics of Welcome: Ceremonies and Constitutional Development in Later Medieval Towns', in Hanawalt and Reyerson, *City and Spectacle*, 208-31.

power vacuum emerged as a result of plague, whilst the rotating offices of mayor and bailiff likewise ensured that the offices were subject to little adverse effect. Although the introduction of attorneys into the civic administration was accelerated by the declining number of officials available to serve after 1349, this predated the onset of plague. Finally, the crisis of the plague years did not stop the civic government from reintroducing the practice of recording the names of its members in the margins of the *Blickling Homilies* as a form of civic posterity, though once again this was not a new practice: it dated to the reforms of the early fourteenth century following the restitution of civil liberties in 1299. These were conscious collective decisions made by civic officials which ensured the smooth running of government even in the most difficult of times.

Despite the limited impact of the Black Death upon local customs and practices, over time the declining population nevertheless began to have an adverse effect on Lincoln's institutions and trade, much like in many other European towns. In particular, the decision of Lincoln's merchants to prioritise the wool trade over and above cloth manufacture was undoubtedly a miscalculation, as exports of the former dwindled in the opening decades of the fifteenth century, with the latter growing commensurately in its stead. The buoyant market for high quality Lindsey wool on a domestic scale never adequately filled the void, with Lincoln losing its status as the main centre of credit in the Midlands to Coventry by the end of the fourteenth century. Lincoln also began to suffer an acute shortage of migrants by the 1420s and 1430s, at much the same time as Boston, Canterbury, Newcastle and Oxford, with many properties decreasing in value or becoming vacant altogether.[8] This points to a general level of decay in towns across much of England, suggesting that Lincoln's experience was certainly no worse than many other urban centres during this period. The impact of this was particularly marked for guilds and chantries, which began to complain of financial difficulties. Taken collectively, it is thus clear that the claims of poverty by the civic government at the turn of the fifteenth century were both exaggerated and politically motivated, a view supported by the fact that during the 1390s the guildhall was rebuilt and the stipend of the mayor and his retinue of staff stood at a fifth of all incoming revenues, hardly the actions of a bankrupt institution. Even so, the problems of English towns were increasing with worse still to come,[9] though the response of the crown and civic government was typically bullish. In 1409, for example, Lincoln was granted urban county status, which bestowed upon the city new powers, revenues and rights of jurisdiction, whilst in 1423 it was named as only one of seven assay towns, highlighting its importance to local manufacture. In the 1430s, too, Lincoln's civic government acquired new methods for raising civic receipts, including the right to export wool tax free, whilst the crown acknowledged and relieved the city of its unfair tax burdens, all of which is testament to the fact that Lincoln's officials fought hard to keep the decline so readily attributed to the cloth industry by their institutional ancestors at bay.

8 Butcher, 'Urban Economy', 42-3; *idem*, 'Economic Change', 75; Rigby, 'Medieval Boston', 16.
9 Hatcher, 'The Great Slump of the Mid-fifteenth Century', 237–72.

Appendix 1

Occupational Sources and Data

The following sources have been analysed to establish Lincoln's occupational profile according to the methodology set down in chapter one.[1] Efforts have been made where possible to provide fair yet comprehensive coverage of each of the four periods reviewed (1289–1319, 1320–49, 1350–79, 1380–1409), though there is an element of bias towards the earlier period, with 952 individuals being noted before 1349 and only 715 after. One source which could have redressed this shortfall but which is not used here is the fragmented Poll Tax of 1377.[2] The reason for its omission relates to the fact that it records the occupations of only a third of all taxpayers (77 of 305), all of whom are named as servants (*famula*). Whilst it is clear that this was a deliberate distinction on the part of the tax assessors, it is nevertheless too biased in favour of this particular group to be included here.

Manuscript Sources

Accounts of Robert le Venur and William Cause (covering the dates 1292/93, 1297/98);[3] two civic registers, the Burwarmote Book (1308–76) and the Blickling Homilies (c.1291–1409);[4] aulnage accounts (1398–1402);[5] civic gaol delivery rolls (1352–55, 1365–68, 1398, 1403);[6] civic deeds (1301, 1353);[7] charters and accounts of the Dean and Chapter (1289–1399);[8] coroners' rolls (1333–97);[9] the Welbeck Cartulary (1302–71);[10] parliamentary accounts (1301, 1305, 1316);[11] the accounts of Henry de

1 See 19–23 and table 2.
2 E 179/240/309. There are no surviving records for 1379 or 1381.
3 E 101/505/24, 28.
4 LCL MS169; Princeton University Library: Scheide Library M71.
5 E 101/339/29–30, E 101/340/2.
6 JUST 3/32/2, m. 42; JUST 3/137A, m. 9; JUST 3/140, m. 24; JUST 3/142, rots 37, 41, 46d–47; JUST 3/149, rot. 14d; JUST 3/177, rot. 102; JUST 3/188, *passim* between rots 100–49.
7 LAO FL/Lincoln St Marks Deeds.
8 LAO Dij and Bj series; *Liber de Ordinationibus Cantariarum*: LAO A/1/8.
9 JUST 2/64, rot. 10; JUST 2/67, rots 42–50d; JUST 2/80, rots 1–4; JUST 2/85, rot. 2; JUST 2/87, rots 1–3; JUST 2/93, rots 1–2, 4–5.
10 LAO MF/2/117.
11 E 101/359/30; E 101/367/10, 28–29. Note that not all accounts associated with the 1301 parliament are considered here as some deal exclusively with traders outside of Lincoln: E 101/568/4–6.

Lacy, earl of Lincoln, for Lincoln castle (1296);[12] the accounts of Hugh de Cressy, constable of Lincoln castle (c.1351);[13] exchequer accounts (1301, 1305);[14] records of the justices of the peace (1332–33, 1351–54, 1395–96);[15] the lay subsidies of 1327, 1332 and 1340;[16] certificates of the statute merchant/staple court (1290–1409);[17] inquisition *ad quod damnum* certificates;[18] and the records of the King's Bench (1331, 1333, 1367, 1374–77, 1395–96).[19]

Printed Primary Sources[20]

Thurgaton Cartulary (1290–1305);[21] patent, close, charter and fine rolls (1290–1409);[22] calendars of inquisitions miscellaneous and post-mortem (1290–1409);[23] ancient deeds (1290–1409);[24] sessions of the peace (1351–54, 1360–75, 1381–96);[25] the 1341 royal inquest;[26] the assize roll of 1298;[27] charters of the Dean and Chapter (1290–1320);[28] bishops' registers and excerpts of wills (1289–1409);[29] and the overseas accounts of Boston (1377–99).[30]

12 DL 29/1/1, m. 9d.
13 DL 29/3884/242.
14 E 101/332/11; E 101/699/23.
15 JUST 1/520, mm. 12d, 13, 14; JUST 1/523; JUST 1/528, mm. 15–15d; JUST 1/532, m. 5; JUST 1/533, m. 5.
16 E 179/135/12, 16, 26.
17 C 241 and C 131 series.
18 C 143 series.
19 KB 29/3, mm. 3d, 5d, 6d, 10, 60d; KB 29/4, m. 7; KB 29/22, m. 26; KB 29/28, mm. 30, 35; KB 29/30, m. 30; KB 29/41, m. 24.
20 For full references to these sources, see bibliography.
21 Foulds, *Thurgarton Cartulary*, 2 vols.
22 *Calendar of Charter Rolls, 1257–1414*; *Calendar of Close Rolls, 1288–1409*; *Calendar of Fine Rolls, 1272–1413*; *Calendar of Patent Rolls, 1281–1413*.
23 *Calendar of Inquisitions Miscellaneous*; *Calendar of Inquisitions Post Mortem*.
24 Maxwell-Lyte, *Catalogue of Ancient Deeds*, 6 vols.
25 Sillem, *Sessions of the Peace*; Kimball, *Sessions of the Peace in the City of Lincoln*; *idem*, *Some Sessions of the Peace in Lincolnshire*, 2 vols.
26 McLane, *1341 Royal Inquest*.
27 Thomson, *Lincolnshire Assize Roll*.
28 Only those *not* considered in manuscript form: Major, *Registrum Antiquissimum*, vols. 8–10.
29 Bennett, *Registers of Bishop Henry Burghersh*, 3 vols; Hill, *Bishop Oliver Sutton*, 8 vols; Gibbons, *Early Lincoln Wills*; Foster, *Lincoln Wills*.
30 Rigby, *Overseas Trade*.

Occupational Data: Full Breakdown

Agriculture	**1289–1319**	**1320–49**	**1350–79**	**1380–1409**
Basketmaker	1	2	1	2
Birdcatcher	1	–	–	–
Dyker	–	2	–	1
Farmer	2	–	–	–
Forester	–	–	–	2
Fowler	3	1	–	–
Herder/herdswoman	2	–	–	1
Huntsmen	–	–	1	–
Seeder	1	–	–	–
Shearer	–	–	1	–
Sheep-breeder	–	1	–	–
Shepherd	1	4	1	2
Tasker	–	1	2	3
Tiller	1	–	–	–
Turfleder	–	–	–	2
Workman	1	3	1	1
	13	**14**	**7**	**14**

Artisans	**1289–1319**	**1320–49**	**1350–79**	**1380–1409**
Archer	2	–	–	–
Botteler	1	–	–	–
Bower	3	12	10	10
Bowlmaker	1	–	–	–
Boxmaker	1	–	–	–
Cartwright	–	–	2	–
Carver	–	–	–	1
Cooper	2	2	1	3
Fletcher	–	4	2	–
Horner	3	–	–	–
Oiler/oilmaker	1	1	–	1
Parchment dealer/maker	5	5	1	2
Potter	3	–	–	3
Soper	2	–	–	–
	24	**24**	**14**	**20**

Building	**1289–1319**	**1320–49**	**1350–79**	**1380–1409**
Brickmaker/kilner	–	2	–	–
Carpenter	8	9	1	3
Glasswright	–	1	1	–
Glazier	2	4	–	1
Joiner	–	–	2	1
Mason	6	5	6	14
Painter	3	8	–	1

Plasterer	1	1	–	–
Pointer	1	–	–	4
Quarrier	–	1	–	2
Thatcher	–	–	–	1
Tiler	3	1	2	3
Wright	–	1	4	5
	24	**32**	**16**	**35**

Clothing: Leather and Fur	**1289–1319**	**1320–49**	**1350–79**	**1380–1409**
Bootmaker	–	–	1	–
Cordwainer	5	13	25	13
Currier	2	1	–	1
Glovemaker	8	3	1	1
Pelter	1	1	–	–
Pouchmaker	–	–	1	–
Saddler	–	11	11	6
Sheather	1	–	–	1
Skinner	5	12	17	5
Souter	–	3	1	–
Tanner	3	11	2	9
Tawyer	1	4	3	–
	26	**56**	**61**	**36**

Clothing: Textiles	**1289–1319**	**1320–49**	**1350–79**	**1380–1409**
Bocher	–	–	3	–
Cardemaker	–	–	1	–
Chaloner	1	–	–	–
Draper/mercer	4	12	10	10
Dyer	1	3	6	4
Embroider	1	–	–	1
Flyer	1	–	–	–
Fuller/walker	1	1	6	4
Girdler	4	–	–	–
Hair-cloth maker	1	–	–	–
Hatcher	–	–	1	–
Hatter	1	2	1	–
Lacemaker	1	–	–	–
Quilter	–	1	–	–
Seamster	2	–	–	–
Sewer	3	–	–	–
Sherman	2	2	2	1
Tailor	19	15	21	26
Upholder	–	1	–	–
Weaver	1	2	21	8
Woad-seller	2	2	–	–
Woolman	2	–	–	–

Woolpacker	–	1	–	1
Woolwinder	–	1	–	–
	47	**43**	**72**	**55**

Distribution	**1289–1319**	**1320–49**	**1350–79**	**1380–1409**
Chandler	5	4	2	1
Chapman	1	2	–	–
Grocer	–	–	3	–
Merchant	100	72	64	19
Wine merchant	1	–	–	3
Wool merchant	–	–	–	3
	107	**78**	**69**	**23**

Metal	**1289–1319**	**1320–49**	**1350–79**	**1380–1409**
Armourer	–	–	–	3
Bell-founder	1	1	1	–
Coppersmith	2	–	–	–
Cutler	2	4	–	1
Farrier	1	1	–	–
Furbour	3	5	1	1
Goldsmith	6	3	5	2
Ironmonger	4	2	1	1
Latoner	2	–	–	–
Lead-beater	1	–	–	–
Locksmith	2	–	1	–
Lorimer	1	–	1	–
Marshal	5	2	–	–
Pewterer	–	–	–	1
Plumber	1	2	–	–
Sealer	4	–	–	–
Shear grinder	1	–	–	–
Smith	7	2	4	6
Spurrier	–	–	–	2
	43	**22**	**14**	**17**

Professional/Administrative	**1289–1319**	**1320–49**	**1350–79**	**1380–1409**
Attorney	1	34	27	8
Bookbinder	1	1	–	–
Clerk	28	69	19	13
Illuminator	2	2	1	2
Notary	–	2	3	–
Physician/surgeon	2	1	1	–
Scribe	3	3	–	1
	37	**112**	**51**	**24**

Service	**1289–1319**	**1320–49**	**1350–79**	**1380–1409**
Apprentice	–	1	–	1
Barber	8	7	4	10
Boatman/shipman/sailor	2	9	9	2
Carter	4	1	2	2
Cellarer	–	4	–	–
Clarion player	1	–	–	–
Cryer	–	1	–	–
Falconer	3	–	–	–
Fiddler	–	1	–	–
Groom	–	1	1	–
Handmaid	1	1	–	–
Hangman	1	–	1	–
Harpist	2	–	–	–
Horse-keeper	1	2	–	–
Jongleur	1	–	–	–
Lavender/laundress	2	–	–	–
Lecher	–	1	–	–
Lute player	–	1	–	–
Messenger	1	–	1	–
Minstrel	–	–	2	–
Nurse/midwife	3	–	–	–
Organ player	1	–	–	–
Packer	–	2	–	–
Piper	–	–	–	1
Porter	–	2	2	1
Rent gatherer	–	1	–	–
Scullion	–	1	–	–
Servant	4	18	1	31
Shield bearer	–	1	–	–
Shipwright	1	–	–	–
Soldier	–	–	–	2
Squire	–	1	–	–
Stacker	–	1	–	–
Summoner	5	2	–	–
Taverner/hosteller	6	5	2	2
Toller	2	–	–	–
Warder	2	–	–	–
	51	**64**	**46**	**52**

Victualling	**1289–1319**	**1320–49**	**1350–79**	**1380–1409**
Apothecary/spicer	7	8	7	2
Baker	14	12	11	4
Brewer	5	3	–	–
Butcher	4	7	10	6
Cheesemaker	2	–	–	–

Cook	4	3	2	3
Fisherman/fishmonger	10	17	11	14
Flanner	3	1	–	–
Fruiterer	1	–	–	–
Fleshewer	–	–	3	–
Food seller	4	–	–	–
Huckster	1	–	–	–
Miller	10	2	3	3
Mustarder	3	–	–	–
Panner	1	–	–	–
Poulter	1	2	1	–
Salter	2	1	–	–
Saucer	–	2	1	–
Tapster	–	1	1	–
Tester	1	–	–	–
Victualler	–	1	–	–
Vintner	2	–	4	1
	75	**60**	**54**	**33**
Totals	**447**	**505**	**405**	**309**

Appendix 2

Lincoln Civic Officials, 1289–1409

Key: † = mayors who did not hold the position of bailiff or coroner prior to their elevation; * = died in 1349. All documents marked Dij are held at Lincoln Archive Office. References to civic office are capped at two per individual; additional references in brackets relate to their occupation if not noted previously. Abbreviated occupations relate to earlier entries where full references are provided. These are att. (attorney), ba. (barber), bar. (barker), bm. (bottle maker), bow. (bower), ch. (chandler), cl. (clerk), drap. (draper), fish. (fisher/fishmonger), ful. (fuller), ir. (ironmonger), li. (litster), mer. (merchant), merc. (mercer), pa. (parchment dealer), po. (porter), sh. (shipman), sk. (skinner), sp. (spicer), wm. (wine merchant). Note that only where omissions are noted is Hill, 'Three Lists', 217–56, used.

Year	**Name**	**Position**	**Occ.**	**Reference(s)**
Easter 1289[1]	*City taken into king's hands*			E 159/63, rot. 2
July 1289	Robert de Chaddeworth[2]	*Custos*	sheriff	C 241/9/122; *Liber Cant.*, no. 613
May 1290/ Sept 1291	Robert le Venur	*Custos*	wine merchant	E 368/61, rot. 14d; Dij 74/2/26 (E 372/135, rot. 17d)
	Alexander s. John s. Martin	bailiff	merchant	Dij 74/2/26 (C 241/56/145, C 241/56/250)
	Adam Cokerel [Kokerel]	bailiff	–	Dij 74/2/26
1291/92	Robert le Venur	*Custos*	wm.	Dij 76/1/41
	John Amesas	bailiff	–	Dij 76/1/41
	John Skinner	bailiff	–	Dij 76/1/41
1292/93	Robert le Venur	*Custos*	wm.	Dij 75/1/13–15; 77/1/44
	William de Paris	bailiff	–	Dij 75/1/13–15; 77/1/44
	Robert ad Fontem [Attewell]	bailiff	–	Dij 75/1/13–15; 77/1/44
1293/94	Robert le Venur	*Custos*	wm.	Dij 76/2/33

1 10 April.

2 *Alias* Shadworth.

or 1294/5[3]	Hugh s. Adam	bailiff	fisher	Dij 76/2/33 (*Liber Cant.*, no. 1173)
	Robert of Binnington	bailiff	–	Dij 76/2/33
1295/96	Robert le Venur	*Custos*	wm.	LCL VC 2/1/252; C 241/82/205
	John Pynell	bailiff	–	LCL VC 2/1/252; Dij 82/1/36
	Jacob Berne[4]	bailiff	merchant	LCL VC 2/1/252; Dij 82/1/36 (*CPR, 1313–17*, 189)
1296/97[5]	Robert le Venur	*Custos*	wm.	Dij 80/3/71
	Nicholas le Grange	bailiff	–	Dij 81/1/42; 80/3/71
	Ralph de Filyngham	bailiff	merchant	Dij 81/1/42; 80/3/71 (KB 27/185, m. 34)
1297/98[6]	William Cause	*Custos*	merchant	E 368/69, rot. 6; Dij 74/2/52 (*CPR, 1313–17*, 189)
	Walter Bayhous	bailiff	merchant	Dij 74/2/52 (*CCR, 1313–18*, 81; *CPR, 1313–17*, 189)
	John Rothinger	bailiff	–	Dij 74/2/52
1298/99	William Cause	*Custos*	mer.	Dij 75/2/25
	John de Normanton	bailiff	merchant	Dij 75/2/25 (C 241/79/110)
	Ralph Russell	bailiff	merchant	Dij 75/2/25 (C 241/79/252)
	Thomas Gamel	bailiff	–	KB 27/164, m. 26
1299/1300	William Cause	mayor	mer.	E 372/146, rot. 15d; Dij 74/2/18
	John de Blyton (senior)	bailiff	merchant	Dij 74/2/18 (*CCR, 1302–07*, 22–3)
	John ad Fontem	bailiff	–	Dij 74/2/18
1300/1	William Cause	mayor	mer.	E 372/146, rots 10–10d; Dij 76/1/34[7]
	Stephen de Stanham	bailiff	merchant	Dij 76/1/34[8] (*CPR, 1307–13*, 36; C 241/34/226, 228–9)
	John de Balliolo	bailiff	–	Dij 76/1/34[9]
1301 (Jan)[10]	Stephen de Stanham	mayor	mer.	Dij 82/1/28

3 No exact date can be given for these officials. Consequently it leaves one year under the wardenship of Venur without any details. This stands in accord with *Reg. Antiq.* 8, 209.
4 *Alias* James Grene.
5 It is possible to date Cause from the evidence of Grange and Filyngham: Dij 81/1/42.
6 Beginning on 26 December 1297: E 368/69, rot. 6.
7 The latter is undated.
8 Undated.
9 Undated.
10 Noted as mayor as early as 29 January 1301: A. Beardwood (ed.), *Records of the Trial of Walter Langeton, Bishop of Coventry and Lichfield, 1307–1312* (London, 1969), 149.

	Henry de Bere	bailiff	merchant	Dij 82/1/28 (C 241/61/85)
	John de Amecotes	bailiff	merchant	Dij 82/1/28; E 372/146, rot. 15 (C 241/79/110)
1301/02	Stephen de Stanham	mayor	mer.	Dij 76/2/44; E 372/147, rot. 12
	Simon Edlington	bailiff	merchant	Dij 76/2/44 (*CCR, 1318–23*, 412)
	John de Horspaye [Horton]	bailiff	–	Dij 76/2/44
1302/03	Stephen de Stanham	mayor	mer.	Dij 75/1/18
	Hugh Thorn	bailiff	merchant	Dij 75/1/18; SC 8/9/416 (*CPR, 1292–1301*, 310)
	Richard of Searby [Severby]	bailiff	merchant	Dij 75/1/18; SC 8/9/416 (KB 27/185, m. 34)
1303/04	Stephen de Stanham	mayor	mer.	Dij 79/2/2; LCL VC 2/1/232
	John de Hadington [Lindington]	bailiff	–	Dij 79/2/2; LCL VC 2/1/232
	Gilbert de Adherby [Atherby]	bailiff	merchant/ fisher	Dij 79/2/2; LCL VC 2/1/232 (*CPR, 1313–17*, 189; Dij 77/1/28)
	Alexander FitzMartin	bailiff	merchant	LCL LCL VC 2/1/232 (C 241/35/326)
	Osbert Long	bailiff	–	LCL LCL VC 2/1/232
1304/05	Stephen de Stanham	mayor	mer.	Dij 74/1/7; 80/3/36
	Gilbert Rodyng	bailiff	–	Dij 74/1/7; 75/1/37
	Geoffrey de Lynn	bailiff	merchant	Dij 74/1/7; 75/1/37 (C 241/82/63)
1305/06	Stephen de Stanham	mayor	mer.	Dij 80/3/34
	Alexander FitzMartin[11]	bailiff	mer.	Dij 77/2/51
	Roger le Copper	bailiff	merchant	Dij 77/2/51; 80/3/34 (C 241/105/142)
	Robert of Oxford [Oxenford]	bailiff	parchment dealer/ merchant	Dij 77/2/51; 80/3/34 (E 101/699/23; E 101/332/11)
1306/07	Alexander FitzMartin	mayor	mer.	Dij 74/2/50; 80/3/2; *CCR, 1302–07*, 485
	John Kempe	bailiff	–	*Ancient Deeds*, vol. 6, 39, no. 4089; Dij 80/3/2

11 Alexander FitzMartin was not the mayor in this year as suggested by Kathleen Major (*Reg. Antiq.*, vol. 8, 209): evidence for this comes from the fact that Dij 77/2/51 records three bailiffs (not the more typical mayor and two bailiffs), which stands in contrast to Dij 80/3/34, which clearly records Stanham as mayor in October 1305.

	Nigel Sistrik	bailiff	–	*Ancient Deeds*, vol. 6, 39, no. 4089; Dij 80/3/2
1307/08	John de Bliton, senior	mayor	mer.	Dij 79/2/20; C 241/76/307
	John le Blake [Noyr]	bailiff	merchant	Dij 79/2/20 (C 241/63/152)
	Gilbert de Leycestre	bailiff	merchant/ clerk	Dij 79/2/20 (Dij 77/1/32; SC 8/71/3518–19)
1308/09	John de Amecotes	mayor	mer.	*BB*, fo. 199; Dij 74/2/51[12]
	Richard Blakdene	bailiff	merchant	*BB*, fo. 199 (*CPR, 1313–17*, 189)
	Walter de Mumby	bailiff	–	*BB*, fo. 199
1309/10	Gilbert le Noir [Blake]†	mayor	merchant	Dij 74/3/14; 77/2/49–50 (*CPR, 1313–17*, 189)
	John de Newcastle[13]	bailiff	ironmonger /merchant	Dij 74/3/14; 77/2/49–50 (*CPR, 1313–17*, 189; *BB*, fo. 78)
	Geoffrey de Kew [Kelworth]	bailiff	–	Dij 74/3/14; 77/2/49–50
1310/11	Alexander FitzMartin	mayor	mer.	Dij 74/3/12;[14] *BH*, fo. 5v
	William de Brayland	bailiff	merchant	Dij 74/3/12 (C 241/40/72)
	Thomas Fayrinou	bailiff	–	Dij 74/3/12
1311/12	Osbert le Lung	mayor	–	Dij 74/2/48; 75/2/18
	Adam de Hibaldstowe	bailiff	merchant	Dij 74/2/48; 75/2/18 (C 241/82/63)
	Hugh Bacon	bailiff	merchant	Dij 74/2/48; 75/2/18; E 372/157, rot. 20 (C 241/82/63)
1312/13	Stephen de Stanham	mayor	mer.	Dij 79/3/89; 82/2/125; *BH*, fo. 4
	David le Tauerner	bailiff	merchant	E 372/158, rot. 13; Dij 79/2/1 (*CPR, 1313–17*, 189)
	Henry de Outhorp	bailiff	clerk/ illuminator	E 372/158, rot. 13; Dij 79/3/89 (C 241/79/252; Dij 79/2/1)
1313/14	Henry Bere	mayor	mer.	*BB*, fo. 75; Dij 79/3/85 (*CPR, 1313–17*, 189; KB 27/185, m. 34)
	Robert de Bardenay	bailiff	–	*BB*, fo. 75; Dij 79/3/85
	John Baron [Barum]	bailiff	–	*BB*, fo. 75; Dij 79/3/85

12 Both Mumby and Blakdene are noted in the charter but not in an official capacity.

13 *Alias* John le Ironmonger.

14 The charter noted in Hill for this year (Dij 75/2/24) is incorrect; he actually means Dij 75/2/26 in which all three officials are noted: *Medieval Lincoln*, 384.

1314/15	Simon de Edelington	mayor	merchant	*BB*, fo. 75v; Dij 81/1/44 (*CPR, 1313–17*, 189)
	John Pinson	bailiff	merchant	*BB*, fo. 75v; Dij 81/1/44 (C 241/82/63)
	Hugh Russell	bailiff	merchant	*BB*, fo. 75v; Dij 81/1/44 (C 241/79/252)
1315/16	John de Blyton, senior	mayor	mer.	Dij 76/1/42; 76/3/33
	John de Leycestre*	bailiff	currier	Dij 76/1/42; 76/3/33 (*BB*, fos 115, 193.)
	Hugh de Edlington, senior	bailiff	merchant	Dij 76/1/42; 76/3/33 (C 241/95/12)
1316/17	Gilbert Atherby	mayor	merchant	*BB*, fo. 77v; Dij 75/3/19 (*CPR, 1313–17*, 189)
	Walter de Ebor [York]	bailiff	merchant	*BB*, fo. 77v; Dij 76/1/35 (*CCR, 1313–18*, 81)
	Walter Bayous	bailiff	mer.	Dij 75/3/19
	Hugh Bacon	bailiff	mer.	Dij 76/1/35
1317/18	John Pinson	mayor	mer.	*BB*, fo. 80v; Dij 74/1/26
	John de Tame	bailiff	–	*BB*, fo. 80v; Dij 74/1/26
	Hugh Tyeghler [Tiler]	bailiff	merchant	*BB*, fo. 80v; Dij 74/1/26 (C 241/82/63)
	Richard Cockrell	bailiff	–	*BB*, fo. 78
1318/19	Robert of Bardeney	mayor	–	Coram Rege Roll, no. 240, Easter 1320, m. 88
	Henry le Lavender	bailiff	merchant/ lavender	Coram Rege Roll, no. 240, Easter 1320, m. 88; JUST 1/520, mm. 12d, 14 (C 241/79/252)
	Richard Petit	bailiff	fisher	Coram Rege Roll, no. 240, Easter 1320, m. 88; JUST 1/520, mm. 12d, 14 (*BB*, fo. 106)
	William Claword	bailiff	–	JUST 1/520, m. 14
1319/20	Hugh Russell	mayor	mer.	Dij 76/1/38; Dij 77/1/43
	Robert Hare	bailiff	bower/ merchant	Dij 76/1/38; Dij 77/1/43 (JUST 1/520, m. 12d; C 241/135/144)
	William Rivet [Ryvet]	bailiff	–	Dij 76/1/38; Dij 77/1/43
1320/21	Richard de Blakdene	mayor	mer.	*BB*, fo. 85; Dij 82/1/17
	Henry Stoile [Stoyle]	bailiff	merchant	*BB*, fo. 85; Dij 82/1/17 (C 241/79/252)
	Adam de Misne	bailiff	salter/ merchant	*BB*, fo. 85; LCL VC 2/1/337 (Dij 82/1/17; *BB*, fo. 78; *CPR, 1313–17*, 189)

1321/22	John de Newcastle	mayor	ir./mer.	*BB*, fo. 89; *BH*, fo. 81v
	Elias de Stubton	bailiff	merchant	*BB*, fo. 89; LCL VC 2/1/261 (SC 8/235/11715)
	Thomas de Kele	bailiff	fisher/ porter	*BB*, fo. 89; LCL VC 2/1/261 *BB*, fo. 176v; E179/135/26, m. 2; BH, f. 59v)
1322/23[15]	Hugh de Edlington, senior[16]	mayor	mer.	*BB*, fo. 93; Dij 82/1/61
	John Ferrar (April–)†	mayor	smith	LCL VC 2/1/351
	William de Snartford	bailiff	merchant	*BB*, fo. 93; Dij 82/1/61 (*CCR, 1339–41*, 177–8)
	Henry de Severby	bailiff	merchant	*BB*, fo. 93; Dij 82/1/61 (C 241/80/221; C 241/82/63)
	John de Thragelthorp	bailiff	merchant	*BB*, fo. 95 (*CCR, 1339–41*, 53)
	William de Hacthorn	coroner	merchant	*BB*, fo. 93 (C 241/82/63)
	John de Thornhagh	coroner	merchant	*BH*, fo. 87v (C 241/82/35, 37)
	William de Hekyngton	coroner	–	*BH*, fo. 87v
1323/24	John de Tame [Thame]	mayor	–	*BB*, fo. 97; *BH*, fo. 65v
	Hamo le Permouner	bailiff	skinner	*BB*, fo. 97; Dij 74/2/39
	Roger de Dalderby	bailiff	merchant	*BB*, fo. 97; Dij 74/2/39 (*CCR, 1339–41*, 52)
	Simon de Ernburgh	bailiff	–	*BB*, fo. 98
1324/25	William de Snartford	mayor	mer.	Dij 77/1/37
	Henry atte Sudeness	bailiff	–	Dij 77/1/37
	Geoffrey de Frothyngham	bailiff	–	Dij 77/1/37
1325/26	Robert de Oxonford	mayor	pa./mer.	Dij 77/2/7, 82/2/124
	William de Blyton	bailiff	merchant	Dij 77/2/7; 82/2/124 (C 241/110/236; C 241/115/331)
	Ralph de Burton	bailiff	–	Dij 77/2/7; *BH*, fo. 68v
	Reginald Cherman	bailiff	–	Dij 82/2/124
1326/27	Hugh de Tyler	mayor	mer.	Dij 80/1/161; *BH*, fo. 50v
	John de Mumby	bailiff	merchant	Dij 80/1/161; *BH*, fo. 50v (KB 27/185, m. 34)
	William de Humberstan	bailiff	attorney	Dij 80/1/161; *BH*, fos 50v, 57v (*BH*, fo. 44v)
	Henry atte Sudeness	coroner	–	*BH*, fo. 50v
	William de Hakthorn	coroner	mer.	*BH*, fo. 50v
	Richard Longes/Lunges	coroner	–	*BH*, fo. 50v

15 Note that the coroners John de Thornhagh and William de Heckyngton were noted as having been (*fuerunt*) previously in office; exactly when this related to is not clear: *BH*, fo. 87v.

16 Edlington died in office no later than April 1323, hence Ferrar's appointment. See SC 6/913/1 for an inquest into his lands in the city.

1327/28	William de Blyton	mayor	mer.	*BB*, fo. 105; Dij 74/2/20
	Hugh de Edelington, junior[17]	bailiff	merchant	*BB*, fo. 105; Dij 74/2/20 (*CCR, 1333–37*, 60)
	Thomas de Bellafago[18]	bailiff	–	*BB*, fo. 105; Dij 74/2/20
	John de Willingham	bailiff	–	*BB*, fo. 104v
	Richard FitzMartin	coroner	–	*BH*, fo. 46v
1328/29	Thomas de Kele	mayor	fish./po.	*BB*, fo. 110; Dij 77/1/25
	Thomas Russell	bailiff	merchant	*BB*, fo. 110; Dij 77/1/25 (C 241/82/63)
	Robert Hare [Herre][19]	bailiff	bow./mer.	*BB*, fo. 110; Dij 77/1/25
	Henry Kemp	bailiff	draper	*BB*, fo. 111v (*BB*, fo. 122v)
	Richard FitzMartin	coroner	–	*BB*, fo. 115v
1329/30	Ralph de Burton	mayor	–	*BB*, fo. 117v; Dij 82/2/96
	John de Blyton, junior	bailiff	merchant	*BB*, fo. 117v; Dij 82/2/96 (C 241/103/144)
	Richard de Kele	bailiff	fisher/ merchant	Dij 82/2/96; E 372/175 rot. 36 (*CCR, 1349–54*, 7; KB 27/540, m. 45)
	Richard Lunges	coroner	–	*BB*, fo. 119; KB 29/3, m. 11d
	William de Hacthorne	coroner	mer.	*BB*, fo. 119
1330/31	Robert de Bellafago [Beafou]	mayor	–	*BB*, fos 124v, 127; Dij 74/2/22
	John de Bristall	bailiff	litster (dyer)	*BB*, fos 124v, 127; Dij 74/2/22 (Dij 74/2/6)
	Robert Quarrell	bailiff	merchant	*BB*, fos 124v, 127; Dij 74/2/22 (C 241/106/249)
	Richard Lungus	coroner	–	*BB*, fos 124v, 127
	William de Hackthorne	coroner	mer.	*BB*, fo. 124v
	Richard FitzMartin	coroner	–	*BH*, fo. 21v
	Thomas le Boteler[20]	coroner	bottle maker?	*BH*, fo. 21v (C 241/108/108)
1331/32	Richard de Kele	mayor	fis./mer.	Dij 76/1/33; *BH*, fo. 48v
	Robert de Welton	bailiff	merchant	Dij 76/1/33; *BH*, fo. 48v (*CCR, 1339–41*, 52)
	Ralph Jolyff*	bailiff	merchant	Dij 76/1/33; *BH*, fo. 48v (*CPR, 1345–48*, 541)
1332/33	Hugh de Edlington, junior	mayor	mer.	Dij 76/1/39; 77/2/1

17 Also identified as Hugh de Belyngton: *LW*, 7.

18 Identified as Robert de Beufou/Beaufou in JUST 1/516, m. 8, 26 and *LW*, 7.

19 This is not the same Robert Hare noted from 1353/54 onwards.

20 Boteler was also noted as the county coroner, though he was relieved of this position the following year: *CCR, 1330–33*, 371.

	Alan de Hodelston	bailiff	merchant	Dij 76/1/39; 77/2/1 (*CPR, 1317–21*, 205)
	Michael de Leicestre	bailiff	spicer	Dij 77/2/1, 76/1/39 (C 241/100/144)
1333/34	John de Blyton, junior	mayor	mer.	Dij 78/2/2; *BH*, fo. 45v
	Ralph de Kyme	bailiff	–	Dij 78/2/2; *BH*, fo. 45v
	Thomas de Hackthorn	bailiff	–	Dij 78/2/2; *BH*, fo. 45v
	Richard Long	coroner	–	KB 29/3. m. 60d
	William de Hakethe[21]	coroner	mer.	KB 29/3. m. 60d
	Richard FitzMartin	coroner	–	KB 29/3. m. 60d
	William Humberston, senior	coroner	att.	KB 29/3. m. 60d
1334/53	Henry de Lavender	mayor	mer.	*BB*, fo. 128v; Dij 75/2/12
	Richard de Ebor	bailiff	–	*BB*, fo. 128v; Dij 75/2/12
	Robert de Appilby	bailiff	mason	*BB*, fo. 128v; E 372/180 rot. 32d (Dij 77/1/38)
	Richard Lungus [Longes]	coroner	–	*BB*, fo. 128v; KB/29, m. 40
	William de Hackthorne	coroner	mer.	*BB*, fo. 128v
1335/36	Richard Lungus	mayor	–	*BB*, fo. 129v; *BH*, fo. 108v
	Henry de Filyngham	bailiff	merchant	*BB*, fo. 129v; *BH*, fo. 108v (*CCR, 1339–41*, 52)
	Robert de Hodilston	bailiff	–	*BB*, fo. 129v; *BH*, fo. 108v
	William de Hackthorne	coroner	mer.	*BB*, fo. 129v
	William de Humberstone, senior	coroner	att.	*BB*, fo. 129v
	Richard s/Adam s/Martin	coroner	–	*BB*, fo. 129v
1336/37	Robert Quarrell*	mayor	mer.	*BB*, fo. 133; Dij 75/2/19
	Adam Moysen	bailiff	merchant	*BB*, fo. 133; Dij 75/2/19 (*CCR, 1343–46*, 153)
	John le Mareschall*	bailiff	–	*BB*, fo. 133; Dij 75/2/19
	Richard Cockerell	bailiff	mer.	*BB*, fo. 136
	William de Hackethorn	coroner	mer.	*BB*, fo. 133
	Richard FitzMartin	coroner	–	*BB*, fo. 133
1337/38	William de Humberston	mayor	att.	*BB*, fo. 138v; Dij 77/1/31
	John de Askeby	bailiff	shipman	*BB*, fo. 138v; Dij 77/1/31 (*BB*, fos 232, 238v)
	John de Canewyke*	bailiff	merchant	*BB*, fo. 138v; Dij 77/1/31 (C 241/109/173)
	Walter de Launesdale	bailiff	–	*BB*, fos 139, 141

21 Presumably a variation of Hackthorne.

	William de Hackthorne	coroner	–	*BB*, fo. 138v; KB 29/4, m. 7
1338/39	John de Bristall	mayor	lit.	*BB*, fo. 141v
	Thomas Frere	bailiff	tanner	*BB*, fo. 141v, 142 (C 241/110/196)
	Richard Bagard	bailiff	merchant	*BB*, fo. 141v, 142; E 372/184 rot. 32 (*CCR, 1339–41*, 52)
	William de Hackthorne	coroner	mer.	*BB*, fo. 141v; KB 29/4, m. 7
	Richard s/Adam s/Martin	coroner	–	*BB*, fo. 141v
1339/40	Thomas Russell	mayor	mer.	*BB*, fo. 143; *BH*, fo. 36v
	Robert de Dalderby	bailiff	merchant	*BB*, fo. 143; *BH*, fo. 36v (*CCR, 1343–46*, 153)
	John Belger	bailiff	–	*BB*, fo. 143; *BH*, fo. 36v
	William de Hackthorne	coroner	mer.	*BB*, fo. 143
	John Mody	coroner	merchant	*BB*, fo. 143 (C 241/130/172)
1340/41	Henry de Fillingham	mayor	mer.	*BB*, fo. 146v; Dij 74/1/17
	Robert de Chesterfeld	bailiff	chandler/ clerk	*BB*, fo. 146v; Dij 74/1/17 (*BB*, fo. 165, *Liber Cant.*, fo. 343v)
	Robert de Maunsfeld*	bailiff	–	*BB*, fo. 146v; *BH*, fo. 55v
	William de Hackthorn[22]	coroner	mer.	*BB*, fo. 146v
1341/42	Robert de Dalderby	mayor	mer.	*BB*, fo. 149v; Dij 80/3/69
	Richard Scarle*	bailiff	tanner/ barker/ mercer	*BB*, fo. 149v; Dij 80/3/69 (*BB*, fos 107, 120v)
	Roger Briddok/ Bredok*	bailiff	draper	*BB*, fo. 149v; *BH*, fo. 35v (Dij 75/2/19)
	Roger de Kele	bailiff	–	Dij 80/3/69
	William de Hacthorn	coroner	mer.	*BB*, fo. 149v
	Richard s/Adam s/Martin	coroner	–	*BB*, fo. 153
	John Mody	coroner	mer.	*BB*, fo. 155v
1342/43	Robert de Hodelston[23]	mayor	–	Dij 77/1/42, *BB*, fo. 162v
	Reginald de Buttyrwike[24]	bailiff	–	*BB*, fo. 159–159v; Dij 77/1/42
	Stephen Russell	bailiff	fisher	*BB*, fo. 159; Dij 77/1/42 (*BB*, fo. 139v)
	Richard FitzMartin	coroner	–	*BB*, fos 159–159v
	William de Hackthorn	coroner	mer.	*BB*, fos 159–159v

22 Also county coroner in this year: JUST 3/133, m. 4.
23 Thomas de Hodelston in *BB*, fo. 159.
24 *Alias* Boterwyk: E 372/188, rot. 17.

1343/44	John Belger*	mayor	–	*BB*, fo. 164v; Dij 74/1/16
	John de Fenton*	bailiff	fisher	*BB*, fo. 164v; Dij 74/1/16 (*BB*, fo. 139v)
	Thomas de Lokton	bailiff	merchant	*BB*, fo. 164v; *BH*, fo. 49 (C 241/131/13)
	Thomas de Norton	bailiff	–	Dij 74/1/16
	Stephen de Totell	bailiff	–	*BB*, fos 166v–167
	Richard FitzMartin	coroner	–	*BB*, fos 159v, 164v
	William de Hackthorn	coroner	mer.	*BB*, fos 159v, 165v
1344/45	Richard s/Adam s/Martin[25]	mayor	–	*BB*, fos 168, 170v; *BH*, fo. 30v
	John de Askeby	mayor	sh.	*BB*, fo. 170v; Dij 82/1/24
	Robert Touk [Toke]	bailiff	painter (*pictor*)	*BB*, fos 168, 170v (*BB*, fo. 170)
	Richard le Paynteur	bailiff	painter	*BB*, fos 168, 170
	John de Dunham	coroner	clerk/ merchant	*BH*, fo. 46v; JUST 2/64, m. 10 (JUST 1/520, m. 13; C 241/126/112)
	William de Humberstone	coroner	att.	JUST 2/64, m. 10
	John de Belger	coroner	–	JUST 2/64, m. 10
	William de Hackthorne	coroner	mer.	*BB*, fo. 173v
1345/46	Robert de Chesterfeld	mayor[26]	ch.	*BB*, fo. 174v; *BH*, fo. 24v
	John de Briggeford	bailiff	–	*BB*, fo. 174v
	John de Outhorp	bailiff	merchant	*BB*, fo. 174v (*CPR, 1358–61*, 260)
	John de Belger	coroner	–	JUST 2/64, m. 10d
	John de Dunham	coroner	cl./mer.	JUST 2/64, m. 10d
	William de Humberston	coroner	att.	JUST 2/64, m. 10d
1346/47	Roger Breddock[27]	mayor	drap.	*BB*, fo. 176v; *BH*, fo. 61v
	Robert Gandes	bailiff	baker/ merchant	*BB*, fo. 176v; *BH*, fo. 61v (*BB*, fo. 219v; *CCR, 1339–41*, 52)
	John de Torkesey[28]	bailiff	taverner/ hosteler	*BB*, fo. 176v; *BH*, fo. 61v (*BB*, fos 175, 193; JUST 1/527, m. 5)
	William de Humberston	coroner	att.	*BB*, fo. 178v; JUST 2/64, m. 10d

25 Richard son of Adam son of Martin died less than four months after becoming mayor [28 January 1345], with John de Askeby being named as his successor: *BH*, fo. 30v; *BB*, fo. 170v.

26 Note that there was also a Robert le Clerk named as mayor in 1345/46. It is possible that this is actually Robert de Chesterfeld: *CIM*, vol. 2, 500, no. 1992.

27 *Alias* Roger de Kele: C 47/41/160.

28 *Alias* Roger de Taverner: C 47/41/160.

	William de Hacthorn	coroner	–	*BB*, fo. 176v
	John de Belger	coroner	–	JUST 2/64, m. 10d
	John de Dunham	coroner	cl./mer.	JUST 2/64, m. 10d
1347/48	Roger de Tirington	mayor	–	Dij 76/2/14
	William de Belay	bailiff	merchant	Dij 76/2/14 (C 241/162/85)
	John de Derfeld	bailiff	merchant	Dij 76/2/14 (*CCR, 1374–77*, 472–4)
	Robert de Hodelston	coroner	mer.	*BH*, fo. 59v
	John Belger	coroner	–	*BH*, fo. 59v; JUST 2/64, m. 10
	William de Humberston	coroner	att.	JUST 2/64, m. 10d
	John de Dunham	coroner	cl./mer.	JUST 2/64, m. 10d
1348/49	John de Fenton*[29]	mayor	fish.	Dij 75/2/22; *BH*, fo. 94v
	John de Outhorp	mayor	mer.	*BB*, fo. 184; Dij 76/2/13
	Walter Kelby	bailiff	merchant	*BB*, fos 183, 184; *BH*, fo. 94v (*CPR, 1358–61*, 260; C 241/126/173)
	John Neubald	bailiff	–	*BB*, fo. 182; Dij 75/2/22
	Robert de Hodelston*	coroner	mer.	*BB*, fo. 186v
	William de Humberston*	coroner	att.	*BB*, fo. 186v
	John de Farburn	coroner	–	*BB*, fo. 184
	John de Dunham	coroner	cl./mer.	*BB*, fo. 193v; JUST 2/64, m. 10
1349/50	John de Outhorp	mayor	mer.	*BB*, fo. 209; Dij 74/2/27
	Robert de Wambewelle	bailiff	–	*BB*, fo. 209; Dij 74/2/27
	William Belle	bailiff	–	*BB*, fo. 209; Dij 74/2/27
	John de Farburn	coroner	–	*BB*, fo. 209
1350/51	Walter de Kelby	mayor	mer.	*BB*, fo. 213; Dij 77/1/39
	William de Herpeswelle	bailiff	merchant	*BB*, fo. 213 (*BB*, fo. 164)
	Walter de Oursby [Oueray]	bailiff	merchant/ fishmonger	*BB*, fo. 213; Dij 77/1/39 (C 241/144/1; Lancashire Archives, DDTO K 10/17)
	William Jolyf	bailiff	merchant	Dij 77/1/39 (*CCR, 1339–41*, 52)
	Roger de Laun	coroner	clerk	*BB*, fo. 213v (*BB*, fos 155v, 178v, 217v)
1351/52	Thomas de Lokton	mayor	mer.	*BB*, fo. 217v; Dij 76/2/11
	William de Hetherby	bailiff	–	*BB*, fo. 217v; Dij 76/2/11
	William de Snellesound	bailiff	merchant	*BB*, fo. 217v; Dij 76/2/11 (C 241/131/56)

29 Fenton died sometime between 25 May and 8 June 1349 (see *BB*, fos 187, 190), undoubtedly of plague. His will was enrolled on 8 June: *BB*, fo. 191.

	Robert de Holm[30]	coroner	clerk	*BB*, fo. 217v (Dij 74/1/24–5, 28, 30–1)
1352/53	William de Herpeswelle	mayor	mer.	*BB*, fo. 220v; Dij 78/2/16
	John de Bole[31]	bailiff	merchant	*BB*, fo. 220v; Dij 78/2/16; JUST 1/523, m. 3 (C 241/139/31)
	William Fynchingfeld	bailiff	–	*BB*, fo. 220v; Dij 78/2/16
	Robert de Holm	coroner	cl.	*BB*, fo. 220v
	John de Dunham	coroner	cl./mer.	*BB*, fo. 222
1353/54	William de Snelleslound	mayor	mer.	*BB*, fo. 223v; *BH*, fo. 70v
	Peter Belaziz [Belasis]	bailiff	spicer	*BB*, fo. 223v; *BH*, fo. 70v (JUST 1/523, m. 15)
	John de Barton	bailiff	–	*BB*, fo. 223v; *BH*, fo. 70v
	Robert de Holm	coroner	cl.	*BB*, fo. 223v
	Robert Hare	coroner	bow./mer.	*BB*, fo. 227
	William Belle[32]	coroner	–	*CCR, 1349–54*, 561
1354/55	Peter de Thornton†	mayor	merchant	*BH*, fo. xi verso; C 241/134/38 (*CCR, 1339–41*, 52; *1349–54*, 6)
	Robert de Holm	bailiff	cl.	*BH*, fo. xi verso
	Thomas de Rasen	bailiff	–	*BH*, fo. xi verso
	Thomas Boteler	coroner	bm.?	*BH*, fo. xi verso
	Robert Hare	coroner	bow./mer.	*BH*, fo. xi verso
1355/56	John de Bergh†	mayor	–	*BB*, fo. 227v; Dij 74/1/10
	John de Rodes	bailiff	saddler	*BB*, fo. 227v; Dij 74/1/10 (Dij 76/2/11)
	Richard de Sixhill	bailiff	mercer	*BB*, fo. 227v; Dij 74/1/10 (*BB*, fo. 147v; C 241/138/171)
	Robert Hare	coroner	bow./mer.	*BB*, fo. 227v
	Thomas Boteler	coroner	bm.?	*BB*, fo. 229
1356/57	Walter de Ouresby	mayor	mer./fish.	*BB*, fo. 230v; Dij 74/2/10
	Richard de Burton[33]	bailiff	–	*BB*, fo. 230v; Dij 74/2/10
	John de Syberton [Sapperton]	bailiff	hosteler/ merchant	*BB*, fo. 230v; Dij 74/2/10 (C 131/10/4; JUST 1/526, 5d)
1357/58	Robert de Holm	mayor	cl.	*BB*, fo. 232; C 241/138/171
	William de Burgh	bailiff	butcher	*BB*, fo. 232 (*BB*, fos 157, 249)
	Gilbert Ferour	bailiff	smith?	*BB*, fo. 232
	Thomas Boteler	coroner	bm.?	*BB*, fo. 232
1358/59	Peter Belasis	mayor	sp.	*BB*, fo. 236; Dij 74/1/8

30 This Robert de Holm (and all subsequent entries noted here) is not the same Robert de Holm listed as county coroner in 1371, as the former died in 1368: *BB*, fo. 265v.

31 *Alias* 'John de Coke de Bole': JUST 3/142, m. 41d.

32 Removed for being insufficiently qualified: *CCR, 1349–54*, 561.

33 Noted as Edward de Burton in Dij 74/2/10 and *BB*, fo. 231.

	Hugh Wake	bailiff	mercer	*BB*, fo. 236; Dij 74/1/8 (*BB*, fos 213v–214)
	William de Paunton	bailiff	merchant	*BB*, fo. 236; Dij 74/1/8 (C 241/63/152)
	Thomas Boteler	coroner	bm.?	*BB*, fos 233, 237
	Robert de Holm	coroner	cl.	*BB*, fo. 237v
1359/60	Peter Belasis	mayor	sp.	*BB*, fo. 240, 241v; Dij 74/1/18
	John de Welton	bailiff	draper/ merchant	*BB*, fo. 240, 241v; Dij 74/1/18 (Sharpe, *Calendar of Letter Books*, Letter Book G, 258; *CPR, 1374–77*, 501–2)
	Adam Blome	bailiff	–	*BB*, fo. 240; Dij 74/1/18
	Robert de Holm	coroner	cl.	*BH*, fo. 41v
	Walter de Kelby	coroner	mer.	*BH*, fo. 41v
	Robert de Themelby	coroner	–	*BH*, fo. 41v
	Thomas de Banham	coroner	merchant	*BH*, fo. 41v (C 241/157/59)
1360/61	Roger de Tatersale†	mayor	fisher	*BB*, fo. 243; Dij 74/2/21 (*BB*, fo. 255v)
	William Bayons	bailiff	cardmaker	*BB*, fo. 243; Dij 74/2/21 (*CPR, 1370–74*, 273)
	Roger Furneux	bailiff	–	*BB*, fo. 243; Dij 74/2/21
	Robert de Holm	coroner[34]	cl.	*BB*, fo. 243
1361/62	John de Bole	mayor	mer.	*BB*, fo. 247; Dij 76/3/30
	William de Spayne	bailiff	merchant	*BB*, fo. 247; Dij 76/3/30 (*CFR, 1377–83*, 40–1)
	Robert Hare[35]	bailiff	bow./mer.	*BB*, fo. 247; *BH*, fo. 86v
	John de Outhorp	coroner	mer.	*BB*, fo. 247
1362/63	William de Thornhagh†	mayor	baker	*BB*, fo. 256; Dij 75/3/18 (*BB*, fos 180v–81, 184v)
	Roger de Tyrington	bailiff	–	*BB*, fo. 256; Dij 75/3/18
	John de Empyngham	bailiff	merchant	*BB*, fo. 256; Dij 75/3/18 (C 241/159/60)
	Robert de Holm	coroner	cl.	*BB*, fo. 256
	John de Outhorp	coroner	mer.	*BB*, fo. 256
1363/64	John de Rodes	mayor	sad.	*BB*, fo. 257v; C 241/145/51
	Simon de Eboraco [York]	bailiff	–	*BB*, fo. 257v; JUST 2/67, rot. 48
	John Milys [Miles]	bailiff	–	*BB*, fo. 257v; JUST 2/67, rot. 48
	John Sutton	coroner	merchant	*BH*, fo. 37 (C 241/150/21)

34 County coroner in this and the following year: JUST 3/157, mm. 7–7d, JUST 3/162, m. 13.

35 Died in office. His will was enrolled 14 March 1362: *BB*, fo. 251. William de Spayne was noted as the 'sole bailiff' (*unicus ballio*) for the remainder of the term: *BB*, fos 252–252v; Dij 74/2/24.

	Thomas de Banham	coroner	mer.	JUST 2/67, rot. 48
	Robert de Holm	coroner	cl.	JUST 2/67, rot. 48
	William de Paunton[36]	coroner	mer.	JUST 2/67, rot. 48, *BH*, fo. 47
	John de Bergh	coroner	–	*BH*, fo. 47
1364/65	John de Welton[Walton]	mayor	drap./mer.	*BB*, fo. 256v; *BH*, fo. 42v
	John Toke	bailiff	merchant	*BB*, fo. 256v; JUST 2/67, rots 48–48d (*CCR, 1374–77*, 472–4)
	Richard de Laun	bailiff	mercer	*BB*, fo. 256v; JUST 2/67, rots 48–48d (*BB*, fo. 217v)
	Thomas de Bannum [Banham]	coroner	mer.	*BB*, fo. 256v; JUST 2/67, rots 48–48d
	Robert de Holm	coroner	cl.	*BB*, fo. 256v; JUST 2/67, rots 48–48d
	William de Paunton	coroner	mer.	JUST 2/67, rot. 48
1365/66	Thomas de Elsham†	mayor	–	*BB*, fo. 260v
	John de Colingham	bailiff	–	*BB*, fo. 260v; JUST 2/67, rots 48d–49
	Robert de Qwytby [Wheteby]	bailiff	–	*BB*, fo. 260v; JUST 2/67, rots 48d–49
	Robert de Holm	coroner	cl.	*BB*, fo. 260v; JUST 2/67, rot. 49
	Thomas de Banham	coroner	mer.	*BB*, fo. 260v; JUST 2/67, rot. 49
	William de Paunton	coroner	mer.	*BB*, fo. 262
1366/67	Richard de Thorp†	mayor	merchant	*BB*, fo. 263v; 79/2/51 (*CCR, 1381–85*, 392)
	John de Eperston	bailiff	bower	*BB*, fo. 263v; 79/2/51 (E 13/100, m. 2)
	John Prentis	bailiff	–	*BB*, fo. 263v; 79/2/51
	Robert de Holm	coroner	cl.	*BB*, fo. 263v; JUST 2/67, rots 49, 50
	William de Paunton	coroner	mer.	JUST 2/67, rots 49, 50d
	Thomas de Banham	coroner	mer.	JUST 2/67, rots 49, 50
	John de Sutton [senior]	coroner	mer.	JUST 2/67, rots 50–50d (C 241/150/21)
1367/68	John de Sutton, senior	mayor	mer.	*BB*, fo. 265; *BH*, fo. 82v
	John de Hodelston	bailiff	merchant	*BB*, fo. 265; *BH*, fo. 82v (*CCR, 1381–85*, 21–2)
	John Belle	bailiff	–	*BB*, fo. 265; *BH*, fo. 82v
	Thomas Banham	coroner	mer.	*BB*, fo. 265
	Thomas Elsham	coroner	–	*BB*, fo. 265v, *BH*, fo. 11v

36 County coroner in this year; removed in 1367 for being unqualified: *CCR, 1364–68*, 348.

	Simon Levelaunce	coroner	attorney	*BB*, fo. 265v, *BH*, fo. 11v (*BB*, fo. 222, 259v, 268v)
	John Denson	coroner	–	*BH*, fo. 11v
1368/69	Roger de Tyrington	mayor	–	*BB*, fo. 266; Dij 76/2/9
	John de Derfeld	bailiff	–	*BB*, fo. 266; Dij 76/2/9
	William de Belay [Beley]	bailiff	merchant	*BB*, fo. 266; Dij 76/2/9 (*CFR, 1377–83*, 40–1)
	Thomas Banham	coroner	mer.	*BB*, fo. 266; JUST 2/67, rots 42, 46
	Simon Levelaunce	coroner	att.	JUST 2/67, rots 42d, 46
	John de Sutton [senior]	coroner	mer.	JUST 2/67, rot. 47
1369/70	John de Colyngham	mayor	–	*BB*, fo. 270; C 241/155/107
	John Norman	bailiff	merchant	*BB*, fo. 270; JUST 2/67, rots 46, 47 (*CFR, 1377–83*, 40–1)
	Walter de Bury	bailiff	skinner	*BB*, fo. 270; JUST 2/67, rots 46, 47 (JUST 3/142, rot.46d)
	Simon Levelaunce	coroner	att.	*BB*, fo. 270; JUST 2/67, rot. 46
	Thomas Banham	coroner	mer.	*BB*, fo. 266; JUST 2/67, rot. 42
1370/71	William Inghes [Ingell]†	mayor	bower	*BB*, fo. 272v; Dij 77/1/21 (*BB*, fo. 247)
	Thomas Horncastre	bailiff	barber	Dij 77/1/21; JUST 2/67, rot. 42 (KB 27/459, m. 22)
	Gilbert de Belesby [Beseby]	bailiff	skinner	Dij 77/1/21; JUST 2/67, rot. 42, 46 (*CPR, 1401–05*, 416–17)
	Simon Levelaunce	coroner	att.	JUST 2/67, rots 42d, 46
	Thomas de Banham	coroner	mer.	JUST 2/67, rots 42d, 46
	Thomas de Elesham	coroner	–	JUST 2/67, rot. 46
	Richard de Ardern	coroner	–	KB 27/459, m. 33
1371/72	William de Belay	mayor	mer.	*BH*, fo. 51v; C 241/153/85
	Nicholas de Cameryngham	bailiff	merchant	JUST 2/67, rot. 42d; E 372/218, rot. 16 (*CCR, 1385–89*, 83)
	John Bene	bailiff	merchant	JUST 2/67, rot. 42d (C 241/159/45)
	Simon Levelaunce	coroner	att.	JUST 2/67, rot. 46d
	Thomas de Banham	coroner	mer.	JUST 2/67, rot. 46d
1372/73	John Toke	mayor	merchant	Dij 75/3/9; 74/2/11 (*CCR, 1374–77*, 472–4)
	Thomas de Banham	bailiff	mer.	Dij 75/3/9; 74/2/11
	John de Farlethorp	bailiff	–	Dij 75/3/9; E 122/188/274
	John Goldesmyth	bailiff	–	Dij 74/2/11

	Simon Levelaunce	coroner	att.	JUST 2/67, rots 43–43d, 45
	Nicholas Werk	coroner	merchant	JUST 2/67, rots 43d, 45 (*CPR, 1377–81*, 429; C 241/164/101)
1373/74	Hugh Garewelle† [Garwell]	mayor	merchant	*Ancient Deeds*, vol. 6, 12, no. C3859; C 241/166/85 (*CFR, 1377–83*, 40–1)
	William Norton	bailiff	tailor/dyer	*Ancient Deeds*, vol. 6, 12, no. C3859; JUST 2/67, rot. 44d (JUST 2/67, m. 48, 49; *BB*, fo. 236v)
	Thomas Pygot	bailiff	merchant	*Ancient Deeds*, vol. 6, 12, no. C3859; JUST 2/67, rot. 44d (*CCR, 1374–77*, 472–4)
	Thomas de Banham	coroner	mer.	JUST 2/67, rot. 46
	Simon Levelaunce	coroner	att.	JUST 2/67, rots 44–44d, 46
	Nicholas Werk	coroner	mer.	JUST 2/67, rots 44d, 45d
1374/75	John de Hodelston	mayor	mer.	*BB*, fo. 101; Dij 80/3/70
	John Bate	bailiff	merchant	*BB*, fo. 101; Dij 80/3/70 (*CCR, 1374–77*, 472–4; *1381–85*, 21–22)
	Thomas de Thornhagh	bailiff	merchant/ barker	*BB*, fo. 101; Dij 80/3/70 (*CCR, 1369–74*, 172; Lancashire Archives, DDTO O 12/79)
	Simon Levelaunce	coroner	att.	*BB*, fo. 101; JUST 2/67, rot. 46
	Thomas de Banham	coroner	mer.	JUST 2/67, rot. 46
	Thomas de Elesham [Aylesham]	coroner	–	JUST 2/67, rot. 46
	Nicholas Werk	coroner	mer.	JUST 2/80, rot. 1
1375/76	Thomas de Horncastre	mayor	ba.	*BB*, fos 102–102v; Dij 74/3/10
	Robert de Farburn	bailiff	–	*BB*, fos 102–102v; Dij 74/3/10
	John de Bultham	bailiff	cooper	*BB*, fos 102–102v; Dij 74/3/10 (JUST 2/67, rot. 49d; *BB*, fo. 238v)
	Simon Levelaunce	coroner	att.	*BB*, fo. 102; JUST 2/67, rot. 44d, 46
	Thomas de Banham	coroner	mer.	JUST 2/67, rot. 46
1376/77	John de Eperston	mayor	bow.	Dij 82/2/98; *CPR, 1374–77*, 489
	Nicholas Werk	bailiff	mer.	Dij 82/2/98; *CPR, 1374–77*, 489
	John Hawardby [Hawerby]	bailiff	mercer/ mason	Dij 82/2/98; *CPR, 1374–77*, 489 (*BB*, fos 252v, 260v–261)

	Simon Levelaunce	coroner	att.	JUST 2/67, rot. 44
	Thomas de Banham	coroner	mer.	JUST 2/67, rot. 46
1377/78	Thomas Bannum [Banham]	mayor	mer.	Dij 82/2/118; C 241/165/22
	Robert de Ledes/Ledys	bailiff	butcher/ merchant	JUST 1/533, m. 5; JUST 3/167, rot. 17 (JUST 2/87, rot. 3)
	Thomas de Donn	bailiff	–	JUST 1/533, m. 5; Dij 82/2/118
1378/79	Walter de Bury	mayor[37]	sk.	Dij 79/2/32; 82/2/131 (JUST 2/67, rot. 49d)
	William de Dalderby	bailiff	merchant	Dij 79/2/32; 82/2/131 (*CFR, 1337–83*, 40–1)
	Simon de Messyngham	bailiff	–	Dij 79/2/32; 82/2/131
	William Dimmok	bailiff	fuller	Hill, 'Three Lists', 229 (*BB*, fo. 269v)
	Thomas de Aylesham	coroner	–	*CPR, 1377–81,* 361
	Nicholas Werk	coroner	mer.	JUST 2/80, rot. 1, 4
1379/80	Robert Sutton†	mayor	merchant	C 241/165/37 (*CPR, 1377–81*, 628; *1385–89*, 415)
	John Hedon	bailiff	mercer	E 372/225 rot. 18; JUST 2/87, rot. 1 (C47/41/155)
	Robert Harewode/ Hareworth	bailiff	merchant/ fustour	JUST 2/87, rot. 1; KB 29/41, m. 24 (*CPR, 1391–96*, 626;
				Rigby, *Overseas Trade*, 95)
	Nicholas Werk	coroner	mer.	JUST 2/80, rot. 1; JUST 3/33/2, m. 10
	Thomas de Horncastre	coroner	ba.	JUST 2/87, rot. 1; JUST 3/33/2, m. 10
1380/81	Gilbert Beseby [Belesby]	mayor	sk.	Dij 82/2/109
	William Dimmok	bailiff	ful.	Dij 82/2/109
	John de Blythe	bailiff	attorney	Dij 82/2/109; E 372/226, rot. 20d (*BB*, fo. 101v)
	Thomas Holme	bailiff	–	Hill, 'Three Lists', 230
	Thomas de Horncastre[38]	coroner	ba.	JUST 2/87, rot. 1
	Nicholas Werk[39]	coroner	mer.	JUST 2/80, rot. 1; JUST 3/167, rot. 36d
1381/82	Simon de Messyngham	mayor	–	Bj/2/7, fos 79, 146; *CCR, 1381–85*, 62

37 Walter de Bury was only named mayor following the death of John Blyton (*cuius post decess' electus fuit*): Hill, 'Three Lists', 229.

38 Also county coroner: JUST 3/167, rot. 29.

39 Also county coroner: JUST 3/167, rot. 29.

	Simon Semans[40]	bailiff	wool merchant	Bj/2/7, fos 79, 146; JUST 3/33/4, m. 14 (*CCR, 1381–85*, 62)
	Thomas Hauke	bailiff	–	Bj/2/7, fos 79, 146
	William de Halton	bailiff	–	Bj/2/7, fos 79, 146
	John de Outhorp	coroner	mer.	JUST 2/85, rot. 2
	Nicholas de Werk	coroner	mer.	JUST 2/80, rot. 1
1382/83	William de Snelleston†	mayor	merchant	*CCR, 1381–85*, 393; Dij 78/2/20 (*CFR, 1377–83*, 40–1)
	Robert Messyngham	bailiff	wool merchant/ barker	Dij 78/2/20; JUST 2/80, rot. 2 (*CPR, 1391–96*, 626; E 13/114, m. 9)
	Alexander Herle[41]	bailiff	merchant	Dij 78/2/20; JUST 2/80, rot. 2 (*CCR, 1381–85*, 268)
	Thomas Haukes	bailiff	–	Hill, 'Three Lists', 230
	John de Outhorp	coroner	mer.	JUST 2/85, rot. 2
	Nicholas de Werk	coroner	mer.	JUST 2/80, rot. 2
	Thomas de Horncastre[42]	coroner	ba.	JUST 2/87, rot. 1
1383/84	William de Dalderby	mayor	mer.	*CIM*, vol. 4, 201; LAO Hill 39/17/1
	Gilbert de Kyme	bailiff	lister (surgeon)	*CIM*, vol. 4, 201; LAO Hill 39/17/1 (*CCR, 1374–77*, 84; *1391–96*, 629)
	Henry Harewode	bailiff	saddler	*CIM*, vol. 4, 201; LAO Hill 39/17/1
	John Hartsholme	bailiff	butcher	*CPR, 1389–92*, 220; LAO Hill 39/17/1
	Nicholas de Werk	coroner	mer.	*CPR, 1381–85*, 552–3; JUST 2/80, rot. 2
1384/85	Robert de Salteby[43]	mayor	merchant	Dij 82/2/127; *Ancient Deeds*, vol. 5, 52, no. A10825 (*ELW*, 139–40
	John Shipman	bailiff	skinner	Dij 82/2/127; *Ancient Deeds*, vol. 5, 52, no. A10825
	John Prentys	bailiff	–	*CPR, 1381–85*, 503–4
	Robert de Lyn	bailiff	lister	Dij 82/2/127; *Ancient Deeds*, vol. 5, 52, no. A10825
	Nicholas de Werk	coroner	mer.	JUST 2/80, rot. 2; *CPR, 1381–85*, 552–3

40 Noted as Simon Semans 'patener' in *CCR, 1381–85*, 62 and 'Simon Laxfeld *alias* Seman de Laxfeld of Lincoln, wool-merchant, *alias* Simon Patener of Lincoln' in *CPR, 1391–96*, 627.

41 *Alias 'esterlyng'*: Dij 82/2/130.

42 Ordered to be removed from office for being insufficiently qualified; this did not happen: *CCR, 1381–85*, 371.

43 Alias Robert de Sutton: *CPR, 1381–85*, 500.

	Thomas de Horncastre	coroner	ba.	JUST 2/87, rot. 1
1385/86	John Norman	mayor	mer.	*CIM*, vol. 4, 201; Dij 79/2/49
	John Bellasise [Belasys]	bailiff	merchant	*CIM*, vol. 4, 201; Dij 79/2/49 (*CPR, 1391–96*, 626)
	Thomas de Hodelston	bailiff	–	*CIM*, vol. 4, 201; Dij 79/2/49
	John de York	bailiff	–	SC 8/214/10651; JUST 2/87, rot. 1
	Nicholas de Werk	coroner	mer.	JUST 2/80, rots 2–3
	William de Norton	coroner	tailor	JUST 2/80, rot. 4 (JUST 2/67, rot. 48)
	Thomas de Horncastre	coroner	ba.	JUST 2/87, rot. 1
1386/87	John Sutton, junior†	mayor	merchant/ barker	JUST 2/87, rot. 1; *CPR, 1389–92*, 220, 271 (*CFR, 1377–83*, 40–1; E 13/119, m. 2)
	William Barkworth	bailiff	–	JUST 2/87, rot. 1; *CPR, 1389–92*, 220, 271
	Walter Faldyngworth	bailiff	–	JUST 2/87, rot. 1; *CPR, 1389–92*, 220, 271
	John Carleton	bailiff	attorney	JUST 2/87, rot. 1; *CPR, 1389–92*, 220, 271 (*BB*, fo. 262)
	John de Outhorp	coroner	mer.	JUST 2/87, rot. 1
	Nicholas de Werk	coroner	mer.	JUST 2/80, rots 2– 3
	Thomas de Horncastre	coroner	ba.	JUST 2/87, rot. 1
1387/88	Robert Ledes[44]	mayor	mer.	*CPR, 1389–92*, 220, 271
	John Nettylham [Netlam]	bailiff	–	JUST 2/87, rot. 2; JUST 1/533, m. 5
	Ralph Skremby	bailiff	–	JUST 2/87, rot. 2; JUST 1/533, m. 5
	Robert Lavender	bailiff	–	JUST 2/87, rot. 2; JUST 1/533, m. 5
	Nicholas de Werk	coroner	mer.	JUST 2/80, rot. 3
	Thomas de Horncastre	coroner	ba.	JUST 2/87, rots 1–2
1388/89	Robert Messingham†	mayor	wm./bar.	*CPR, 1389–92*, 220; C 241/178/66
	Richard Reepham	bailiff	–	JUST 2/87, rot. 1; Arnold, *Select Cases of Trespass*, 59
	John Biryngtoun	bailiff	–	JUST 2/87, rot. 1; Arnold, *Select Cases of Trespass*, 59
	Jacob Pye	bailiff	–	JUST 2/87, rot. 1; Arnold, *Select Cases of Trespass*, 58

44 According to *Rot. Parl.*, vol. 3, 403, Ledes was mayor alongside Barkworth, Faldyngworth and Carleton, the previous year's bailiffs, not Nettylham, Skremby and Lavander. It is unclear which is accurate.

	Nicholas de Werk	coroner	mer.	JUST 2/80, rot. 3
	Thomas de Horncastre	coroner	ba.	JUST 2/87, rots 1–2
1389/90	Simon Laxfelde[45]	mayor	wm.	Dij 74/1/14; KB 27/518, m. 63
	John Boston	bailiff	weaver/ cordwainer	Dij 74/1/14; KB 27/518, m. 63 (*BB*, fo. 243; E 13/110, m. 1d)
	John Syklyng	bailiff	barber	Dij 74/1/14; KB 27/518, m. 63 (*CPR, 1391–96*, 626)
	Thomas de Horncastre	coroner	ba.	JUST 2/87, rot. 2
1390/91	Thomas Thornhagh	mayor	mer./bar.	Dij 82/2/110
	Peter Saltby	bailiff	merchant	Dij 82/2/110; JUST 2/87, rot. 2 (*CPR, 1391–96*, 626)
	Robert Bury	bailiff	–	Dij 82/2/110; JUST 2/87, rot. 2
	John Candelesby	bailiff	–	JUST 2/87, rot. 2; JUST 1/533, m. 5
	Thomas de Horncastre[46]	coroner	ba.	JUST 2/87, rot. 2; JUST 1/533, m. 5
	John de Outhorp	coroner	mer.	JUST 2/85, rot. 2
1391/92	John Driffeld/Derfeld	mayor	merchant	C 241/181/35; E 13/110, m. 13 (*CCR, 1381–85*, 21–2)
	John Thorlay	bailiff	–	JUST 1/532, m. 5
	John Severby	bailiff	–	JUST 1/532, m. 5; E 372/237, rot. 24
	John de Outhorp	coroner	mer.	JUST 2/85, rot. 2
1392/93	Henry Harewood	mayor	sad.	*BH*, fo. 57; JUST 2/87, rot. 2
	John Sparrow	bailiff	pewterer	*BH*, fo. 57 (*CCR, 1396–99*, 348; JUST 2/93, rots 1, 4)
	John Ryppon	bailiff	cordwainer	*BH*, fo. 57; JUST 2/93, rot. 4 (*BB*, fo. 102)
	William Stretton	bailiff	litster (dyer)	*BH*, fo. 57; JUST 2/93, rot. 4 (*CCR, 1396–99*, 348)
	John de Outhorp	coroner	mer.	JUST 2/85, rot. 2
	Thomas de Thornhagh	coroner	mer./bar.	JUST 1/532, m. 5; JUST 2/93, rots 1–2, 4
	Thomas de Castell[47]	coroner	–	JUST 1/532, m. 5; JUST 2/93, rots 1–2, 4
1393/94	Robert Harewood/ Haworth	mayor	mer./fus.	JUST 1/532, m. 5; JUST 2/93, rots 1, 3
	Adam Rausse [Raus/Rauff]	bailiff	–	JUST 1/532, m. 5; JUST 2/93, rots 1, 3
	Thomas attehall	bailiff	–	JUST 1/532, m. 5; JUST 2/93, rots 1, 3

45 See Simon Semans at 1381/82.
46 Removed in this year for being 'sick and aged': *CCR, 1389–92*, 471.
47 Coroner until no later than 1404: *CPR, 1401–05*, 451.

	John Kaye [Kays]	bailiff	–	JUST 1/532, m. 5; JUST 2/93, rots 1, 3
	Thomas de Thornhagh	coroner	mer./bar.	JUST 1/532, m. 5; JUST 2/93, rots 1–3
	Thomas de Castell	coroner	–	JUST 1/532, m. 5; JUST 2/93, rots 1–3
1394/95	John Belasys [Bellasise]	mayor	mer.	JUST 1/532, m. 5; JUST 2/93, rots 1–3
	John Barkworth	bailiff	–	JUST 2/93, rot. 1, 3; JUST 3/188, rot. 103d
	John Hawerby [Hawardeby]	bailiff	merc./mas.	JUST 2/93, rot. 1, 3
	William Dan	bailiff	–	E 372/241, rot. 19
	Thomas de Thornhagh	coroner	mer./bar.	JUST 1/532, m. 5; JUST 2/93, rots 1–2
	Thomas de Castell	coroner	–	JUST 1/532, m. 5; JUST 2/93, rots 1–2
1395/96	John Hedon	mayor	merc.	*ELW*, 59
	John Fen [at the Fenne]	bailiff	–	JUST 1/532, m. 5
	Thomas Aston	bailiff	–	JUST 1/532, m. 5
	Richard Marum	bailiff	–	JUST 1/532, m. 5; KB 29/41, m. 24
	Thomas de Thornhagh	coroner	mer./bar.	JUST 1/532, m. 5; JUST 2/93, rots 1–2
	Thomas de Castell	coroner	–	JUST 1/532, m. 5; JUST 2/93, rots 1–2
1396/97	John Schipman	mayor	sk.	JUST 3/177, rot. 102
	John Balderton	bailiff	merchant	JUST 3/177, rot. 102 (*CPR, 1401–05*, 416–17)
	Robert Appulby	bailiff	merchant	JUST 3/177, rot. 102; E 372/242, rot. 23 (*ELW*, 107–8)
	William Maioy[48]	coroner	mer./bar.	JUST 3/188, rot. 118d
1397/98	John Toreley [Thorley]	mayor	–	*BH*, fo. 29v; LCL VC 2/1/327
	John Hoghton	bailiff	–	*BH*, fo. 29v; LCL VC 2/1/327
	Nicholas Hoddelston	bailiff	merchant	*BH*, fo. 29v; LCL VC 2/1/327 (*CPR, 1401–05*, 416–17; *1436–41*, 210)
	Richard Staynfeld	bailiff	–	*BH*, fo. 29v; LAO Diocesan Misc. Roll 1
1398/99	John de Severby	mayor	–	*CCR, 1396–99*, 348; *BH*, fos 29v, 104v
	Hugh de Netylham	bailiff	–	*BH*, fo. 104v
	William Peeke	bailiff	–	*BH*, fos 29, 104v

48 *Alias* Thomas de Thornhagh: JUST 3/188, rot. 118d.

	John Wykeforth	bailiff	–	*BH*, fo. 104v; E 372/245, rot. 23
	John Scarburght	bailiff	–	*BH*, fo. 48
	Thomas de Castell	coroner	–	JUST 3/188, rot. 103
1399/ 1400	John Balderton	mayor	mer.	*BH*, fo. 118v; *CPR, 1399–1401*, 214
	William de la Ile	bailiff	–	*BH*, fos 57v, 118v
	Henry Dyke	bailiff	–	*BH*, fos 57v, 118v
	Thomas Russel	bailiff	merchant	*BH*, fos 57v, 118v (*CPR, 1399–1401*, 362)
1400/01	Robert Bury	mayor	–	C 260/115
	Richard Wyrsop [Worsop]	bailiff	–	C 260/115; JUST 3/188, rot. 107
	John Fuystour	bailiff	–	C 260/115; JUST 3/188, rot. 107
	Thomas Forster	bailiff	–	C 260/115; JUST 3/188, rot. 107
	Thomas de Castell	coroner	–	JUST 3/188, rot. 107
1401/02	Robert Appulby	mayor	mer.	*BH*, fo. 31v
	Richard Tytheby	bailiff	–	*BH*, fo. 31v; JUST 3/188, rot. 119
	Robert Markyn	bailiff	–	*BH*, fo. 31v; JUST 3/188, rot. 119
	Alexander Carlele	bailiff	–	JUST 3/188, rot. 119
	Thomas Multon	bailiff	–	JUST 3/188, rot. 119
	Thomas de Castell	coroner	–	JUST 3/188, rots 109, 123d
1402/03	William Blyton†	mayor	spurrier	*BH*, fo. 124v
	Richard Cok	bailiff	–	E 13/119, m. 2
	Stephen Bradenham	bailiff	–	*BH*, fo. 124v; E 13/119, m. 2
	Robert Athern	bailiff	–	*BH*, fo. 124v; E 13/119, m. 2
	John Doket	bailiff	–	*BH*, fo. 124v; E 13/119, m. 2
	Thomas de Castell	coroner	–	JUST 3/188, rots 116d, 117d
1403/04	John Hoghton	mayor	–	*BH*, fos vii, 54
	John Waltham	bailiff	sheather	*BH*, fos vii, 54 (C 241/179/2)
	Thomas Fulham	bailiff	–	*BH*, fos vii, 54
	John Sheffeld	bailiff	–	*BH*, fos vii, 54
	John Alneth	bailiff	–	Hill, 'Three Lists', 232
1404/05	Peter de Salteby	mayor	mer.	*BH*, fos viii, 23v
	Thomas Archer	bailiff	mercer/ attorney	*BH*, fos viii, 23v (*CPR, 1408–13*, 137; E 13/119, m. 2)
	Richard Bell	bailiff	merchant	*BH*, fos viii, 23v (Archer, *Bishop Philip Repingdon*, no. 410)
	William Walshe	bailiff	–	*BH*, fos viii, 23v; E 372/252, rot. 20

	Jacob de Staynton	bailiff	–	*BH*, fos viii, 23v; E 372/252, rot. 20
	William Dalderby	coroner	–	JUST 3/188, rot. 120
1405/06	Nicholas Hoddelston	mayor	mer.	*CPR, 1405–8*, 494
	Henry Dyke	bailiff	–	E 13/199, m. 16; E 13/120, m. 7
	William of the Ile	bailiff	–	E 13/199, m. 16; E 13/120, m. 7
	Thomas Russell	bailiff	–	E 13/199, m. 16; E 13/120, m. 7
	William Skott de Lincoln	bailiff	–	E 372/252, rot. 20
	William Dalderby	coroner	–	JUST 3/188, rot. 126
1406/07	William Darkworth[49]	mayor	–	Hill, 'Three Lists', 232
	William Burton	bailiff	–	JUST 3/188, rot. 130d
	Thomas Donne	bailiff	–	JUST 3/188, rot. 130d
	William Markeby	bailiff	–	JUST 3/188, rot. 130d
	John Neuyll	bailiff	–	JUST 3/188, rot. 130d
	Thomas Fulham	coroner	–	JUST 3/188, rot. 131
1407/08	Thomas Forster	mayor	–	*CCR, 1405–9*, 465
	William Kyrkeby	bailiff	–	*CCR, 1405–9*, 465
	John Ryle	bailiff	–	*CCR, 1405–9*, 465
	John Raysyn	bailiff	–	*CCR, 1405–9*, 465
	John Tonarde	bailiff	–	*CCR, 1405–9*, 465
1408/09	Walter Faldyngworth	mayor	–	*BH*, fo. 15v
	John Messyngham	bailiff	weaver	*BH*, fo. 15v (*WB*, fo. 2v)
	William Chesterfeld	bailiff	–	*BH*, fo. 15v
	John Gryssyngton	bailiff	–	*BH*, fo. 15v
	William Dauy	bailiff	–	*BH*, fo. 15v

49 This is almost certainly 'Barkeworth', who was bailiff in 1386/87.

Appendix 3

Lincoln Members of Parliament, c.1290–1410

Source: *Return of the Name of Every Member of the Lower Parliament of England, Scotland and Ireland*, vol. 1 (London, 1878), 1–275.

Key: **bold** entries denote parliaments held (or due to be held) at Lincoln; * = individual not serving as a civic official; ^ = biography of MP available in J. S. Roskell, L. Clark and C. Rawcliffe, *The History of Parliament: the House of Commons, 1386–1421* (London, 1993). Note: no attempt has been made to standardise surnames. All dates relate to the original summons, not prorogued parliaments.

1290 (15 July)	*unknown*
1294 (12 Nov)	*unknown*
1295 (27 Nov)	William Cause, Peter de Thornehawe
1296 (3 Nov)	*unknown*
1297 (6 Oct)	*unknown*
1298 (25 May)	Richard de Bellafago, Alexander son of John son of Martin
1299–1300 (6 March)	*unknown*
1300 (20 May)	*unkown*
1300–01 (20 Jan)	Stephen de Stanham, William Cause
1302 (29 Sept)	William Cause, John son of Richard
1304–05 (16 Feb)	Stephen de Stanham, John Blake
1306 (30 May)	John de Amecotes, Gilbert le Blake
1306–07 (20 Jan)	Hugh Skarlet,* Henry de Wyndesonore*
1307 (13 Oct)	William Cause, Alexander son of Martyn
1309 (27 April)	William Cause, Alexander son of Martyn
1311 (8 Aug)	Thomas Gamel, Henry Wyndesore
1311 (12 Nov)	Roger de Totil, Thomas Gamel
1311–12 (13 Feb)	*unknown*
1312–13 (18 Mar)	Thomas Gamel, Henry Stoile
1313 (8 July)	*unknown*
1313 (23 Sept)	Thomas Gamel, Henry Stoile
1314 (21 April)	*unknown*
1314 (9 Sept)	William de Pontefracto,* Henry Stoyl
1314–15 (20 Jan)	Hugh Scarlet, Henry Stoyl
1315–16 (27 Jan)	*unknown*
1316 (25 April–24 May)	*unknown*
1316 (29 July)	*unknown*

1318 (27 Jan)	*did not meet on account of the Scottish invasion*
1318 (20 Oct)[1]	Thomas Gamel, Henry Stoyl
1319 (6 May)	William de Hakethorn, Simon de Leycestre
1320 (6 Oct)	William de Hakthon, Nicholas de Welton
1321 (15 July)	*unknown*
1322 (2 May)	Henry de Hakethorn, Thomas Gamel
1322 (14 Nov)	*unknown*
1323–24 (20 Jan)	Walter de Ebor, Alan de Hodeleston
1324 (20 Oct)	*unknown*
1325 (18 Nov)	Alan de Hodeleston, Andrew de Norton*
1326–27 (14 Dec)	John de Tame, William de Hakethorn
1327 (15 Sept)	John de Tame, William de Hakethorn
1327–28 (7 Feb)	William de Hakethorn, Walter de Ebor
1328 (24 April)	William de Hakethorn, Walter de Ebor
1328 (31 July)	John de Tame, Alan de Huddeleston
1328–29 (16 Oct)	Walter de Ebor, William de Hakethorn
1329–30 (11 March)	William de Hakethorn, William Virley*
1330 (26 Nov)	William de Hakethorn, Hugh de Carleton
1331 (30 Sept)	*unknown*
1331–32 (16 March)	William de Hakethorn, Thomas Cause*
1332 (9 Sept)	Thomas de Carleton,* William de Hakethorn
1332 (4 Dec)	Hugh de Carleton,* William de Vyrly
1333–34 (21 Feb)	Thomas de Carleton, William de Hakthorn
1334 (19 Sept)[2]	William de Hakthorn, William Vyrly
1335 (26 May)	William de Hakthorn, Simon de Grantham*
1335–36 (11 March)	William de Hakthorn, William Virly
1336 (23 Sept)	Hugh de Edlyngton, William de Hakthorn
1336–37 (3 Jan)	*unknown*
1336–37 (3 Mar)	*unknown*
1337 (26 Sept)[3]	William de Hakthorn, Richard son of Martyn
1337–38 (3 Feb)[4]	Thomas Botiller, William Vyrly
1338 (26 July)	*unknown*
1338–39 (14 Jan)[5]	Hugh Stokes,* John Judkin*
1339 (13 Oct)[6]	William de Dalderby, William de Virly
1339–40 (20 Jan)	*unknown*
1340 (29 March)	William de Virly, William de Hackthorn
1340 (12 July)	*unknown*

1 For expenses relating to this parliament: *CCR, 1318–23*, 116.
2 Expenses: *CCR, 1333–37*, 349–50.
3 Expenses: *CCR, 1337–39*, 244.
4 Expenses: *CCR, 1337–39*, 388.
5 Stokes and Judkin did not attend parliament despite appropriating funds for doing so. The attendees and defrauded individuals were William Virly and Richard son of Martin: *1341 Inquest*, no. 867. For fraudulently claimed expenses: *CCR, 1339–41*, 97.
6 Expenses: *CCR, 1339–41*, 275.

1341 (21 April)	William Virly, William de Hakthorn
1342 (16 Oct)	*unknown*
1343 (28 Apr)[7]	William Virly
1344 (7 June)	William de Humberston, William Virly
1346 (11 Sept)	William Virly, Simon de Erneburgh
1347–48 (14 Jan)	Robert de Dalderby, William de Humberston
1348 (31 March)	Walter de Kelleby, Thomas de Lokton
1348–49	*parliament suspended due to plague*
1350–51 (9 Feb)	Walter de Kelby, Robert de Dalderby
1351–52 (13 Jan)	*unknown*
1352 (16 Aug)	John de Outhorp
1353 (23 Sept)	Robert de Dalderby, Walter de Kelly (*viz.* Kelby)
1354 (28 Apr)	*unknown*
1355 (12 Nov)	*unknown*
1357 (17 Apr)	*unknown*
1357–58 (5 Feb)	John de Outhorp, John de Bole
1360 (15 May)	John de Outhorp, William de Wyhum*
1360–61 (24 Jan)	Walter de Kelby, Peter Belsayse
1362 (13 Oct)	Walter de Kelby, John de Rodes
1363 (6 Oct)	*unknown*
1364–65 (20 Jan)	Walter de Kelby, John de Bole
1366 (4 May)	John de Rodes, John de Welton
1368 (1 May)	Walter de Kelby, John de Welton
1369 (3 June)	Walter de Kelby, John de Sutton
1370–71 (24 Feb)	*unknown*
1371 (8 June)	John de Outhorp
1372 (13 Oct)	Walter de Kelby, John de Sutton
1373 (21 Nov)[8]	John de Sutton, Roger de Tateshale
1375–76 (12 Feb)[9]	William Belay, John de Hodleston
1376–77 (27 Jan)	John de Hodelston, John de Derfeld
1377 (13 Oct)	*unknown*
1378 (20 Oct)[10]	John de Outhorp, Hugh de Garwell
1379 (24 April)[11]	Thomas Horncastre, Roger Tiryngton
1379–80 (16 Jan)	John de Hodelston, John de Driffeld
1380 (5 Nov)	*unknown*
1381 (16 Sept)	John de Sutton, Roger de Messyngham
1382 (7 May)[12]	Robert de Sutton, Robert de Ledes
1382 (6 Oct)	John de Derfeld, Gilbert de Beseby

7 Expenses: *CCR, 1343–46*, 136.
8 Expenses: *CCR, 1369–74*, 612.
9 Expenses: *CCR, 1374–77*, 429.
10 Expenses: *CCR, 1377–81*, 222.
11 Expenses: *CCR, 1377–81*, 253.
12 Expenses: *CCR, 1381–85*, 134.

1382–83 (23 Feb)[13]	Thomas de Horncastre, Robert de Salteby
1383 (26 Oct)	Robert de Sutton, William de Dalderby
1384 (29 Apr)[14]	William de Snelleston, Nicholas de Werk
1384 (12 Nov)	Robert de Sutton, John de Derfeld
1385 (20 Oct)	Robert de Sutton, Simon de Messyngham
1386 (1 Oct)^	Robert de Sutton, Robert de Saltby
1388 (3 Feb)^	Robert de Sutton, John de Sutton
1388 (9 Sept)^[15]	Gilbert de Beseby, Robert de Harworth
1389–90 (17 Jan)^	Nicholas de Werk, Robert de Peek
1390 (12 Nov)	*unknown*
1391 (3 Nov)^	Robert de Sutton, Robert de Ledes
1392 (14 Oct)	*unknown*
1393 (20 Jan)^[16]	Thomas de Thornhagh, John Belassise
1393–94 (27 Jan)^[17]	Robert de Sutton, Robert de Messyngham
1394–95 (27 Jan)^[18]	Robert de Ledes, Robert de Harworth
1396–97 (22 Jan)^	Robert de Sutton, Robert de Appleby
1397 and 1397–98 (17 Sept)^[19]	Seman de Laxfeld, John Thorley
1399 (30 Sept)	*parliament suspended due to king's abdication*
1399 (6 Oct)^[20]	William de Blyton, Robert de Sutton
1401 (27 Oct)^[21]	Gilbert de Beseby, William de Harworth
1401–02 (30 Jan)	*unknown*
1402 (13 Sept)^	William Bliton, John Balderton
1403 (3 Dec)^	Seman Laxfeld, William de Daldirby
1404 (6 Oct)^	Robert de Appelby, Nicholas Hodelston
1405–06 (15 Feb)^[22]	Richard Worsop, Thomas Forster
1407 (20 Oct)^	Richard Worsop, Richard Balle (*viz.* Belle)
1409–10 (27 Jan)	*unknown*

13 Expenses: *CCR, 1381–85*, 291.
14 Expenses: *CCR, 1381–85*, 454.
15 Expenses: *CCR, 1385–89*, 658.
16 Expenses: *CCR, 1392–96*, 116.
17 Expenses: *CCR, 1392–96*, 279.
18 Expenses: *CCR, 1392–96*, 419.
19 Expenses: *CCR, 1396–99*, 304.
20 Expenses: *CCR, 1399–1402*, 108.
21 Expenses: *CCR, 1399–1402*, 331.
22 Expenses: *CCR, 1405–09*, 283.

Appendix 4

The Fraternal Year

Sources: C 47/40/134–50, C 47/41/151–60. Note: BVM = Blessed Virgin Mary

Guild	**Parish church**	**Event**	**Date**
Purification of the BVM	St Benedict, Wigford	Single Mornspeche	Sunday after the feast of the Epiphany (6 Jan)
Corpus Christi (Sailors)	*unknown*	Procession	To the Mother Church on the festival of John Dalderby (16 Jan)
St Mary and Nicholas (Clerks)	St John, Wigford	Mornspeche (1 of 2)	Sunday after the feast of the conversion of St Paul (25 Jan)
Purification of the BVM	St Benedict, Wigford	Feast	Purification of the BVM (2 Feb)
Corpus Christi	St Michael on the Hill	Single Mornspeche	Sunday after the feast of the Purification (2 Feb)
Holy Cross (Archers)	Holy Cross, Wigford	Mornspeche (1 of 3)	Ninth Sunday before Easter [*Septuagesima*] (24 Jan–27 Feb)
Resurrection	St Martin	Mornspeche (1 of 4)	Feast of Albinus (1 March)
Holy Sepulchre	Holy Cross, Wigford	Mornspeche (1 of 4)	First Sunday of Lent (14 Feb–13 March)
St George	St George	Mornspeche (1 of 4)	Sunday in the middle of Lent (21 Feb–20 March)

Guild	Parish church	Event	Date
BVM	St Benedict, Wigford	Mornspeche (1 of 2)	Feast of St Mary (25 March)
BVM (Cordwainers)	St Lawrence	Feast	BVM (25 March)
St Anne	St Peter in the Skinmarket	Mornspeche (1 of 2)	Sunday after the feast of BVM (25 March)
St Mary	St Rumbold	Mornspeche (1 of 3)	Sunday after the feast of BVM (25 March)
St Lawrence	St Lawrence	Mornspeche (1 of 2)	Sunday after the feast of BVM (25 March)
St Margaret	St Margaret, the Close	Mornspeche (1 of 3)	Sunday after the feast of BVM (25 March)
Corpus Christi (Tailors)	*unknown*	Mornspeche (1 of 4)	Sunday after the feast of BVM (25 March)
St Bavon	St Bavon	Mornspeche (1 of 3)	Sunday after Easter (29 March–2 May)
St George	St George	Feast	St George (23 April)
All Saints (Masons)	All Saints, the Bail	Single Mornspeche	Morrow of Easter (23 March–26 April)
Resurrection or Holy Sepulchre	St Cuthbert	Single Mornspeche	Wednesday of Easter Week (25 March–28 April)
Resurrection	St Martin	Feast	Wednesday of Easter Week (25 March–28 April)
St Mary	St Rumbold	Procession	To the Mother Church on the feast of the Assumption (30 March–3 June)
Corpus Christi (Tailors)	*unknown*	Mornspeche (2 of 4)	Octave of Easter (30 March–3 May)
St George	St George	Mornspeche (2 of 4)	Sunday after the feast of St George (23 April)
St Margaret	St Margaret, the Close	Mornspeche (2 of 2)	Sunday after the feast of St Mark the Evangelist (25 April)
St Anne	St Peter in the Skinmarket	Mornspeche (2 of 2)	Sunday before Ascension Day (25 April–29 May)

Guild	Parish church	Event	Date
St John the Evangelist (Barbers)	St John the Poor	Mornspeche (1 of 3)	Sunday after the feast of the Apostles Philip and Jacob (1 May)
Holy Cross (Archers)	Holy Cross, Wigford	Mornspeche (2 of 3)	Sunday after the feast of Holy Cross [*inventionem sancte crucis*] (3 May)
Minstrels and Entertainers	*unknown*	Procession	To the Mother Church on Wednesday of Whitsun Week (13 May–16 June)
BVM (Mercers)	*unknown*	Procession	To the Mother Church on Sunday after the Feast of Pentecost (17
			May–20 June)
Corpus Christi	St Michael on the Hill	Feast and procession	Eve of Corpus Christi (20 May–23 June) and Corpus Christi (21 May– 24 June)
Corpus Christi (Tailors)	*unknown*	Procession	To the Mother Church on the feast of Corpus Christi (21 May–24 June)
Corpus Christi	*unknown*	Procession	To the Mother Church on the feast of Corpus Christi (21 May–24 June)
Corpus Christi (Sailors)	*unknown*	Feast	Feast of Corpus Christi (21 May–24 June)
Corpus Christi (Tilers)	*unknown*	Feast	Feast of Corpus Christi (21 May–24 June)
St Martin	St Martin	Procession	To the Mother Church on the Translation of St Martin (4 July)
Resurrection	St Martin	Mornspeche (2 of 4)	Sunday after the translation of St Martin (4 July)
St Margaret	St Margaret, the Close	Feast	St Margaret (20 July)
St Anne	St Peter in the Skinmarket	Feast	St Anne (26 July)
BVM	St Benedict, Wigford	Mornspeche (2 of 2)	Feast of St Peter ad Vincula (1 Aug)
St Mary	St Rumbold	Mornspeche (3 of 3)	Sunday after the feast of St Peter ad Vincula (1 Aug)
Holy Cross (Archers)	Holy Cross, Wigford	Mornspeche (3 of 3)	Sunday after the feast of St Peter ad Vincula (1 Aug)

Guild	Parish church	Event	Date
St Lawrence	St Lawrence	Mornspeche (2 of 2)	Sunday after the feast of St Lawrence (10 Aug)
BVM (Cordwainers)	St Lawrence	Mornspeche (1 of 4)	Sunday before the feast of St Lawrence (10 Aug)
Holy Sepulchre	Holy Cross, Wigford	Mornspeche (2 of 4)	Sunday before the feast of St John [the Baptist] (29 Aug)
St Bavon	St Bavon	Mornspeche (2 of 3)	Sunday after the feast of St John the Baptist (29 Aug)
Exaltation of the Cross (Weavers)	*unknown*	Feast and procession	Exaltation of the Cross (14 Sept); procession to the cathedral
St Mary and Nicholas (Clerks)	St John, Wigford	Mornspeche (2 of 2)	Sunday after the feast of St Mathew (21 Sept)
St George	St George	Mornspeche (3 of 4)	Sunday after the feast of St Mathew (21 Sept)
Holy Sepulchre	Holy Cross, Wigford	Mornspeche (3 of 4)	Sunday before the feast of the Archangel Michael (29 Sept)
St Margaret	St Margaret, the Close	Mornspeche (3 of 3)	Feast of St Michael (29 Sept)
Corpus Christi (Tailors)	*unknown*	Mornspeche (4 of 4)	Sunday after the feast of the Archangel Michael (29 Sept)
St Nicholas, St Mary and All Saints	St Nicholas, Newport	Mornspeche (1 of 2)	Sunday after the feast of the Archangel Michael (29 Sept)
St Edmund	All Saints, Hungate	Mornspeche (1 of 2)	Sunday after the feast of the Archangel Michael (29 Sept)
St Bavon	St Bavon	Feast	St Bavon (1 Oct)
Resurrection	St Martin	Mornspeche (3 of 4)	Feast of the translation of St Hugh (6 Oct)
St John the Evangelist (Barbers)	St John the Poor	Mornspeche (2 of 3)	Feast of the translation of St Hugh (6 Oct)
St Mary and Nicholas (Clerks)	St John, Wigford	Feast and procession	To the Mother Church on the Monday after the feast of the translation of St Hugh (6 Oct)
BVM (Cordwainers)	St Lawrence	Mornspeche (2 of 4)	Sunday after the feast of St Lucas (18 Oct)

Guild	Parish church	Event	Date
St Edmund	All Saints, Hungate	Feast and procession	Sunday after the feast of St Edmund (15 Nov); procession to the
		Mornspeche (2 of 2)	'ymage of St Edmund'
Holy Sepulchre	Holy Cross, Wigford	Mornspeche (4 of 4)	Third Sunday before Christmas (4–9 Dec)
St Nicholas, St Mary and All Saints	St Nicholas, Newport	Feast	St Nicholas (7–14 Dec)
St Nicholas, St Mary and All Saints	St Nicholas, Newport	Mornspeche (2 of 2)	Sunday after the feast of the St Nicholas (7–14 Dec)
Resurrection	St Martin	Mornspeche (4 of 4)	Feast of St Thomas the Martyr (21 Dec)
St George	St George	Mornspeche (4 of 4)	Sunday after the feast of St Thomas the Martyr at Christmas [*in Natali*] (21 Dec)
St John the Evangelist (Barbers)	St John the Poor	Feast	St John the Evangelist (28 Dec–5 Jan)
St John the Evangelist (Barbers)	St John the Poor	Mornspeche (3 of 3)	Sunday after the feast of the St John the Evangelist (28 Dec–5 Jan)
Certificates Damaged			
St Bavon	St Bavon	Mornspeche (3 of 3)	*illegible*
BVM (Cordwainers)	St Lawrence	Mornspeche (3 of 4)	*illegible*
BVM (Cordwainers)	St Lawrence	Mornspeche (4 of 4)	*illegible*
Information Missing			
Holy Sepulchre	Holy Cross, Wigford	Feast	Not noted; presumably Good Friday (20 March–23 April)

Guild	Parish church	Event	Date
Holy Cross (Archers)	Holy Cross, Wigford	Feast	Not noted; presumably Good Friday (20 March–23 April)
St Mary and Nicholas (Clerks)	St John, Wigford	Feast	Not noted; presumably BVM (25 March) or St Nicholas (7–14 Dec)
Resurrection or Holy Sepulchre	St Cuthbert	Feast	Not noted; presumably Good Friday (20 March–23 April)
BVM (Great Guild)	St Andrew, Wigford	Feast	Not noted; presumably BVM (25 March)
Holy Cross (Fullers)	Holy Cross, Wigford	Feast	Feast noted, no date; presumably Good Friday (20 March–23 April)
St Mary	St Rumbold	Mornspeche (2 of 3)	Omitted in error
No Mornspeches noted			
BVM (Great Guild)	St Andrew, Wigford		
Holy Cross (Fullers)	Holy Cross, Wigford		
BVM (Mercers)	*unknown*		
Corpus Christi (Tilers)	*unknown*		
Corpus Christi (Sailors)	*unknown*		
Exaltation of the Cross (Weavers)	*unknown*		
Minstrels and Entertainers	*unknown*		

Appendix 5

Perpetual Chantry Foundations

Key: † = goods alienated under a general licence.

Foundation	Name	Church
1284[1]	Roger FitzBenedict	St Peter, Eastgate
1301[2]	Beatrice Colet	St Michael on the Mount
1303[3]	Alexander FitzMartyn	St Lawrence
1315[4]	John de Blyton	St Margaret, Wigford
1324[5]	John Pinzun	St Swithun
1327[6]	Edward I and II/ John de Blyton	Friars of the Penance of Jesus Christ (of the Sack)
1329[7]	Thomas de Wykford	St Benedict
1339[8]	Thomas de Carleton	St Mary Crackpole
1342[9]	William de Baiocis	St Botolph
1347[10]	Ralph Jolyff	St Peter, Wigford

1 *CPR, 1281–92*, 117; *CPR, 1281–92*, 162; *CPR, 1292–1301*, 31; *CPR, 1307–13*, 343; C 143/7/16; C 143/18/23; *Liber Cant.*, fos 165–181; LAO Reg/10, fos 106v–107; LAO Reg/11, fos 45–45v; LAO FL/Transcripts/J/33, 65, 73.

2 *CPR, 1292–1301*, 576; C 143/37/15; *BB*, fos 271, 272v; *Liber Cant.*, fo. 162v.

3 *CPR, 1301–07*, 114; *Chantry Certificates*, 201–4; C 143/43/11; LAO Reg/2, fos 14–15; LAO Reg/11, fo. 85; *Liber Cant.*, fos 40–42, 244–245v; LAO Dij 51/2/1.

4 *CPR, 1313–17*, 284; *Chantry Certificates*, 204–5; C 143/105/14; *Liber Cant.*, fos 292–3. *CIM, 1348–77*, 303–4, no. 807.

5 C 143/170/7; *BB*, fo. 165v; *BB*, fo. 209v.

6 *CPR, 1327–30*, 30–1; *CPR, 1330–34*, 160; SC 8/163/8121; C 143/187/6.

7 Re-foundation of the chantry located in the chapel of St Thomas founded in the twelfth century (see 202–3 for details). *CPR, 1327–30*, 414; *BB*, fo. 157; C 143/207/30; LAO Reg/5, fo. 368v; *Historical MSS*, 26–7, 32, 35, 38; LAO Dij 74/2/2, 7.

8 *CPR, 1338–40*, 301–2; C 143/249/15; *BB*, fo. 159v.

9 *CPR, 1340–3*, 566; *BB*, fo. 194v; C 143/264/5; LAO Reg/6, fo. 14; Reg/10, fos 84v, 98, 116v; Reg/11, fos 35v, 50, 67, 78v; Reg/13, fo. 174.

10 *CPR, 1345–8*, 541; *BB*, fo. 188; LAO Reg/9, fo. 128v; Reg/13, fos 155, 169; *Liber Cant.*, fos 310–11. The surviving inscription of Jolyff's chantry reads *Radulphus Jolyf & sua coniux ac Amisia/Hic simul humantur quibus ista capella paratur/Virgine Mater Theos qui sibi salvet eos/Pro quibus oretis opus hoc qui cumque videtis*: F. A. Greenhill, *Monumental Slabs in the County of Lincoln* (Weston-Super-Mare, 1986), 84–5.

1348[11]	Great Guild of BVM (two chantries)	St Andrew, Wigford
1350[12]	Thomas de Kele	St Mary Crackpole
1351[13]	Robert de Chesterfeld (Whitwell)†	St Swithun
1351[14]	Robert de Dalderby (two chantries)	St Benedict
1371[15]	John de Hodelston	St Peter at Pleas
	Re-founded in 1465[16]	
1378[17]	Agnes Cause	Cathedral
1378[18]	Roger de Tatersale	St Benedict
1382[19]	Robert Sutton	St Andrew, Wigford
1392[20]	Walter de Kelby	Priory of St Katherine
c.1425[21]	William de Blyton	St Stephen, Newland
c.1463[22]	'Chandeler chauntere'	*unknown*
1500[23]	Vicar General	St Peter, Wigford
1521[24]	Robert Dygton	St Michael on the Mount

11 Later known as the chantry of the guild of St Anne. *CPR, 1348–50*, 12; C 143/287/22; *Chantry Certificates*, 205–6; *Historical MSS*, 16, 34–5; C 143/349/21.

12 *CPR, 1348–50*, 466; C 143/295/7; *CPR, 1358–61*, 175; LAO Reg/8, fos 123–123v, 134.

13 *CPR, 1350–54*, 378; C 143/301/20; *Liber Cant.*, fos 343v–344v; *BB*, fos 220v–221; *WB*, fo. 85.

14 *CPR, 1350–54*, 116; *1364–67*, 384; *Chantry Certificates*, 199–200; C 143/301/24; C 143/308/6; LAO Reg/9, fos 44–5; *Liber Cant.*, fos 290v–292v.

15 C 143/376/22; C 143/447/8; *Liber Cant.*, fos 162v–163; *CCR, 1454– 61*, 124–5; *WB*, fos 39v, 96.

16 *CPR, 1461–67*, 382 (re-founded as 'John Huddilston's chaunterie').

17 *CPR, 1378–81*, 279; C 143/394/18; Bradshaw and Wordsworth, *Statutes of Lincoln Cathedral*, vol. 2, 443; LAO, A/3/1, fo. 80v.

18 Later known as the chantry of 'St Benedict'? *CPR, 1377–81*, 157; C 143/393/19; *ELW*, 82; *WB*, fo. 99.

19 *CPR, 1381–85*, 96, 443; *CPR, 1389–92*, 196; *CPR, 1391–96*, 112; C 143/399/20; C 143/408/16; C 143/412/23.

20 *CPR, 1391–96*, 105; C 143/413/23.

21 No exact date can be ascribed to Blyton's foundation. However, is it possible that the manor of Boultham, called Blyton Manor, sold for 300 marks to Hamon Sutton, John Kyghley, John Langholm of Salmonby, Robert Walssh of Lincoln and Simon Swaby, chaplain, in 1425, was in fact cover for this foundation? LAO Cragg 2/3, fo. 1; CP 25/1/145/156, no. 14. See 205–6 for more on chantries being established by trustees.

22 This chantry held tenements in St Swithun and St Stephen. No other details are known. *WB*, fos 39, 96.

23 Founded by Richard Johnson (city sheriff 1506/7); LAO Reg/23, fo. 56v; Hill, 'Three Lists', 241.

24 LAO L1/3/1, fos 108v–109, 141v; *Historical MSS*, 24.

Bibliography

Unpublished Primary Sources

Lincoln, Lincoln Archive Office

A/1/13
A/2/35–6
A/3/1
A/4/2/8–11, 16, 19/1–2, 21
A/4/2/17–18
Bj series
Cragg 2/3
Dean and Chapter, A/1/8, *Liber de Ordinationibus Cantariarum*
Dij series
Diocesan Miscellaneous Roll 1
FL/MISC/1/1/6
FL/transcripts/J/33
L/1/1/1, L/1/1/2
L1/3/1, *The White Book*
MF/2/38, 41, 45
Registers 2–25
LCL VC 2/1

Lincoln, Lincoln Cathedral Library

MS169, *The Burwarmote Book*

London, The National Archives

Public Record Office

Chancery
C 47 Chancery Miscellanea
C 60 Fine Rolls
C 62 Liberate Rolls
C 66 Patent Rolls
C 131 Extents for Debts, Series I
C 143 Inquisitions Ad Quod Damnum, Henry III to Richard III
C 241 Certificates of Statute Merchant and Statute Staple
C 267 Files, Tower and Rolls Chapel Series, Certificates of Elections

C 270 Ecclesiastical Miscellanea

Court of Common Pleas
CP 25 Feet of Fines

DL Duchy of Lancaster, Records

Exchequer
E 13 Exchequer of Pleas: Plea Rolls
E 101 King's Remembrancer: Accounts Various
E 122 King's Remembrancer: Particulars of Customs Accounts
E 159 King's Remembrancer: Memoranda Rolls and Enrolment Books
E 179 King's Remembrancer: Particulars of Account and other records relating to Lay and Clerical Taxation
E 356 Pipe Office: Customs Accounts
E 368 Lord Treasurer's Remembrancer: Memoranda Rolls
E 372 Pipe Office: Pipe Rolls

Justices Itinerant
JUST 1 Justice in Eyre, of Assize, of Oyer and Terminer, and of Peaces, etc: Rolls and Files
JUST 2 Coroner's Rolls and Files, with Cognate Documents
JUST 3 Justices of Gaol Delivery: Gaol Delivery Rolls and Files

King's Bench
KB 27 Court of King's Bench
KB 29 Controlment Rolls and other Memoranda Rolls of the Clerk of the Crown

Special Collections
SC 8 Ancient Petitions

Princeton, USA, Princeton University Library

Digital Collections, *The Blickling Homilies* (Scheide Library M71): online at http://pudl.princeton.edu/objects/x346d4176

Published Primary Sources

Archer, M. (ed.), *The Register of Bishop Philip Repingdon, 1405–19*, 3 vols (Lincoln Record Society, 1963–82)
Arnold, M. S., *Select Cases of Trespass from the King's Courts, 1307–1399*, 2 vols (London, 1985–87)
Ballard, A., and J. Tait (eds), *British Borough Charters, 1216–1307* (Cambridge, 1923)
Bateson, M. (ed.), *Borough Customs*, 2 vols (London, 1904–06)
—— *Cambridge Gild Records* (London, 1903)

—— *Records of the Borough of Leicester* (London, 1899)
Beardwood, A. (ed.), *Records of the Trial of Walter Langeton, Bishop of Coventry and Lichfield, 1307–1312* (London, 1969)
—— *The Statute Merchant Roll of Coventry, 1392–1416* (Oxford, 1939)
Bell, A., C. Brooks and P. Dryburgh (eds and trans), *Advance Contracts for the Sale of Wool, c.1200–c.1327* (List and Index Society, vol. 315) (Chippenham, 2006)
Bennett, N. (ed.), *The Registers of Bishop Henry Burghersh, 1320–1342*, 3 vols (Lincoln Record Society, 1999–2011)
Birch, W. de Gray (ed.), *The Royal Charters of the City of Lincoln* (Cambridge, 1911)
Bliss, W. H., and J. A. Twemlow (eds), *Calendar of Papal Registers Relating to Great Britain and Ireland*, vol. 3, 1342–1362 (1897)
—— *Calendar of Papal Registers Relating to Great Britain and Ireland*, vol. 4, 1362–1404 (1902)
Bradshaw, H., and C. Wordsworth (eds), *Statutes of Lincoln Cathedral*, 2 vols (Cambridge, 1892–97)
Calendar of Close Rolls (London, 1900–63)
Calendar of Fine Rolls (London, 1911–62)
Calendar of Inquisitions Miscellaneous (London, 1916–68)
Calendar of Inquisitions Post Mortem (London, 1904–87)
Calendar of Liberate Rolls (London, 1917–64)
Calendar of Patent Rolls (London, 1891–1986)
Carus-Wilson, E. M., and O. Coleman, *England's Export Trade, 1275–1547* (Oxford, 1963)
Chaplais, P. (ed.), *The War of Saint-Sardos (1323–1325)* (London, 1954)
Fenwick, C. C. (ed.), *The Poll Taxes of 1377, 1379 and 1381: Part 2, Lincolnshire-Westmorland* (Oxford, 2001)
Flower, C. T. (ed.), *Public Works in Medieval England*, vol. 1 (London, 1915)
Foster, C. W. (ed.), *Lincoln Wills, vol. 1: 1271–1526* (Lincoln Record Society, 1914)
—— *The Registrum Antiquissimum of the Cathedral Church of Lincoln*, vols 1–3 (Lincoln Record Society, 1933–35)
Foster, C. W., and K. Major (eds), *The Registrum Antiquissimum of the Cathedral Church of Lincoln*, vol. 4 (Lincoln Record Society, 1937)
Foster, C. W., and A. H. Thompson (eds), 'The Chantry Certificates for Lincoln and Lincolnshire returned in 1548 under the Act of Parliament of 1 Edward VI', *AASRP*, 36, 2 (1922): 183–295
Foulds, T. (ed.), *The Thurgaton Cartulary*, 2 vols (Donington, 1994)
Fowler, J. T. (ed.), *Extracts from the Account Rolls of the Abbey of Durham*, vol. 2 (Durham, 1899)
Fryde, E. B. (ed.), *The Wool Accounts of William de la Pole* (York, 1964)
Gibbons, A. (ed.), *Early Lincoln Wills* (Lincoln, 1888)
Given-Wilson, C., et al. (ed.), *The Parliament Rolls of Medieval England* (Leicester, 2005), CD-ROM version
Gras, N. S. B., *The Early English Customs System* (Cambridge, 1918)
Greenway, D. E. (ed.), *John Le Neve: Fasti Ecclesiae Anglicanae 1066–1300: III Lincoln* (London, 1977)
Hall, H. (ed.), *Select Cases Concerning the Law Merchant*, vol. 2 (London, 1930)
Hearne, T. (trans), 'Peter Langtoft's Chronicle', in *The Works of Thomas Hearne* (London, 1810).
Hector, L. C., and B. F. Harvey (eds and trans), *The Westminster Chronicle, 1381–1394* (Oxford, 1982)
Hickman, D. (ed.), *Lincoln Wills: 1532–4* (Lincoln Record Society, 2004)

Hill, M. T. (ed.), *The Rolls and Register of Bishop Oliver Sutton, 1280–1299*, 8 vols (Lincoln Record Society, 1948–86)

Hoskin, P. (ed.), *Robert Grosseteste as Bishop of Lincoln: The Episcopal Rolls, 1235–1253* (Lincoln Record Society, 2015

Horrox, R. (ed.), *The Black Death* (Manchester, 1994)

Hudson, A. (ed.), *Selections from English Wycliffite Writings* (Toronto, 1997)

Hudson, W. (ed.), *Leet Jurisdiction in the City of Norwich*, Selden Society, vol. 5 (London, 1892)

Hunter, J. (ed.), *The Great Rolls of the Pipe for the Second, Third, and Fourth Years of the Reign of King Henry the Second, A.D. 1155, 1156, 1157, 1158* (London, 1844)

Introduction to the Study of the Pipe Rolls (London, 1884)

Kahrl, S. J. (ed.), *Records of Plays and Players in Lincolnshire, 1300–1585* (Oxford, 1974)

Kelly, R. J. (ed.), *The Blickling Homilies: Edition and Translation* (London, 2003)

Kimball, E. G. (ed.), *Sessions of the Peace in the City of Lincoln, 1351–1354, and the Borough of Stamford 1351* (Lincoln Record Society, 1971)

—— *Some Sessions of the Peace in Lincolnshire, 1381–96*, 2 vols (Lincoln Record Society, 1953–62)

Latham, R. E. (ed.), *Revised Medieval Latin Word-List from British and Irish Sources* (Oxford, 2008)

Leadam, I. S. (ed.), *Select Case in the Court of Requests, AD 1497–1569* (London, 1898)

List of Sheriffs for England and Wales (List and Index Society, vol. 9) (New York, 1963)

Macray, W. D. (ed.), *Historical MSS, 14th Report: The Manuscripts of Lincoln, Bury St Edmunds and Great Grimsby Corporations and of the Deans and Chapters of Worcester and Lichfield, etc.* (London, 1895)

Madox, T. (ed.), *Firma Burgi, or an Historical Essay Concerning the Cities, Towns and Buroughs of England* (London, 1726)

—— *The History and Antiquities of the Exchequer of the Kings of England*, 2 vols (London, 1769)

Major, K. (ed.), *The Registrum Antiquissimum of the Cathedral Church of Lincoln*, vols 5–10 (Lincoln Record Society, 1940–73)

Maxwell-Lyte, H. C. (ed.), *A Descriptive Catalogue of Ancient Deeds in the Public Record Office*, 6 vols (London, 1890–1915)

McHardy, A. K. (ed.), *Clerical Poll-Taxes of the Diocese of Lincoln, 1377–1381* (Lincoln Record Society, 1992)

—— *Royal Writs addressed to John Buckingham, Bishop of Lincoln, 1363–1398: Lincoln Register 12b: a Calendar* (Lincoln Record Society, 1997)

McLane, B. W. (ed.), *The 1341 Royal Inquest in Lincolnshire* (Woodbridge, 1988)

Merle, William, *Consideraciones Temperieri Pro 7 Annis: The Earliest Known Journal of the Weather, 1337–1344*, trans and ed. by G. J. Symons (London, 1891)

Poos, L. R. (ed.), *Lower Ecclesiastical Jurisdiction in Late-Medieval England: The Courts of the Dean and Chapter of Lincoln, 1336–1349, and the Deanery of Wisbech, 1458–1484* (Oxford, 2001)

Raine, J. (ed.), *Fabric Rolls of York Minster* (Durham, 1858)

Return of the Name of Every Member of the Lower Parliament of England, Scotland and Ireland, vol. 1 (London, 1878)

Rich, E. E. (ed.), *The Staple Court Books of Bristol* (Bristol, 1934)

Rigby, S. (ed.), *The Overseas Trade of Boston in the Reign of Richard II* (Lincoln Record Society, 2004)

Rotuli Hundredorum, 2 vols (London, 1812–18)

Rotuli Parliamentorum ut et petitiones et placita in Parliamento, vol. 3 (1783)

Sharpe, R. R. (ed.), *Calendar of Letter Books* (London, 1950)
—— *Calendar of Letters from the Mayor and Corporation of the City of London, c.1350–1370* (London, 1885)
Sillem, R. (ed.), *Some Sessions of the Peace in Lincolnshire, 1360–1375* (Lincoln Record Society, 1937)
Simpson, G. G., and J. D. Galbraitth (eds), *Calendar of Documents Relating to Scotland*, vol. 5 (Edinburgh, 1881)
Smith, T. (ed.), *English Guilds* (Oxford, 1870)
Statutes of the Realm, vols 1–2 (Record Commission, London, 1810–16)
Stevenson, W. H. (ed.), *Records of the Borough of Nottingham*, vol. 1: *1155–1399* (Nottingham, 1882)
Stokes, J. (ed.), *Records of Early English Drama: Lincolnshire*, 2 vols (London, 2009)
Thomas, A. H. (ed.), *Plea and Memoranda Rolls, 1413–17* (London, 1943)
Thomson, S. E. M. (ed.), *Chronicon Galfridi le Baker de Swynebroke* (London, 1889)
Thomson, W. S. (ed.), *A Lincolnshire Assize Roll for 1298* (Lincoln Record Society, 1944)
Tillot, P. M. (ed.), *Victoria County History of the County of York* (London, 1961)
Twiss, T. (ed.), *The Black Book of the Admiralty*, vol. 2 (London, 1873)
Venables, E., *The Chronicle of Louth Park Abbey*, trans A. R. Maddison (Lincoln Record Society, 1891)
Willard, R. (ed.), *The Blickling Homilies: the John H. Scheide Library, Titusville, Pennsylvania* (Copenhagen, 1960)
Williams, W. J. (ed. and trans), 'Certificate of the Guild of Masons', *Ars Quatuor Coronatorum*, 42 (1931): 64–7
Wood, A. C., *List of Escheators for England and Wales* (List and Index Society, vol. 72) (London, 1971)

Secondary Sources

Abulafia, D., M. Franklin and M. Rubin (eds), *Church and City, 1000–1500: Essays in Honour of Christopher Brooke* (Cambridge, 1992)
Alcock, N. W., 'The Catesbys in Coventry: A Medieval Estate and its Archive', *Midland History*, 15 (1990): 1–36
Allen, J. (ed.), *The English Hospice in Rome* (Leominster, 2005)
Andrews, F. (ed.), *Ritual and Space in the Middle Ages: Proceedings of the 2009 Harlaxton Symposium* (Donington, 2011)
Armstrong, L., and I. Elbl (eds), *Money, Markets and Trade in Late Medieval Europe* (Leiden, 2007)
Arnade, P. J., M. C. Howell and S. Walter, 'Fertile Spaces: The Productivity of Urban Space in Northern Europe', *Journal of Interdisciplinary History*, 32, 4 (2002)
Arnold, J. H., *Belief and Unbelief in Medieval Europe* (London, 2010)
—— 'Margery's Trials: Heresy, Lollardy and Dissent', in J. H. Arnold and K. J. Lewis, *A Companion to the Book of Margery Kempe* (Cambridge, 2004)
Aston, M., 'Death', in R. Horrox (ed.), *Fifteenth-Century Attitudes: Perceptions of Society in Late Medieval England* (Cambridge, 1994)
—— *Lollards and Reformers: Images and Literacy in Late Medieval Religion* (London, 1984)
Attreed, L., 'The King's Interest: York's Fee Farm and the Central Government, 1482–92', *Northern History*, 17 (1987): 24–43

—— *The King's Towns: Identity and Survival in Late Medieval English Boroughs* (Oxford, 2001)

—— 'Medieval Bureaucracy and Bureaucracy and York's Fee Farm during the Fifteenth Century', *York Historian*, 6 (1985): 24–31

—— 'The Politics of Welcome: Ceremonies and Constitutional Development in Later Medieval Towns', in B. A. Hanawalt and K. L. Reyerson (eds), *City and Spectacle in Medieval Europe* (London, 1994)

—— 'Poverty, Payments, and Fiscal Policies in English Provincial Towns', in S. K. Cohn and S. A. Epstein (eds), *Portraits of Medieval and Renaissance Living* (Ann Arbor, 1996), 325–48

—— 'Urban Identity in Medieval English Towns', *Journal of Interdisciplinary History*, 32, 4 (2002): 571–92

Bailey, M., '*Per impetum maris*: natural disaster and economic decline in eastern England, 1275–1350', in B. M. S. Campbell (ed.), *Before the Black Death: Studies in the 'Crisis' of the Early Fourteenth Century* (Manchester, 1991), 184–208

Bailey, M., and S. Rigby (eds), *Town and Countryside in the Age of the Black Death* (Turnhout, 2012)

Bainbridge, V., *Gilds in the Medieval Countryside* (Woodbridge, 1997)

Barley, M. W., 'Lincolnshire Rivers in the Middle Ages', *Lincolnshire Architectural and Archaeological Society Reports and Papers*, 1 (1936): 1–21

Barron, C. M., *London in the Later Middle Ages: Government and People 1200–1500* (Oxford, 2004)

—— 'The London Middle English Guild Certificates of 1388–9', *Nottingham Medieval Studies*, 39 (1995): 108–45

—— 'The Parish Fraternities of Medieval London', in C. M. Barron, and C. Harper-Bill (eds), *The Church in Pre-Reformation Society* (Woodbridge, 1985)

Barron, C. M., and C. Harper-Bill (eds), *The Church in Pre-Reformation Society* (Woodbridge, 1985)

Barron, C. M., and A. F. Sutton (eds), *The Medieval Merchant: Proceedings of the 2012 Harlaxton Symposium* (Donington, 2014)

Bartlett, J. N., 'The Expansion and Decline of York in the Later Middle Ages', *Economic History Review*, Second Series, 12 (1959–60): 17–33

Beal, P., and J. Griffiths (eds), *English Manuscript Studies, 1100–1700*, vol. 4 (London, 1993)

Beattie, C., 'Living as a Single Person: Marital Status, Performance and the Law in Late Medieval England', *Women's History Review*, 17, 3 (2008): 327–40

Bedos-Rezak, B., 'Civic Liturgy and Urban Records in Northern France, 1100–1400', in B. A. Hanawalt and K. L. Reyerson (eds), *City and Spectacle in Medieval Europe* (London, 1994), 34–55

Bell, A. R., C. Brooks and P. R. Dryburgh, *The English Wool Market, c.1230–1327* (Cambridge, 2007)

Benedictow, O. J., *The Black Death, 1346–1353: The Complete History* (Woodbridge, 2008)

Binnall, P. B. G., 'Notes on the Medieval Altars and Chapels in Lincoln Cathedral', *Antiquaries Journal*, 42 (1962): 68–80

Bischoff, J. P., '"I Cannot Do't without Counters": Fleece Weights and Sheep Breeds in Late Thirteenth-Century and Early Fourteenth-Century England', *Agricultural History*, 57, 2 (1983): 143–60

—— 'Pegolotti: an Honest Merchant?', *Journal of European Economic History*, 6 (1977): 103–8

Black, C. F., *Italian Confraternities in the Sixteenth Century* (Cambridge, 2003)

Blair, J., and N. Ramsey (eds), *English Medieval Industries* (London 1991)

Bolton, J., '"The World Upside Down": Plague as an Agent of Economic and Social Change', in M. W. Ormrod and P. G. Lindley (eds), *The Black Death in England* (Stamford, 1996)

Bonney, M., 'The English Medieval Wool and Cloth Trade', *Local Historian*, 22, 1 (1992): 18–40

Bothwell, J., P. J. P. Goldberg and W. M. Ormrod (eds), *The Problem of Labour in Fourteenth- century England* (York, 2000)

Braid, R., 'Behind the Ordinance of Labourers: Economic Regulation and Market Control in London before the Black Death', *Journal of Legal History*, 34, 1 (2013): 3–30

Bridbury, A. R., 'The Black Death', *Economic History Review*, New Series, 26, 4 (1973): 577–92

—— 'English Provincial Towns in the Later Middle Ages', *Economic History Review*, 34, 1 (1981): 1–24

—— *Medieval English Clothmaking: An Economic Survey* (London, 1982)

Britnell, R., 'Bailiffs and Burgesses in Colchester, 1400–1525', *Essex Archaeology and History*, 21 (1990): 103–9

—— 'The Black Death in English Towns', *Urban History*, 21, 2 (1994): 195–210

—— *Britain and Ireland, 1050–1530: Economy and Society* (Oxford, 2004)

—— *The Commercialisation of English Society, 1000–1500* (Manchester, 1996)

—— 'The East Midlands', in J. Thirsk (ed.), *The Agrarian History of England and Wales*, vol. 3: 1348–1500 (Cambridge, 2011)

—— 'The Economy of British Towns 1300–1540', in D. M. Palliser (ed.), *Cambridge Urban History of Britain, vol. 1: 600–1540* (Cambridge, 2008), 326

—— 'Forstall, Forestalling and the Statute of Forestallers', *English Historical Review*, 102 (1987): 89–102

—— *Growth and Decline in Colchester, 1300–1525* (Cambridge, 1986)

—— 'Sedentary Long-distance Trade and the English Merchant Class in Thirteenth-Century England', in P. R. Coss and S. D. Lloyd (eds), *Thirteenth Century England V* (Woodbridge, 1995)

—— 'Town Life', in R. Horrox and W. M. Ormrod (eds), *A Social History of England: 1200–1500* (Cambridge, 2006)

—— 'Urban Demand in the English Economy, 1300–1600', in J. A. Galloway (ed.), *Trade, Urban Hinterlands and Market Integration, c.1300–1600* (London, 2000)

Britnell, R., and J. Hatcher (eds), *Progress and Problems in Medieval England* (Cambridge, 2002)

Brödt, B., 'East Anglia', in D. M. Palliser (ed.), *Cambridge Urban History of Britain, vol. 1: 600–1540* (Cambridge, 2008), 656

Brown, A. D., *Popular Piety in Late Medieval England: The Diocese of Salisbury, 1250–1550* (Oxford, 1995)

Burgess, C., '"By Quick and by Dead": Wills and Pious Provisions in Late Medieval Bristol', *English Historical Review*, 102, 405 (1987): 837–58

—— 'Chantries in the Parish, or "Through the Looking-glass"', *Journal of the British Archaeological Association*, 164 (2011): 100–29

—— '"A fond thing vainly invented": An Essay on the Pious Motive in Later Medieval England', in S. J. Wright (ed.), *Parish, Church and People: Local Studies in Lay Religion, 1350–1750* (London, 1988), 56–84

—— '"For the Increase of Divine Service": Chantries in the Parish in Late Medieval Bristol', *Journal of Ecclesiastical History*, 36, 1 (1985): 46–65

—— 'Making Mammon Serve God: Merchant Piety in Later Medieval England', in

C. M. Barron and A. F. Sutton (eds), *The Medieval Merchant: Proceedings of the 2012 Harlaxton Symposium* (Donington, 2014)

—— 'Strategies for Eternity: Perpetual Chantry Foundation in Late Medieval Bristol', in C. Harper-Bill (ed.), *Religious Belief and Ecclesiastical Careers in Late Medieval England* (Woodbridge, 1991), 1–33

Butcher, A. F., 'Rent and the Urban Economy: Oxford and Canterbury in the Later Middle Ages', *Southern History*, 1 (1979): 11–43

—— 'Rent, Population and Economic Change in Late Medieval Newcastle', *Northern History*, 14 (1978): 67–77

Cam, H. E., 'Shire Officials: Coroners, Constables, and Bailiffs', in J. F. Willard, W. A. Morris and W. H. Dunham (eds), *The English Government at Work, 1327–1336*, vol. 3 (Cambridge: Massachusetts, 1950), 149–65

Cameron, K., *The Place-names of Lincolnshire, Part One: The Place-names of the County of the City of Lincoln* (Cambridge, 1985)

Campbell, B. M. S. (ed.), *Before the Black Death: Studies in the 'Crisis' of the Early Fourteenth Century* (Manchester, 1991)

—— 'Benchmarking Medieval Economic Development: England, Wales, Scotland, and Ireland, c.1290', *Economic History Review*, 61, 4 (2008): 896–945.

Campbell, B. M. S., and K. Bartley, *England on the Eve of the Black Death* (Manchester, 2006)

Campbell, B. M. S., J. A. Galloway, D. Keene and M. Murphy, *A Medieval Capital and its Grain Supply: Agrarian Production and Distribution in the London Region, c.1300* (London, 1993)

Campbell, M., 'Gold, Silver and Precious Stones', in J. Blair and N. Ramsey (eds), *English Medieval Industries* (London 1991), 107–66

Carpenter, C., 'Gentry and Community in Medieval England', *Journal of British Studies*, 33, 4, (1994): 340–80

Carrel, H., 'Disputing Legal Privilege: Civic Relations with the Church in Late Medieval England', *Journal of Medieval History*, 35 (2009): 279–296

—— 'The Rituals of Town–Crown Relations in post-Black Death England', in F. Andrews (ed.), *Ritual and Space in the Middle Ages: Proceedings of the 2009 Harlaxton Symposium* (Donington, 2011)

Carter, H., *The Study of Urban Geography* (London, 4th edn, 1995)

Carus-Wilson, E. M., 'The Aulnage Accounts: A Criticism', *Economic History Review*, 2, 1 (1929): 114–23

—— 'The English Cloth Industry in the Late Twelfth and Early Thirteenth Centuries', *Economic History Review*, 14, 1 (1944): 32–50

—— *Medieval Merchant Venturers* (London, 2nd edn, 1967)

—— 'The Medieval Trade of the Ports of the Wash', *Medieval Archaeology* (1962–63): 182–201

Cassidy, R., '*Recorda splendidissima*: the Use of Pipe Rolls in the Thirteenth Century', *Historical Research*, 85, 227 (2012): 1–12

Cherry, J., 'Leather', in J. Blair and N. Ramsey (eds), *English Medieval Industries* (London 1991), 295–318

Chew, H. M., 'Mortmain in Medieval London', *English Historical Review*, 236 (1945): 1–15

Childs, W., 'A Paradise Hit is to Behold: Opportunities for Profit in Spain and Portugal in the Later Middle Ages', in C. M. Barron and A. F. Sutton (eds), *The Medieval Merchant: Proceedings of the 2012 Harlaxton Symposium* (Donington, 2014), 1–19

Christianson, C. P., 'Evidence for the Study of London's Late Medieval Manuscript-Book

Trade', in J. Griffiths and D. Pearsall (eds), *Book Production and Publishing in Britain, 1375–1475* (Cambridge, 1989), 87–108

Clanchy, M. T., *From Memory to Written Record: England 1066–1307* (London, 1979)

Clark, L., and C. Rawcliffe (eds), *The Fifteenth Century XII: Society in an Age of Plague* (Woodbridge, 2013)

Clark, P. (ed.), *Cambridge Urban History of Britain, 1540–1840*, vol. 2 (Cambridge, 2000)

Clemens, R., and T. Graham, *Introduction to Manuscript Studies* (Ithaca, 2007)

Cohn, S., 'After the Black Death: Labour Legislation and Attitudes towards Labour in Late- medieval Western Europe', *Economic History Review*, 60, 3 (2007): 457–85

—— 'Renaissance Attachment to Things: Material Culture in Last Wills and Testaments', *Economic History Review*, 65, 3 (2012): 984–1004

Cole, R. E. G., 'The Priory of St Katherine without Lincoln, of the Order of St Gilbert of Sempringham', *AASRP*, 27 (1903–04): 264–336

—— 'Proceedings Relative to the Canonisation of John de Dalderby', *AASRP*, 33 (1915): 143–76

—— 'Proceedings Relative to the Canonisation of Robert Grosseteste, Bishop of Lincoln', *AASRP*, 33 (1915): 1–34

Conway Davies, J. 'The Memoranda Rolls of the Exchequer to 1307', in *idem* (ed.), *Studies Presented to Hilary Jenkinson* (Oxford, 1957)

Cooper, A., 'The King's Four Highways: Legal Fiction Meets Fictional Law', *Journal of Medieval History*, 26, 4 (2000): 351–70

Corfield, P. J., and D. Keene (eds), *Work in Towns, 850–1850* (Leicester, 1990)

Coss, P. R., and S. T. Lloyd (eds), *Thirteenth Century England V* (Woodbridge, 1995)

Cragoe, C. D., 'The Custom of the English Church: Parish Church Maintenance in England before 1300', *Journal of Medieval History*, 36, 1 (2010): 20–38

Craig, H., 'The Lincoln Cordwainers' Pageant', *PMLA*, 32, 4 (1917): 605–15

Crouch, D. J. F., *Piety, Fraternity and Power: Gilds in Late Medieval Yorkshire, 1389–1547* (York, 2000)

Crum, R. J., and J. T. Paoletti (eds), *Renaissance Florence: A Social History* (Cambridge, 2006)

Curry, A., and E. Matthew (eds), *Concepts and Patterns of Service in the Later Middle Ages* (Woodbridge, 2000)

Curtis, M., 'The London Lay Subsidy of 1332', in G. Unwin (ed.), *Finance and Trade under Edward III* (Manchester, 1918), 35–60

Davies, J., 'Selling Food and Drink in the Aftermath of the Black Death', in M. Bailey, and S. Rigby (eds), *Town and Countryside in the Age of the Black Death* (Turnhout, 2012), 351–406

Davies, M., and A. Prescott (eds), *London and the Kingdom* (Donington, 2008)

Davies, R. G., and J. H. Denton (eds), *The English Parliament in the Middle Ages* (Manchester, 1981)

DeWindt, E. B. (ed.), *The Salt of Common Life: Individuality and Choice in the Medieval Town, Countryside, and Church* (Kalamazoo, 1995)

Dobson, J., and R. Milnes Walker, *Barbers and Barber Surgeons of London* (Oxford, 1979)

Dobson, R. B., 'Admissions to the Freedom of the City of York in the Later Middle Ages', *Economic History Review*, 26, 1 (1973): 1–22

—— 'Citizens and Chantries in Late Medieval York', in D. Abulafia, D., M. Franklin, and M. Rubin (eds), *Church and City, 1000–1500: Essays in honour of Christopher Brooke* (Cambridge, 1992), 311–32

—— 'The Foundation of Perpetual Chantries by the Citizens of Medieval York', in G. J. Cuming (ed.), *Studies in Church History*, vol. 4 (Leiden, 1967), 22–38

—— 'General Survey, 1300–1540', in D. M. Palliser (ed.), *Cambridge Urban History of Britain, vol. 1: 600–1540* (Cambridge, 2008), 276

—— 'Urban Decline in Late Medieval England', in R. Holt and G. Rosser (eds), *The Medieval Town, 1200–1540: A Reader in English Urban History* (Harlow, 1990), 265–86

Dodd, G., 'Corruption in the Fourteenth-Century English State', *International Journal of Public Administration*, 34, 11 (2011): 720–30

—— 'Richard II, Fiction of Majority Rule', in C. Beem (ed.), *The Royal Minorities of Medieval and Early Modern England* (New York, 2008), 103–60

Dodds, B., and C. Liddy (eds), *Commercial Activity, Markets and Entrepreneurs in the Middle Ages: Essays in Honour of Richard Britnell* (Woodbridge, 2011)

Drendel, J. (ed.), *Crisis in the Later Middle Ages: Beyond the Postan–Duby Paradigm* (Turnhout, 2015)

Duffy, E., 'Mater Dolorosa, Mater Misericordiae', *New Blackfriars*, 69, 816 (1988): 210–27

—— 'Religious Belief', in R. Horrox, and W. M. Ormrod (eds), *A Social History of England: 1200–1500* (Cambridge, 2006)

—— *The Stripping of the Altars: Traditional Religion in England, 1400–1580* (London, 1992)

Dunn, P., 'Trade', in C. Rawcliffe and R. Wilson (eds), *Medieval Norwich* (London, 2004), 213–34

Dyer, A., 'Appendix 5: Ranking of Towns by Taxpaying Population: the 1377 Poll Tax', in D. M. Palliser (ed.), *Cambridge Urban History of Britain, vol. 1: 600–1540* (Cambridge, 2008), 758

—— *Decline and Growth in English Towns, 1400–1600* (Cambridge, 1991)

—— 'Midlands', in P. Clark (ed.), *Cambridge Urban History of Britain, 1540–1840*, vol. 2 (Cambridge, 2000), 109–10

—— 'The Political Economy of Urban Decline in the Renaissance', in T. Slater (ed.), *Towns in Decline, AD100–1600* (Aldershot, 2000)

Dyer, C., 'The Consumer and the Market in the Later Middle Ages', *Economic History Review*, 42, 3 (1989), 309–10

—— *Everyday Life in Medieval England* (London, 2000)

—— 'Luxury Goods in Medieval England', in B. Dodds and C. Liddy (eds), *Commercial Activity, Markets and Entrepreneurs in the Middle Ages: Essays in Honour of Richard Britnell* (Woodbridge, 2011)

—— 'Market Towns and the Countryside in Late Medieval England', *Canadian Journal of History*, 31 (1996): 17–35

—— 'Medieval Small Towns and the Late Medieval Crisis', in J. Drendel (ed.), *Crisis in the Later Middle Ages: Beyond the Postan–Duby Paradigm* (Turnhout, 2015)

—— 'Small-town Conflict in the Later Middle Ages: Events at Shipston-on-Stour', *Urban History*, 19, 2 (1992): 183–210

—— 'Small Towns, 1270–1540', in D. M. Palliser (ed.), *Cambridge Urban History of Britain, vol. 1: 600–1540* (Cambridge, 2008), 505–40

—— *Standards of Living in the Later Middle Ages: Social Change in England, c.1200–1520* (Cambridge, 1998)

—— 'Taxation and Communities in Late Medieval England', in R. Britnell and J. Hatcher (eds), *Progress and problems in medieval England* (Cambridge, 1996), 168–90

—— 'Trade, Urban Hinterlands and Market Integration, 1300–1600: A Summing Upup', in J. A. Galloway (ed.), *Trade, Urban Hinterlands and Market Integration, c.1300–1600* (London, 2000)

Dyer, C., and T. Slater, 'The Midlands', in D. M. Palliser (ed.), *Cambridge Urban History of Britain, vol. 1: 600–1540* (Cambridge, 2008)

Epstein, S. R., 'Regional Fairs, Institutional Innovation, and Economic Growth in Late Medieval Europe', *Economic History Review*, 47, 3 (1994): 459–82

Faith, R., 'The Structure of the Market for Wool in Early Medieval Lincolnshire', *Economic History Review*, 65, 2 (2012): 674–700

Farnhill, K., *Guilds and the Parish Community in Late Medieval East Anglia, c.1470–1550* (York, 2001)

Ferris, S., 'Chaucer at Lincoln (1387): The "'Prioress's Tale" as a Political Poem', *Chaucer Review*, 15, 4 (1981): 295–321

Fleet, P., 'Markets in Medieval Lincolnshire', *East Midland Historian*, 3 (1993): 7–14

Fleming, P. W., 'Charity, Faith, and the Gentry of Kent, 1422–1529', in T. Pollard (ed.), *Property and Politics: Essays in Later Medieval English History* (Gloucester, 1984), 36–58

Fraser, C. M. 'The Pattern of Trade in the North-East of England, 1265–1350', *Northern History*, 40 (1969): 44–66

French, K. L., *The Good Wife of the Parish* (Philadelphia, 2008)

Frost, R. H., 'The Urban Elite', in C. Rawcliffe, and R. Wilson (eds), *Medieval Norwich* (London, 2004), 235–54

Fryde, E. B., 'Edward III's Wool Monopoly: A Fourteenth-Century Royal Trading Adventure', *History*, New Series, 37 (1952): 8–24

Gadd, I. A., and P. Wallis (eds), *Guilds and Association in Europe, 900–1900* (London, 2006)

Galloway, J. A. (ed.), *Trade, Urban Hinterlands and Market Integration, c.1300–1600* (London, 2000)

Gerchow, J., 'Gilds and Fourteenth-Century Bureaucracy: The Case of 1388–9', *Nottingham Medieval Studies*, 40 (1996): 109–48

Giles, K., *An Archaeology of Social Identity: Guildhalls in York, c. 1350–1630*, BAR British Series 315 (Oxford, 2000)

Given-Wilson, C., 'Service, Serfdom and English Labour Legislation, 1350–1500', in A. Curry and E. Matthew (eds), *Concepts and Patterns of Service in the Later Middle Ages* (Woodbridge, 2000), 21–37

Glennie, P., and I. Whyte, 'Towns in an Agrarian Economy', in P. Clark (ed.), *Cambridge Urban History of Britain, 1540–1840*, vol. 2 (Cambridge, 2000), 183–90.

Goddard, R., 'Church Lords and English Urban Investment in the Later Middle Ages', *Past and Present*, Supplement 2 (2007): 148–65

—— 'Commercial Contraction and Urban Decline in Fifteenth-century Coventry', *Dugdale Society Occasional Papers*, 46 (2006): 1–33

—— *Credit and Trade in Later Medieval England, 1353–1532* (Basingstoke, forthcoming, 2016)

—— *Lordship and Medieval Urbanisation: Coventry, 1043–1355* (Woodbridge, 2004)

—— 'Medieval Business Networks: St Mary's Guild and the Borough Court in Later Medieval Nottingham', *Urban History*, 40, 1 (2013): 3–27

Goff, J. le, *The Birth of Europe* (Oxford, 2005)

—— *The Birth of Purgatory*, trans A. Goldhammer (London, 1984)

Goldberg, P. J. P., *Medieval England: A Social History, 1250–1550* (London, 2004)

—— 'Urban Identity and the Poll Taxes of 1377, 1379 and 1381', *Economic History Review*, 43, 2 (1990): 194–216

—— 'What Was a Servant?', in A. Curry and E. Matthew (eds), *Concepts and Patterns of Service in the Later Middle Ages* (Woodbridge, 2000), 1–20

—— *Women, Work, and Life Cycle in a Medieval Economy: Women in York and Yorkshire, c.1300–1520* (Oxford, 1992)

Good, J., 'The Alien Clothworkers of London, 1337–1381', in L. E. Mitchell, K. L French

and D. L. Biggs (eds), *The Ties that Bind* (Farnham, 2011)
Gray, H. L., 'The Production and Exportation of English Woollens in the Fourteenth Century', *English Historical Review* 39, 153 (1924): 13–35
Green, A., *Town Life in the Fifteenth Century*, 2 vols (London, 1894)
Green, B., and R. M. R. Young, *Norwich: The Growth of a City* (Norwich, 1963)
Greenhill, F. A., *Monumental Slabs in the County of Lincoln* (Weston-Super-Mare, 1986)
Griffiths, J., and D. Pearsall (eds), *Book Production and Publishing in Britain, 1375–1475* (Cambridge, 1989)
Gurevich, A. J., 'Popular and Scholarly Medieval Traditions – Notes in the Margins of Jacques Le Goff's Book', *Journal of Medieval History*, 9 (1983): 71–90
Hadwin, J. F., 'The Medieval Lay Subsidies and Economic History', *Economic History Review*, 36, 2 (1983): 200–17
Hamilton, J. S. (ed.), *Fourteenth Century England VIII* (Woodbridge, 2014)
Hanawalt, B. A., 'Keepers of the Lights: Late Medieval English Parish Gilds', *Journal of Medieval and Renaissance Studies*, 41, 1 (1984)
Hanawalt, B. A., and K. L. Reyerson (eds), *City and Spectacle in Medieval Europe* (London, 1994)
Hanham, A., 'Profits on English Wool Exports, 1472–1544', *Bulletin of the Institute for Historical Research*, 55 (1982): 139–47.
Hare, J. 'Inns, Innkeepers and the Society of Later Medieval England, 1350–1600', *Journal of Medieval History* 39, 4 (2013): 477–97
—— 'Salisbury: The Economy of a Fifteenth-Century Provincial Capital', *Southern History*, 31 (2009): 1–26
Harper-Bill, C., 'The English Church and English Religion after the Black Death', in W. M. Ormrod and P. G. Lindley (eds), *The Black Death in England* (Stamford, 1996)
—— (ed.), *Medieval East Anglia* (Woodbridge, 2005)
Harriss, G. L., 'Aids, Loans, Benevolences', *Historical Journal*, 6, 1 (1963): 1–19
—— 'Political Society and the Growth of Government in Late Medieval England', *Past and Present*, 138 (1993): 28–57.
Harvey, B. F., 'Introduction: the "Crisis" of the Early Fourteenth Century', in B. M. S. Campbell (ed.), *Before the Black Death: Studies in the 'Crisis' of the Early Fourteenth Century* (Manchester, 1991), 1–24
Harvey, E., 'Pavage Grants and Urban Street Paving in Medieval England, 1249–1462', *Journal of Transport History*, 31, 2 (2010): 151–63
Harvey, M., *Lay Religious Life in Late Medieval Durham* (Woodbridge, 2006)
Hatcher, J., 'England in the Aftermath of the Black Death', *Past and Present*, 144 (1994): 3–35
—— 'The Great Slump of the Mid-fifteenth Century', in R. Britnell and J. Hatcher (eds), *Progress and Problems in Medieval England* (Cambridge, 1996), 237–72
—— *Plague, Population and the English Economy 1348–1530* (London, 1977)
Hatcher, J., and M. Bailey, *Modelling the Middle Ages* (Oxford, 2001)
Heath, P., 'Before Reform and Reformation: The English Church in the Fourteenth and Fifteenth Centuries', *Journal of Ecclesiastical History*, 41, 4 (1990): 647–78
—— 'Urban Piety in the Later Middle Ages: the Evidence of Hull Wills', in B. Dobson (ed.), *The Church, Politics and Patronage in the Fifteenth Century* (Gloucester, 1984), 209–29
Heaton, H., *The Yorkshire Woollen and Worsted Industries* (Oxford, 1920)
Henderson, J., *Piety and Charity in Late Medieval Florence* (Chicago, 1997)
Hewitt, M. J., *The Organization of War under Edward III, 1338–62* (Manchester, 1966)
Hicks, M., 'Chantries, Obits and Almshouses: the Hungerford Foundations, 1325–1478',

in C. M. Barron and C. Harper-Bill (eds), *The Church in Pre-Reformation Society* (Woodbridge, 1985), 123–42

—— (ed.), *English Inland Trade, 1430–1540: Southampton and its Region* (Oxford, 2015)

Hill, J. W. F., 'The Manor of Hungate, or Beaumont Fee, in Lincoln', *AASRP*, 38 (1926–27): 175–208

—— *Medieval Lincoln* (Cambridge, 1948; reprint, Stamford, 1990)

—— 'Three Lists of Mayors, Bailiffs and Sheriffs of the City of Lincoln', *AASRP*, 39, 2 (1929): 217–56

—— *Tudor and Stuart Lincoln* (Cambridge, 1956; reprint, Stamford, 1991)

Hill, R. M. T., '"A Chaunterie for Soules": London Chantries in the Reign of Richard II', in F. R. H. Du Boulay and C. M. Barron (eds), *The Reign of Richard II* (London, 1971), 242–55

—— *Oliver Sutton, Bishop of Lincoln, 1280–1299* (Lincoln, 1950)

Hilton, R., *English and French towns in feudal society: A comparative study* (Cambridge, 1992)

—— 'Small Town Society in England before the Black Death', *Past and Present*, 105 (1984): 53–78

Hodgett, G. A. J., *Tudor Lincolnshire* (Welwyn Garden City, 1975)

Holt., R., 'Society and Population, 600–1300', in D. M. Palliser (ed.), *Cambridge Urban History of Britain, vol. 1: 600–1540* (Cambridge, 2008), 79–104

Holt, R., and G. Rosser (eds), *The Medieval Town, 1200–1540: A Reader in English Urban History* (Harlow, 1990)

Horrox, R., 'Purgatory, Prayer and Plague', in P. C. Jupp and C. Gittings, *Death in England: An Illustrated History* (Manchester, 1999), 90–118

—— 'The Urban Gentry in the Fifteenth Century', in J. A. F. Thomson (ed.), *Towns and Townspeople in the Fifteenth Century* (Gloucester, 1988), 22–44

—— (ed.), *Fifteenth-Century Attitudes: Perceptions of Society in Late Medieval England* (Cambridge, 1994)

Horrox, R., and W. M. Ormrod (eds), *A Social History of England: 1200–1500* (Cambridge, 2006)

Hughes, 'The Parliament of Lincoln, 1316', *Transactions of the Royal Historical Society*, New Series 10 (1896): 41–58

Hunnisett, R., *The Medieval Coroner* (Cambridge, 2008)

James, M., 'Ritual, Drama and Social Body in the Late Medieval English Town', *Past and Present*, 98 (1983): 3–29

James, M. K., *Studies in the Medieval Wine Trade* (Oxford, 1971)

Johnson, C., and S. Jones, *Steep, Strait and High: Ancient Houses of Central Lincoln* (Woodbridge, 2016)

Johnston, A. F., 'English Guilds and Municipal Authority', *Renaissance and Reformation*, 25 (1989): 69–88

—— 'The Guild of Corpus Christi and the Procession of Corpus Christi in York', *Mediaeval Studies*, 38 (1976): 372–84

Jones, S., K. Major, and J. Varley, *The Survey of Ancient Houses in Lincoln*, 3 vols (Lincoln, 1984– 90)

Jones, S., K. Major, J. Varley and C. Johnson, *The Survey of Ancient Houses in Lincoln: IV: Houses in the Bail: Steep Hill, Castle Hill, and Bailgate* (Lincoln, 1996)

Jordan, W. C., *The Great Famine: Northern Europe in the Early Fourteenth Century* (Princeton, 1996)

Jupp, P. C., and C. Gittings (eds), *Death in England: An Illustrated History* (Manchester, 1999)

Kaeuper, R. (ed.), *Medieval Law and its Practices, vol. 14: Law, Governance, and Justice: New Views on Medieval Constitutionalism* (Leiden, 2013)

Keene, D., 'Changes in London's Economic Hinterland as Indicated by Debt Cases in the Court of Common Pleas', in J. A. Galloway (ed.), *Trade, Urban Hinterlands and Market Integration, c.1300–1600* (London, 2000), 59–81

—— 'Continuity and Development in Urban Trades: Problems of Concepts and the Evidence', in P. J. Corfield and D. Keene (eds), *Work in Towns, 850–1850* (Leicester, 1990), 1–16

—— 'Crisis Management in London's Food Supply, 1250–1500', in B. Dodds and C. Liddy (eds), *Commercial Activity, Markets and Entrepreneurs in the Middle Ages: Essays in Honour of Richard Britnell* (Woodbridge, 2011)

—— 'English Urban Guilds, c.900–1300', in I. A. Gadd and P. Wallis (eds), *Guilds and Association in Europe, 900–1900* (London, 2006), 3–26

—— *Survey of Medieval Winchester*, 2 vols (Oxford, 1985)

Kemp, B., 'The Acta of English Rural Deans in the Later Twelfth and Early Thirteenth Centuries', in P. Hoskin, C. Brooke and B. Dobson (eds), *The Foundations of Medieval English Ecclesiastical History: Studies Presented to David Smith* (Woodbridge, 2005), 139–58

Kemp, E. W., 'The Attempted Canonization of Robert Grosseteste', in D. A. Callus, *Robert Grosseteste: Scholar and Bishop* (Oxford, 1955), 241–6

Kermode, J., 'The Greater Towns, 1300–1540', in D. M. Palliser (ed.), *Cambridge Urban History of Britain, vol. 1: 600–1540* (Cambridge, 2008), 453–4

—— 'Medieval Indebtedness: the Regions versus London', in N. Rogers (ed.), *England in the Fifteenth Century* (Stamford, 1994), 72–88

—— *Medieval Merchants: York, Beverley and Hull in the Later Middle Ages* (Cambridge, 1998)

—— 'Merchants, Overseas Trade, and Urban Decline: York, Beverley, and Hull c.1380–1500', *Northern History*, 23, 1 (1987): 51–73

—— 'Money and Credit in the Fifteenth Century: Some Lessons from Yorkshire', *Business History Review*, 65, 3 (1991): 475–501

—— 'Sentiment and Survival: Family and Friends in Late Medieval English Towns', *Journal of Family History*, 24, 5 (1999): 5–18

—— 'Urban Decline? The Flight from Office in Late Medieval York', *Economic History Review*, New Series, 35, 2 (1982): 179–98

—— (ed.), *Enterprise and Individuals in Fifteenth Century England* (Stroud, 1991)

Kershaw, I., 'The Great Famine and Agrarian Crisis in England, 1315–1322', *Past and Present*, 59 (1973): 3–50

Kissane, A., '*Manibus Violentis*: Touch and Sanctuary in Medieval Lincoln', in U. Krampl, R. Beck and E. Retaillaud-Bajac (eds), *Les cinq sens de la ville du Moyen Age à nos jours* (Tours, 2013), 315–27

Kissane, A., and J. Mackman, 'Aliens and Local Justice in Late Medieval Lincolnshire', in W. M. Ormrod, N. McDonald, C. Taylor (eds), *Resident Aliens in Later Medieval England* (Turnhout, forthcoming, 2017)

Kleineke, K., 'Civic Ritual, Space and Conflict in Fifteenth-Century Exeter', in F. Andrews (ed.), *Ritual and Space in the Middle Ages: Proceedings of the 2009 Harlaxton Symposium* (Donington, 2011), 169–70

Kreider, A., *English Chantries: The Road to Dissolution* (Cambridge, 1979)

Kowaleski, M., 'The Demography of Maritime Communities in Late Medieval England', in M. Bailey and S. Rigby (eds), *Town and Countryside in the Age of the Black Death* (Turnhout, 2012), 87–118

—— 'The History of Urban Families in Medieval England', *Journal of Medieval History*, 14 (1988): 47–63

—— *Local Markets and Regional Trade in Medieval Exeter* (Cambridge, 2002)

—— 'Port Towns: England and Wales 1300–1540', in D. M. Palliser (ed.), *Cambridge Urban History of Britain, vol. 1: 600–1540* (Cambridge, 2008), 476–87

—— 'Town and Country in Late Medieval England: The Hide and Leather Trade', in P. J. Corfield and D. Keene (eds), *Work in Towns, 850–1850* (Leicester, 1990)

—— 'Warfare, Shipping, and Crown Patronage: The Impact of the Hundred Years War on the Port Towns of Medieval England', in L. Armstrong and I. Elbl (eds), *Money, Markets and Trade in Late Medieval Europe* (Leiden, 2007), 233–54

Kowaleski, M., and J. M. Bennett, 'Crafts, Gilds, and Women in the Middle Ages: Fifty Years after Marian K. Dale', *Signs: Journal of Women in Culture and Society*, 14, 2 (1989): 74–88

Kowaleski, M., J. Langdon and P. R. Schofield (eds), *Peasants and Lords in the Medieval English Economy* (Turnhout, 2015)

Lambert, B., and M. Pajic, 'Drapery in Exile: Edward III, Colchester and the Flemings, 1351–1367', *History*, 99, 338 (2014): 733–53

Laughton, J., *Life in a Late Medieval City: Chester, 1275–1520* (Oxford, 2008)

Laughton, J., E. Jones and C. Dyer, 'The Urban Hierarchy in the Later Middle Ages: A Study of the East Midlands', *Urban History*, 28, 3 (2001): 331–57

Lee, J. S. 'The Role of Fairs in Late Medieval England', in M. Bailey and S. Rigby (eds), *Town and Countryside in the Age of the Black Death* (Turnhout, 2012), 407–37

Liddy, C., *War, Politics and Finance in Late Medieval English Towns: Bristol, York and the Crown, 1350–1400* (Woodbridge, 2005)

Lilley, K., *Urban Life in the Middle Ages, 1000–1450* (Basingstoke, 2002)

Lindley, P., 'The Black Death and English Art', in W. M. Ormrod and P. G. Lindley (eds), *The Black Death in England* (Stamford, 1996)

—— (ed.), *The Early History of Lincoln Castle* (Lincoln, 2004)

Livingstone, M., 'A Snapshot in Time: The Weather as Seen in the Record of the *Nonae* (1339–41)', in M. Kowaleski, J. Langdon and P. R. Schofield (eds), *Peasants and Lords in the Medieval English Economy* (Turnhout, 2015)

Lloyd, T. H., *The English Wool Trade in the Middle Ages* (Cambridge, 1977)

—— 'The Movement of Wool Prices in Medieval England', *Economic History Review Supplement*, 6 (Cambridge, 1973)

Lutton, R., *Lollardy and Orthodox Religion in Pre-Reformation England* (Woodbridge, 2006)

Lydon, J. F., 'Survey of the Memoranda Rolls of the Irish Exchequer, 1294–1509', *Analecta Hibernica*, 23 (1966): 51–74

Maddicott, J. R., 'The English Peasantry and the Demands of the Crown, 1294–1341', in T. H. Aston (ed.), *Landlords, Peasants and Politics in Medieval England* (Cambridge, 1987), 285–359

Major, K., 'The Finances of the Dean and Chapter of Lincoln from the Twelfth to Fourteenth Century', *Journal of Ecclesiastical History*, 5 (1954): 149–67

—— *Minster Yard* (Edinburgh, 1974)

Martin, G. H., 'The English Borough in the Thirteenth Century', in R. Holt and G. Rosser (eds), *The Medieval Town, 1200–1540: A Reader in English Urban History* (Harlow, 1990)

Mason, E., 'The Role of the English Parishioner, 1100–1500', *Journal of Ecclesiastical History*, 27, 1 (1976): 17–29

Masschaele, J., *Peasants, Merchants, and Markets: Inland Trade in Medieval England,*

1150–1350 (New York, 1997)

—— 'Tolls and Trade in Medieval England', in L. Armstrong and I. Elbl (eds), *Money, Markets and Trade in Late Medieval Europe* (Leiden, 2007), 146–83

McClure, P., 'Patterns of Migration in the Late Middle Ages: The Evidence of English Place-Name Surnames', *Economic History Review*, New Series, 32, 2 (1979): 167–82

McHardy, A. K., 'Ecclesiastics and Economics: Poor Priests, Prosperous Laymen, and Proud Prelates in the Reign of Richard II', in W. J. Sheils and D. Wood (eds), *The Church and Wealth* (Oxford, 1987), 129–37

—— 'The Lincolnshire Clergy in the Later Fourteenth Century', in W. M. Ormrod (ed.), *England in the Fourteenth Century: Proceedings of the Harlaxton Symposium* (Woodbridge, 1986), 145–51

McNall, C., 'The Business of Statutory Debt Registries, 1283–1307', in P. R. Schofield and N. J. Mayhew (eds), *Credit and Debt in Medieval England, c.1180–c.1350* (Oxford, 2002)

McRee, B. R., 'Charity and Gild Solidarity in Late Medieval England', *Journal of British Studies*, 32, 3 (1993): 195–225

—— 'Peacemaking and its Limits in Late Medieval Norwich', *English Historical Review*, 109, 433 (1994): 831–66

—— 'Religious Gilds and Civil Order: The Case of Norwich in the Late Middle Ages', *Speculum*, 67, 1 (1992): 69–97

—— 'Religious Gilds and the Regulation of Behaviour in Late Medieval Towns', in J. Rosenthal and C. Richmond (eds), *People, Politics and Community in the Later Middle Ages* (Gloucester, 1987), 108–22

—— 'Unity or Division? The Social Meaning of Guild Ceremony in Urban Communities', in B. Hanawalt and K. L. Reyerson (eds), *City and Spectacle in Medieval Europe* (London, 1994), 189–207

Meekings, C. A. F., 'The Pipe Roll Order of 12 February 1270', in J. Conway Davies (ed.), *Studies Presented to Hilary Jenkinson* (Oxford, 1957), 222–53

Mercer, M., 'King's Armourers and the Growth of the Armourer's Craft in Early Fourteenth-Century London', in J. S. Hamilton (ed.), *Fourteenth Century England VIII* (Woodbridge, 2014), 1–20

Merrick, P., 'Taxing Medieval Cloth', *Local Historian* 32, 4 (2002): 218–33

Meyer, E. T., 'Boroughs', in J. F. Willard, W. A. Morris and W. H. Dunham (eds), *The English Government at Work, 1327–1336*, vol. 3 (Cambridge, Massachusetts, 1950), 107–8

Michael, M. A., 'English Illuminators, c.1190–1450: A Survey from Documentary Sources', in P. Beal and J. Griffiths (eds), *English Manuscript Studies, 1100–1700*, vol. 4 (London, 1993), 62–113

Miller, E., 'The Fortunes of the English Textile Industry during the Thirteenth Century', *Economic History Review*, 18, 1 (1965): 64–82

Miller, E., and J. Hatcher, *Medieval England: Towns, Commerce and Crafts, 1086–1348* (Harlow, 1995)

Mitchell, L. E., K. L. French and D. L. Biggs (eds), *The Ties that Bind* (Farnham, 2011)

Moore, E. W., *The Fairs of Medieval England: An Introductory Study* (Wetteren, 1985)

Morris, C., and P. Roberts (eds), *Pilgrimage: the English Experience from Becket to Bunyan* (Cambridge, 2002)

Mundill, R. R., *England's Jewish Solution: Experiment and Expulsion, 1262–1290* (Cambridge, 1998)

Munro, J., 'Before and after the Black Death: Money, Prices, and Wages in Fourteenth-century England', *New Approaches to the History of Late Medieval and Early Modern*

Europe, 104 (2009): 335–64

—— 'The "Industrial Crisis" of the English Textile Towns, c.1290–c.1330', in M. Prestwich, M. R. Britnell and R. Frame (eds), *Thirteenth Century England VII: Proceedings of the Durham Conference, 1997* (Woodbridge, 1999), 105–15

Musson, A., 'Centre and Locality: Perceptions of the Assize Justices in Late Medieval England', in R. Kaeuper (ed.), *Medieval Law and its Practices, vol. 14: Law, Governance, and Justice: New Views on Medieval Constitutionalism* (Leiden, 2013), 211–42

—— 'New Labour Laws, New Remedies? Legal Reaction to the Black Death 'Crisis'', in N. Saul (ed.), *Fourteenth Century England I* (Woodbridge, 2000), 73–88

—— (ed.), *Medieval Law in Context* (Manchester, 2004)

New, E. A., 'Fraternities in English Cathedrals in the Later Medieval Period', in T. Thornton (ed.), *Social Attitudes and Political Structures in the Fifteenth Century* (Stroud, 2000), 33–51

Nightingale, P., 'Alien Finance and the Development of the English Economy, 1285–1311', *Economic History Review*, 66, 2 (2013): 477–96

—— 'Capitalists, Crafts and Constitutional Change in Late Fourteenth-Century London', *Past and Present*, 124 (1989): 3–35

—— 'The Growth of London', in R. Britnell and J. Hatcher (eds), *Progress and Problems in Medieval England* (Cambridge, 2002), 89–106

—— 'The Intervention of the Crown and the Effectiveness of the Sheriff in the Execution of Judicial Writs, c.1355–1530', *English Historical Review*, 123, 500 (2008): 1–34

—— 'Knights and Merchants: Trade, Politics and the Gentry in Late Medieval England', *Past and Present*, 169, 1 (2000): 36–62

—— 'The Lay Subsidies and the Distribution of Wealth in Medieval England', *Economic History Review*, 57, 1 (2004): 1–32

—— 'Monetary Contraction and Mercantile Credit in Later Medieval England', *Economic History Review*, 43, 4 (1990): 560–75

—— 'Some New Evidence of Crises and Trends of Mortality in Late Medieval England', *Past and Present*, 187 (2005): 33–68

—— 'The Rise and Decline of Medieval York: A Reassessment', *Past and Present*, 206, 1 (2010): 3–42

Nilson, B., *Cathedral Shrines of Medieval England* (Woodbridge, 2001)

Ormrod, W. M., 'The Crown and the English Economy, 1290–1348', in B. M. S. Campbell (ed.), *Before the Black Death: Studies in the 'Crisis' of the Early Fourteenth Century* (Manchester, 1991), 149–83

—— (ed.), *England in the Fourteenth Century: Proceedings of the 1985 Harlaxton Symposium* (Woodbridge, 1986)

Ormrod, W. M., and P. G. Lindley (eds), *The Black Death in England* (Stamford, 1996)

Owen, D. M., *Church and Society in Medieval Lincolnshire* (Welwyn Garden City, 1971)

—— (ed.), *A History of Lincoln Minster* (Cambridge, 1994)

Page, W. (ed.), *The Victoria History of the County of Lincolnshire*, vol. 2 (London, 1906)

Palliser, D. M., 'Urban Decay Revisited', in J. A. F. Thompson (ed.), *Towns and Townspeople in the Fifteenth Century* (Gloucester, 1998)

—— 'Urban Society', in R. Horrox (ed.), *Fifteenth-Century Attitudes: Perceptions of Society in Late Medieval England* (Cambridge, 1994), 132–49

—— (ed.), *The Cambridge Urban History of Britain*, vol. 1 (Cambridge, 2000)

Palmer, R. C., *The County Courts of Medieval England, 1150–1350* (Princeton, 1982)

Pantin, W. A., *The English Church in the Fourteenth Century* (Cambridge, 1955)

Pelham, R. A., 'The Provisioning of the Lincoln Parliament of 1301', *University of Birmingham Historical Journal*, 3 (1951–52): 16–32

Phythian-Adams, C., 'Ceremony and the Citizen: The Communal Year at Coventry 1450–1550', in R. Holt, and G. Rosser (eds), *The Medieval Town, 1200–1540: A Reader in English Urban History* (Harlow, 1990)

—— *Desolation of a City: Coventry and the Urban Crisis of the Later Middle Ages* (Cambridge, 1979)

Platt, C., *King Death: The Black Death and Its Aftermath in Late-Medieval England* (London, 1997)

—— *Medieval Southampton: The Port and Trading Community, A. D. 1000–1600* (London, 1973)

Platts, G., *Land and People in Medieval Lincolnshire* (Lincoln, 1985)

Postan, M. M., *Medieval Trade and Finance* (Cambridge, 1973)

Postles, D., 'Lamps, Lights and Layfolk: "Popular" Devotion before the Black Death', *Journal of Medieval History*, 25, 2 (1999): 97–114

—— 'Migration and Mobility in a Less Mature Economy: English Internal Migration, c.1200–1350', *Social History*, 25, 3 (2000): 285–99

—— *The North through its Names: A Phenomenology of Medieval and Early-Modern Northern England* (Oxford, 2007)

Power, E., *The Wool Trade in English Medieval History* (Oxford, 1941)

Prestwich M., *Armies and Warfare in the Middle Ages: The English Experience* (New Haven, 1996)

—— *Edward I* (Berkeley, 1988)

Prestwich, M., R. Britnell and R. Frame (eds), *Thirteenth Century England VII* (Woodbridge, 1999)

Putnam, B. H., 'Maximum Wage-Laws for Priests after the Black Death, 1348–1381', *American Historical Review*, 21 (1915): 12–32

Raban, S., *Mortmain Legislation and the English Church, 1279–1500* (Cambridge, 1982)

Rawcliffe, C., 'Dives Redeemed? The Guild Almshouses of Late Medieval England', in L. Clark (ed.), *The Fifteenth Century VIII: Rule, Redemption and Representations in Late Medieval England and France* (Woodbridge, 2008), 1–27

—— 'The Hospitals of Later Medieval London', *Medical History*, 28, 1 (1984): 1–21

—— *Urban Bodies: Communal Health in Late Medieval English Towns and Cities* (Woodbridge, 2013)

Rawcliffe, C., and R. Wilson (eds), *Medieval Norwich* (London, 2004)

Rees Jones, S., 'God and Mammon: The Role of the City Estate of the Vicars Choral in the Religious Life of York Minster', in R. Hall and D. Stocker (eds), *Vicars Choral at English Cathedrals: Cantate Domino, History, Architecture and Archaeology* (Oxford, 2005), 192–9

—— 'Household, Work and the Problem of Mobile Labour: the Regulation of Labour in Medieval English Towns', in J. Bothwell, P. J. P. Goldberg and W. M. Ormrod (eds), *The Problem of Labour in Fourteenth-century England* (York, 2000), 133–53

—— 'Richard Scrope, the Bolton Hours and the Church of St Martin in Micklegate: Reconstructing a Holy Neighbourhood in Later Medieval York', in P. J. P. Goldberg (ed.), *Richard Scrope, Archbishop and Martyr* (Donington, 2007), 214–36

—— *York: The Making of a City, 1068–1350* (Oxford, 2013)

—— (ed.), *The Government of Medieval York: Essays in Commemoration of the 1396 Royal Charter* (York, 1997)

Reynolds, S., 'Decline and Decay in Late Medieval Towns', *Urban History Yearbook* (1980): 76–8

—— 'The Farm and Taxation of London, 1154–1216', in S. Reynolds, *Identities and Solidarities of the Medieval Laity* (Aldershot, 1995), 211–28

—— *Identities and Solidarities of the Medieval Laity* (Aldershot, 1995)

—— *An Introduction to the History of English Medieval Towns* (Oxford, 1977)*Kingdoms and Communities in Western Europe, 900–1300* (Oxford, 2nd edn, 1997)

—— 'Medieval Urban History and the History of Political Thought', *Urban History*, 9 (1982): 14–23

Rich, E. E., 'The Mayors of the Staples', *Cambridge Historical Journal*, 4, 2 (1933): 120–42

Rigby, S. H., '"John of Gaunt's Palace" and the Sutton Family of Lincoln', *Lincolnshire History and Archaeology*, 35 (2000): 35–9

—— 'Late Medieval Urban Prosperity: The Evidence of the Lay Subsidies', *Economic History Review*, 39, 3 (1986): 411–16

—— 'Medieval Boston: Economy, Society and Administration', in S. Badham and P. Cockerham (eds), *'The beste and fairest of al Lincolnshire': The Church of St Botolph, Boston, Lincolnshire and its Medieval Monuments*, British Archaeological Reports, 554 (2012), 6–28

—— *Medieval Grimsby: Growth and Decline* (Hull, 1993)

—— '"Sore Decay" and "Fair Dwellings": Boston and Urban Decline in the Later Middle Ages', *Midland History*, 18 (1995): 47–61

—— 'Urban Decline in the Later Middle Ages: the Reliability of the Non-statistical Evidence', *Urban History Yearbook*, 11 (1984): 45–60

—— 'Urban "Oligarchy" in Late Medieval England', in J. A. F. Thomson (ed.), *Towns and Townspeople in the Fifteenth Century* (Gloucester, 1988)

—— 'Urban Population in Late Medieval England: the Evidence of the Lay Subsidies', *Economic History Review*, 63, 2 (2010): 393–417

—— 'Urban Society in Early Fourteenth Century England: the Evidence of Lay Subsidies', *Bulletin of the John Rylands Library*, 72, 3 (1990): 169–184

Rigby, S. H., and E. Ewan, 'Government, Power and Authority', in D. M. Palliser (ed.), *Cambridge Urban History of Britain, vol. 1: 600–1540* (Cambridge, 2008), 291–312

Rimmer, J., 'The Language and Property: Vernacular in the Context of Late Medieval Urban Identities', in E. Salter and H. Wicker (eds), *Vernacularity in England and Wales, c.1300–1500* (Turnhout, 2011), 269–93

Roach, J. C. (ed.), *A History of the County of Cambridge and the Isle of Ely, vol. 3: The City and University of Cambridge* (1959)

Robson, M., 'The Greyfriars of Lincoln c.1230–1330: the Establishment of the Friary and the Friars Ministry and Life in the City and its Environs', in M. Robson and J. Rohrkasten (eds), *Franciscan Organisation in the Mendicant Context: Formal and Informal Structures of the Friars' Lives and Ministry in the Middle Ages* (Berlin, 2010), 113–37

—— 'Robert Grosseteste: his Memory among the Greyfriars, his Cult in Lincoln Cathedral and the Petition for his Canonisation', *Miscellanea Francescana*, 104 (2004): 306–23

Rogers, A., 'The Lincolnshire County Court in the Fifteenth Century', *Lincolnshire History and Archaeology*, 1 (1966): 64–78

—— *Noble Merchant: William Browne (c.1410–1489) and Stamford in the Fifteenth Century* (Bury St Edmunds, 2012)

Roskell, J. S., L. Clark and C. Rawcliffe (eds), *The History of Parliament: the House of Commons, 1386–1421* (London, 1993)

Ross, J., *Civitas Lincolnia* (Lincoln, 1870)

Rosser, G., 'The Anglo-Saxon Guilds', in J. Blair (ed.), *Minsters and Parish Churches: The Local Church in Transition, 950–1200* (Oxford, 1988), 31–5

—— *The Art of Solidarity in the Middle Ages: Guilds in England, 1250–1550* (Oxford, 2015)

—— 'Big Brotherhood: Guilds in Urban Politics in Late Medieval England', in I. A. Gadd and P. Wallis (eds), *Guilds and Association in Europe, 900–1900* (London, 2006), 27–42

—— 'Communities of Parish and Guild in the Late Middle Ages', in S. J. Wright (ed.), *Parish, Church and People: Local Studies in Lay Religion, 1350–1750* (London, 1988), 29–55

—— 'Conflict and Political Community in the Medieval Town: Disputes between Clergy and Laity in Hereford', in T. R. Slater and G. Rosser (eds), *The Church in the Medieval Town* (Aldershot, 1998), 20–42

—— 'Going to the Fraternity Feast: Commensality and Social Relations in Late Medieval England', *Journal of British Studies*, 34, 4 (1994): 430–46

—— 'The Guild of St Mary and St John the Baptist, Lichfield: Ordinances of the Late Fourteenth Century', *Collections for a History of Staffordshire*, 4, 13 (1988): 19–26

—— *Medieval Westminster, 1200–1540* (Oxford, 1989)

—— 'Parochial Conformity and Voluntary Religion in Late-Medieval England', *Transactions of the Royal Historical Society*, Sixth Series, 1 (1991): 173–89

Rousseau, M. H., *Saving the Souls of Medieval London, Perpetual Chantries at St Paul's Cathedral, c.1200–1548* (Farnham, 2011)

Rubin, M., *Charity and Community in Medieval Cambridge* (Cambridge, 1987)

—— *Corpus Christi: The Eucharist in Late Medieval Culture* (Cambridge, 1999)

—— 'Corpus Christi: Fraternities and Late Medieval Piety', *Studies in Church History*, 23 (1986): 97–109

—— 'Identities', in R. Horrox and W. M. Ormrod (eds), *A Social History of England: 1200–1500* (Cambridge, 2006), 402–12

—— 'Sacramental Life', in M. Rubin and Walter Simons (eds), *Cambridge History of Christianity*, vol. 4 (Cambridge, 2009), 217–37

—— 'Small Groups: Identity and Solidarity in the Late Middle Ages', in J. Kermode (ed.), *Enterprise and Individuals in Fifteenth Century England* (Stroud, 1991)

Rubin, M., and Walter Simons (eds), *Cambridge History of Christianity*, vol. 4 (Cambridge, 2009)

Ruffer, V., and A. J. Taylor (eds), *Medieval Studies Presented to Rose Graham* (Oxford, 1950)

Rutledge, E., 'Economic Life', in C. Rawcliffe and R. Wilson (eds), *Medieval Norwich* (London, 2004), 157–88

—— 'Lawyers and Administrators: the Clerks of Late-Thirteenth Century Norwich', in C. Harper-Bill (ed.), *Medieval East Anglia* (Woodbridge, 2005), 83–98

Saul, A., 'English Towns in the Late Middle Ages: the Case of Great Yarmouth', *Journal of Medieval History*, 8 (1982): 75–88

Sawyer, P. *Anglo-Saxon Lincolnshire* (Lincoln, 1998)

Scammell, G. V., 'English Merchant Shipping at the End of the Middle Ages: Some East Coast Evidence', *Economic History Review*, Second Series, 13, 3 (1961): 327–41

Schofield, J., and G. Stell, 'The Built Environment', in D. M. Palliser (ed.), *Cambridge Urban History of Britain, vol. 1: 600–1540* (Cambridge, 2008), 371–94

Schofield, P. R., and N. J. Mayhew (eds), *Credit and Debt in Medieval England, c.1180–c.1350* (Oxford, 2002)

Shaw, D. G., *The Creation of a Community: The City of Wells in the Middle Ages* (Oxford, 1993)

Shull, V., 'Clerical Drama in Lincoln Cathedral, 1318–1561', *PMLA*, 52, 1 (1937): 946–66

Slater, T. (ed.), *Towns in Decline, AD 100–1600* (Aldershot, 2000)

Slavin, P., 'The Great Bovine Pestilence and its Economic and Environmental

Consequences in England and Wales, 1318–50', *Economic History Review*, 65, 4 (2012): 1239–66
—— 'Market Failure during the Great Famine in England and Wales (1315–1317)', *Past and Present*, 22 (2013), 34–42
Sloane, B., *The Black Death in London* (Stroud, 2011)
Spufford, P., *Money and its Use in Medieval Europe* (Cambridge, 1988)
Steel, A., 'The Practice of the Assignment in the Later Fourteenth Century', *Economic History Review*, 43, 170 (1928): 172–80
Stenton, F. M., 'The Road System of Medieval England', *Economic History Review*, 7, 1 (1936): 1–21
Stocker, D., 'The Lincoln Stonebow and the Flattery of Princes', *Journal of the British Archaeological Association*, 150 (1997): 96–105
—— 'The Tomb and Shrine of Bishop Grosseteste in Lincoln Cathedral', in W. M. Ormrod (ed.), *England in the Thirteenth Century: Proceedings of the 1984 Harlaxton Symposium* (Woodbridge, 1985), 143–8.
—— '"A Very Goodly House Longging to Sutton ...": a Reconstruction of 'John of Gaunt's Palace', Lincoln', *Lincolnshire History and Archaeology*, 34 (1999): 5–15
—— (ed.), *The City by the Pool: Assessing the Archaeology of the City of Lincoln* (Oxford, 2003)
Stokes, J., 'Staging Wonders: Ritual and Space in the Drama and Ceremony of Lincoln Cathedral and its Environs', in F. Andrews (ed.), *Ritual and Space in the Middle Ages: Proceedings of the 2009 Harlaxton Symposium* (Donington, 2011), 197–212
Storey, R. L., 'Recruitment of English Clergy in the Period of the Conciliar Movement', *Annuarium Historiae Conciliorum*, 7 (1975): 290–313
Summerson, H., 'Calamity and Commerce: the Burning of Boston Fair in 1288', in C. M. Barron and A. F. Sutton (eds), *The Medieval Merchant: Proceedings of the 2012 Harlaxton Symposium* (Donington, 2014)
Sutton, A. F., and L. Visser-Fuchs, 'The Sun in Splendour and the Rose Reborn: A Yorkist Mayor of Lincoln and his Book of Hours', *Nottingham Medieval Studies*, 57 (2013): 195–245
Swanson, H., 'Artisans in the Urban Economy: the Documentary Evidence from York', in J. Corfield and D. Keene (eds), *Work in Towns, 850–1850* (Leicester, 1990), 42–56
—— 'The Illusion of Economic Structure: Craft Guilds in Late Medieval Towns', *Past and Present*, 121 (1988): 29–48.
—— *Medieval Artisans* (Oxford, 1989)
—— *Medieval British Towns* (Basingstoke, 1999)
Swanson, R. N., *Church and Society in Late Medieval England* (Oxford, 1989)
—— 'Indulgences for Prayers for the Dead in the Diocese of Lincoln in the Early Fourteenth Century', *Journal of Ecclesiastical History*, 52, 2 (2001): 197–219
—— 'Universities, Graduates and Benefices in Later Medieval England', *Past and Present*, 106 (1985): 28–61
Sweetinburgh, S., *The Role of the Hospital in Medieval England: Gift-Giving and the Spiritual Economy* (Dublin, 2004)
—— (ed.), *Later Medieval Kent* (Woodbridge, 2010)
Tait, J., *The Medieval English Borough: Studies on Its Origins and Constitutional History* (Manchester, 1968)
Tanner, N., *The Church in Late Medieval Norwich, 1370–1532* (Toronto, 1984)
Tanner, N., and S. Watson, 'Least of the Laity: the minimum requirements for a medieval Christian', *Journal of Medieval History*, 32 (2006): 395–423
Thirsk, J. (ed.), *The Agrarian History of England and Wales, vol. 3: 1348–1500* (Cambridge,

2011)

Thomas, S. S., *Creating Communities in Restoration England* (Leiden, 2013)

Thompson, A. H., 'Diocesan Administration in the Middle Ages: Archdeacons and Rural Deans', *Proceedings of the British Academy*, 15 (1943): 153–94

—— 'The Registers of John Gynewell', *Archaeological Journal*, 68 (1911): 301–60

Thomson, J. A. F., 'Piety and Charity in Late Medieval London', *Journal of Ecclesiastical History*, 16 (1965): 178–95

—— (ed.), *Towns and Townspeople in the Fifteenth Century* (Gloucester, 1988)

Thomson, R. M., *Catalogue of the Manuscripts of Lincoln Cathedral Chapter Library* (Woodbridge, 1989)

Thrupp, S. L., 'Medieval Gilds Reconsidered', *Journal of Economic History*, 2 (1942): 164–73

—— *The Merchant Class of Medieval London, 1300–1500* (Ann Arbor, 1989)

Tucker, P., *Law Courts and Lawyers in the City of London, 1300–1550* (Cambridge, 2007)

Unwin, G. (ed.), *Finance and Trade under Edward III* (Manchester, 1918)

Veale, E. M., *The English Fur Trade in the Later Middle Ages* (Oxford, 1966)

—— *Studies in the Medieval Wine Trade* (Oxford, 1971)

Venables, E., 'A List and Brief Description of the Churches of Lincoln Previous to the Period of the Reformation', *AASRP*, 19, 2 (1887): 326–54

—— 'The Shrine and Head of St Hugh of Lincoln', *AASRP*, 50, 1 (1893): 131–51

Verduyn, A., 'The Revocation of Urban Peace Commissions in 1381: the Lincoln Petition', in S. Mews (ed.), *Religion and National Identity* (Oxford, 1982), 108–11

Vince, A., 'Lincoln in the Early Modern Era (c.1350–c.1750)', in D. Stocker (ed.), *The City by the Pool: Assessing the Archaeology of the City of Lincoln* (Oxford, 2003)

—— 'The New Town: Lincoln in the High Medieval Era (c.900 to c.1350)', in D. Stocker (ed.), *The City by the Pool: Assessing the Archaeology of the City of Lincoln* (Oxford, 2003)

Wade, J. F., 'The Overseas Trade of Newcastle upon Tyne in the Late Middle Ages', *Northern History* 30, 1 (1994): 31–48

Walton, P., 'Textiles', in J. Blair and N. Ramsey (eds), *English Medieval Industries* (London 1991), 319–46

Webb, D., *Medieval European Pilgrimage, c.700–c.1500* (Basingstoke, 2002)

—— *Pilgrimage in Medieval England* (London, 2000)

Weddle, S., 'Identity and Alliance: Urban Presence, Spatial Privilege, and Florentine Renaissance Convents', in R. J. Crum and J. T. Paoletti (eds), *Renaissance Florence: A Social History* (Cambridge, 2006), 394–412

Westlake, H. F., *The Parish Gilds of Mediaeval England* (London, 1919)

Wickenden, J. F., 'John de Dalderby, Bishop of Lincoln, 1300–20', *Archaeological Journal*, 40 (1883): 215–24

Wilkinson, L. J., *Women in Thirteenth-Century Lincolnshire* (Woodbridge, 2007)

Willard, J. F., *Parliamentary Taxes on Personal Property, 1290–1334* (Cambridge: Massachusetts, 1934)

Willard, J. F., W. A. Morris and W. H. Dunham (eds), *The English Government at Work, 1327–1336*, vol. 3 (Cambridge: Massachusetts, 1950)

Williams, G. A., *Medieval London, from Commune to Capital* (London, 1963)

Wood-Legh, K. L., *Perpetual Chantries in Britain* (Cambridge, 1965)

—— *Studies in Church Life under Edward III* (Cambridge, 1934)

Wordsworth, C., *Notes on Mediaeval Services in England* (London, 1898)

Ziegler, P., *The Black Death* (London, 1998)

Unpublished Secondary Sources

Bean-King, J., 'Lists of Mayors, Bailiffs, Sheriffs, Chamberlains, Town Clerks and Recorders of the City of Lincoln, 1202–1945': LAO LCL/5206

Bevan, K. L., 'Clerks and Scriveners: Legal Literacy and Access to Justice in Late Medieval England' (Unpublished Ph.D Thesis, University of Exeter, 2013)

Bischoff, J. P., 'Economic Change in Thirteenth-Century Lincoln: Decline of an Urban Cloth Industry' (Unpublished Ph.D Thesis, Yale University, 1975)

Brooks, F. W., 'Calendar of the Rolls of the Lincoln Court of Burghmanmote', LAO FL/Transcripts/U/28

Candy, C. A., 'The Scottish Wars of Edward III, 1327–1338' (Unpublished Ph.D Thesis, University of Durham, 2004)

Dinn, R., 'Popular Religion in Late Medieval Bury St Edmunds' (Unpublished Ph.D, University of Manchester, 1990)

Gee, S., '"At the Sygne of the Cardynalles Hat": The Book Trade and the Market for Books in Yorkshire, c.1450–1550' (Unpublished D.Phil Thesis, University of York, 1999)

Mackman, J., 'The Lincolnshire Gentry and the Wars of the Roses' (Unpublished Ph.D Thesis, University of York, 1999)

Mundill, R. R., 'The Jews in England, 1272–1290' (Unpublished Ph.D Thesis, University of St Andrews, 1988)

Rigby, S. H., 'Boston and Grimsby in the Middle Ages' (Unpublished Ph.D Thesis, University of London, 1982)

Uhler, S. G., 'English Customs Ports, 1275–1343' (Unpublished Ph.D Thesis, University of St Andrews, 1977)

Wilson, M., 'Community, Kinship and Piety: Lincoln Cathedral Close, c.1450–1500' (Unpublished Ph.D Thesis, University of Nottingham, 2014)

Index

Printed and bound by CPI Group (UK) Ltd, Croydon, CR0 4YY

15/09/2026

14962416-0007